# READING HEINRICH HEINE

This comprehensive study of the nineteenth-century German poet
Heinrich Heine is the first to be published in English for many years.
Anthony Phelan examines the complete range of Heine's work, from
the early poetry and 'Pictures of Travel' to the last poems, including personal polemic and journalism. Phelan provides original and
detailed readings of Heine's major poetry and throws new light on
his virtuoso political performances that have too often been neglected
by critics. Through his critical relationship with Romanticism, Heine
confronted the problem of modernity in startlingly original ways that
still speak to the concerns of postmodern readers. Phelan highlights
the importance of Heine for the critical understanding of modern
literature, and in particular the responses to Heine's work by Adorno,
Kraus and Benjamin. Heine emerges as a figure of immense European significance, whose writings now need to be seen as a major
contribution to the articulation of modernity.

ANTHONY PHELAN is a Faculty Lecturer in German at Oxford and
Fellow of Keble College.

CAMBRIDGE STUDIES IN GERMAN

*General editors*
H. B. Nisbet, University of Cambridge
Martin Swales, University of London

*Advisory editor*
Theodore J. Ziolkowski, Princeton University

Also in the series

J. P. STERN: *The Dear Purchase: A Theme in German Modernism*

SEÁN ALLAN: *The Plays of Heinrich von Kleist: Ideals and Illusions*

W. E. YATES: *Theatre in Vienna: A Critical History, 1776–1995*

MICHAEL MINDEN: *The German 'Bildungsroman' Incest and Inheritance*

TODD KONTJE: *Women, the Novel, and the German Nation 1771–1871 Domestic Fiction in the Fatherland*

STEPHEN BROCKMANN: *Literature and German Reunification*

JUDITH RYAN: *Rilke, Modernism and Poetic Tradition*

GRAHAM FRANKLAND: *Freud's Literary Culture*

RONALD SPIERS: *Brecht's Poetry of Political Exile*

NICHOLAS SAUL: *Philosophy and German Literature, 1700–1990*

STEPHANIE BIRD: *Women Writers and National Identity: Bachmann, Duden, Özdamar*

MATTHEW BELL: *The German Tradition of Psychology in Literature and Thought, 1700–1840*

# READING HEINRICH HEINE

ANTHONY PHELAN

CAMBRIDGE
UNIVERSITY PRESS

CAMBRIDGE UNIVERSITY PRESS
Cambridge, New York, Melbourne, Madrid, Cape Town, Singapore, São Paulo

Cambridge University Press
The Edinburgh Building, Cambridge CB2 2RU, UK

Published in the United States of America by Cambridge University Press, New York

www.cambridge.org
Information on this title: www.cambridge.org/9780521863995

© Anthony Phelan 2007

First published 2007

Printed in the United Kingdom at the University Press, Cambridge

*A catalogue record for this publication is available from the British Library*

ISBN-13 978-0-521-86399-5 hardback
ISBN-10 0-521-86399-6 hardback

# Contents

v

PART IV EPILOGUE

# Acknowledgements

I started to read Heine under the guidance of Trevor Jones in Cambridge, and then found myself teaching him at the University of Warwick. Elisabeth Stopp encouraged some early thinking about his bear fable, *Atta Troll*; and I am grateful to the German Academic Exchange Service for a scholarship that first enabled me to get to know the texts of Heine's critical and creative reception in the twentieth century, and to make a start on some of the secondary literature; and to the University of Warwick, the University of Oxford, and Keble and Trinity Colleges for research leave.

Unless otherwise stated, translations are my own. I am particularly grateful to the Suhrkamp Verlag, Frankfurt am Main, for permission to use the English version of *The Complete Poems of Heinrich Heine* by Hal Draper.

Chapter 10 on *Romanzero* and the later poetry appeared as a contribution to *A Companion to the Works of Heinrich Heine*, ed. Roger F. Cook (Rochester, NY, and Woodbridge: Camden House, 2002). The Epilogue was first presented in *Heine und die Weltliteratur*, ed. T. J. Reed and Alexander Stillmark (Oxford: legenda, 2000). In each case I am grateful to the original editors for their constructive criticism. Parts of the study were read by Helmut Schmitz and the late Gillian Rose at the University of Warwick, and by Tom Kuhn in Oxford; Martin Swales has always been a great source of encouragement over the years. The manuscript as a whole was read by Rowland Cotterill, Heidrun Friese, and Michael Perraudin. I am very grateful to all of them, and to a relatively anonymous American reader, for their critical comments, which have corrected many errors and clarified much that was obscure. Some things I persist in – and that is no one's fault but my own.

What I owe to Liz Dowler for her patience and persistence, as we head for an anniversary of our own one year after this Heine year, is more than words can tell.

A. P.

# Introduction

1997 saw the two hundredth anniversary of the birth of Heinrich Heine, and the one hundred and fiftieth anniversary of his death falls in 2006. In the fifty years since the centenary of his death in 1956 his reputation, his canonical status, and perhaps even his popularity have been consolidated by enormous scholarly and critical activity. Towards the end of the last century, however, two commentators speaking from widely different positions challenged the prospects for Heine's continuing vitality, both within the academy and more generally in the future of literary culture.

Over a number of years Jeffrey Sammons, Heine's most important English biographer, has kept an acerbic eye on the mounting critical literature. He recently suggested that the intense preoccupation with Heine since the late 1960s has run its course and become exhausted. In response to this state of affairs, he has called for (and contributed to) a fuller understanding of the reception of Heine's work, and a return to careful readings of his style.[1] The playwright Heiner Müller, on the other hand, responded to the award of the Darmstadt academy's Büchner prize in 1985 with a speech claiming that 'Heine the Wound has begun to heal over, crooked; Woyzeck is the open wound.'[2] Müller's comment acknowledges the disturbance in German literary awareness caused by Heine, and evoked by Adorno's lecture 'Die Wunde Heine' ('Heine the Wound')[3] in 1956, but suggests that it has been settled – though not set to rights. The remaining sore point is Büchner's *Woyzeck*. Heiner Müller's intuition was that Büchner more sharply addresses the North–South divide, and the residual claims made on our Western consciousness by democracy, which Müller understood as entailing the social and economic emancipation of working classes, and a solution to the problem of poverty that Büchner summarized as the 'bread question'. Faced with these doubts, the question of what continues in Heine, what lives on to provoke and disturb – what survives two historical-critical editions and a scholarly yearbook – is more important than ever to our understanding of the history of modernity and its current shadow, the so-called postmodern. It is the purpose of this study to reassess Heine's relation to and articulation of modernity, both as writer and as critic, as 'talent' and 'character'.

Generally the *Modern* implies two historical definitions: within the general period since the Renaissance, the specific development of the industrialized and urban culture of the nineteenth century which extends to our own time. In Germany, the experience of modernity was typically dominated by quite sudden demographic and economic changes. In the latter part of the nineteenth century there was a shift in the German population from the country and an essentially agrarian economy to the metropolitan centres of Berlin and Munich and the growth of manufacturing industry. In the tradition of German sociology these changes are associated with a rationalization of social action and a corresponding curtailment of affect (described by Georg Simmel's fundamental study 'The Metropolis and Mental Life')[4] and with increasing alienation, secularization, and disenchantment. Heine's experience is, on the whole, of an earlier phase of this development, but in a number of respects he recognizes structures which become dominant in later social formations: the capital-led changes in the intensification of industrial production, and the consequent importance of capital mobility; the social and political significance of the emerging proletarian response; and the collapse of traditional forms of religious belief. Heine's relationship with his uncle Salomon, and his reflections on the significance of Baron James Rothschild testify to his sense of the mechanisms and effects of capital investment; his awareness of the growing importance of the communist movement and its cultural consequences bears witness to his understanding of the democratic claims of the working class beyond the scope of bourgeois liberalism; and the repeated images of old gods in exile clearly address the question of the secular – whatever we make of Heine's personal return to religious belief towards the end of his life.

Heine's importance two hundred years after his birth is closely tied to his self-understanding, his understanding of the process of modernity, and to twentieth-century readings of the forms in which these understandings were articulated. In the first instance, however, Heine defines his position as a modern in relation to Romantic poetry: 'with me the old German lyrical school was closed, while at the same time the new school, the modern German lyric was inaugurated by me' (B 6/1, 447).[5] He happily accepts this assessment by the literary historians of his own day; and his *Geständnisse* (*Confessions*) go on to identify his recovery of religious belief (the so called 'theological revision') by reference to Judaism as well as the Christian tradition, and of course in relation to the 'communist' atheism which he has come to abjure.

In this sense, it is also possible to see Heine's modernity as defined also by his relationship to tradition – or rather to distinct traditions. In his memoir of Ludwig Börne, Heine structures his recollections by reference to three contexts: the July Revolution and the political future of Europe, the traditions of Judaism (in the Frankfurt ghetto) and of German nationalism (in the Hambach Festival). There is little doubt that he sees himself as engaging more adequately with problems of politics and aesthetics than his critical contemporary and sparring partner. The figure of Börne is presented as simply old-fashioned, but not, Heine claims, because there is any fundamental ideological disagreement between them. No doubt there were disagreements, but Heine understands his own position as defined by his written *style*.

In turn, this commitment to a modern writing has its own tradition. At the end of the first book of *Zur Geschichte der Religion und Philosophie in Deutschland* (*On the History of Religion and Philosophy in Germany*), Heine identifies the true origin of the modern style in Luther; again and again, in other work, Luther is associated with Lessing, the great literary and critical figure of the late Enlightenment, and, surprisingly, with the classicist translator and poet Johann Heinrich Voß, in a trinity of polemical and democratic *stylists*. Such modern writing has three essential characteristics in Heine's view. First, it addresses the material interests of the present in a way which is combative and adversarial; Romantic writing in the previous generation, on the other hand, which is *not* modern, attempts to combine the national and the religious. Modern writing, secondly, returns to classical models of decorum and genre, while its Romantic predecessor is extravagant. Finally, it is rational, individualist and sceptical. These are the qualities which have encouraged recent critics to identify Heine as a precursor and ally of modern intellectual critique. Peter Sloterdijk, in his *Critique of Cynical Reason*,[6] endorses his modernity by aligning the modern tradition Heine defined with the representatives of his own 'Higher Kynicism'. Sloterdijk's allusion attempts to harness Heine to the argument of his 'postmodernism of resistance';[7] and in another quarter Jürgen Habermas has claimed him for the genealogy of the post-war German intellectual. Habermas sees him, perhaps more importantly, as presenting the form in which critical distance and political commitment to questions of German identity can be established.

Modernity in turn made its own historic claims on Heinrich Heine. They are the very conditions of his life and work which bring him within the scope of Habermas's problematic. In the (old, pre-unification) Federal Republic of Germany several aspects of political culture made the intellectual model provided by Heine vitally relevant: the electronic media, an expanded educational sector, the uneasy relations between parties and their 'supporters', and the constant demoscopic testing of 'public opinion'. Heine's sense of distance as a critical intellectual can be specified: his years in Paris provide the occasion for his close observation of the French administrations as well as of political culture in the capital, on its streets as much as in its salons. Yet it is not only the political imperatives of the July Monarchy or 'communism' that bind him to Paris. He acknowledges the power of urban experience in his critical prose and in his decisively modern poetry. There are perhaps few moments in his work that better express his acknowledgement of this urban imperative than the structure deployed in *Ludwig Börne: eine Denkschrift* (*Ludwig Börne: A Memorial*),[8] where Paris appears as the particular site of modern politics seen from the geographical remoteness of Heligoland (in the interpolated 'Briefe aus Helgoland' ('Letters from Heligoland')) and in comparison with the provincial follies of the Hambach festival ('O land of fools, my fatherland').[9] Paris provides a geographical focus for Heine's engagement with the themes of the city; in terms of style and tone, his critical prose and journalism make formal commitments which will finally alter the lyric register in his late poems beyond all recognition.

These changes have given rise to the claims made by moderns for and against Heine's writing ever since Nietzsche. Friedrich Nietzsche hailed Heine as his greatest predecessor in the art of German style – and in 1908 Thomas Mann emphasized that judgement.[10] Although Heine's canonical authority seems secure, Mann's remarks also coincide with the earliest reflections on Heine's status by his most virulent critic, Karl Kraus. As later chapters show, Kraus's work began a critical debate about Heine which has been conducted more or less in public and to which Habermas's essay is perhaps the most recent contribution. This intense and sustained engagement with Heine as a *problem*, in the critical tradition since Kraus, as well as Heine's continuing life in contemporary poetry make it possible, now, to consider a century view of him based not on the volumes of literary scholarship and critical editions, but on the disturbance his writing continues to make in the reflexes of modernity in Germany.

A couple of years ago a colleague in a British university remarked that he could never think of anything to say about Heine's poetry. This came as a surprise since the scholar in question had no trouble writing about difficult poets like Paul Celan. Heine's simplicity and, often, brevity can be deceptive. In the present study I attempt to follow the logic and implications of his writing as closely as possible, and to assess it in the light of strong readings in the twentieth century. The first part of the discussion traces the critical debate about Heine in a polemical tradition which Kraus initiated. His enormous anxiety in relation to Heine's style has constantly embarrassed later Heine critics. My purpose, however, is not simply to document this aspect of a difficult reception. Rather, by tracing the development of Kraus's case, its influence on Adorno's centenary talk in 1956, and the counterclaims made for Heine by Helmut Heißenbüttel, it is possible to identify a recurring biographical impulse. Kraus and Adorno need to fix the disturbances of Heine's writing in a corresponding *personality* with whom ultimate moral responsibility lies. Heißenbüttel responds by insisting on *textual* effects, and a formal and constructivist aesthetics which he associates with the documentary and the end of lyric metaphor. This argument provides a framework in which the poetry of *Das Buch der Lieder* (*The Book of Songs*) can be reconsidered as a text directly addressing the possibility of lyric subjectivity. Heine himself plays a kind of hide-and-seek with the expectations of autobiographical reference to make his collection a compendium of forms for supposed self-expression. In a close parallel to this game with self-revelation, the *Reisebilder* or pictures of travel, which first made Heine's name, explore the material and ideological constraints imposed on literary subjectivity.

Heine finds many ways of dismantling the poetic language of selfhood. In a further investigation of the forms in which he refracts modernity for the twentieth century, I examine the serious problems his ironies and cynicism presented for the German poets who established a durable symbolist aesthetic from the turn of the century. Here, anthologies compiled by Stefan George and Rudolf Borchardt show how strongly Heine's poems simultaneously lend themselves to and resist atmospheric vagueness. Within the framework of this symbolist aesthetic, Heine's writing in *Atta Troll. Ein Sommernachtstraum* (*Atta Troll. A Summer Night's Dream*) can be seen to deploy the lyrical discourse of personality and *character* with a calculated political edge. His celebration of 'l'art pour l'art' in poetry written *for its own sake* negotiates the relationship between poetry and politics on the terrain of style and form, and so defends his own art from the encroachments of mere ideology.

The work which most fully theorizes and practises the suspension of the personal in order to maintain the political freedom of the aesthetic is the memoir of Ludwig Börne – a work which on the face of it appears to flaunt personality and private resentments more than any other. In the history of Heine's reception it has been, strikingly, writers who have recognized the achievements of this notorious polemic. Heine's whole strategy in the memoir quizzically and smilingly upsets every possible assumption about public authorship and personal commitment, so that *style itself* becomes the instrument of the most rigorous and scathing political analysis.

In the third part of the book, Heine's encounter with the urban political life of Paris is examined. The political journalism of *Lutetia* exploits the destabilization of metaphor, begun in *Buch der Lieder*, in order to set in play a stylish political emblematics. To borrow a phrase from Jacques Derrida, Heine the famously 'elusive poet' derives the strength of his encounter with Paris and Parisian politics from 'knowing how not to be there'. Heine's other great encounter with Paris is conducted in verse, in the poems of *Romanzero* and his later poems of 1853 and 1854, and in posthumous collections. In examining this mature work, I first return to Adorno's claim that Heine did not achieve 'archetypes of modernity' of the kind created by his younger contemporary Charles Baudelaire; and then, following a hint in one of Adorno's letters to Walter Benjamin, I consider the ways in which Heine's late poetry very precisely articulates his relationship to modernity understood as the disruption of tradition.

Tradition disrupted continues to define the experience of modernity for the older generation of German poets writing at the moment. Here an epilogue considers the vitality of Heine's legacy in the verse of Peter Rühmkorf, Günter Kunert and Wolf Biermann. Heine emerges as a poet confronting modernity because he engages so profoundly with history, and does so at the point where he is most vulnerable and most exposed – in the secular defeat of poetry itself.

# PART I

# *The biographical imperative*

# CHAPTER I

# The biographical imperative: Karl Kraus

Heine saw himself as the founder of a radically modern school of German poetry. Such claims have been treated to a mixed reception, however; and Karl Kraus provided one of the most intelligent and influential readings. His virulent attack on Heine's innovative effect as a writer set the agenda for many subsequent critics in the twentieth century.[1] The essay remains an embarrassment;[2] but equally Kraus identifies problems in Heine that are still difficult to resolve. Chief among these is a failure of authenticity, which Kraus believes Heine bequeaths to contemporary journalists, and his strategy is to insist on Heine's *personal* responsibility for this effect of modernization. Like many hostile critics before him, Kraus is forced to submit to a biographical imperative which will also guide Adorno's attempt at rehabilitation in 1956. Kraus's critique, cast in the terms of his own transcendental understanding of literature, may be allergic, but his response to the peculiar stylistic expression of Heine's modernity is extremely acute.

## HEINE THE PROBLEM

'Heine und die Folgen' ('Heine and the Consequences', 1910) is central to a critical attack extending from 'Um Heine' ('Around Heine'), written for the fiftieth anniversary of the poet's death in 1906, to Kraus's major essay on rhyme of 1927.[3] The continued use and abuse of Heine over this period is striking. Kraus's essay powerfully associates Heine with central issues in modernity, while simultaneously attempting to block his reception. His status within the canon in 1910 is not a matter of great interest to Kraus, though he is well aware of recent new editions. Rather, Kraus takes his stand as an expert on writing ('Schriftsachverständiger') to identify a cultural crisis. He believes that intellectual 'anti-culture' has now taken two forms, each moving away from an unnamed centre. The spatial metaphor soon shifts towards a geographical one in which Germany and France stand at opposite poles. This confrontation plays a significant part in Heine's critical essays on German literature and thought and on French politics, but for Kraus it is also part of the common currency of his own time. The source of the contrast that identifies France with form and Germany with content is almost certainly Nietzsche's essay 'On the Use and Abuse of History', the second of the *Unzeitgemäße Betrachtungen (Untimely Meditations)*. Nietzsche attacks the German habit of mind that confuses inwardness ('Innerlichkeit') with content ('Inhalt'), eschewing all outward, formal expression.[4] Kraus, taking up the German preoccupation with substance, glosses the tendencies as two varieties of an identical weakness – a vulnerability either to matter or to form.

The relation of 'Form' to 'Stoff' is traditionally that of form to content, but Kraus uses 'Stoff' to include the substance of the world or even 'experience' itself. The Germanic 'defencelessness before the material', in Kraus's terms, concentrates on the content of a work of art. The Romance tendency, on the other hand, finds aesthetic qualities in the substance of experience *already*, prior to the work of form. In May 1917 Kraus added a 'final word' to his polemic in which he asserts his own unqualified allegiance to human values. Taking up a theme already touched on in 1910, he identifies in contrast to such values the corrosive force of the commodity. Whatever else his Franco-German terms may intend, they have little to do with differing national allegiances.

The 'German' dominance of content over form is welcome to Kraus because it frees the imagination and poses afresh the question of beauty. In the Romance preference, 'good taste' and 'culture' have penetrated everyday phenomena so completely that 'any Parisian newspaper-seller has more grace than a Prussian publisher'.[5] The ultimate effect of this, in Kraus's view, is that the well-spring of art in the interior life is obliterated by a universal superficiality. Echoing Richard III's remark about every Jack becoming a gentleman, Kraus observes that when every fool is possessed of individuality, then the real autonomous 'individualities' are bound to be vulgarized.

When Kraus claims that the 'German' mentality makes of art a mere *instrument* for its content, while its 'Romance' counterpart transforms life exclusively into *ornament*, he uses terminology borrowed from the architect Adolf Loos. The instrumentalization of art is the lesser of two evils, Kraus suggests, because it leaves intact the substantial objectivity and priority (both logical and chronological) of 'content'. However functionally it may be conceived, the autonomy of art is preserved, since the relation between 'life' and 'art' can still be understood in terms of reflection or mimesis. The 'Romance' mentality, on the other hand, already experiences the aesthetic in the material from which art might otherwise be made. This is where the complexity of Kraus's argument begins to emerge. If the German mentality recognizes in art only the sphere of its reference – what it is *about* – it must nevertheless concede a kind of epistemological power to the aesthetic as the form in which that field of reference is 'truly' revealed, in the mimetic process. The French preference, the ornamentalization of life, however, dissolves these relations: the relocation of the aesthetic in the sphere of the material itself simply abolishes the mimetic relation. Every Jack becomes a gentleman, and both life and art are equalized in relations of homogeneity. There can no longer be a platform for art because life itself has ceased to exercise any privilege as content. Art ceases to be art because the mimetic distance which makes possible the criteria of adequacy in relations of form and content is closed. 'Every man his own poet' is Kraus's summary, and mimesis has been replaced by mere repetition.

Heine is presented as the symptom and origin of this condition. Yet his dubious achievement is also recognized as the response to a need in the 'German' mentality. Kraus calls it 'a longing that has to rhyme somewhere or other', and the metaphor of rhyme will be cashed in when Kraus discusses Heine's verse technique.[6] To illustrate his case, Kraus describes the German desire for a direct, if subterranean, route from the realm of secular practicality in the accounts office ('Kontor') to the kitsch 'blue grotto' of a decayed Romantic imagination. The separation of the two is familiar from Thomas Mann's contrast between the bourgeois and the artist, in *Tonio Kröger*, for example, or *Buddenbrooks*. Kraus is much more exercised by the immediacy of the connection between them.

Heine not only brings the 'French' message to Germany, he also supposedly seeks to combine the two opposed impulses. Kraus objects to a levelling out of strict distinctions: form and content, in such writing, are merely contiguous and perspicuous – but where there is no conflict, art cannot create true unity either. Just this *confusion* of forces has been inherited by its worst contemporary expression in journalism, the true object of Kraus's polemic. But within the terms of his critique, Heine's crime is to have rejected the fundamental oppositions on which art depends, to have displaced the boundary by taking on the role of a dangerous *mediator* between art and life, and hence, in a further very striking metaphor, becoming parasitic on each. Another way in which Kraus's point can be understood is to see the autobiographical theme which insinuates itself into

Heine's writing as an occupation of the boundary dividing art from life. Writing for Heine, Kraus's essay suggests, dissolves these distinctions and demarcations.

Kraus's polemic recognizably works with two main metaphors, one sexual and the other economic. The 'feuilleton' of Kraus's slogan 'No feuilleton without Heine' is of course a French word, and Kraus suggests that the impressionistic journalism of his day has taken its lead from a certain ease of writing originally imported by Heine from France. Stylistic facility is evidence of the absence of conflict between content and form. Kraus does not believe that the relationship between the two, in language, is obvious or given. Rather the bond between word and essence ('Wesen') must be pursued in a constant process of critical doubt. If the writer should once 'stop calling the connexion into question . . . the association between linguistic form and conceptual meaning becomes attenuated'.[7]

In French writing, then, and in French culture generally, this sense of necessary difficulty is absent. French is simply lazy in matters of thought. Subsequently the French and German languages will be personified as women or Muses, via an image that comes from Kraus's description of the feuilleton as 'the French disease' Heine brought from Paris, where 'you easily get infected'. In fact Heine is implied in each of these images. The French disease Kraus means is syphilis, and Heine's paralysis during his last years in Paris was widely thought to have been syphilitic in character. From this biographical detail Kraus extends the sexual force of his polemic to a systematic comparison of the French and German languages. If French is intellectually idle, she is also 'easy': she gives herself to any rogue, effortlessly, 'with that perfect deficiency of restraint and inhibition which is perfection in a woman but a deficiency in a language'.[8] Contact with French weakens the moral fibre of German *Sprachgefühl* so that the most level-headed writer will start to have bright ideas.[9] German, on the other hand, is a 'companion who only creates and thinks for the man who can give her children'. Here a new element has appeared in the sexual metaphor, perhaps derived from the earlier image of the parasite. It is now clear that the French linguistic and cultural principle is ultimately unproductive. It can produce only phantom pregnancies.

Since Heine, Kraus tells us, German-language journalism, at least in Vienna, can dispense with creativity. Hack-work will achieve the necessary ends: 'German journalists can fetch themselves some talent in Paris as a matter of pure diligence'.[10] The reference to talent alludes to a central theme of Heine's disagreement with his contemporary and friend Ludwig Börne, who had also claimed that Heine was merely a talent, lacking the moral substance of *character* to give him political direction. For the immediate victims of Kraus's polemic, a trip to Paris is no longer necessary. As he says, parodying the tag 'hic Rhodus, hic salta', 'these days a cripple who stays in Vienna is credited with a cancan'. Nevertheless, a certain exotic remoteness, whether of Paris or of the 'jungles' made popular by Kipling and his German imitators, provides an easy approach to subject matter through 'foreign costume'.[11]

Kraus complains that Paris provided both substance *and* form – like the superficiality of foreign costume – but that this form is 'merely clothing to the body and not flesh to the spirit'. The phantom pregnancies engendered in the French language cannot be the result of truly fruitful intercourse between writer and language. They are the result of a trick. In describing it, Kraus introduces the second of his two metaphors.

The great trick of this linguistic racket, which pays a lot better than the greatest achievement of linguistic creativity, continues through successive newspaper generations, and provides anyone and everyone who thinks of reading as a pastime with the most agreeable pretext for avoiding literature.[12]

Kraus's argument relates this point to the issue of inauthenticity by observing that modern feuilletons can be written without anyone needing to 'sniff their way to the Champs Elysées personally'. The image of clothing to the body (as against flesh to the spirit) stresses the idea of an assumed appearance, an inauthentic surface, hollowed out and lacking real interiority. This inauthenticity is now focussed in the notion of linguistic fraudulence. An economic metaphor is deployed from the moment this con trick in language is formulated. The journalistic trick substitutes a forgery for real literary value. In a further image Kraus suggests that talent is uncentred and weightless ('schwerpunktlos') in the world, so that writing in the feuilleton makes plausible the false, and indeed impossible, prospect of 'setting curls on a bald head'. Once more Kraus returns to Heine as the origin of all this corruption. Like the magician in Goethe's ballad, he allowed essentially ungifted apprentices to discover how they might come by a little talent.

Here Kraus alludes directly to Adolf Loos's essay on 'Ornament and Crime'. The architect's analysis of contemporary design provides a context in which Kraus's Heine critique can be properly understood. Kraus claims that what Loos identified as the devaluation of practical life by 'ornament' corresponds to the even more catastrophic confusion created by the admixture of spiritual or intellectual elements ('Geistelemente') in modern journalism. Far from following Loos's policy and removing anything decorative from its efforts, the modern press constantly renovates and updates its ornamental styles and modes of writing. Loos himself parodies such a need for constant renovation in a passage of his essay on ornament and crime which is worth quoting at length:

> The Austrian ornamentalists say: 'We far prefer a consumer who has furnishings that are intolerable to him after only ten years, and who is therefore compelled to get everything redone every ten years, to one who never buys a new thing until the old one is worn out. It's what industry demands. Millions are kept in work by the rapid turn-over.' This seems to be the secret of the Austrian national economy; how often do we hear these words on the outbreak of a fire: 'Thank God, folk will have something to do.' Well, I have a good solution. Let's set fire to a city, let's set fire to the whole realm, and everything will be swimming in money and affluence.[13]

Although Loos was formally attacking the mixture of 'craft', design, and marketing in early twentieth-century art nouveau, he is clearly describing the origins of consumer society with its need for 'built-in obsolescence'.[14] In substance, however, he is addressing an advanced stage of commodity production; and if this line of thought is read back into his argument, the economic metaphors appear in a sharper light.

Literary ornament, says Kraus, is never pulped, it is simply 'modernized'. The element of the *modern* in this process, then, is not a local question of style so much as a matter of the economic and historical conditions of its production. Kraus hence explicitly rejects the modernizing tendencies in industrial society. While allowing a place for the press 'as a social institution . . . in a progressive social order' (as well he might), he sets out to resist the modernizing force of the industrial economy. In a rather precise metaphor, Kraus identifies *usury* as the root cause of the corruption he attacks. Here the parallel with Loos's argument is clear enough – the practical use of various goods is reduced and, in the developing consumer economy, concealed by the fashionable aspect of 'ornamentation'. In the same way, the immediacy of language is lost in writing which needs to 'render the exterior of its bad intention attractive'.[15] The 'insubstantial' wealth produced by usury – the apparent generation of value without goods – is an unnatural creation and so parallels the infertility of the French language in Kraus's sexual metaphor; it specifically recalls the sorcerer's apprentice, and the weightlessness of mere talent.

The ornament generated by 'modernizing' production is reflected explicitly in form: the decorative writing of the Sunday supplement (these are

Kraus's words!) goes hand in hand with the advertisements that accompany it because both are part of an economic system, founded on the circulation of commodities without reference to any practical use. What makes the triumph of this form of 'robbery' in the Viennese press even worse is its ornamentation with the qualities of 'Geist' – its superficial acquisition of artistic characteristics. In this respect, the press shares in the same structure of desire as the circulation of commodities: the vacuum of a 'poverty of the imagination' is stuffed full of 'facts', the fetishized substitute for 'content' which for Kraus, as we have seen, provides the essential substance of reality. In this corrupt ornamentation of the banal and inauthentic, even aesthetes undertake the metaphorical journey to Paris, world capital of the easy and seductive turn of phrase.

Kraus's second, economic metaphor in the drift of his polemic can now be summarized. In the basic opposition of 'Germanic' and 'Romance' cultures, the French pole is thought to see the substance of life itself as mere ornament. Relying on Loos, Kraus develops this view in relation to the connection between a particular kind of writing, in the press, and the development of consumer society. In this context the structure of the commodity is of interest not only because, as in Marx, it conceals the alienated labour of its producer and, in circulation, occludes the actual nature of social relations. Kraus realizes that commodity relations have already affected consumer perceptions, and stimulated a new kind of discourse in the press. Even 'quality newspapers', of the kind attacked by Kraus, produce a 'writing of the commodity' in several important senses. First, and most simply, the feuilleton is perceived to be in a relation of equivalence with the remainder of the advertising section of the Sunday supplement – the paper itself is a commodity and is marked as belonging to the discourses of and about commodities by proximity. Secondly, language takes on a function separate from any direct communication through a concentration on phrase-making for its own sake, which involves a commodification of language itself. And finally 'experience' is transformed into a series of dead, objective (fetishized) 'facts', interchangeable and ultimately unknowable.

The aesthetic attitude associated with this stress on the stylish or eye-catching turn of phrase is well illustrated in Kraus's attack on Hermann Bahr's beard, which he regarded as merely fashionable: 'not an organic necessity, but merely a feuilletonistic prop, an adjective, a phrase. It need not exist.'[16] The colloquial German of journalism and of ordinary social exchange is no more than the reflex of the corrupting capitalist mode of production, which so exploits and occupies the sphere of 'Spirit' that the latter entirely serves the imperatives of the commodity. Walter Benjamin was among the first to recognize the importance, in Kraus, of this sense of the phrase:

The empty phrase. It, however, is an abortion of technology . . . The empty phrase of the kind so relentlessly pursued by Kraus is the [brand] label that makes a thought marketable ['verkehrsfähig'], the way flowery language ['Floskel'], as ornament, gives a thought value for the connoisseur. But for this very reason the liberation of language has become identical with that of the empty phrase – its transformation from reproduction to productive instrument.[17]

According to Benjamin, then, the phrase which Kraus tirelessly pursues is both a brand-name and the mark of the commodity *per se* ('Waren-zeichen' means literally 'sign of wares') which enables ideas to circulate and 'traffic', just as in classical Marxist economics goods must be transformed into commodities before they can enter into circulation. Benjamin's further remarks may be read as relating this condition of language to advertising. The connoisseur-value to which he refers indicates a sense of specificity con-ferred by the ornamental distinction of the catch-phrase. Benjamin finally turns Kraus's critique of the phrase on its head: this condition of lan-guage must be transformed from the mark merely imprinted ('Abdruck') on an unchanged reality to an instrument of production which might change the world. Nevertheless the extension of Kraus's case, by inversion, still confirms his perception of a commodification of language as prac-tised in the feuilleton of Viennese journalism, and originally, he claims, *in Heine*.

The third and final consequence of this 'writing of the commodity' is neatly summarized by Benjamin. In Kraus's critique, the 'phrase' makes possible the circulation of ideas by giving them 'currency', as it were, and guarantees a (spurious) specificity of reference, the connoisseur-value derived from a supposedly subjective and individual origin. (Once again Heine is cited to take the blame for having prostituted language so that every salesman can have his say. Kraus's imagery is sexual again: Heine, he says, so loosened the bodice ('Mieder') of the German language that every shop-boy ('Kommis') can finger her breasts. The metaphor of prostitution does not itself occur, though it clearly lies close to hand in this mixture of sexual and economic metaphors.) The creation of a personal note in jour-nalistic writing since Heine, Kraus claims, in reality masks an appalling similarity. All such 'talents' are identical, and all experience becomes inter-changeable when converted into the common currency of falsely subjective reporting. Kraus's essay reaches a minor climax when he pillories this sense of journalistic indifference:

This type [of new talent] is either an observer who bountifully harvests in lux-uriant adjectives what nature has denied to him in substantives, or else he is an aesthete who stands out through a love of colour and a sense of nuance, and per-ceives as much of the things of the phenomenal world as there is dirt under his finger-nails.[18]

The contrast implied here is identical with the one deployed in the opening of Kraus's essay, between a culture given over to content and one given over to form, the Germanic and the Romance. In each case the dignity of the real is undermined or obliterated, drowned out by an excess of interiority. The last trace of the real, says Kraus, is the grubby remainder of a life with the gutter press, the black ink of the journalist's trade.

The coda of this passage crystallizes the sense of the pre-formed and ready-made nature of such experiences. Kraus complains that such banal-ities are presented (by their authors) in a tone of discovery which 'pre-supposes a world which was only created when God made the Sunday supplement and saw that it was good'. The sense of the original creation and its objective validity, which is a constant criterion in Kraus's critical thought, has been replaced by an infinity of journalistic representations. The replacement is total: the very possibility of mimesis falls to the forces of *repetition* unleashed in commodity production. As Kraus remarks bit-terly, everything always fits everything else. And in this way experience itself is stripped of its authenticity and becomes part of a generalized series of repetitions.

Kraus illustrates this depletion of experience by comparing reports of a tram-accident in Berlin and in Vienna. What is still specific to a particular incident in the German capital is reduced to a false essence in Viennese journalism, tricked out with registrations of mood, 'scraps of poetry', and colour. The commodification of language in the aesthetics of the phrase entails a parallel process in experience itself, of our knowledge of it and hence of the world. At every level the effects of commodity production are apparent: in the form of the feuilleton as a literary artefact, in its linguistic medium, and in its experiential content. In Kraus's view both Heine's writing and the journalism of his own contemporaries bear the moral responsibility for this impoverishment. The importance for Kraus of the way in which *Die Fackel* was produced emphasizes the awareness of the 'forces of the commodity' which underlies his polemic against Heine. Kraus went to great lengths to guarantee absolute independence from com-mercial publishing, to the point indeed of ensuring that his paper made less money than it might otherwise have done. Indeed, Pfabigan suggests that Kraus developed anachronistic forms of production derived from the early

nineteenth century rather than the early twentieth.[19] More importantly,
Kraus finds ways to realize his resistance to the power of the commodity
which crushes 'all the elemental drives out of life in order to hand it all
over to the industrial process', as he remarks in his final comments of May
1917.

Ironically enough, Kraus might have found support for his position
in Heine's criticism of Sir Walter Scott's biography of Napoleon. In the
*Englische Fragmente* (*English Fragments*) Heine is clear about the close parallel between Scott's style and monetary exchange:

But to tell the truth, he was like a millionaire whose whole fortune was in small
change, and who has to drive up with three or four wagon loads of pennies and
farthings whenever he has to pay over a large sum . . . (B 2, 549)

Yet for Kraus it is still Heine who not only happened to originate this
transformation in writing, but who is also still directly implicated in the
processes of repetition he is supposed to have unleashed. Heine's centrality to the argument has been relativized by some commentators, but any
attempt to reconstruct the reception of Heine's modernity needs to take
Kraus at the word of his argument and in the context of his understanding
of writing and literature.

First, we should note that two quite different contemporary readings of
'Heine and the Consequences' were in no doubt about its polemical focus.
Rose Ausländer, for instance, gives a very vivid account of the aesthetic
limitations imposed by Kraus's anathematization. As a Jewish intellectual,
rooted in Yiddish culture and moving in the linguistically hypersensitive
literary circles of Czernowitz in the Bukovina, she found that Kraus's ban
made any defence of Heine hopeless. (Interestingly enough, Ausländer
misdates the essay to the late 1920s or early 30s, thus associating the argument with the period of high modernism in the interwar years.)[20] On
the other hand, and in a quite different vein, Alf Jörgensen's pamphlet
on Kraus's attack identifies the importance of his self-regarding style and
remarks wryly, 'When he picked on Heine to bully, he picked the wrong
victim.'[21]

Such responses provide only circumstantial evidence. In two respects,
however, Heine is genuinely central to the argument Kraus puts forward;
and this argument is itself consonant with the ahistorical forms of his critical procedure. His fiercely guarded economic and ideological independence
also projected and asserted a total separation from the social or psychological forces which constituted its actual context. This real foundation
is replaced, in what Pfabigan calls the *Fackel*-ideology, by an exclusively

aesthetic sphere as the only context in which antecedents and contemporaries can be understood:

In the first place there is [Kraus's] assertion that there is a continuity of satirical argument between himself and the authors with whom he identified, who had for instance lived in quite different contexts such as Gogol and Nestroy.[22]

It is clear from the arguments surrounding Heine in 'Heine and the Consequences' that an inverse critical relationship is established on the same grounds. The authors against whom Kraus took up a position, including Heine, are also judged in the context of this aesthetic continuum, and are therefore, in this absolute sense, timeless contemporaries. When Hans Mayer remarks that in Karl Kraus's metaphysics causality is suspended, he offers no more than a *mise au point* of Kraus's own contention that there is finally no distinction between 'Heine' and 'the consequences'.[23]

When Kraus returns to his whipping-boy, it is to see Heine (for the first time in the essay) as the problematic meeting-point of the two conflicting tendencies – of those who 'live in form' and those who 'live in content'. In each case Heine's influence and effect is universal: they 'take their life from him and he lives on in them'. In the sphere of aesthetic judgement the rules of sequence, consequence, and causality are disturbed and paradoxical. Kraus sees each of Heine's 'successors' removing one stone from the 'mosaic' of his work until it disappears entirely. The original is thrown into the shade by the copy. Thus for Kraus Heine's originality is paradoxical – he positively loses what he can give to others, and Kraus is forced to ask what kind of originality is in question if its imitators outdo it.

In this account, Heine's writing is located in the development (and serial production) of modern journalism, which has been perfected as a 'modern machine'. His supposed qualitative identity with his successors effectively abolishes any sense of originality. Although, as Kraus concedes, no subsequent writer can challenge Heine in quantity of output or range of interests, his writing is somehow *already* involved in the processes of repetition which give the 'copy' a plausible superiority to the 'original'. Heine is timelessly implicated in the mechanisms of journalism because he had himself destroyed the very structures – whether they be psychological, epistemological, or aesthetic – which made the authentic representation of reality possible.

### HEINE THE POET

The wide range of Kraus's invective makes it clear that he is speaking of more than some general history of journalism. The strategy of the essay now takes Kraus towards Heine's verse as a case of the same problem. The poetry too has its imitators, and so also falls foul of the implication of repetition and repeatability. In feeling and gesture, minor wit for small-scale melancholy, in the exhaustion of its formal line ('der ausgeleierte Vers') and its cheap rhymes, Heine's poems – as Kraus reads them – are ideally suited to reproduction.

His diatribe against Heine the poet is launched in terms of experience (in the traditional sense of 'Erlebnis') and human maturity. Heine the poet, writes Kraus, lives on as a conserve of youthful love ('eine konservierte Jugendliebe'). Kraus suggests that the poems provide an experience of youthful passion artificially preserved, like bottled fruit. The poems continue to present to their readers experiences and values they should long since have recognized as worthless. Heine profits from these associations to such an extent that an attack on him is perceived as an attack on everyone's private life – because memories of Heine read in adolescence seem to represent authentic personal experiences. In reality they are at best immature features of the interior life, and at worst they were already falsified by their association with the Heine-texts which helped to generate them in the first place. In adult maturity such happy associations must be objectively re-examined, and that will involve recognizing the true sources of Heine's popularity. For Kraus, all that can be and has been said in Heine's defence, by way of 'musicality', wit, or sentiment, attests merely to a systematic distraction from the fundamental question of language itself, represented in Kraus's rather passé pantheon by Liliencron and Gottfried August Bürger. For similar reasons Kraus thinks that contemporary arguments about Heine's standing in the context of German anti-Semitism entirely miss the point. True poets, he believes, restore a primal chaos and have nothing at all to do with any existing social order. Heine, by contrast, is the last resort of all who believe that rhyme constitutes a kind of contract or guarantees some sort of sympathy between writer and reader within society as a whole.

The extent to which such poetry has an integrative function and is itself socially integrated destroys any sense of the primal or elemental, as Kraus requires them in poetry. Appropriately, he returns to metaphors of technology and inauthenticity. Heine becomes a technician, practised in joy and sorrow, as if they are part of a standard repertoire; he efficiently puts on pre-existing moods.[24] At its most acute, this argument sees Heine's early poetry in *Buch der Lieder* as a decoy or non-functional imitation ('Atrappe') in which it is not the revelation of some truth in nature that is experienced by the reader (this is claimed for Goethe's 'Wandrers Nachtlied' ('Wanderer's

Night Song')) but a desire or yearning on Heine's part for which nature serves merely as the allegory (in 'Ein Fichtenbaum steht einsam' ('A pine is standing lonely')).

This is the second occurrence of the idea of allegory in Kraus's argument. He had already said that Heine is ideally suited to those who want to watch a poet in search of extensive allegories. In *Lyrisches Intermezzo* (*Lyric Intermezzo*) XXXIII ('Ein Fichtenbaum Steht einsam' ('A pine is standing lonely')) it may be that the evidently emblematic character of the pine and palm suggested the possibility of an allegorical reading to Kraus; what is certain is that this is a negative quality. It indicates a forced and random imposition of meaning on those elements of reality which it selects for its procedures. This is, of course, consonant with the absence of aesthetic necessity in Heine's work and its consequences, in Kraus's view; and it is entirely in line with the standing of allegory in the literature of German classicism and where it is dismissed, in Benjamin's words, as constituting a merely 'conventional relationship between a significant image and its meaning'.[25]

Kraus's attack on the Heine of *Buch der Lieder* is little short of allergic; but even here his metaphors maintain a fundamental coherence. Kraus suggests that Heine can only be ranked above Goethe by a reader who 'wishes to betread' ('zu betreten wünscht') a poet in search of distended allegories. This is the exact opposite of what is claimed for Goethe and Liliencron, who are said to make available an objective landscape which the sympathetic reader can enter imaginatively – without any of the lexical or grammatical violence of the comment about 'betreading' Heine. There is a sense in Kraus's reading of *Buch der Lieder* that the emblematic status of 'palm' and 'pine' leaves nature deserted, fragmentary, and devoid of any meaning of its own – as Benjamin recognized in baroque allegory a dozen or so years later.

If the writing in the lone pine poem, 'Ein Fichtenbaum steht einsam', *imposes* meanings, Kraus thinks that the substance of Heine's verse must be marked linguistically by the same process. Kraus identifies false sentiment, therefore: it is not nature 'holding her head in her hands' as seen in Liliencron's image, but Heine's hand against his own cheek that we perceive. This supposed banality can then be registered in the embarrassing ease with which 'Herz' rhymes with 'Schmerz'. The rhyme embarrasses through its facility, derived from the merest accident of German vocabulary.[26] But this chance conjunction of sound and sense, the contingency of the poetic substance, also extends to the poetic line. Here too Kraus registers an interchangeability of the sort he has criticized in the Viennese feuilleton with the bleak remark that 'anything will fit anything else'. Thus, 'new' texts by Heine could be 'invented' by intercalating lines from verso and recto pages of *Buch der Lieder* more or less at random.

Such a possibility of transference and exchange exists within a particular range of lyrical writing. So Kraus believes that *Buch der Lieder* could well include texts by Offenbach's librettists but lacks their sense of artistic necessity in the operetta. Perhaps the brilliance of the music leads to this overestimation of Halévy's skill as a writer. Offenbach, says Kraus, is music; Heine simply turns out 'lyrics'. As a result, the witty turns of his verse can never be more than ornamental – and once again Heine is firmly associated with the ornamentality which Loos saw as distinguishing a certain modern form of production. Heine can be condemned out of his own mouth when he says that his pain had been delicately *put into* verse. On Kraus's reading, the poet is rewarded by the mass-effect of his mass production, designed explicitly with one eye on his publisher's profits. The rhymes are symptomatic of the ornamental approach, and that in turn underlines Heine's involvement with the market as a commercial author.

At this point Kraus attempts to relate his criticism of *Buch der Lieder* poems to what he has had to say about that other variety of commercialized writing, journalism. Once again, a false subjectivity, which keeps the reader informed about the author's moods, rubs shoulders with an objectivity which is incapable of any authentic moral or emotional communication. Apropos of Heine's later poem 'Vitzliputzli', Kraus claims to detect a disintegration of mood and substance, of sentimentality and wit: 'Poetry and satire – the phenomenon of the bond between them becomes tangible –: they are neither of them there; they meet on the surface, not in the depths.'[27] What links sentiment to wit is their shared absence, at least at the depth Kraus requires. Lacking any profounder cohesion, they exist only contiguously within a plane, in the spatial disposition of the text. (This sense of a textual surface is perhaps reflected in the previous image of Heine's work as a plundered mosaic.)

Kraus now needs to deal with Heine's supposed wit as a residue of this disintegration. In one of the most interesting and telling criticisms of the essay, he argues that Heine's wit is an 'asthmatic cur' without any of the pathos which could give his 'pointes' real force. Instead, he can only make promises which remain forever unfulfilled: so the verse polemic promised in 'Wartet nur', for instance, is blocked, perhaps by the prevarication of wit itself. As a result of this separation of forces, Heine's technique gives rise to two distinct sorts of reading, one trapped in the realm of sentiment which wit cannot breach, the other parading a false enlightenment and intellectualism which has no sense of pathos. Yet neither of these impulses can sustain real imaginative power because the texts in which they are generated constantly fall apart.

This unachieved nature of Heine's wit leads Kraus to a broad statement of his own view of what can only be called the 'precession of thought'. This is the transcendental doctrine that the creative personality is only a 'chosen vessel' for ideas and indeed poems which pre-date their historical articulation. True thought is immediate, like a 'miasma', a direct infection carried by the air, while opinion ('Meinung') is contagious and only mediated by aesthetic or intellectual contact. Because of the immediacy of true inspiration, the historical paradox I have already noted becomes possible: a creative mind can conceive an idea 'originally' which, in crudely chronological terms, lesser spirits have already imitated. So, for Kraus, Heine merely imitated Nietzsche's notion of the Nazarenic, and all he can truly be said to have anticipated is Maximilian Harden's homophobic prudery.

Once again, in connecting Heine's notorious attack on August von Platen's sexual proclivities in *Die Bäder von Lucca* (*The Baths at Lucca*) with his own polemics against anti-homosexual legislation and mores, Kraus sees Heine as a still contemporary foe. His intolerance towards Platen is party to an unholy alliance with the worst excesses of sensationalist journalism. In such company Heine's word-play is understood as superficial, fragmentary and unintegrated. What is true of Heine's puns is equally true of his other great polemic, the memoir of Ludwig Börne:

The parts without order, the whole without composition, that short windedness that has to start afresh in every paragraph, as if he had to say over and over again: right, and now we'll speak of something else.[28]

In word-play, rhetorical syntax, and overall structure, Heine's work is criticized for its inability to integrate parts within a whole.

In a brief return to economic metaphor, Kraus identifies this failure with a lack of ethical resources. Although the late verse is excluded from this general condemnation, Kraus quotes Heine's remark shortly before his death ('dieu me pardonnera, c'est son métier') to confirm his obsession with trade! From here it is a short step back to the metaphors of production and reproduction I have considered. The invention of the 'feuilleton style' is now attributed to Heine, but those who fear their work may be revealed as an imitation need only transform themselves into forgers to go into mass-production under his name, without fear of discovery.

In the last resort there is some uncertainty of judgement in 'Heine and the Consequences'. While Kraus concedes major and catastrophic achievements to Heine, he generally insists that he did no more than exploit his talent to establish the dominance of technique over creativity. This would be entirely in keeping with the aesthetic doctrine embraced in the essay.[29] As he discusses the function of talent, however, Kraus becomes increasingly involved in Heine's own arguments. He can even quote him for his own ends. Yet the two remain forever at odds. Heine can only be a technician, popularizer, trickster, incapable of that higher writing that gathers the fragmentary and refracted shards which material experience has made of the transcendental idea, and re-forms them into intact virginal thought. Whatever the process may have been which brought about this Fall and disintegration, Heine has certainly never benefitted from the prevenient and saving grace of language, as Kraus understands it.

It should now be possible to identify the major themes of Kraus's critique. We need not accede to his underlying theory of literary creativity to recognize that the principle of Heine's continued *implication* in various kinds of modern writing is important, and recurs in other influential readings of his work in the twentieth century. The idea of Heine's responsibility is twofold: it presents a genetic model of popular writing which he made possible ('Ohne Heine kein Feuilleton') by radically divorcing 'talent' from character; and it understands a whole movement from Heine to the period before the First World War as in some sense unitary.

The easy sexual morals of the French language are associated with Loos's category of the ornamental, which in turn can be understood in relation to a certain sense of the commodity in Heine's style. In an explicit way, writing is grasped in essentially economic terms, identified with a modern mode of production, and realized in the manipulation of the 'phrase'. In its turn this allows Kraus to identify fundamental forms in Heine. *Buch der Lieder* provides the paradigm because its dominant features are repetition and transposition. Kraus can therefore present Heine's text as an extended surface without depth and without authentic mimesis. In the course of the critique, Kraus finally identifies these elements as associated with the structures of *allegory*. Yet in Heine's case the allegorical form has been, so to speak, secularized. The refraction of thought into linguistic elements through the prism of material experience does not allow him to form the lost organic totality of the idea. Instead he builds the fragments of experience into mosaics which his successors can cheerfully pillage.

In all of these major themes, Kraus's reading acutely describes elements of Heine's modern style, its mood and structures, which go at least some way towards clarifying the 'problem Heine' Kraus discovers at the end of his essay. To take his reading, to this extent, seriously need not formally contravene his own account of its intention. In response to criticism (from predictable journalistic quarters) Kraus insisted in his 'Afterword' of August 1911 that he set out neither to be unjust nor to do full justice to Heine. Kraus had not written a literary essay, he claimed – and in his view the problem remained unexhausted. Whatever the value of Heine's verse, in the mirror of Heine's style Kraus had recognized a 'form of life' – perhaps the origins of a modern form of literary production.

# CHAPTER 2

# The biographical imperative: Theodor Adorno

When Kraus speaks of a 'form of life', he is using a moral category. It seems likely that Kraus himself remained blind to the full impact of the economic metaphor underlying his polemic and only marginally aware, through his own journalistic and publishing practices, of those fundamental changes in cultural production which gave the true direction of his attack on the contemporary press. His major successor in the analysis of Heine as a cultural problem, the philosopher and critic Theodor Adorno, was acutely aware of the questions raised by 'political economy' for Heine's work and its reception.

## HEINE, THE MARKET, AND THE COLD WAR

Adorno's essay 'Die Wunde Heine' sets out to be a commemorative talk for the one-hundredth anniversary of the poet's death in 1956. Adorno claims that, as a result of some dialectical reversal, what had been failure is transformed into success when after a hundred years an 'intentionally false folksong becomes a great poem'.[1] This suggests that Adorno is aware of the paradoxical nature of such anniversaries.[2] For post-war readers, he argues, Heine seems to mean something other than what he had 'intended' or what he had meant to his contemporaries, seen as historical readers; but this problem for commemoration is also historically determined: 'Heine' is seen as an effect – as well as a symptom – of the way in which the Third Reich had been repressed in the old Federal Republic, as much as of the actual suppression of Heine's works by the Third Reich. These two distinct elements may perhaps be seen as a single, though differentiated history. But the commemoration of Heine is crossed by history in another way, which is also present in Adorno's essay. As Gerhard Höhn points out, 1956 marks a time when Heine was being appropriated energetically by scholars and critics in the German Democratic Republic, in a specifically socialist spirit.[3] Bringing Heine home from exile involved his 'return' to the *West* German post-war restoration, and hence the calculation of the political feasibility of such a return. That calculus is the underside of Adorno's self-identification with Heine. Adorno's own role can only be 'fulfilled' as a legacy of Heine's original critical potential as an intellectual or 'poète diffamé', forced into exile but bringing a critical humanism back with him.

The extent of Adorno's reliance on Kraus is important in itself if we are to understand his subsequent inflection of this critique. Adorno says himself that Kraus's verdict is ineradicable;[4] and precisely because it is of a different order from the banalities of the National Socialists and the obvious nationalism of the aesthetic and critical circle around Stefan George, Kraus's judgement can continue to influence modern readers as a convenient instrument of the repression of Heine's treatment in the Third Reich by the post-war restoration.[5] It is because of the strength of Kraus's case that it continues to be part of the guilt and embarrassment associated with Heine's reputation. Implicitly Adorno distances himself from Kraus's critique. Nevertheless, certain major themes of Adorno's text as well as a number of incidental details are conceived in close parallel to Kraus's linguistic focus and central thesis. Adorno essentially shares the belief that *Das Buch der Lieder* is guilty of having started a process which ultimately brought lyric poetry down to the level of commerce and the press.[6]

This claim establishes one of the poles of Adorno's argument – the function of the market and market relations in the history of art. The other is constituted by a social and psychological history of Heine's reception which is, at the same time, a history of Jewish repression. Heine's work is placed in the tension between these two moments by which it is, therefore, doubly determined. The most notorious example of such repression and its failure is the story (nowadays considered apocryphal) that Heine's Loreley poem (*Die Heimkehr, The Homecoming*) II) was included in Nazi anthologies with the attribution 'Anonymous' ('Dichter unbekannt'). Kraus had used the same poem as an example of the assimilation of Heine's writing by the most rabidly philistine and anti-Semitic elements of society:

[The satirical journal] *Simplicissimus* once made fun of those German clans who make the sign of the cross at the mention of Heine, only immediately thereafter to sing the Loreley, 'all the same', blissfully drunk on sentimentality.[7]

Adorno, while offering a parallel judgement, interprets such assimilation – via the categorization as 'folksong' which supposedly permitted Heine's poem a place in the fascist canon – as an avoidance of the secretly scintillating and enigmatic ('insgeheim schillernd') power of the lines. This is a significant departure from Kraus's point of view, as is Adorno's suggestion that 'Die Lorelei' ('The Lorelei') recalls long forgotten works by Offenbach – as if Heine's siren presented Wagnerian Rhine-maidens seen through the prism of *Orpheus in the Underworld* or *La Belle Hélène*. Kraus, of course, had made out the exactly contrary case. For him, in the spirit of *prima la musica doppo le parole*, Offenbach is music, while Heine merely provides lyrics. Both departures from Kraus's interpretation indicate a re-evaluation of Heine's writing in relation to the forces of the market, whether specifically in the realm of literature or where writing and market forces meet in the press.

Adorno's argument sidesteps the question, raised by Kraus, of Heine's prose as a source for the 'ornamentalization' of journalism. In Adorno's view, Heine's prose style is sustained by its attention to real human existence, a concern supposedly derived from Heine's Enlightenment inheritance. However friendly Heine may seem, he retains in Adorno's view a critical edge which links him with Spinoza and which generates a certain uneasiness from the air of that more radical time. (It will not have escaped Adorno's notice that Spinoza is celebrated in Heine's essay *Zur Geschichte der Religion und Philosophie* as a Jewish martyr expelled from Spain by the Catholic kings only to be expelled in turn as a heretic from the Amsterdam synagogue [B 3, 562–3].) Here too Adorno recalls a theme of Kraus's polemic which recognized the rationalist origins of Heine's wit. It is important to Adorno, on the basis of his remarks on Heine's prose, to establish Heine as an individualist with only a vague allegiance to the claims of socialism. Because his own commemorative address is formulated as a counter-position to contemporary GDR reception, he is keen to present Heine as anticipating Stalinist repression and the inability of centralized communist economies to satisfy consumer demand: 'His aversion to revolutionary purity and stringency is indicative of Heine's distrust of mustiness and asceticism.'[8] To this end, the image of Heine as a troublesome sensualist in the ranks of the republican and early socialist movements is useful;[9] perhaps more importantly, it is designed to make room for Heine in the context of the Cold War by promoting his individualism and an 'existentialism' more in line with contemporary progressive tastes.

The individualism celebrated in the polemical force of Heine's autobiographical and semi-autobiographical prose is seen in dialectical tension with a contrary force leading to the *loss* of identity. Adorno's suggestion that the Nazis brought Heine a degree of recognition is only half ironic: the supposed anonymity of the 'folksong' that achieves official approval grants Heine's writing public acceptability at the price of just such a loss of identity. If the poem is acknowledged, the poet must remain unknown – as 'Dichter unbekannt'. This aspect of the social and psychological repression which is the history of Heine's reception is symmetrically balanced by a further factor making for anonymity in the field of market relations; and it is this anonymity which, Adorno believes, marks Heine's verse in a special way because it is among the first attempts to come to terms with advanced capitalist society:

It is just this that later generations find embarrassing. For since the existence of bourgeois art in which artists have to earn their livelihoods without patrons, they have secretly acknowledged the law of the marketplace alongside the autonomy of their law of forms, and have produced for consumers. It was only that this dependency was not visible behind the anonymity of the marketplace.[10]

Here Adorno refines part of the argument deployed by Kraus in relation to Loos's view of modern modes of production. But the balance of anonymity is also plain: if Heine's poem can reputedly appear in the framework of Nazi ideology only as the product of an unknown author, the application of market principles to the production of art ultimately has the same effect. Direct personal relations of the kind involved in a system of patronage disappear, and the author becomes an anonymous producer. Or, to put it another way, his or her name and *signature* – as a written identity and identification – are at a premium because it is this authenticity that the connoisseur is willing to pay for.

In this relatively minor text, it is hence possible to discern the dynamics of Adorno's theories of the culture-industry and of the relationship between art and commodity production deployed in his later aesthetic theory. Adorno had little to say about Heine subsequently, but this account of his writing within the framework of the transition of cultural production to developed capitalist conditions makes him a key figure in Adorno's cultural history. The dialectical relations between the creative autonomy of the private individual and his or her loss of individuality and autonomy through subjection to the law of an anonymous market inform the whole of Adorno's account in 1956. Hence, at another level, Heine's supposedly inoffensive prose writings, with their immediate interest in real human existence, are symmetrically opposed in 'Heine the Wound' to the representation of 'experience' in Heine's verse, above all in *Buch der Lieder*. Adorno sees Heine's understanding of the poetry of experience, developed by Goethe in poems occasioned by some specific event, as a broad generalizing of terms – such that 'every occasion finds its poem and everyone agrees that the occasion for verse is appropriate'.[11]

The shadow of Kraus's critique falls across Adorno's judgement here once more. Kraus had complained that impressionistic journalism deems every possible minor event worthy of a 'treatment' in which experience, stripped of any genuine particularity, takes on the contours of the commodity; and Adorno detects exactly the same process in Heine's earlier poems:

> For them as for the feuilletonist, the experiences they [the poems] processed secretly became raw materials that one could write about. The nuances and tonal values which they discovered, they made interchangeable, delivered them into the power of a prepared, ready made language.[12]

This description of a kind of industrial mechanization of the lyric process is very closely derived from Kraus's argument that in journalism the real sensuous particular is displaced by mere impressionism. Similarly in Heine, the apparent immediacy of the verse is *itself* mediated as a commodity; not for the first time the poet emerges as a middleman leaping in to bridge the gap between art and 'an everyday world bereft of meaning'. What seems 'pure and autonomous', the immediacy of experience expressed in Heine's poetry, is the very thing that it *reproduces* for the market: in the terms of Benjamin's Kraus essay, the signs of intimacy and individuality in this verse are those clichés ('Floskel') which 'as ornaments give it a certain collectors' value [Liebhaberwert]', and individuality is no more than a brand-name;[13] or to speak with Adorno again, the vitality of the poems is simply saleable, their spontaneity at one with their reification.

By a perceptive turn of the argument, Adorno defines this structure as specific to the lyric. He observes that, in this poetry, sound itself falls prey to the power of commodity exchange when it had previously been the essential negation of that circulation. By this Adorno means that the tradition which had always identified poetry with sound (vocal rhythm or even song), and hence with the intimacy and interiority of the human voice, is contested in *Buch der Lieder*: far from being the guarantors of some realm of subjective experience, by making such authenticity generally accessible – by marketing it – the poems sell out to the forces of commodity exchange.

However, the dialectical pair of spontaneity and reification conjured up by Adorno was perfectly capable of being read as straightforward ambiguity, or even as unsuccessful irony. The forces of the market may well have set out to occupy the territory of 'sound', but in the first round at least the outcome was not a foregone conclusion. It has been suggested that Heine's success with the poems of *Buch der Lieder* was achieved relatively slowly in the early part of the publishing history, between 1822 and 1829. In large measure this was because of the public's inability to read the poems successfully.[14] More striking, however, in the light of Adorno's remarks, is the enormous musical literature which gathered round this book of songs, and so reclaimed for subjective authenticity what 'sound' seemed to have lost to reification. This is presumably Adorno's point when he speaks of the Heine 'whose poems were still set to music by Schubert' – as if such compositions were now clearly unthinkable.[15] In such a case the contradiction between the song as an expression of full interiority and as a saleable artefact on the market was not yet acute. Yet there is inevitably a final turn of the dialectical screw when the success of musical settings, such as Mendelssohn's 'Auf Flügeln des Gesanges' ('On wings of song'), let alone Silcher's version of the 'Loreley', effectively confirm the anonymity of the author and reinforce the transformation of sound in conditions of commodity exchange. Such popularity is what lent a certain plausibility to the supposed Nazi ascription to an anonymous author that Adorno has invoked: as Kraus had testified, many of the anti-Semitic 'nationalists' who sang Heine's words would not have recognized his authorship.

Adorno is partly aware of the correspondences between his view of *Buch der Lieder* and the prose works which he thinks are less offensive. The transformation of what could be paraphrased as 'acoustic inwardness' into commodity and exchange is parallel to the unmasking of Romantic individualism by Heine's undiluted rationalist impulse, the Enlightenment legacy; it then appears that the autonomy conferred on the writer by the market conceals a significant degree of commodification. In Heine's prose, the same impulse refuses to smuggle back in – through some backdoor of literary profundity (Adorno calls it 'the basement door to the depths' ('Kellertür der Tiefe')) – the very thing it has just demolished. It is in this sense that Heine's individualism, in Adorno's phrase, 'did not bend to the individualistic concept of inwardness'; his utopia of sensual fulfilment includes some fulfilment in external things ('die Erfüllung im Auswendigen').[16] What in this sense is fulfilled 'externally' has turned outwards, to a world that opposes the inwardness of Romantic subjectivity. Adorno's account of Heine's prose defines it in terms of exteriority and a rejection of depth which parallels and inverts Kraus's mistrust of the ornamental surface generated by a modernist contiguity of 'art' and 'life'. For Adorno these are characteristics that give Heine's prose-style its critical and existential immediacy; what he fails to make clear is that this immediacy is exactly parallel to the 'spontaneity' which in the *verse* writing coincides with its reification. In both cases it is the obliteration of 'real' subjectivity, dense, inward, and ultimately reliable, that is at issue.

Heine's personal engagement, so to speak, with the forces of the market informing his work gives offence: if Adorno believes that the offence of the poet can be avoided by concentrating on the prose author, he does so at the price of an unusual paradox. For Adorno unusually accepts Heine's attack on Platen's homosexuality in *Die Bäder von Lucca* as an example of Heine's subjective powers as a polemicist. In doing so, he challenges Kraus's moral indignation at the same attack which, he said, would have extinguished Heine's reputation if there had been any feeling for true polemical power in Germany. In a direct echo of Kraus's phrase, Adorno identifies in Heine 'a polemical power unrestrained by any kind of servility' and so endorses the attack on Platen's homosexual preference. The paradox of Adorno's account lies in the fact that in the next breath this commitment to 'real human existence' is dismissed as bravura, a florid display of temperament and technique, which is much less important than the general range of his subject-matter. In this way another version of 'spontaneity' (polemical force) gives way in the face of the exteriority it supposedly addresses.

## HEINE AND/OR BAUDELAIRE

As an historical individual, Heine is seen by Adorno as doubly vulnerable to this subjection of individuality to the world around it. His weakness can be represented by the nature of the commodity in the market, or by the society that created the market. First, Heine is seen to be severely limited by the phase of capitalism which provokes and develops his techniques of writing in the first place. In Adorno's view, Heine began to write (roughly between 1815 and 1830) at the point when poetry could no longer ignore the emerging power of 'capitalist society' without falling back into a kind of cosy provincialism ('ins provinziell Heimelige' – 'provincial folksiness').[17] This specifically responds to Kraus, who cited Liliencron's direct expression of an immediate relationship to landscape and language as a stylistic foil for Heine's 'ornamentalism'.[18] It is Heine's inability or refusal to maintain such appearances of unbroken naivety that puts him, in Adorno's view, alongside Baudelaire in the modern movement of the nineteenth century. If 'experience' – the field of knowledge and self-knowledge of an autonomous individual – has been transformed into 'raw material for writing about' ('über die sich schreiben läßt'), then the process of writing itself also comes under the aegis of industrial production. Adorno sees this aspect of Heine in a moral contrast with Baudelaire: the younger poet resisted the process of destruction and dissolution set in motion by modernization, and so 'heroically wrests dream and image from modernity itself; indeed he transfigures the loss of all images, transforming that loss itself into an image';[19] Heine, on the other hand, gives way to the historical current and develops 'a poetic technique of reproduction' appropriate to the industrial age. In doing so he becomes caught up in the market and its corresponding social structures, and so fails to attain to the archetypes of modernity attributed to Baudelaire.

It seems that Heine's failure in this respect is not simply a consequence of Adorno's preference for Baudelaire,[20] nor is it attributable to the fact that Adorno's own canons are derived from the classical and full-blooded Romantic traditions of German verse and so lead him to repeat Benjamin's exclusion of Heine from an aesthetics of modernity.[21] Rather, Heine is seen as a transitional figure – provoked by the effects that an emerging capitalism has on the human and natural worlds, but unable to rise to its challenges. Having understood the threat posed by the market and its commodity forms to the writer and his or her autonomous work of art, Heine unmasks the inwardness of late Romantic subjectivity through and as a merely superficial replication. The effect of this rationalist impulse, however, is to deliver poetry entirely into the power of the market process. It should perhaps be said at this point that Adorno's argument ought not to depend solely on a critique of repetition or replication. For, in Heine's partial contemporary Eichendorff (to whom Adorno devoted an essay and whose poetry is constructed over an extremely narrow thematic and lexical range), Adorno also discovers an impulse towards replication arising from the exhaustion of the Romantic lexicon. In this case, however, the sense of loss which presides over the utterance of 'the departed words' positively guarantees their viability.[22] Heine's writing celebrates the opposite tendency: he cannot recall the lost immediacy of landscape and language but only the condition of alienation which has overwhelmed them and him.

### LANGUAGE AND AUTHENTICITY

According to Adorno, Heine is vulnerable to the exterior world of commodities and markets, and to the market society, which is simultaneously the world in which Heine believed full human, sensual fulfilment was to be found. This sensitivity is historically conditioned, but Adorno goes on to define Heine's responses as both racially and psychologically predetermined; ultimately Heine's vulnerable relationship to the social and economic environment is biological and, according to Adorno, its chief symptom is to be found in Heine's use of German and his relationship with the language.

Adorno believes he can detect in Heine a totally smooth linguistic structure ('das glatte sprachliche Gefüge').[23] This sort of virtuoso writing, he claims, is only possible for an author whose relationship to the medium of their self-expression is somehow tangential – as if Heine were using something other than the language of his birth. In order to clarify his sense of a linguistic smoothness, Adorno makes two remarks, both of which retain the earlier sense of imitation. In relation to the 'muteness' of Heine's language, as he calls it, he refers to 'the virtuosity of this man who imitated language as if he were playing it ['nachspielte'] on a keyboard', where the image depends on the idea of playing through music written by someone *else*. Similarly, near the start of his discussion, he speaks of a 'fluency ['Geläufigkeit'] and self-evidence ['Selbstverständlichkeit'], which is derived from the language of communications'.[24] As Robertson has shown, such images of performance, impersonation, and echo, associated with a sense of linguistic surface and virtuosity, form part of a depressing critique of Jewish 'mimicry' among German anti-Semites, which is also taken up by assimilated Jews in their anxiety to obliterate marks of linguistic difference.[25] At bottom the idea of impersonation is clearly a version of the old complaint, launched by Ludwig Börne and his friends, that Heine's talent exceeds his character.

It comes as no surprise to find in Adorno's discussion of the inauthenticity of Heine's language a largely Krausian context. Instead of dwelling securely in language, Heine has language *at his disposal*. The complaint that he lacks resistance ('Widerstandslosigkeit') to merely current vocabulary recalls Kraus's notion of 'defencelessness'('Wehrlosigkeit'). It is more surprising to recall that the common source of this imagery of inauthentic virtuosity is in fact Heine himself, though it remains unclear whether Kraus or Adorno were aware of Heine's comments on Platen in *Die Bäder von Lucca*: 'Unlike the true poet language never became master in him; on the contrary, he became a master in language, or rather a master on language like a virtuoso on an instrument' (B 2, 455). Adorno makes every effort, however, to reverse the polarity of the earlier use of this metaphor in Kraus, and reconstructs such themes in Heine's favour. He is now to become a representative modern figure in the very moment of his failure. It will be the universality of Heine's Jewish experience which renews his insight. For the need to impersonate current language, Adorno argues, is directly produced by the continued exclusion of Jews from positions of responsibility in post-Napoleonic Prussia. The failure of assimilation generates precisely an excess of linguistic identification. It is the absence of Jewish emancipation which enables Heine to recognize artistic autonomy dependent on the anonymity of the market as a phantasm: that is why the language of spontaneous subjectivity (the speech of the emancipated and autonomous individual, released into the extraterritorial realm of Romantic 'Wander-lieder') turns out in *Buch der Lieder* to be identical with the language of reification (the dependence of all on alienating exchange value).

In order to define the kind of subject whose own language is or has become to all intents and purposes foreign ('fremd') – who 'deploys language like something that has gone out of stock' (or perhaps 'like a book that is out of print': 'wie ein vergriffenes Ding')[26] – Adorno is reduced to an extraordinary level of biographical supposition. To establish this disturbed relationship with German as Heine's mother tongue, Adorno remarks 'Heine's mother, whom he loved, did not have full command of German'.[27] A number of things are odd about this. Most obvious is the rhythmic and rhetorical disruption which the sentence brings to its rather abstract context. It is not at all clear what difference the fact that Heine loved his mother is supposed to make to the case – though his relationship with his parents continues to be a matter of some debate.[28] Jeffrey Sammons comments that his mother's German was 'somewhat faulty'.[29] Presumably the claim would be that, subsequently, Heine needed to overcompensate for this inadequacy in his mother's command of German as his own mother tongue. Yet it is not at all clear that his acquisition of language was adversely affected by his mother's youthful grammatical errors.

The same general point could as well have been made by describing Heine's relationship with his father. In the *Memoiren* (*Memoirs*) he says that his father was the one he most loved 'on this earth' (B 6/1, 586); yet if anyone was going to reveal the illusory character of the autonomous bourgeois subject, it was surely Samson Heine. After all, Heine's father was both himself an example of failed independence, forced to rely on the wealth and acumen of his brother Salomon, who finally liquidated his business and had him declared incompetent to manage his own affairs. Samson Heine must also have made a significant contribution to his son's discovery that independence and autonomy could not be achieved through commodity exchange (Adorno's 'Ware und Tausch') when he hit upon the notion of paying his own debts with bills of exchange drawn upon the company his brother had set up for his son.[30] There is also evidence to suggest that the fundamental trauma of the young Heine's psychological development lay in the realization, alluded to in a veiled way in the *Memoiren*, that his childhood happiness and particularly his sunny image of his father were based on illusion – indeed, that his father lived his life as pure illusion.[31] In this respect too Samson Heine might have served the purposes of Adorno's argument concerning the false sense of independence conjured up by the process of commodity exchange in an author writing for the market.

It is striking that in precisely the passage of the *Memoiren* in question, Heine refers to his father's manner of speech. It is difficult to believe that, by 1956, Adorno was not aware that Heine comments on his father's voice and dialect:

> He spoke the dialect of Hanover, where – as also in the vicinity to the south of this city – German is pronounced best. It was a great advantage for me that from childhood onwards my ear was used to good German pronunciation. (B 6/1, 584)

Heine was in a position to acquire a good accent, at any rate in comparison with what he calls the double Dutch of the Lower Rhine spoken in Düsseldorf and Cologne. Of his father's voice he recalls that it was virile and rich, but also childlike – reminiscent in some way of woodland sounds, and perhaps of the cries of robins! (B 6/2, 584). This too may be a compensatory memory. It clearly indicates the association of aesthetic qualities with language, while the birdsong provides both a symbol of Heine's attempt to recover a primitive 'natural sound' through art, and a veiled hint that the language which most integrally expressed his father's identity remained Yiddish, carefully masked by precise elocution. From Adorno's point of view this in turn would suggest that Samson Heine's mastery of Hanoverian High German was also a 'performance' in a foreign tongue rather than a Krausian security in language.

Any or all of these accounts might have been grist to Adorno's mill. It is also true, however, that Heine had only the dimmest recollections of Hebrew, as his requests to school-friends for help with quotations from Scripture demonstrate. The story he tells about walking through the Frankfurt ghetto with Börne and failing to recognize Psalm 137 when he heard it in Hebrew seems to admit as much.[32] This is the kind of evidence Adorno would need if he were to substantiate his sketch of Heine's alienation from the German language. Yet the 1956 commemoration not only avoids material which might damage Adorno's case, it entirely ignores Heine's own recollections relating to language acquisition. Instead, Adorno prefers anecdotal material relating to Betty van Geldern, Heine's mother.

There are two reasons for this preference. First, throughout the text Adorno approaches the provocation which Heine represents in terms of his Jewishness. Platen's scurrilous anti-Semitism is said to have provoked the exemplary polemics of *Die Bäder von Lucca* and the prose works generally – literary and philosophical commentary and the ideological critique of *Ludwig Börne eine Denkschrift*. When Adorno turns to the verse, however, it is once again the Jewish middleman who is in evidence when the poems are seen as willing mediators ('prompte Mittler') of marketable spontaneity. Furthermore, this is only possible because the failure of Jewish emancipation and assimilation after 1815 allows Heine to see that the apparent autonomy conferred by the market is illusory. According to Adorno, it is because Heine remains Jewish and unassimilated that he is able to create from a borrowed, *naturalized* fluency the polished construct of a language become entirely commodity. Ultimately, it is not Heine's exile or his baptism that is important so much as his Jewish birth and, therefore, his mother. Only Betty Heine guarantees her son's place in the congregation of Israel, and so she must also be the point at which his tangential, alienated relation to the mother tongue is instituted.

Secondly, Adorno prefers anecdotal material concerning Heine so long as it provides a form in which popular images of the poet can be confronted. He retells the story of Heine's visit to Goethe in Weimar, when he replied to an enquiry about his current work that he was engaged on a *Faust*. Adorno could have known that there are several versions of this unreliable reminiscence even in Heine's published accounts. But the anecdote is ideally suited to demonstrate Heine's position as an outsider who needs to feel he is in a position central to the culture as a whole, but whose very desire for inclusion becomes the occasion for his continued exclusion. The desire for acceptance, Adorno writes, is 'doubly irritating to those [natives] who are already established, who drown out their own guilt at excluding him by reproaching him for the vulnerability of his assimilation'.[33] Irrespective of its relevance to what passed between Goethe and Heine on 2 October 1824, this brings Adorno back to the theme of Heine as excluded and guilty Jew. In this capacity, he can also point the way forward to the social salvation by which the trauma of Heine's name can be healed. For it is through the failure of assimilation that his great achievement as a poet of modern alienation becomes possible.

Heine's virtuosity in playing through language like some forgotten or reconstructed melody is so great that the very inadequacy of his speech becomes the means he is given 'to say what he suffers'. The allusion to *Torquato Tasso* suggests that Heine's inadequacy did indeed rival Goethean self-expression. For the Tasso who says

> Und wenn der Mensch in seiner Qual verstummt
> Gab mir ein Gott zu sagen, wie ich leide,[34]

> When man falls silent in his pain,
> a god gave me the power to express how I suffer.

the utterance given to the poet amid human silence is of divine origin. As Adorno reads the poet's power of expressivity, Heine raises the issue of human linguistic failure himself. Divine inspiration of Heine the speechless

Jew would make him a prophet. In the banal sense, he would be one whose words come to fulfilment in the future – 'now that the destiny which Heine sensed has been fulfilled literally';[35] in the more strictly biblical sense, we might conjecture, he would be a man whose life and form of existence bear witness to a truth and to a fall from grace. These two senses come together as Adorno develops the musical metaphor to claim that Heine's true being was not revealed in the various settings of Heine-*Lieder*, but only in the music of Mahler, who could also make 'the brittleness of the banal and the derivative' express what was most real.[36] And Mahler, of course, was also a baptized Jew.

The focus for Adorno's critique is biographical and both recapitulates and re-evaluates Kraus's critical procedure. Adorno's insistence on Heine as a Jew crucially underlies his understanding of how language can relate to the false autonomy conferred by market relations. A traditional image of the role of commercial activity in Jewish life provides the link, and so the same ethnic dimension and its social consequences project Heine as a talent who instrumentalizes language and experience, commercializes poetry, and ultimately faces anti-Semitic hatred to the point of the unspeakable horror of the Holocaust. It is therefore only by restoring Heine's *Jewish* name, to the poet who has been reduced to public anonymity by the Nazis, that it will be possible to see in the exile of the Diaspora the universal homelessness of modern alienation.

In all these respects Adorno has developed the implicit anti-Semitism of Kraus's essay, but he gives a new and positive turn to the clichés of Jewish commercial expertise.[37] The residue of negativity is also Krausian. If Heine's success was to devise a kind of writing consonant with a particular phase of capitalist development, it was also his failure, since, on Adorno's reading, he could not create the 'archetypes of modernity' which might have transcended that development, as its critique. At least, this is Adorno's claim at the historical level. The paradox of his conclusion lies in the fact that a poem from the 'Homecoming' section in *Buch der Lieder* has now attained an archetypal significance it could not have possessed historically. Such paradoxes proliferate: the more the 'false' and perhaps falsified folksong is read in the specific context of Heine's Jewishness, the more it turns out to speak for an experience of modern isolation and alienation of a different order from Heine's own. His manipulation of the inauthenticity of his own language makes it a *true* and authentic reflection of ours.[38]

# CHAPTER 3

# The biographical imperative: Helmut Heißenbüttel – pro domo

> . . . bei solchem Streit
> Verliert man seine Ähnlichkeit.
> . . . after such pugnacity
> You lose your selfsame similarity.
>
> (Wilhelm Busch)

Karl Kraus's critique and Adorno's talk taking up and extending its themes are the most important texts in the public debates about Heine in the first half of the twentieth century. An unusual and provocative coda to their arguments was provided by Helmut Heißenbüttel in two essays published a decade apart. Until his death in 1996 Heißenbüttel was one of the leading figures in the experimentalist avant-garde of the former West Germany. His essays 'Materialismus und Phantasmagorie in Gedicht' ('Materialism and Phantasmagoria in the Poem' (1972)) and 'Karl Kraus und die Folgen' ('Karl Kraus and the Consequences'. Heinrich Heine as a Journalist'(1982, broadcast on South German Radio in 1979)) set out to throw new light on the views of Kraus and Adorno, and to reinterpret them. Heißenbüttel understands perfectly well the political and economic framework of Kraus's polemic and Adorno's manipulation of its arguments. His strategy, however, inverts their assessment in order to claim that Heine achieved a fundamental change of direction in post-Romantic aesthetics. The suggestion is not new in itself: academic criticism had long applied categories of 'belatedness', of the epigonic, and of the transitional to Heine's work. Heißenbüttel has an independent and intriguing view of Heine's novelty which confirms the major themes in the literary understanding of his work which have emerged in the work of Kraus and Adorno, but gives an original inflection to his importance as a modern poet.

The volumes in which Heißenbüttel's two Heine essays are collected both present sketches for an alternative and even revisionist literary history. The earlier collection on the tradition of modernism, *Zur Tradition der Moderne* (*On the Tradition of Modernism*), surveys both the literary past and the salient figures of contemporary writing. Heißenbüttel would like to consider the younger generation of West German writers within a new historical perspective. In doing so he seeks precedents for the innovations of contemporary writing. This search provides the framework when Heißenbüttel asks 'how [Heine's] oeuvre appears today', and as a consequence he is also arguing *pro domo*, for an understanding of literary history that provides a background to the experiments he seeks to promote in his own day.[1] To understand Heine in this contemporary context is also to make claims for his patronage and antecedence in respect of Heißenbüttel's contemporaries and ours. This context also explains why Heißenbüttel addresses himself to his two critical antagonists in chronologically reverse order. The late 1960s had given Adorno a prominence in the student movement and in the universities generally which made his view of Heine a necessary target for Heißenbüttel. Indeed, it would be possible to go further and say that the barely concealed contempt for Adorno, which emerges in Heißenbüttel's quotations and near quotations from 'Die Wunde Heine', are symptomatic of the farewell to Adorno which came after 1968 – if not earlier.

To ask what force Heine's writing has now, 'how it seems' to us, is to reverse Adorno's point of departure, while in another sense this question also repeats it. Adorno's major conclusion, after all, had been to identify in Heine a modern sense of alienation which emerges, after the event, in a dialectical reversal of his failure, his supposed 'speechlessness'. Heißenbüttel sets out to reverse the premise of Adorno's argument – namely the belief that there is in Heine an unbridged gap, a failure or absence. This deficiency appears, in Adorno's case, as the non-attainment of 'archetypes of modernity' of the kind achieved by Baudelaire. But Heißenbüttel goes further. By comparison with popular literary history, illustrated in the 1954 edition of the Brockhaus encyclopaedia and Otto von Leixner's *Literaturgeschichte* (*Literary History*) of 1893, he demonstrates that the registration of inadequacy is a standard manoeuvre in critical assessments of Heine. The reality of a break in lyrical feeling, expression, or style is admitted, in this traditional view, but Heine is only ever considered in comparison with different, and presumably more successful, responses to it. Where traditional lyrical language persists under the sign of melancholy or irony in poets such as Eichendorff and Mörike, and its loss is transcended into modern forms of expression in Baudelaire, Heine is judged a failure on both counts. It is a central strategy of Heißenbüttel's essays to recognize this absence or lacuna and use it to give a positive account of Heine's supposed inadequacy. The result is familiar in two ways. First, if Eichendorff and Mörike appear to hang on to fading modes of expression, while Baudelaire's creative negativity is a decisive measure of their disappearance, Heine can be correspondingly seen as the writer *at the break* itself, as the great witness to it; in both senses, therefore, as the writer of the break. Secondly, in a gesture that few writing about him avoid, Heine becomes the hero of this moment, not subjected to it, but mastering and manipulating it.

According to Heißenbüttel, the break occurs in the relationship between metaphorical language and subjectivity. This, he claims, is the terrain which Heine's *Buch der Lieder* shares with the Romantic poets and with Baudelaire. In fact, this relationship, between metaphor and subjectivity, is seen as the site of the break in Heine's work, from *Buch der Lieder* onwards; the failure of that relation is itself the break:

The ability to express subjective things – feelings, moods, love, pain, despair, disappointment etc. – in the form of linguistic images, in the form of metaphors is thwarted again and again by the irony or even cynicism that earned Heine a hundred years of censure.[2]

Metaphor is understood here as an adequate and appropriate expression of emotion through poetic imagery, which corresponds to or is anchored in an accessible subjectivity. In Heine, however, according to Heißenbüttel, the anchoring of metaphor in a stable relation of expressivity is upset by the effects of irony and cynicism; that is to say, the 'subject' veers away from the security of the metaphor, and perhaps means something else (irony), or, in a more extreme way, exploits metaphorical discourse for other purposes and abandons all claim to expressivity (cynicism). Heißenbüttel generalizes these two indications by saying that the (expectations of) metaphorical discourse are not fulfilled, and then goes on to paraphrase this process as an 'emptying out', an evacuation, of metaphor. To varying degrees the bond between the subjective experience or 'feeling' of an historical personality and its expression in imagery is attenuated or severed. In each case what Heißenbüttel addresses is the recourse to *biographical* explanation, which can be identified as an imperative in Kraus and in Adorno.

Michael Perraudin's account of Heine's use of Wilhelm Müller as a source of such dead metaphors (and symbols) fleshes out historically what Heißenbüttel identified phenomenologically. With reference to *Lyrisches Intermezzo* LIX he remarks:

For this poet, his feeling is represented neither by the falling star, nor the falling blossom, nor the swan-song but by their absence; in one sense he bemoans their loss, in another he acknowledges their inadequacy for the expression of his condition of mind.[3]

Heißenbüttel might well feel that any claim of this kind about this poet's 'condition of mind' is really rather risky. It is perhaps at best a positivist version of Adorno's idea of Heine's 'speechlessness'. For once metaphor has been emptied or hollowed out in this way, what remains is perceived as stereotyped and formulaic. Heißenbüttel illustrates this kind of formulaic writing with an example from *Heimkehr* (LII: 'Andre beten zur Madonne'), particularly its variational final couplet and its careless rhymes. But he suggests that *Buch der Lieder* reveals two other related strategies. The first is Heine's exploitation of motifs of death, annihilation and transitoriness as a means to breaking with subjectivity; the other sets out explicitly to unmask the illusion of metaphor and therefore of subjectivity itself. The effect of this last strategy is to generate a new linguistic relation (that is, a new relation of referentiality) in the poem. *Heimkehr* XVIII provides Heißenbüttel's case, where the second strophe abandons the residually metaphorical language of the first, in which the house of the faithless beloved is described as 'empty and abandoned' ('Das [i.e. Haus] steht so leer und verlassen'), for simple utterances ('einfache Aussagesätze') expressed as exclamations ('Die Straßen sind doch gar zu eng!' ('The streets are cramped and narrow!')). Speech here is indicated by the vernacular particles 'doch gar' and, I suppose, by the lost metaphor entailed in describing the pavement in the next line as 'unbearable'. Although such utterances might issue from affect, Heißenbüttel argues that they have been stripped of any metaphorical form to become merely propositional, constative – as it were, facticious.

Heißenbüttel understands this element in *Buch der Lieder* as marking the exhaustion of a traditional technique, in which metaphor had always been safely grounded in subjectivity. But although Heine seems, in Heißenbüttel's scenario, to have perceived this Alexandrian condition of the late Romantic lyric, he is not thought of as exploiting it for other ('ironic') purposes. Rather, he queries the status of the whole realm of subjective feeling. We are not to see this account as aggressive or deliberately shocking, however; it is simply the effect of the inadequacy of that 'metaphorical' relation of language to the factors conditioning contemporary life. The factors determining this sense of the times will have to be defined historically and, in particular, in relation to a changing mode of production. Like Kraus and Adorno, Heißenbüttel opts for the mystified representation of alienated social relations in Marx's idea of the fetishism of the commodity as the dominant characteristic of his own time to which Heine responds. But Heißenbüttel also remains within the general sphere of poetry in order to locate Heine's positive achievement. Hence, within the same trajectory, late Mörike is cited as cancelling out his own earlier poetry of mood; and an alternative poetic succession is sketched which moves through the verse of the novelist Theodor Fontane (!) to the cartoon satires of Wilhelm Busch.

Heißenbüttel returned to Busch in a later collection of essays, *Von fliegenden Fröschen* (*On Flying Frogs*), in which his second Heine essay also appears.[4] There, Wilhelm Busch, the painter, satirical poet, and cartoonist, is read as a critic of the bourgeoisie and of clericalism; and the final illustration of the force of Busch's technique strikingly returns to the problem of metaphor and subjectivity. 'Verlust der Ähnlichkeit' ('Loss of Similarity') describes the fate of a drunkard who is badly stung by moralistic bees when he approaches their hive:

> Und als er wiederum erscheint,
> Erkennt ihn kaum sein bester Freund.
> Natürlich, denn bei solchem Streit
> Verliert man seine Ähnlichkeit.[5]

> When finally his woes have reached their end
> He's hardly recognized by his best friend.
> No wonder – after such pugnacity
> You lose your selfsame similarity.

The clash between narrow-minded morality and hedonistic excess brings about a failure of similitude which, Busch's title hints, could be generalized. This throws further light on Heißenbüttel's view of Heine. The conflicts he experienced in moral and ideological domains – with Prussian censorship on the one hand, and with hot-house politics of exiled republicanism on the other – leads to a similar 'loss of similitude' of the kind Heißenbüttel earlier identifies as the evacuation of metaphor.

This revision of the history of German poetry continues with Karl Kraus (who turns out to have been 'of the devil's party' all along), and would no doubt conclude with Heißenbüttel himself. The discovery of 'simple utterances', claimed for *Heimkehr* XVIII, is extended to a general practice of quotation which Heißenbüttel identifies in the well-known opening of Heine's *Harzreise* (*Harz Journey*) with its parody of tourist information on Göttingen, famous for its university and its sausages. This is reckoned to be innovatory, in as much as Heine is thought to be the first writer to 'stick to facts, conventional talk'. In short, 'He quotes.' And this attention to fact is glossed with an Adornian phrase which was also current in the theoretical debates of the student movement when Heißenbüttel claims 'he abstains from the affirmative, as we say today'. This strategy, it turns out, also has an historical pedigree, but one in which once again the primacy of Heine's innovation is maintained. Heißenbüttel sees both Lawrence Sterne and Denis Diderot as possible antecedents on Heine's path to modern writing, but in each case he is thought to risk more, by refusing the security of Sterne's tone of personal irony that can lend a human warmth to ironic distance, and by launching a critique – in *Die Bäder von Lucca* – without philosophically secured foundations.

By making the break into the purely citational, whether it is understood as facts, as common parlance and received wisdom, or as direct quotation, Heine, in Heißenbüttel's account, severs the link to a self-expressive subject which conventional reading needs as a guarantee of metaphorical discourse. In so doing, he moves towards a constructivist aesthetic – with obvious similarities to Heißenbüttel's own work in the *Textbücher* (*Textbooks*) and the succeeding 'projects'. The discovery of a practice of quotation, further, opens up the possibility of writing as reproduction, in exactly the sense addressed by Adorno when he criticizes Heine's reliance on 'ready-made' language. But here Adorno's judgement is turned on its head, so that the technique of poetic reproduction is welcomed as a fundamentally positive characteristic of Heine's oeuvre. And yet by a dialectical reversal very like Adorno's, it will now be this citational, or even documentary, strategy in Heine which establishes his canonical authority in a revisionist literary history.

Heißenbüttel culls a famous passage from the epistle dedicatory to Heine's second collection of his Paris journalism, *Lutetia*, which provides a focus for this new technique. There, Heine compares his own procedure to the early photographic process of the daguerreotype:

An honest daguerreotype must render a fly just as well as the proudest horse, and my reports are a history book made of daguerreotypes in which each day provided its own portrait. Through the conjunction of such pictures the ordering mind of the artist has produced a work in which what is represented documents its faithfulness authentically through itself. (B 5, 239)

Heißenbüttel subsequently seeks to appropriate the notions of daguerreotype, of documentation, and of authenticity for a general reading of Heine's aesthetic project. Such categories, he believes, run counter to traditional ideas of the true, the beautiful, and the sublime, against generic preconceptions such as tragedy and comedy, and against any understanding of art as reflection or imitation. In identifying a break with the idea of artistic mimesis, Heißenbüttel may well be responding to Karl Kraus's remarks on art and the centrality of the mimetic relation in his criticism of Heine.

More importantly, he returns to the break in the relationship between metaphor and subjectivity which had been his starting point, by claiming that Heine's categories in *Lutetia* abandon the standards of 'Goethe and the Romantics' which had presupposed the 'linguistic-metaphorical expression of subjectivity'. As a result Heine has simply been misread, in the light of false and prejudicial expectations. It is precisely in the failure of such traditional models to deal with the provocation of Heine's methods that the alternative tradition and its different criteria can be glimpsed. However tentatively, Heißenbüttel believes that this is the tradition of modernity and modernism ('die Moderne') to which his whole book is addressed. In the twentieth century such writing continued to appear alien, arbitrary and 'apoetic'[6] – and the last term will recur in the critical essays of the late 1970s, which celebrate literature as 'Verarschung' or piss-taking.

In applying the standards of the daguerreotype to Heine's work as a whole, Heißenbüttel is aware of a certain risk. But he believes that *Deutschland. Ein Wintermärchen* (*Germany. A Winter's Tale*) most readily demonstrates that the photographic process is an appropriate model. As an example, he quotes from the poem the very stanza which had attracted Kraus's particular censure:

> Von Köllen bis Hagen kostet die Post
> Fünf Taler sechs Groschen Preußisch.
> Die Diligence war leider besetzt
> Und ich kam in die offene Beichais!
>
> (B 4, 596)

> The fare from Cologne to Hagen is
> Five Prussian thalers six groschen.
> The coach was full; an open chaise
> Was my means of locomotion.
>
> (D 498)[7]

While Kraus had bitterly criticized the nasal, 'Jewish' pronunciation necessary to make this notorious rhyme work properly, Heißenbüttel sees 'five thalers six groschen' as a documentary fact and the loan-words 'Diligence' (the French name for a stagecoach) and 'Beichais', with its curious German prefix, as documentation of current terminology. As a literary method the daguerreotype can thus have two distinct functions. It may record facts (the fare from Cologne to Hagen) or topography in the manner of the travel-journal, or it may fix and merely reproduce linguistic material, without any attention to referentiality. This second version of the photographic method (with its obvious affinities, in these terms, with his own procedures) is the one Heißenbüttel prefers, and he makes a relatively unsubstantiated claim that this second sense of the daguerreotype dominates in Heine's 'late poetry' – in which he includes the two satires *Atta Troll* and *Deutschland. Ein Wintermärchen*. This understanding of the import of Heine's style once again reverses an earlier judgement. Just as Adorno's negative view of reproduction had been turned round, here Heißenbüttel gives his approbation to the very thing Kraus complains of – that the 'ornamental' style dissolves the differences between art and the world to generate the homogeneity which sees 'form' everywhere and already. Heine, in short, becomes a linguistic realist.

This whole development is premised on the anti-metaphorical moves of *Buch der Lieder*. Heißenbüttel sees in them a radicalized version of Romantic irony which, far from setting up a self-transcending subject of the kind Friedrich Schlegel's classical definition outlined in *Athenäum* (*Athenaeum*), reveals the evacuation of subjectivity ('Entleerung der Subjektivität'). Heißenbüttel takes the late poem 'Schnapphahn und Schnapphenne' ('Thieving cock and thieving hen') as a demonstration of the extent to which this irony *abandons* subjectivity, however decadent or corroded, in order to open up political, social, and material dimensions. This new perspective is hence 'produced from the abandoned realm of the subjective' ('stellt sich her aus dem aufgegebenen Bereich des Subjektiven').[8] Society evacuates the subject, which survives now only as a memory in the play of wit – yet even this is often generated within language (without any real subjective, or even social, dimension) as 'Sprachwitz', a pure word-play. If wit is therefore symptomatic of Heine's nostalgia for a lost subjectivity, Heißenbüttel also believes that the same double-edged experience of discontinuity can be seen in the poet's relationship to communism, which both terrifies and charms him.

This well-known ambivalence is cited in the German version of the French preface to *Lutetia*, in which 'ces sombres iconoclastes', the communists, (B 5, 224), become 'diese finstern Bildstürmer' (gloomy image-breakers) rather than retaining the Greek derivative. The Germanization of the loan-word yields a much stronger link to the disruption of metaphor which, in Heißenbüttel's account, is consequent upon the advent of a certain new social dynamic. The political and material forces which gain access to poetry, in 'Schnapphahn und Schnapphenne', in the wake of a now abandoned subjectivity are themselves the driving power of communism, which makes an earlier form of metaphorical language impossible by 'breaking the images'.

When metaphor apparently returns, in some parts of the *Romanzero*, it is encountered, Heißenbüttel believes, in a constant movement between enchantment and disenchantment. The characteristic case he cites is the poem 'Prinzessin Sabbat' ('Princess Sabbath') from the 'Hebräische Melodien' ('Hebrew Melodies'):

> Und wir schauen plötzlich wieder
> Seine königliche Hoheit
> in ein Ungetüm verzottelt.
>
> (B 6/1, 125)

> And again all of a sudden
> We behold his royal highness
> Retransmuted to a monster.
>
> (D 651)

Just as the thematic material of *Buch der Lieder* associated with ghosts, death, even the failure of romantic love, is understood in such an interpretation as extending the argument against subjectivity by dwelling on dissolution, so too in the disenchantments of *Romanzero* Heißenbüttel sees a strategy which brings Heine into alliance with Marx's definitions in *Capital* of the commodity as fetishistic and phantasmagorical.[9] Heißenbüttel associates Marx's own term 'phantasmagorische Form' (obscured in the standard English translations as 'fantastic') with a moment in Heine's ballet-scenario *Doktor Faust*. Heine's choreographic version of the legendary material in his 'poem for dancing' has its own materialist point to make by conceiving the early scenes of the action as a series of transformations or 'coups de théâtre', while a female Mephistophela is engaged to teach Faust to dance: Faust's pact with the devil is to be enacted as an acquisition of the physical skills of this stage. Subsequently, the disappearance of Faust's knights at the end of the second act is said to be 'like a phantasmagoria'. The effects of 'disenchantment' are thus seen in parallel to Marx's critical understanding of the 'fetishism of the commodity'; Heißenbüttel's interpretation reappropriates the alienation of social relations as the historical characteristic marking out Heine's work, just as Kraus and Adorno had done before him.

While Kraus locates this damaging alienation in a mode of literary production associated with the press, and Adorno presents it in the very dissolution of reliable subjectivity caused by the marketing of human spontaneity, Heißenbüttel suggests that Heine actually recognizes the phantasmagoric (and therefore, perhaps, fetishistic) character of traditional poetic language. This insight then enables him to initiate a quite new kind of writing, and to reveal the commodity (through and as poetic diction) as itself a poetic object, the object of modern poetry par excellence. The revisionist view of Heine's importance which this would entail is not seen merely as a relocation within the canon, but as a redrawing of aesthetic categories to make way for the possibility of the 'linguistic document' which Heißenbüttel believes he has uncovered.

What is at stake in such a reformulation of the function of poetry can be summarized in a couple of sentences from Heißenbüttel's essay 'Über den Begriff der Verarschung als literarisches Kriterium' ('On the Notion of the Piss-take as a Literary Criterion'). Speaking of Brecht's 'Lied der preiswerten Lyriker' ('Song of the Cut-price Poets'), he remarks: 'It is a matter of what is negotiated in the poem according to the agreement that has been reached individually and in society. It is a question of the ideology of the poetic.'[10] What is now negotiated in the poem is the whole set of expectations associated with lyrical writing, within the terms of the social contract in force. The same would be true of Heine in an earlier phase of that development. The first victim of the encroachment of commodity-form into the language of poetry is, we have seen, the secure bond between metaphor and subjectivity. Heißenbüttel returns to that rupture in his essay on Heine's journalism, 'Karl Kraus und die Folgen', by emphasizing the *canard* Kraus had borrowed from Heine's contemporaries and, for that matter (in *Atta Troll* XXIV), from Heine himself: that he was a *talent* precisely because he lacked character ('a talent because not a character', inverting the epitaph given to the artistic bear Atta Troll in the comic epic – 'No talent, and yet a character for all that' ('Kein Talent und doch ein Charakter'), B 4, 563). Here the subjectivity of a recognizable and familiar personality ceases to be available to secure the movement of writing under the aegis of new social and cultural relations. That older ideology of poetry has been challenged by a wholly new practice.

Heißenbüttel claims that Heine's Paris journalism for the *Augsburger Allgemeine Zeitung*, later gathered together in *Lutetia*, provided a new form of resistance to the increasing popularity, and hence assimilation, of *Buch der Lieder* and the early *Reisebilder*. What had been, as early as *Buch der Lieder*, in some sense citational, and had developed in *Deutschland. Ein Wintermärchen* into a material and linguistic registration of bare facts, is elevated in the French preface to *Lutetia* to the status of a general form, 'the form of fact' (B 5, 230).[11] In this context an important aspect of the logic of Heine's modern reception becomes apparent: while 'facticity' may disclose a genuine personal preference for what has become 'reportage', it is

nevertheless recognized as a mere form – as Heine himself remarks, the flags
under which censorship forced him to sail often bore emblems suggesting
a tendency quite different from his own (B 5, 230). Such camouflage is
identified by Heißenbüttel in terms such as anecdote, insult, and gossip.[12]
Paradoxically in the logic of this reception, the more Heine makes use of
such personal and intimate forms, the more his credibility and his character
are called into question. And more generally, the more Heine tells us directly
about himself, the less securely we seem to know it.

Hermann Marggraff's review of *Lutetia* in 1857 is quoted by Heißenbüttel
(see B 5, 969) to demonstrate that personal judgements, however 'authentic', are deemed so scurrilous that they succeed only in calling Heine's
(moral) character into question. Gossip and anecdote, which Heine himself calls 'Anekdotenkrämerei' (trading in anecdotes) and even 'Commerage'
(ill-natured gossip) (B 5, 231), are the products of a social idleness, according to Marggraff, characteristic of the 'flâneur'. We need hardly recall that
this representative of the new urbanism was subsequently identified by
Walter Benjamin as the typical figure of the metropolitan streets of Paris,
in his study of Baudelaire and of Paris as the 'capital of the 19th century'.
Marggraff speaks of this idleness as 'Müßiggang', literally a kind of idle
*walking* which provides 'superficial pleasure' (B 5, 969). For Heißenbüttel,
such 'Flanieren' and the devotion to the randomly anecdotal which marks
its superficial movement can be defended (and are so defended by Heine
himself) as parables of Heine's pro-republican and even pro-communist
ideas.

However much this journalism is rendered more complex in intention
and reception by Heine's profound hatred of German nationalist xenophobia, he recognized and actively promoted the historical and political intrication of his writing. So whenever a Kraus or, by implication, a
Rudolf Borchardt demands from Heine some 'eternal treasury of German
poetry',[13] they quite specifically ask for the impossible from a writer who
demonstrated the *necessary* relations between poetry and history. Heine,
Heißenbüttel claims, is the first German author to realize that the political-
historical actuality is indispensable for an author.[14]

This unavoidable determination by the historical context of his or her
work also involves the author in certain risks, as well as providing certain
gains. While historical context guarantees the unity of Heine's oeuvre in one
sense, and Heißenbüttel resists all attempts to separate the lyric poet from
the journalist, it does so at the price of the traditional unity of reading which
secures all difference within the processes of a single biography. Where, in

the development of Heine's later poetry, society had evacuated the subject, on Heißenbüttel's account, here in the journalism of *Lutetia* any subjective selectivity gives way before the documentation of historicity:

Everything that belongs within the domain of social, historical and experiential actuality is sayable and must be said.[15]

In attempting to define the new aesthetic project envisaged in Heine's work, Heißenbüttel returns to the passage from the epistle dedicatory to *Lutetia* where Heine proposes the daguerreotype as a model of his journalism. His earlier Heine essay used the same image to identify the alternative to 'metaphorical discourse', which Heißenbüttel sees in Heine's commitment to a variety of linguistic documentary, precluding the old aesthetic categories of reflection (and of reflexivity). In the later case, Heißenbüttel identifies the 'daguerreotypical' method of Heine's texts with the elements of polemic and prurience, deviance and frivolity which make the most personal aspects of Heine's writing so signally short of (moral) character ('Charakterlosigkeit' is the word Heißenbüttel uses, parodying the shocked tones of Marggraff). Heine's virulent polemic against the homosexual Platen (a commonplace in the tradition of Heine criticism since Kraus) is cited in illustration, but one might as readily think of his prurient interest in Börne's domestic arrangements in *Ludwig Börne: eine Denkschrift*, or the celebration of the goddess Hammonia at the end of *Deutschland. Ein Wintermärchen.*

The daguerreotype represents the fly as well as it does the noblest horse, Heine had written; for Heißenbüttel this method opens up those areas of language and experience which previously had been foreclosed by the imposition of moral categories. Seen in this way, Heine's notorious attack on Platen can be understood in broader terms. For in his *Memoiren*, Heißenbüttel reminds us, Heine also drew a parallel between his own maternal dependency and the public gossip surrounding Grabbe's relationship with his mother.[16] Heißenbüttel believes that, in this respect, Heine even anticipates Freud: the dark side of the Romantics is turned outwards from the Gothic and supernatural to suggest an account of political and social, and literary behaviour in terms of primal drives, the libido and the unconscious.

Such a reading presents a final response to Karl Kraus. Heißenbüttel's earlier essay 'Materialismus und Phantasmagorie im Gedicht' had recalled Kraus's complaints of irony and cynicism, a lack of seriousness, and a linguistic randomness in Heine. Here, in the later study, Heißenbüttel identifies such randomness as the principle of literary selectivity established by a linguistic materialism. Such new writing leaves the subject as a function, no longer in control of the metaphors through which it had once found 'self-expression'; instead it is decentred, as we have seen, socially, historically, and (not least) psychologically. And yet this writing is also the only available measure of these transformations, itself fetishized and suborned by the iconoclastic impulses of communism, which, as we all know, Heine feared would finally settle accounts with his own poetry and its project, the most feared goal of his whole trajectory.

# CHAPTER 4

# *From the private life of Everyman: self-presentation and authenticity in* Buch der Lieder

> . . . nur sein eigener Nachahmer
> merely his own impersonator
>
> (Gustav Pfizer)

Kraus and Adorno are anxious about Heine's style because it seems inauthentic or alienated. In their different ways, they understand Heine's relationship to writing in the context of modern modes of production, but ultimately make him, in his character or upbringing and socialization, personally responsible for the effects of modernity. In Kraus's account, Heine secularized the transcendental business of literary creativity, and therefore demeaned the chaste embrace of the German Muse by making her accessible. Adorno recognizes the same process at work, though he is willing to credit Heine as a *Jew* with important insights into modern social and economic alienation; but that in turn is only made possible by matching the biography to the writing it produced. Only Heißenbüttel makes the positive move and so turns Adorno's sense of alienation into a postmodern collapse of the structures of metaphor; in this way Heine can become the engineer of a constructivist poetics who actively and necessarily engages his writing with the exigencies of the social and historical context. Such work goes against the grain of bourgeois reading habits in the very process of exploiting their prurience. In Kraus and Adorno, Heine's writing is an involuntary reflex of his experience of the modern. In Heißenbüttel it is a conscious and deliberate critical practice. In this chapter I read *Das Buch der Lieder* along these lines, as the product of an encounter between preferred representations of subjectivity and social and historical forces encountered in the commodity.

## THE PREFACE TO THE SECOND EDITION

In reflecting on his poems, Heine is well aware that his theme of unrequited love is repetitive. In a letter to his friend Immermann he calls it 'the same little theme' (10 June 1823),[1] and at Christmas the previous year he acknowledged that the tone of his malicious sentimentality is ambiguous ('maliziös-sentimental', to Immermann, 24 December 1822). Not long after the appearance of the collection, Heine happily accepts both aspects of this popular image. In *Die Bäder von Lucca*, he revels in his reputation for sentimentality while simultaneously projecting the Byronic image of a wildly riven soul ('Zerrissenheit'). In programmatic statements in later editions of *Buch der Lieder*, however, Heine is carefully quizzical about these personal images.

The preface to the second edition in 1837 begins with an insistence on prose which the third edition in 1839 will allude to and cancel out. In 1837 Heine writes

I do not know what strange sentiment keeps me from writing the kind of foreword that is customary in poetry collections, versified in nice rhythms. For some time something in me has balked at any poetic language . . . (B 1, 9; D 3)

He goes on to note that he is not alone in his generation to feel uncomfortable about the constraints of metre implied in the German term 'gebundene Rede' (literally 'bound speech'), which includes the forms of verse as well as its diction. This disturbance is characteristic of what has been called, in Stendhal's phrase, 'l'ère du soupçon',[2] the shift, which Heine himself identified with Goethe's death, to historically and politically engaged prose and away from flights of the imagination. He puts the point elegantly: 'It would seem that all too many lies are told in beautiful verse, and that the truth shrinks from appearing in metrical garb' (B 1, 9; D 3). The truth, it seems, cannot appear in verse under present conditions. Yet the very next paragraph lays claim to an almost adolescent authenticity which can scarcely survive the rigours of print without risking the final evaporation of its essential oils and aromatics. Poetry, at any rate early poems ('erste Gedichte') of this personal kind, demand an immediacy of reference which can only be properly retained in manuscript, like the original handwriting of love-letters, scattered with dried and wilted flowers, locks of hair, and fading ribbons. In this way Heine's prose preface begins to investigate the relationship between writing and subjective authenticity which troubled later readers and, as we shall see, some of Heine's contemporaries.

Such prerequisites recall the assumptions of 'Erlebnislyrik' as a poetry of genuine personal experience, though they also parody certain sentimental habits of reading. The visible 'track of a tear' on a fading manuscript – the last mark of authenticity Heine mentions – would constitute a trace of the immediate which confounds the possibilities of representation in a medium of multiple transmission such as the printed book.

First poems, however, that have been printed, printed in harsh black on horribly smooth paper have lost their sweetest, most virginal charm, and arouse in the author a ghastly ill temper. (B 1, 9; D 3 (modified))

Print, says Heine, robs his work of its attractive innocence and evokes instead a sense of irritation mixed with a sense of dread and perhaps of the uncanny ('einen schauerlichen Mißmut'). Norbert Altenhofer reads this disturbance as a reflection of Heine's uncertainty in the first part of *Buch der Lieder*, in which the poems seem to hesitate between authentic immediacy and the effects of their organization in a *pattern* of productivity based on the lyric cycle.[3] In the light of Adorno's critique of lyric subjectivity in his Heine essay, however, it is possible to see this loss of 'personal' reference as a feature of the anonymous market for which Heine is now quite explicitly writing: it is after all a *second* edition. In his preface, then, there are signs that Heine is learning to reassess his own output strategically, as a function of his own historical position and context.

These worries about authenticity and a certain irritation with Heine's sentimentality can be documented among the earliest readers of *Buch der Lieder*. Wienbarg reported uncertainty about the biographical truth of the poems as early as 1830;[4] and Werner Kraft cites a remarkable review by Gustav Pfizer in 1838 which clearly anticipates Kraus's criticisms of Heine as a self-plagiarist who impersonates his own style, as well as Kraus's notion of the poetry as a fragmentary whole ('mosaic') constantly pillaged by its imitators.[5] From another point of view, however, Heine's registration of ghastly ill-temper ('einen schauerlichen Mißmut') suggests a different context. The sense, in both Pfizer and Kraus, of self-plagiarism and self-impersonation becomes a thematic concern of *Buch der Lieder* in poems typified by the 'Doppelgänger' effect of *Heimkehr* XX ('Still ist die Nacht, es ruhen die Gassen' ('The night is still')), but also more generally by the poetry of haunting and hauntedness which recurs throughout the volume, and indeed through Heine's whole oeuvre. Apart from its antecedents in Romantic variations on departure and return,[6] the larger literary context of this poetry is the darker side of Romanticism which imagines the return as that of a revenant. Such a haunting by some mirage of the self may indeed register 'grief over the lost simplicity of grief', as Siegbert Prawer says;[7] in *Heimkehr* XX it may do so by miming the gestures of 'Romantic emotionality' in the self-consciousness of 'a new, post-Romantic complexity'.[8] The preface of 1837, however, pursues a different course.

Printing, and in this case *re*printing to satisfy the needs of the publishing market, may well, in Heine's view, attenuate to the point of anonymity the original experience of unrequited or lost love; but that is not to say that the poems have no present context. The passage of time, the fading passion of the first embrace of the Muse under the pressure of political difficulties and financial hardship – all this offers a different, retrospective scenario for the texts that follow. In one sense, what has been lost to time can readily be restored. Original dedications have been omitted, Heine explains, for reasons of space. Nevertheless, he can summon up his respect for his uncle Salomon, which had originally found expression in the dedication of the volume that first included *Lyrisches Intermezzo*. Similarly, *Heimkehr* triggers memories of Rahel Varnhagen von Ense who had showed concern for Heine at a time when his 'passion for truth had generated more heat than light'. The passage of time, Heine believes, both brings the cooler illumination of retrospection, but also provides a revised perspective for the assessment of 'truth'. In immediate self-proximity it is impossible, he says, to negotiate our own most pressing concerns: hence Heine's puzzling anecdote about Paganini who, after being passionately complimented on his playing, most wishes to know not how his performance has been received, but how his acknowledgement of the audience's applause in bows and curtseys ('Komplimente, Verbeugungen') has gone down.

My account has been tracing Heine's thought quite closely and, characteristically, the preface has now come rather badly adrift, but the feints of Heine's argument are worth following. What had begun with a sense that truth could no longer appear in metre led to the suggestion that print and hence commercial publication falsify the truthful immediacy of writing; one set of mementos and souvenirs could still be replaced with other triggers for the memory – such as the suppressed dedications, recalling Salomon Heine and Rahel Varnhagen. She initiates the final shift which will lead to Paganini's inappropriate question. For the original flame of truth, it now turns out, had always generated more heat than light, and so led to the experience of exile which transforms Rahel into a type of the biblical Rachel weeping 'when her children were led into captivity'. Attempts to 'see' oneself are misguided and misleading: 'We are casual about our own excellences; we try to deceive ourselves about our weaknesses so long that we end up taking them for eminent virtues' (B 1, 11; D 5). The passage of time and the reassessment of personal talents provide the thematic link between the opening of the preface and its provisional commitment of the volume to the care and indulgence of the public. This act is performed 'in all modesty

and craving the public's indulgence' immediately after the maxim concerning self-deception has been illustrated by the tale of Paganini. Authenticity,
in 1837 at any rate, no longer seems to present a problem. However, the
moral point of the whole passage is that we fail to recognize the worth of
those gifts we receive from nature ('Ah, among the unhappiest blunders a
man makes is this, that he childishly misjudges the value of the gifts that
nature bestows on him most easily . . .': D 5) This strikingly anticipates
Heine's comments on self-representation in his *Geständnisse*: 'each of us
would like to appear before the public in a colour different from the one
fate has painted us in' (B 6/1, 449).

This parallel suggests that Heine is overconfident in dismissing the problem of self-portrayal to the realms of ethical commonplace. This is confirmed by the unwillingness of the preface, as it were, to accept its author's
rhetoric. His book cannot be sent on its way without one further remark
which simply reopens the argument – and incidentally brings back the
opening question concerning the relative merits of prose and verse:

In all modesty and asking the public's indulgence, I submit this *Book of Songs*;
perhaps my political, theological and philosophical writings make some amends
for these poems' weaknesses. (B 1, 11; D 5)

The final cadence that begins here is not sufficient to avoid the need for
some supplement. No sooner has this been conceded than a further remark
becomes necessary, and Heine insists that his work in verse and in prose
springs from 'one and the same thought', consistently present to his soul
in spite of any perceived need to moderate or even suppress his polemics:
'Only in the minds of certain narrow-minded people could my greater
moderation in speech, or indeed my enforced silence, appear as recantation
on my own part' (B 1, 11–12: 'als ein Abfall von mir selber'). For a moment,
amid the manoeuvres of the preface, there appears here a clear sense of
Heine's identity as he himself perceives it, briefly, in unproblematic unity:
'But I have a right to be tired . . .'

This grip on the self is short-lived, however. Heine's sense of exhaustion
is illustrated and evoked by a couple of lines from Raimund's *Der Bauer
als Millionär* (*The Millionaire Peasant*). And the same play provides a trope
for Heine's sense of decline in the allegorical figures of youth and age.

> Und scheint die Sonne noch so schön,
> Am Ende muß sie untergehn!
>
> (B 1, 12)

And though so fair the sun may glow
Down at last it yet must go!

(D 5)

Heine points out that this is a setting ('Untergang') not the kind of falling
off ('Abfall') that detractors had claimed to find in his work; Heine sees
it not as a dereliction but as part of the natural process of time. It is the
'wintry figure' of age who now approaches – so that Heine prays he may
retain the virtues of youth in idealism and fearless honesty. This 1837 Preface will conclude with a moment of local colour, as Heine suggests that
his beautiful female companion ('die schöne Freundin') in Paris, stroking
his curls with her rosy fingers, had found there white hairs. The identity
of this female figure is ambiguous. The Homeric epithet indicates that she
is Hebe, the dawn itself as a further symbol of Youth which has already
put in an allegorical appearance in Raimund. Yet there are other figures
in the text which may be recalled here: the Muse had been seen as 'this
good lass' ('diese gute Dirne'), but because the rosy-fingered woman is
simply called 'die schöne Freundin' the figurative and mythological sense
slides closer to the kind of realism that reads here a straightforward allusion to Heine's wife, Frau Mathilde, or at the very least to some youthful
grisette.[9]

Through their personal tone and their light-hearted allusions, these final
paragraphs recover the whimsy and gentle irony of the opening. The scene
of intimacy in Paris recalls the emblems of youthful passion – the wilted
flowers, lock of hair and faded ribbon – of the opening, just as the site of
Heine's signature ('written in Paris') confirms the distance and space opened
by the adjective trans-Rhenish ('überrheinisch') in Heine's opening greeting
to his public. But by now the self has been dispersed in time and space,
and through writing and publication. To retain the virtues of youth will
be precisely *not* to attempt, any longer, the registration of immediacy. The
law of time, which all must obey (B 1, 12; cf. D 5) means that freshness can
only reside in meaning, not in the specific form of an expression:

Let me become a graybeard who loves youth and who despite age's infirmities still
partakes of its games and risks! Anyhow let my voice tremble and quaver as long
as the meaning of my words remains fresh and undaunted! (B 1, 13; D 6)

Meaning ('Sinn') can retain some sort of priority, even though beautiful
verse has far too often been used for lying. Fresh and fearless, Heine's
sense shares in the games and dangers of youth – because it is libertarian,
unserious, and politically radical. Yet the final turn of his prose preface

underlines the difficulty of reaching meaning. The beautiful friend with her rosy fingers hesitates on the dividing line between 'sense' or 'meaning' ('Sinn'), and some sort of biographical authenticity. A figurative reading makes possible the meanings attaching to age and the passage of time, but it does so at the cost of personal experience. On the other hand, if we are privy, now, to the intimacies of Paris, that is paradoxically because we are structurally excluded, by the falsehood and unreliability of 'beautiful verse', from those of Hamburg or Düsseldorf, where the poems of *Buch der Lieder* are 'set'.

### THE PREFACE TO THE THIRD EDITION

In 1839 Heine's third preface returns to the issues of verisimilitude and veracity in verse. This preface (which also appeared in the *Zeitung für die elegante Welt* under the title 'Liebe') consists of thirteen quatrains, rhymed abcb, and followed by one paragraph of prose beginning, 'All of this I could have said very well in good prose . . .' The ellipse is Heine's own, the first of six in the preface as a whole, and seems to anticipate a quizzical or querulous reader wanting to know why he did not do just that. That demand is anticipated by Heine's complaints about the mendacity of verse writing in the 1837 preface, as we have seen. In this second preface, however, the same occasion – correction of the text in preparation for a reprint – has the reverse effect. The strange feeling prohibiting versification in 1837 is replaced by 'the jingling habit of rhyme and meter' (D 8) which brings Heine, inadvertently as it were, to write a poetic preface after rereading his old poems. As we shall see, this hint of inadvertency offers a fairly precise reading of the poem. Nevertheless, Heine remains confident in his apostrophe to the god of poetry that, even if the resulting poem is poor, Apollo will forgive him. The remainder of the preface is then addressed to the god, and explains that the absence of lyrical writing in Heine's output during the period preceding the second and third editions of *Buch der Lieder* is explicable in relation to demands made on his talents and energies by political and aesthetic struggles. Apollo can sympathize with these conflicting claims, Heine suggests, because the god is accustomed to exchange the lyre for his mighty bow and mortal arrows (B 1, 16), as the preface to the third edition claims after more ellipses; the implication being that the god in his bright and dark aspects provides an archetype of Heine's own activity which both 'delighted the world in brilliant fireworks' but, as political and aesthetic polemic, turned its energy to 'far more serious fires'. It is this polemical activity that first suggests the flaying of Marsyas, the inadequate artist in competition with a great one. By positioning himself in this parallel as Apollo, Heine leaves open the possibility that he may be guilty of hubris. Marsyas may more appropriately represent Heine – for the smile of Apollo with which the preface concludes is ambiguous and, therefore, threatening.

The flaying of Marsyas (by or as Heine) in the prose section of this preface is echoed by the flaying of a poet by a living sphinx in the passage of verse which opens the third preface.

> Das ist der alte Märchenwald!
> Es duftet die Lindenblüte!
> Der wunderbare Morgenglanz
> Bezaubert mein Gemüte.
>
> Ich ging fürbaß, und wie ich ging,
> Erklang es in der Höhe.
> Das ist die Nachtigall, sie singt
> Von Lieb und Liebeswehe.
>
> Sie singt von Lieb und Liebesweh,
> Von Tränen und von Lachen,
> Sie jubelt so traurig, sie schluchzet so froh,
> Vergessene Träume erwachen. –
>
> Ich ging fürbaß, und wie ich ging,
> Da sah ich vor mir liegen
> Auf freiem Platz ein großes Schloß,
> Die Giebel hoch aufstiegen.
>
> Verschlossene Fenster, überall
> Ein Schweigen und ein Trauern;
> Es schien, als wohne der stille Tod
> In diesen öden Mauern.
>
> Dort vor dem Tor lag eine Sphinx,
> Ein Zwitter von Schrecken und Lüsten,
> Der Leib und die Tatzen wie ein Löw,
> Ein Weib an Haupt und Brüsten.
>
> Ein schönes Weib! Der weiße Blick!
> Er sprach von wildem Begehren;
> Die stummen Lippen wölbten sich
> Und lächelten stilles Gewähren.
>
> Die Nachtigall, sie sang so süß –
> Ich konnt nicht widerstehen –
> Und als ich küßte das holde Gesicht,
> Da wars um mich geschehen.

Lebendig ward das Marmorbild,
Der Stein begann zu ächzen –
Sie trank meiner Küsse lodernde Glut
Mit Dürsten und mit Lechzen.

Sie trank mir fast den Odem aus –
Und endlich, wollustheischend,
Umschlang sie mich, meinen armen Leib
Mit den Löwentatzen zerfleischend.

Entzückende Marter und wonniges Weh!
Der Schmerz wie die Lust unermeßlich!
Derweilen des Mundes Kuß mich beglückt,
Verwunden die Tatzen mich gräßlich.

Die Nachtigall sang: 'O schöne Sphinx!
O Liebe! was soll es bedeuten,
Daß du vermischest mit Todesqual
All deine Seligkeiten?

O schöne Sphinx! O löse mir
Das Rätsel, das wunderbare!
Ich hab darüber nachgedacht
Schon manche tausend Jahre.'

                                        (B 1, 14–15)

This is the fabled wood of old!
The linden scents the dell.
Upon my heart the fairy moon
Casts a magic spell.

I walked along, and as I walked
A song rang out above.
The nightingale it is – she sings
Of love and the pain of love.

She sings of love and the pain of love,
The love that laughs and cries;
Her joy's so sad, her sobs so glad,
Forgotten dreams arise.–

I walked along, and as I walked
Through the enchanted wood,
I came to an open glade and there
A gabled castle stood.

Silence and sorrow hung upon
Barred casements, empty halls;
It seems as if mute death dwelt there
In its deserted walls.

Before the gate there lay a Sphinx. –
Terror and lust cross-bred!
In body and claws a lion's form,
A woman in breast and head.

A lovely woman! Her white eyes
Spoke of desire grown wild;
Her lips gave silent promises,
Her mute lips arched and smiled.

The nightingale! She sang so sweet –
I yielded, passion-tossed –
And as I kissed that lovely face
I knew that I was lost

The marble image came alive,
Began to moan and plead –
She drank my burning kisses up
With ravenous thirst and greed.

She drank the breath from out my breast,
She fed lust without pause;
She pressed me tight and tore and rent
My body with her claws.

O rapturous torment and exquisite pain!
Anguish and bliss evermore!
While the kiss of her mouth was thrilling joy,
Her lion claws ripped and tore.

The nightingale sang: 'O lovely Sphinx!
O love, explain to me:
Why do you blend the pain of death
With every ecstasy?

'O lovely Sphinx! O read me right
This riddle of sages and seers!
I've thought and thought about it now
For many thousand years.'

(D 7–8)

'Das ist der alte Märchenwald!' falls into four parts: after an opening qua-
train, the nightingale and its song first hold the poem's attention; this is
followed by a castle marked by mourning and silence as if it were the
dwelling of death ('der stille Tod'); then comes the embrace of the sphinx
which lies at its gates; and finally the poem returns to the nightingale's song
and the riddle of the sphinx as a figure of Love. This narrative appears to
introduce images and allegories which are already familiar, as the opening

cry of recognition suggests (it is a familiar *fairy-tale* wood rather than any other kind) – and the assurance is confirmed by the scent of 'linden blossom'. The exclamation marks in the poem's opening lines confirm, perhaps, the quality of the already-literary or of the citational which Karl Kraus, Adorno, and Heißenbüttel, in different ways, are all aware of. My purpose now, however, is to ask in what way this poem reads as a preface to the volume it precedes, and how it takes up the question of authenticity.

Although the ordering of the poem in four narrative units is apparently straightforward, this is complicated by the 'Chinese box' effect of the frames in which the story unfolds. These are in turn undercut by patterns of repetition in the opening and closing stanzas and by the temporal structure of the verbs, suggesting other and disruptive patterns. The narrative within a narrative is identified at the end of stanza 3 (by the dash or 'Gedankenstrich') as a 'forgotten dream', as 'Vergessene Träume erwachen'. The vision of the melancholy castle and the sphinx thus appears to be securely framed as a dream awakened by the nightingale's song – or possibly as the substance of the song itself. The identification of the nightingale's song appears in a repeated phrase whose second occurrence shifts the rhyme 'singt' to the position of first stress in the line and abolishes an enjambement. It therefore highlights both the metrical and acoustic effects of the writing. The other repeated pattern, of assertion, in the first and seventh lines ('Das ist der alte Märchenwald'; 'Das ist die Nachtigall') apparently gives a symmetrical organization to the first twelve lines. However, another repetition undercuts this pattern. The andante of 'Ich ging fürbaß, und wie ich ging' (reminiscent of Goethe's poems 'Im Vorübergehen' and 'Gefunden': 'Ich ging im Walde/ So für mich hin') occurs both in the frame within which the forgotten dreams awake, and in the opening line of the dream sequence itself. The dash preceding the second occurrence of the phrase, which seems to mark a transition, is thus undercut by the continuity of the lyric forms: 'Das ist ...' – 'Das ist ...'; 'Ich ging fürbaß ...' – 'Ich ging fürbaß und wie ich ging ...' The interaction of narrative framework and rhetorical figure has the effect of leaving the perspective of the poem ambiguous. Our expectation that the framework narrative will have a clear rule about which elements belong where is disturbed and disappointed.

This difficulty recurs with the returns of the nightingale. The lyric self encounters a sphinx outside a silent and mournful castle; but the sphinx is only embraced after a further recollection of the nightingale: 'Die Nachtigall, sie sang so süß – / Ich konnt nicht widerstehen –'. The punctuation here leaves all questions of cause and effect entirely open, so that the function of the nightingale's song within the larger logic of the unfolding narrative is uncertain. Now, it is clear that in one sense it does not matter at all whether we regard this nightingale as inhabiting the world of the awakened dream, or as being (or being identical with) the nightingale of the 'framework' who intervenes from beyond the visionary world in such a way as to propel the dream action into its most painful phase. A similar uncertainty occurs in the last two stanzas. Here the nightingale's song seems to offer a commentary on the dream action which has reached a rhetorical conclusion in the ironic rhyme of 'unermeßlich' with 'gräßlich'. As a result the reader may be initially inclined to see this song as part of the dream sequence like the one which apparently causes the lyric subject to embrace the sphinx in stanza 8. On the other hand, the substance of the song 'O Liebe! was soll es bedeuten' clearly parallels the 'Lieb und Liebeswehe' of the second stanza. But even if this connection is possible, the framing devices of the poem seem to lack final conviction. The level of the opening narrative – on any reading – does not achieve closure; and to see the final stanzas as decisively within the dream frame is only the most radical reading of this open-endedness.

There is another way in which this uncertainty is subtly sustained in the course of the poem. The pattern of tenses hints at a present-tense action-of-narrative framing the past-tense story of the awakened dream. Confronted by and entering 'der alte Märchenwald', the narrator hears the song of the nightingale. With the exception of the first lines of stanza 2, the tenses here are all present indicatives. In the dream sequence from stanza 4 to stanza 10 the main verbs are all simple past, and the past tense is sustained in the opening phrase of stanza 12 and hence to the end of the text, given that the words of the nightingale's song are reported in stanzas 12 and 13. Within this sequence (4–13), however, there is a further exception.

The first deviation from the pattern of present-tense frame and past-tense dream-narrative appears in the second stanza. The first appearance of the formula 'Ich ging fürbaß' establishes a simple past which, like its reappearance in stanza 4, introduces a sequence of past tenses. 'Ich ging fürbaß, und wie ich ging,/ Erklang es in der Höhe.' The tense of this second line is therefore parallel to that of the second line of stanza 4: 'Da sah ich vor mir liegen'. This confirms a sense that the repeated formula needs to operate in parallel ways: the opening of the dream narrative would thus be located at the start of the second stanza, an effect of the spell cast on the poet's sensibilities by the miraculous moonlight. In formal terms the demarcations between one movement of the poem and another seem to have become blurred. The present tenses describing the nightingale's song and its effects ('Vergessene Träume erwachen') then need to be seen as a gloss on the general function of nightingales, pulling us back to the identificatory 'Das ist' of the opening: the bitter-sweet art of the nightingale's song always reawakens forgotten dreams. A second reading is possible, which is familiar from a well-known poem in *Buch der Lieder* itself. It may be that the second 'das ist' initiates a second but illusory framework within which, in turn, the dream-narrative will be set. Such a pattern would reproduce the dream-within-a-dream structure that S. S. Prawer identified in *Lyrisches Intermezzo* IX, 'Auf Flügeln des Gesanges'('On wings of song' (D 54)), in which a flight of the imagination debilitatingly culminates in the proposal that the lovers 'dream their blessed dream' (B 1, 78).[10] *Atta Troll* provides another obvious case. In the preface of 1839 the important point is that these patterns are indecisive – gestured at but unfulfilled.

My reading might be thought to tax an innocent text with too much ambiguity, were it not for the fact that the second exception to the apparently stable pattern of tenses in narrative and narration occurs at the rhetorical climax of the 'dream'. Stanza 11 begins with two exclamations: 'Entzückende Marter und wonniges Weh!/ Der Schmerz wie die Lust unermeßlich!' The second of these seems to imply a suppressed verb in the past tense ('waren'), even though in the first there is no real need to supply any sense of 'what I experienced in the arms of the sphinx was . . .' And the feeling of ellipsis is sustained and developed in the third line: 'Derweilen des Mundes Kuß mich beglückt' sounds as though it expects the reader to supply an auxiliary 'hat' to give a perfect tense within the temporal perspective established by 'Derweilen' – which will then foreground the wounds inflicted by the sphinx at the end of the stanza. These expectations are disappointed, however. 'Beglückt', it turns out, is a *present* tense which does not require any auxiliary; but this will only be grammatically confirmed by the clearly present-tense form of 'verwunden' in the last line. As we have seen, the coda provided by the nightingale's final song is introduced by the simple past tense 'sang', which returns us safely to the retrospective dream-narrative.

The status of the present tense of 'beglückt' and 'Verwunden' is not at all clear. It would be possible to regard the tense here, and in stanzas 2 and 3, as instances of an historic present, adding vitality and immediacy to a story which would then begin decisively in stanza 2. The blurring of levels of narration and narrative by formal patters of repetition ('Das ist', 'Ich ging') would leave the incomplete series of Chinese boxes to turn on the question of where, precisely, the dream sequence is supposed to begin and end; and the tense of the nightingale's song (stanzas 2, 3, 8, and 12) would be random and even opportunistic in its pursuit of effect. If we can recognize this effect as *casual*, it should perhaps be seen as parallel to the discursive drift of the preface to the second edition, which becomes most marked at the point where Paganini appears. If Heine's approach to argument were more obviously controlled, this aspect of his writing in the prose preface could be seen as digression. In practice, here and elsewhere, Heine allows his writing to drift, giving more a suggestion of indirection or even insouciance.

This also describes the effects I have examined in 'Das ist der alte Märchenwald'. Without close attention to tense and structure we have a sense of vague generality, almost a kind of emotional blankness – as if the poem were merely reworking familiar material. Yet, however much the poem appears to be casual, its movement back to the present tense in stanza 11 remains unaccountable. The participial phrases in stanza 10 ('Mit den Löwentatzen zerfleischend') prepare the ground for two lines without any verb, which in turn ease the movement into the present. But that present must indicate a direct and immediate experience of the pains and joys of love which have been mediated by the allegory of the preceding narrative. That is what the changing tenses mean. The perception may only last for seconds, but as it slips into the present the poem conveys, for a moment, an intimate private emotion, glimpsed as a fragment of experience which can be directly associated with 'Heine himself'. The defences and masks of allegory and convention seem to be down; this is not 'Liebeswehe' at some metaphorical remove but a statement of experience in the here and now.

The equivocal relationship of the literary and allegorical dream narrative and its framework to any present moment of real experience can even be traced in the manuscript evidence of the poem. Grappin notes that the 'ist' in the very first line – 'Das ist der alte Märchenwald!' – appears in a correction where the word 'war' has been crossed out. This alteration may seem very minor, but in the context of the time structure at work in the poem it is also very striking. The suppression of the earlier titles of the poem – 'Die Sphynx' and 'Die Liebe' – whose significance would amount to more or less the same thing (i.e. the 'plaisirs' and 'chagrins d'amour' seen from within the text, as it were, and glossing it from without respectively) raises the question of reference: what, precisely, 'ist der alte Märchenwald'?[11]

It seems at first sight to refer to the world of moonlight, linden blossom, and general sensibility which the first stanza catalogues among the props of Romantic sentiment; but in reading the poem as the first line of a preface, we are bound to see the fairy-tale forest as a metaphor for the poems which we are about to read. Nor are we the only readers: after Heine's disingenuous claim, in the text following the poem, that he could have conveyed the poem's meaning quite adequately in decent prose, he suggests that his own rereading of the poems in *Buch der Lieder* has delivered him once again into the power of poetry, just as in the poem the lyric self is delivered by the song of the nightingale to the painful experience of the sphinx – whose mystery has endured for thousands of years: a literary experience (rereading his earliest poems – 'erste Gedichte') becomes the occasion of revived memories ('Vergessene Träume erwachen') which are felt, now, as utterly immediate personal experience. The equivocation of the manuscript, as between 'Das ist' and 'Das war' (which would more precisely refer to a volume of poetry recently *re*read in preparation for a new edition) raises just this question of autobiographical relevance very sharply. If the DHA editor is correct, the tense of the final version makes its reference more immediate and less generally Romantic in tone:

In 1839 Heine looked back on the poems of his youth as on to a now remote past. As he reviewed them and reread them critically the opening topos of the fairy tale spontaneously came to mind: 'once upon a time' ['Es war einmal']. (DHA 1/2, 1239)

I see no reason to think anything much in this poem is the result of sponta-neous inspiration. The substitution of the present tense indicates that the poetry of the volume, with its typical Romantic features, can still be a living issue for the poet even though it consists of fairy-tales. The first version, 'Das war der alte Märchenwald', would leave us in no doubt that the *Buch der Lieder* was a matter of no more than historical interest for its author, twelve years after its original appearance.

   The continued relevance of the book and its Romantic impulses antici-pates what Heine had to say later in the *Geständnisse* about his own recidivist Romanticism:

After I had dealt the feeling for Romantic poetry the most mortal blows, an infinite longing for the blue flower in the dream-land of Romanticism crept up on me once again. (B 6/1, 447)

The opening of the poem then becomes a response to and even a description of Heine's own reading of *Buch der Lieder*. Nightingales and linden blossom are the attributes of his own writing and the dream a pastiche of charac-teristic themes from the collection. It is in the course of such a self-reading that the alarming immediacy of the present tenses of stanza 11 has its place. What seemed to be retrospect or dream – what seemed to be 'Romantic poetry' – shifts for a moment into autobiographical truth. The allegorical elements of the poem, particularly of the dream-sequence, achieve their fullest possible realization in this way. The song of the nightingale delivers the lyric subject to the contradictory powers of the sphinx; and reading the poems delivers their reader *and author*, once again, to the immediacy of joy and pain in love. Heine becomes a victim of his own skill, Marsyas in yet another sense. However, the coda of the poem leaves us once again with the allegory of the sphinx decoded, but relatively secure within the imagery of the poem itself and in the language of what was already one of Heine's most famous poems, the 'Lorelei' of *Heimkehr* II:

> Die Nachtigall sang: 'O schöne Sphinx!
> O Liebe! was soll es bedeuten . . .'

The poem, then, presents itself as a reading of literary and allegorical material in the apparent form of a chance encounter. This explains its casual allusion to Goethe's poems 'Im Vorübergehen' and 'Gefunden' ('In passing', 'Found'), in both of which the poet assures us that he intended to seek nothing in particular ('. . .nichts zu suchen,/ Das war mein Sinn').[12] The looseness of structure within what seem at first sight to be strict patterns, the relative unpredictability of the temporal order of the poem – all these elements indicate an easiness of style, which intimates something like whimsy: a sense of wilfulness that finally takes on the contours of personality and experience glimpsed in the oddness of the tenses. Ultimately what is incoherent or, at best, inconclusive within the structure of the text points to an easiness which we attribute *to Heine himself*.[13] That sense of blurred demarcations and drift corresponds to what is evident in the second preface and which is brilliantly deployed in Heine's critical prose. So it is no surprise to find in the prose text that follows the poem a meditation on the conditions and circumstances of its composition, punctuated by a succession of ellipses. For the ellipse dramatizes 'on the page' the movement of a mind, between experience and its metaphors. If the poem presents us with a sense of musing on its own substance, however, it can be simultaneously very general ('love is an infinitely problematic experience') and intimate ('as I know only too well'), while marking its authenticity in loose and inconclusive structures. For the poem is constructed, both by its prose rider and by its unexpected emergence into vivid intimacy, as a self-consciously fragmentary glimpse of a real life: that is to say, it moves towards the *anecdotal* in much the same way that the allegorical figures from Raimund's play at the end of the second preface are replaced by the ambiguous 'schöne

Freundin . . . mit ihren rosigen Fingern' who slides indeterminately from
the mythical to the autobiograpical.

In proposing this term to define an aspect of Heine's writing in *Buch der
Lieder*, I am drawing on Frank Lentricchia's work on anecdote. In an essay
on Wallace Stevens in his book *Ariel and the Police*, the American critic
points out that the Greek root 'anekdota' means unpublished items and
hence, in English, comes to mean a short narrative of an incident from
private life – which has therefore not been 'given out' or published. In this
sense, the traces of adolescent authenticity, invoked by Heine in the second
preface as the tracks of his tears, belong to the territory of anecdote –
or, if Heine is right in thinking that some personalia are incapable of
public transmission in print, to the category that the anecdote can only
gesture towards. This involves two kinds of larger coherence, one grounded
in the author's life and the other in some recognized area of human or
social experience. In each case the anecdote, and hence the poem, has a
representative quality. Lentricchia comments that

a hitherto unpublished little story . . . apparently stands in for a bigger story, a
socially pivotal and culturally pervasive biography which it illuminates – in an
anecdotal flash it reveals the essence of the larger unspoken story, and in that
very moment becomes exegesis of a public text; the unpublished items become
published. [14]

These are the rhetorical manoeuvres that Kraus denounces in the name
of true maturity and 'experience' when he claims that an attack on Heine
amounts to an attack on everyone's private life. The poems of *Buch der Lieder*
appear to give voice to individual experience – the pangs of unrequited
love – by declaring the individual case to be an instance of a culturally
pervasive biography. In broader terms, we might say that Heine elevates
the banal particular to the condition of universality, the 'essence of the
larger unspoken story', in Lentricchia's terms, which would then be the very
process of individuation. The preface to the third edition demonstrates the
point: these poems deal with and 'work through' subjectivity as their theme
and problematic, by setting the process of subjectivity to work, and raising
over and over again the question of 'personal experience' as the commonly
circulating idea of which the poems provide an exegesis. The dimension
of the personal and original, to which we suppose we can gain access as an
autobiographical 'reference', is hence itself a function of that reading.

Norbert Altenhofer has described the way in which the architecture of *Buch der Lieder* introduces an element of reflexivity. The first and last poems of various cycles often draw attention to the lyric enterprise. Thus 'Traumbilder I' ('Dream Images I') of the *Junge Leiden* (*Young Sorrows*) already plays on the tension between the autobiographical and the literary. The recurrence of this kind of self-consciousness at the end of 'Romanzen' in the well-known 'Wahrhaftig' ('Believe me!' (D 45), 'Romanzen' ('Romances') XX), which was written even earlier, and then successively in the 'prologues' to *Lyrisches Intermezzo* and *Heimkehr*, establishes a pattern of retrospection, involving elements of both personal history and literary self-consciousness. As Altenhofer demonstrates in the case of the *Homecoming* poem *Heimkehr* LXXXVIII, 'Sag, wo ist dein schönes Liebchen' ('Tell me, where's the shining love'), what appears to transform the autobiographical into literary self-awareness is in fact literary *already*. Heine's letter to Christiani of 4 September 1824 reveals that the first stanza of the poem was conceived as a parody of his friend Heinrich Straube. In this way, priority is given to the *textual* dimension over any supposed element of biography. An important counter-argument might well point out that this literary dimension of the poem is no less 'autobiographical' for being a parody. In fact the force of the poem moves in precisely the opposite direction: it converts the purely literary into a feature of Heine's psychological self-portrait, as Heine called his book ('psychologiches Bild von mir'),[15] but the focus for the autobiography is now the practice of writing itself. Once more we encounter Heine reading and rereading.

## METAPHOR AND LYRIC SUBJECT

The parade of subjectivity and the uncovering, at every turn, of the process of individuation which are at work in the prefaces to *Buch der Lieder* serve to confirm Adorno's claims. Spontaneity of emotion does indeed become a saleable commodity, however much the preface to the second edition may worry about the inauthenticity of writing for reproduction by the book-trade. But something more radical is at work here than the sell-out envisioned by Adorno. Heine can simultaneously exemplify and undermine the notion of a dense realm of private experience by his very equivocations about authenticity.

Adorno himself recognizes the ideological function of the idea of 'private life' in his review of Kraus's book on morality and crime, *Sittlichkeit und Kriminalität* (*Morality and Criminality*):

The concept of privacy, which Kraus honors without criticism, is fetishized by the bourgeoisie and becomes 'my home is my castle.' Nothing, on the other hand, neither what is most holy nor what is most private, is safe from the exchange principle. Once concealed delight in the forbidden provides capital with new opportunities for investment in the media, society never hesitates to put on the market the secrets in whose rationality its own irrationality is entrenched.[16]

Such fetishization of the private sphere – making capital out of intimacy – is satirized in *Buch der Lieder* itself. One of the best-known examples is *Lyrisches Intermezzo* L, 'Sie saßen und tranken am Teetisch'. The small scale of this conversation, like the limited scope of Heine's usual four-liners, makes the poem a duodecimo response to the complaints Goethe voices in his second 'Roman Elegy' ('Ehret wen ihr auch wollt! . . .'), in which the world of the erotic provides a safe haven from the encroachments of prurient gossip. For Heine in this poem the intimate and the erotic are hopelessly bound up with the cheapening effect of social mores and doubles ententdres. That is why the opening rhyme is so outrageous. 'Teetisch/ästhetisch' achieved an early notoriety and draws a particularly acid commentary from Kraus. After admitting to Heine's extraordinary intellectual range, he adds:

Without doubt every witty yid can outdo him these days at skilfully rhyming aesthetic with tea-table ['ästhetisch auf Teetisch'], and using rhyme and rhythm to make the candied hull of an idea into a real cracker.[17]

Here anti-Semitism stands in for the commercialization of poetic language of which Kraus generally complains.[18] The empty shell of a now absent idea has been 'candied' over to produce a mere cracker – a surprise effect with no serious consequences. But, in its context, this is exactly the point of Heine's rhyme. 'Sie saßen und tranken am Teetisch' addresses the space of social intimacy, the conversations around the tea-table:

> Sie saßen und tranken am Teetisch,
> Und sprachen von Liebe viel.
> Die Herren, die waren ästhetisch,
> Die Damen von zartem Gefühl.

> Die Liebe muß sein platonisch,
> Der dürre Hofrat sprach.
> Die Hofrätin lächelt ironisch,
> Und dennoch seufzet sie: Ach!

> Der Domherr öffnet den Mund weit:
> Die Liebe sei nicht zu roh,
> Sie schadet sonst der Gesundheit.
> Das Fräulein lispelt: Wie so?

Die Gräfin spricht wehmütig:
Die Liebe ist eine Passion
Und präsentieret gütig,
Die Tasse dem Herren Baron.

Am Tische war noch ein Plätzchen,
Mein Liebchen, da hast du gefehlt.
Du hättest so hübsch, mein Schätzchen,
Von deiner Liebe erzählt.

(B 1, 95–6)

They talked of love and devotion
Over the tea and the sweets –
The ladies, of tender emotion;
The men talked like aesthetes.

'True love must be platonic,'
A wizened old councillor cried.
His wife, with a smile ironic,
Bent down her head and sighed.

The canon opened his fat face:
'Love must not be coarse, you know,
It's bad for the health in that case.'
A young girl lisped 'Why so?'

The countess sadly dissented:
'Oh, love must be wild and free!'
And graciously presented
The baron a cup of tea.

You should have been there, my treasure;
An empty chair stood near.
You'd talk of your love and its pleasure
So charmingly, my dear.

(D 68–9)

The poem locates the supposed density of subjective inwardness ('Die Liebe ist eine Passion') precisely in this social discourse, as a function of public speech. The possibility of truth in self-expression is collapsed in the first rhyme; for the aesthetic has been taken over by the banality of social intercourse. A similar argument is in place when Heine rhymes 'Passion' with 'Baron' in the penultimate stanza where, as usual, the French loan-word 'präsentieret' is minted to dialectical effect. When the 'Hofrätin' does manage something like a sigh of passion in stanza 2, she is trapped in a Romantic role which her own sense of irony cannot fail to unmask.

This society has lost touch with, and lost its control over, the figurative aspect of language. Because the aesthetic is now assimilable to the
most jejune drawing-room conversation, language and especially metaphor
become dangerously unstable – subject to the principle of exchange Adorno
describes. These instabilities are exploited by Heine as part of his satire.
The conversation he describes restages the debate of the Symposium, as
the insistence on Platonic love on the part of the councillor indicates. His
academicism – the scholarly approach to an otherwise passionate subject –
is explained as an aspect of his 'dry' conversation: 'Die Liebe muß sein
platonisch,/ Der dürre Hofrat sprach'. In the public sphere, however, this
can be recognized as an intimate secret: the councillor is impelled to justify
himself in the presence of his wife, whose ironic smile makes the whole
exchange readable – if only for Heine, the observer and victim of such
tea-time scourgings ('theegesellschaftliche Geißelung')[19] – as a revelation
of sterility and impotence.

The middle stanza of the poem, dealing with the cleric from the cathedral
chapter, the 'Domherr', operates the same kind of transferred sense, when
the canon issues his health warning about love. Love should not be too
'raw' is the primary sense, as the cleric's mouth gapes to make his remark.
Presumably he means something like 'coarse', as Draper suggests, or perhaps
'rough', but in conjunction with his gesture the metaphor slides over into
a gastronomic context. This can yield at least two more possibilities: love
must be enjoyed à point – raw but not too raw, as it were: the speaker
is a gourmet of passion; or he may mean that it should be well cooked,
as an example of 'gut bürgerliche Küche', and hence kept within strict
limits. Either of these meanings will satisfy the rider that one's health might
otherwise be threatened by anything too rough. In any event, love is an
object of consumption, and intimacy is revealed as an isolable commodity
like any other. No wonder the hopeful spinster is puzzled.

The poem ends with a stanza suggesting that the unfaithful beloved
would fit in only too well with this arid and calculating company with 'their
chorus of hypocrisy and frustration'.[20] Here Heine achieves his most acid
tone by the use of diminutives: 'Am Tische war noch ein Plätzchen;/ Mein
Liebchen, da hast du gefehlt.' Laura Hofrichter, writing about the *Homecoming* poem *Heimkehr* XXIX, 'Das ist ein schlechtes Wetter' ('This surely
is dreadful weather'), calls this recurrent feature of *Buch der Lieder* Heine's
tricky diminutives ('die vertrackten Diminutiva'). Just as in *Lyrisches Intermezzo* L, Heine's use of diminutives here functions in a moral judgement:
'Ein Mütterchen mit dem Laternchen / Wankt über die Straße dort.' –
'With lantern a little old mother / is tottering down the lane' (D 89). The

verb, with its suggestion of painful effort, indicates a mismatch between the cosiness enacted by the folksy diminutives and the represented human situation. This incommensurability is present as a visual effect of distance in *Heimkehr* III, the poem read by Adorno as a document of modern alienation:

> Jenseits erheben sich freundlich,
> In winziger, bunter Gestalt,
> Lusthäuser, und Gärten, und Menschen,
> Und Ochsen, und Wiesen, und Wald.
>
> (B 1, 108)

> Beyond in coloured patches
> So tiny below, one sees
> Villas and gardens and people
> And oxen and meadows and trees.
>
> (D 77)

The friendliness of the idyll serves only to stress the remoteness of such an unspoilt world from the lyric subject. The young soldier in his diminutive sentry-box ('Schilderhäuschen') confirms the discontinuity and, of course, initiates the final movement of the poem towards its death-wish: 'Ich wollt, er schösse mich tot.' The disconnection of the suicidal speaker from the world of conventionalized Romantic responses converts the idyllic scene into a list of objective tokens or emblems, signalled by their diminutive scale.

The grammatical diminutives put in another satirical appearance in *Lyrisches Intermezzo* XXXVII. 'Philister in Sonntagsröcklein' ('Burghers in Sunday clothes strolling') begins quite simply by *belittling* its object: the Sunday promenade of the bourgeoisie becomes for Heine another opportunity to measure the disparity between a sentimental appropriation of nature as a kind of 'objective correlative' and the philistine mentality – the 'bourgeois subject' – which sees itself reflected there.

> Sie jauchzen, sie hüpfen wie Böcklein,
> Begrüßen die schöne Natur.
>
> (B 1, 89)

> Like frisky young goats caracoling,
> Salute nature's beauties again.
>
> (D 63)

The poem 'Götterdämmerung' ('Twilight of the Gods') at the end of *Die Heimkehr* provides a more extended treatment of the same topic.[21] Here the Romantic false consciousness that is pilloried is glossed as an explicitly literary phenomenon when, amid 'the eddying throngs' (D III) 'The poets of the town put in their pockets / Pencil, paper and lorgnette'. Their efforts serve merely to maintain the currency and popularity of the metaphors that a letter calls 'emotional garbage' ('Gemüthskehricht', HSA 20, 179) and which other diminutives have already dismissed at the end of the 'Ballads' in 'Wahrhaftig': 'No matter how much you like such stuff, / To make a world they're just not enough' ('Wie sehr das Zeug auch gefällt, / So machts doch noch lang keine Welt').[22]

### 'ES FÄLLT EIN STERN HERUNTER'

From the tea-party of 'Sie saßen und tranken . . .' to the absurd philistinism that greets 'die schöne Natur', the metaphorical repertoire of the pathetic fallacy demonstrates its bankruptcy. The poem 'Es fällt ein Stern herunter' ('A star is falling slowly'), *Lyrisches Intermezzo* LIX, provides a more complex case of such a withdrawal of metaphor's guarantees; but the questions it poses merit more detailed consideration.

> Es fällt ein Stern herunter
> Aus seiner funkelnden Höh!
> Das ist der Stern der Liebe,
> Den ich dort fallen seh.
>
> Es fallen vom Apfelbaume
> Der Blüten und Blätter viel!
> Es kommen die neckenden Lüfte
> Und treiben damit ihr Spiel.
>
> Es singt der Schwan im Weiher,
> Und rudert auf und ab,
> Und immer leiser singend,
> Taucht er ins Flutengrab.
>
> Es ist so still und dunkel!
> Verweht ist Blatt und Blüt,
> Der Stern ist knisternd zerstoben,
> Verklungen das Schwanenlied.
>
> (B I, 100)

> A star is falling slowly
> From the twinkling sky above!
> I see its shining pathway –
> It is the star of love.

> From apple trees are falling
> Buds and leaves away.
> The merry breezes gather
> And whirl them round in play.
>
> On the lake a swan is singing,
> Floating on its grave,
> And singing soft and softer
> It sinks beneath the wave.
>
> It is so dark and silent!
> The trees are blighted and bare,
> The star is dust and ashes,
> The swan song fades on the air.
>
> (D 68–9)

In the first place, it is clear that this poem is not an instance of the ironic 'Stimmungsbrechung' for which Heine is generally well known in *Buch der Lieder*. Equally, because no such disruption clarifies the status of the imagery, the reticence of the text proves to be provocative. Hofrichter sees in it a series of available images reduced to their absolute essentials, until in the silence and darkness of the final verse the poem itself appears to participate in the dissolution it has registered.[23] Grappin dramatically develops this suggestion: he explains that 'It is so dark and silent' in the final stanza of the poem

. . . because all that is transient is scattered, dispersed or faded [verweht, zerstoben oder verklungen] the lifeless and loveless night remains, the empty night of loneliness after the star of love fell from the sky. (DHA, I/2, p. 846)

As we know from the final lines of Goethe's *Faust* (though Heine could not, at the time), 'All that is transient / is but a parable' – or metaphor ('Alles Vergängliche / Ist nur ein Gleichnis'). The DHA editor attempts an account of the poem in terms of personal experience, but in doing so suppresses the power of metaphor which his casual allusion recalls. The figurative language of this poem in fact registers a good deal more than the naive sentimentalism of Romantic solitude.

Klaus Briegleb takes a different tack and devises a general decoding of Heine's imagery by means of what he defines as the four fundamental motifs of *Buch der Lieder*: love, freedom, poetry, and death.[24] In this case the falling star and the song of the dying swan yield love, poetry, and death; the playful breezes of stanza 2 then stand in for freedom by way of a comparison with *Heimkehr* LXI:

Ich wollt, meine Schmerzen ergössen
Sich all in ein einziges Wort,
Das gäb ich den lustigen Winden,
Die trügen es lustig fort.

(B1, 136)

I would I could pour my sorrow
All into a single word,
Thrown to the merry breezes
And borne on the wings of a bird.

(D 100)

Wind is understood as 'messenger of love', combined in this context with its use as image and bearer ('Bild und Träger') of freedom. But the real basis for this meaning, as Briegleb himself admits, is its relation to the common phrase 'as free as the wind'.[25] Briegleb's critical method reads Heine integrally by trying to identify his personality and intentions dispersed through his writing as a 'perspectival existence in writing' ('perspektivisches Sein in der Schrift');[26] but this interpretation must hold fast to a fundamentalist faith in the complete perspicuity of the Heine corpus: the construction of a concordance and systematic harmonization of the texts are supposed to give the critical reader access to that original integrity of the author.

In varying degrees, these very different readings confidently return us to the author as the secure psycho-social foundation for whatever force of identity or meaning we can cull from the poem. Even Michael Perraudin, at once more sophisticated than the sentimentality of Grappin and more straightforward than Briegleb's cryptography, claims that 'This poet's feeling' is represented by the absence of the star, the blossom, and the swan-song.[27] However, *Lyrisches Intermezzo* LIX also seems to provide an instance of the destabilization we have encountered, in a perhaps more studied form, in the verse preface of 1839. Patterns of repetition are again exploited to suggest a consistency in the metaphors which is constantly questioned and disturbed.

The organizing repetition that sustains the whole structure is established by the series of impersonal verbs: 'Es fällt', 'Es fallen', 'Es kommen', 'Es singt', 'Es ist'. In the first, second, and fourth stanzas these impersonal forms are found in exclamations reminiscent of what Heißenbüttel had called 'simple utterances'. They are veridical statements, and one might almost understand the opening two lines as a generalized possibility – 'somewhere a star is falling from its glittering height'; something similar is true for the first sentence of stanza 2 also. The second sentence of stanza 1 can then be seen to expand perception into significance. The lyric subject sees the star and identifies it as the star of love, and the indefinite article – as it were the random star – of the opening is clarified and made definite in a metaphor. The shooting star and its personal significance are held in balance by the structure of the stanza. The repetition of the impersonal form in following lines suggests that this pattern will continue. Formally it does so, as we have noted, but the identification of meaning is not forthcoming. The second part of the stanza opens with another impersonal verb, sustaining a different pattern, and the figurative language remains generally unspecific: 'the merry breezes' at play in the leaves are not cashed in by the lyric speaker.

The third stanza with its swansong moves into a different mode altogether from what has gone before. 'Es singt der Schwan im Weiher' cannot be veridical in the sense of the previous statements of perception. The song of the dying swan derives from myth alone, which means that it is a meaningful image *already*, and so does not need even the appearance of exegesis which survives in stanza 2. It would need to signify something like ultimate and ultimately beautiful articulacy, in an undivided unity of expression and experience.[28] The song and the death are one; and it is perhaps unnecessary to add that Apollo's gift to the songless bird already undoes its identity: that a swan that sings is no longer a swan. These implications and the mythical mode of the third stanza in general inevitably destabilize the limited consistency established in the first half of the poem. To the extent that a continuity of consciousness is discernible over the three stanzas, it is now sensed as a mind contemplating – or casting about for – metaphor, without settling to any with authority and conviction. The implied topography of the poem, with repeated falling movements traversing a space between the sky and the surface of the water, is less a landscape out in the world and much more an interior space in which each metaphor leads a peculiarly isolated existence. In the stillness and darkness of the final lines, the order of these elements is altered, with more than a hint that they belong temporally to a remote past. As the plural blossoms and leaves ('Blüten und Blätter viel') of stanza 2 become generic (in 'Blatt und Blüt') and rhetorical, in the chiasmus suggested by the refiguring, the rococo challenge of 'the merry breezes' to the veridical spring of stanza 2 is confirmed. Shooting stars and apple-blossom time have gone the way of the swan-song: the poem cites and rereads topoi of its own exhaustion, as Hofrichter correctly perceived.

## EMBLEMATIC AND ALLEGORICAL READING

This reading has suggested that the logic of *Lyrisches Intermezzo* LIX displays that 'loss of similitude' and evacuation of metaphor described by Heißenbüttel; or that it articulates the alienated 'loss of language' described

by Adorno, and for which the swansong provides a kind of dialectical image.
To the extent that 'Es fällt ein Stern herunter' also retains the force of an
anecdote, it intervenes in the public discourse which desires authentic personal experience as a foundation for poetic language. The poem works
on the process of subjectivity even as it blocks it. Yet, as the poem scans
the possibilities it lists, the opening move appears to propose a figurative
relationship; this is the kind Heißenbüttel believes to have been utterly
hollowed out. The falling star becomes emblematic, allegorized as 'the star
of love', which thus becomes the meaning subjoined to the emblem. (After
all, in other cultures a falling star might signify good luck; before it fell, it
might be something to catch or even wish upon.) But the security of the
allegorical relation is subsequently displaced by the powers of variation and
differentiation that the poem invokes.

In varying ways the poems of *Lyrisches Intermezzo* weigh up the possibili-
tites of figuration, but rarely leave any sense that metaphorical expectations
have been fulfilled. Over and over again the symmetries of such figurative
language are withheld or exaggerated. The withdrawal of metaphor's guarantees is apparent in 'Es fällt ein Stern herunter' and in many of the poems
preceding it (from XLII), up to the suicidal sequence (LXI–LXIV). The
confrontation with allegory by exaggeration, on the other hand, occurs elsewhere. *Lyrisches Intermezzo* III, 'Die Rose, die Lilie, die Taube, die Sonne'
('The rose and the lily, the sun and the dove'), for instance, well known from
Schumann's *Dichterliebe* (*A Poet's Love*) cycle, presents its own catalogue of
allegorical ciphers.

> Die Rose, die Lilie, die Taube, die Sonne,
> Die liebt ich einst alle in Liebeswonne.
> Ich lieb sie nicht mehr, ich liebe alleine
> Die Kleine, die Feine, die Reine, die Eine;
> Sie selber, aller Liebe Bronne,
> Ist Rose und Lilie und Taube und Sonne.
>
> (B 1, 76)

> The rose and the lily, the sun and the dove,
> I loved them all once with the rapture of love
> I love them no more, they cannot outshine one –
> My fair one, my rare one, my fine one, divine one,
> She herself is love's pure source and the spirit of
> The rose and the lily, the sun and the dove.
>
> (D 52)

Grappin suggests that the poem concentrates the conventions of the French
rondel form in a mannerist way, and that such a process of concentration
is repeated in its treatment of figuration.[29] The lyric subject confesses to

having loved each of the individual figures of the first line, but then acknowledges that his new love for 'Die Kleine, die Feine, die Reine, die Eine' has
displaced all of these in his affections because, as the source of love, she is
now in herself rose and lily and dove and sun.

Two possibilities emerge in the figuration of the opening: either the
poet confesses to having loved a number (four) of women, each of whom
figured as one of the listed emblems, almost as if they were pet-names; or he
claims that once, for sheer joy of being in love, he had loved the real roses,
lilies, doves, and sun because they were the multiform allegorical figures of
love encountered in the real world, empirically.[30] The object of his present
passion is represented adjectivally ('Die Kleine', etc.) in the middle section
of the poem, before the fine rallentando of 'Sie selber, aller Liebe Bronne'
explains that the sheer inclusivity of the current beloved means that she is
figured in not one but all of the allegorical figures of the opening. The new
beloved may be the singular and unique ('die Reine, die Eine') origin of
'true' love, but figuration can do no more than bind this singularity by the
repetitive force of convention. The poem has made little or no progress.
The dense identity of 'she herself' is little more, to speak with Kraus for
a moment, than the ground for the ornamentalization which abolishes
mimesis and equalizes life (or subjective authenticity) and art in relations
of repetitive homogeneity. The aesthetics of the 'phrase' – here the hollow
remainder of a lost emblematic art – appears to give access to individual
spontaneity and psychological depth, but in reality makes individuality so
universal as to be utterly interchangeable.

Similar or related debates with the rhetorical means of poetry in allegory, metaphor, and simile recur in a number of the succeeding poems.
The theme is finally abandoned when the poems controlled by character
and affect intervene at XVIII, with their 'grolle nicht' ('I'll not complain')
catch-phrase. In the exhausted figuration of *Lyrisches Intermezzo* III we can
identify the kind of fake or con-trick that Karl Kraus calls a 'decoy'. Allegorical intuition, Benjamin observes of the Baroque, converts the image into
a fragment or illegible rune ('Bruchstück, Rune'); beneath its superficial
splendours it bears 'the confinement, incompletion, brokenness of sensual,
beautiful physis [nature]'.[31] It is that failure of the organic and individual
which Kraus rightly reads in *Buch der Lieder*, and which so many of the
poems work at with a wide and varied range of techniques.

If we consider Kraus's example of this allegorical dissolution, *Lyrisches
Intermezzo* XXXIII, we do not have to settle for his particular brand
of fin-de-siècle language-mysticism to recognize that there is something
unsatisfactory and blank about its imagery or allegory, if indeed it is
one.

Ein Fichtenbaum steht einsam
Im Norden auf kahler Höh.
Ihn schläfert; mit weißer Decke
Umhüllen ihn Eis und Schnee.

Er träumt von einer Palme,
Die, fern im Morgenland,
Einsam und schweigend trauert
Auf brennender Felsenwand.

(B 1, 88)

A pine tree standing lonely
In the North on a bare plateau.
He sleeps; a bright white blanket
Enshrouds him in ice and snow.

He's dreaming of a palm tree
Far away in the Eastern land
Lonely and silently mourning
On a sunburnt rocky strand.

(D 62)

The most obvious manoeuvres of the poem are derived from the uncertain status of the dream in stanza 2: is it entirely framed by the narrative of the previous four lines, as a dream which the pine tree has, quite simply; or does the palm tree really exist as an object of the pine tree's desire? Is the anthropomorphism of the *blanket* of snow a dead metaphor; or does it seriously imply some vitalistic sympathy among the elements? (And in any case is it not excessively domestic?) If these uncertainties conjure up Heine, his hand against his cheek as Karl Kraus thought, the poet we encounter is withdrawing from the biographical, rather than acceding to it. The evacuation of metaphor and the exhaustion of allegory allow many possibilities, and insist on the powers of reading and interpretation. One recent reader, for instance, Martin Walser, relates the allegory to Heine's nostalgic relations with Judaism, conceived in the poem as a profound natural sympathy between the Germanic North and the East.[32] The power of Walser's fine reading has not been sufficiently recognized, but it too is qualified by the implausibility of the anthropomorphic trees and a later poem, the comic parody 'Der weiße Elefant' ('The White Elephant') in *Romanzero*, takes it back in the same way that 'Romanzen' VI of the *Neue Gedichte* (*New Poems*), with the loaded title 'Unstern' ('Unlucky Star'), gives the game away on *Lyrisches Intermezzo* LIX.[33]

There are perhaps two reasons why this risky openness to reading should come about. Confidence in the adequacy of nature to reflect and express human emotion has dwindled to mere convention and repetition: this is the underlying logic of 'Philister in Sonntagsröcklein' (*Lyrisches Intermezzo* XXXVII) where the idea that bourgeois promenaders greet the beauties of nature directly addresses the immediacy of Goethe's 'Erlebnislyrik' ('poetry of experence') in general and his famous 'Mailied' ('May Song') in particular; and the same would also be true of so many failed or excessive conceits in *Lyrisches Intermezzo* (such as the whispering hair-curler of XXXIV). Walter Benjamin's 'beautiful nature' is deserted, fragmentary, bereft of meanings in these poems because, as Heißenbüttel recognized, the social contract that defines what a poem can negotiate has been redefined. Secondly, in such conditions of formulaic repetition, when meaning can no longer be securely lodged in the thing itself – in some veridical correspondence between the natural and the human – then both intratextual and intertextual relations become correspondingly more important: in Briegleb's view the formulaic units open up a resonant space in which the utopian immediacy of natural sounds ('Naturlaute') can still be calibrated – as an inscription of echoes from the world of 'natural' spontaneity which is now ultimately lost to alienation.[34] This understanding conceives of Heine's texts as a virtually infinite series of connections. The further consequence is that the pathos of allegorical meaning (in falling stars or lone pines) can readily be undone by counter-examples elsewhere in the collection or in the oeuvre as a whole. In this way, natural symbols of human emotion are shown to be inadequate to the individual case, at least. This appears to provide a third position, in which sarcasm and the rejection of poetic language and poetic imagery apparently offer the ground for a genuinely authentic spontaneity – but with the paradoxical logic that residual subjectivity is guaranteed by an anti-poetic refusal of literary 'self-expression'. (*This* swan is not taken in by Apollo's generosity.)

### SYMBOLIC NETWORKS AND POETIC CYCLES

Klaus Briegleb has written of Heine's 'transcendental sarcasm' and seems to mean by this Heine's immense self-consciousness and self-confidence as master of his mythical reconstruction of the world;[35] if it is appropriate to apply the term 'transcendental' at all, I would wish rather to do so in the sense that Heine displays the *conditions of possibility* of such powerful identity, within the currencies of the literature of personal experience or 'Erlebnis' – and does so, radically, by operating along the boundary between the aesthetic and the (auto-) biographical and hence *occupying* the distinction.

Nevertheless, sarcasm (or 'irony' or the disruption of mood known as 'Stimmungsbrechung': all of these terms appear to designate the same range of effects) is not the only possible response to the illegibility of natural emblems and hieroglyphs. Nor can they necessarily be successfully integrated in the system of some greater textual network. The *Homecoming* poem *Heimkehr* LVIII, 'Zu fragmentarisch ist Welt und Leben', itself rejects the systematizations of German idealism:

> Zu fragmentarisch ist Welt und Leben!
> Ich will mich zum deutschen Professor begeben.
> Der weiß das Leben zusammenzusetzen,
> Und er macht ein verständlich System daraus;
> Mit seinen Nachtmützen und Schlafrockfetzen
> Stopft er die Lücken des Weltenbaus.
>
> (B 1, 135)

> Life and the world's too fragmented for me!
> A German professor can give me the key.
> He puts life in order with skill magisterial,
> Builds a rational system for better or worse;
> With nightcap and dressing-gown scraps as material
> He chinks up the holes in the Universe.
>
> (D 99)

The singular verb of the opening line is very canny: its vernacular imprecision articulates exactly the discontinuities the poems examined here seem to display. Are the world and life severally fragmentary, or is their condition one and the same? Life and the universe drift apart in the following lines in spite of their *rimes croisées* – life becomes merely comprehensible, while the lacunae of the world-fabric are filled up with stop-gaps. Certainly in *Buch der Lieder* even the conception of the poems in a cycle or cycles undermines the possibility of perspicuous cross-referencing. As Norbert Altenhofer shows, Heine restructures the whole basis of referentiality in the poems.

The link between the text and the experiential structure of an extra-literary subject is replaced by an intra-literary reference to other texts. In Heine's lyric cycles this reference mostly takes the form of a self-critical or poetological commentary in verse.[36]

But against this, it is also important to bear in mind that Heine resists the encyclopaedic impulse of his Romantic predecessors, which would have looked for an infinitely rich series of connections between the written text and the world. Far from steadying our focus on the subjectivity of the texts (in both senses), it can be increasingly disturbed.

A sequence of three poems in the *Homecoming* (*Heimkehr* XXXVII–XXXIX) usefully demonstrates what is at stake. The first of these is 'Die heilgen drei Könige aus Morgenland' – a poem probably best known because of Richard Strauss's setting. The three stanzas retell the journey of the Magi to Bethlehem:

> Die heilgen drei Könige aus Morgenland,
> Sie frugen in jedem Städtchen:
> 'Wo geht der Weg nach Bethlehem,
> Ihr lieben Buben und Mädchen?'
>
> Die Jungen und Alten, sie wußten es nicht,
> Die Könige zogen weiter;
> Sie folgten einem goldenen Stern,
> Der leuchtete lieblich und heiter.
>
> Der Stern blieb stehn über Josephs Haus,
> Da sind sie hineingegangen;
> Das Öchslein brüllte, das Kindlein schrie,
> Die heilgen drei Könige sangen.
>
> (B 1, 126)

> The three holy kings from eastern lands
> Ask everyone who passes:
> 'Where is the road to Bethlehem,
> My dear little lads and lasses?'
>
> Not young nor old can tell them where,
> The kings go on aweary;
> They follow a star of golden light
> That shines down bright and cheery.
>
> The star stands still at Joseph's house,
> They go in gifts abringing;
> The little ox lows, the little child bawls,
> The three holy kings are singing.
>
> (D 91–2)

Both the 'four-square' rhyming (of 'weiter' with 'heiter' in stanza 2 and 'hineingegangen' with 'sangen' in stanza 3) and the cacophony that ends the poem suggest a degree of irony which is hard to define or fix. Strauss's setting probably provides the finest commentary, with the penultimate line sliding chromatically across a sequence of diminished sevenths, full of uncertainties, before arriving in the last line at C major, towards the end of the cadenza for the voice, on the word 'sangen'. The cantilena leads into an orchestral postlude in which, with a last flicker of rising melody, the voice nevertheless leaves us feeling that not quite everything has been said.

If there is an asymmetry or disproportion between the din of the stable and the song of the Wise Men, their effort at least legitimates the poem's place in a Book of Songs. Nevertheless, a blankness remains in the narrative which is reminiscent of *Lyrisches Intermezzo* LIX: this is caused in part by the complete absence of any explicitly subjective dimension in the poem, but also by a series of rhetorical devices parallel to the differential frames in 'Es fällt ein Stern herunter'. In the case of the Magi poem, the context of the succeeding poems gives access to the shifting perspective that Heine has constructed. *Heimkehr* XXXVIII, 'Mein Kind, wir waren Kinder' sharpens the uncertain focus of the preceding poem:

> Mein Kind, wir waren Kinder,
> Zwei Kinder, klein und froh;
> Wir krochen ins Hühnerhäuschen,
> Versteckten uns unter das Stroh.
>
> Wir krähten wie die Hähne,
> Und kamen Leute vorbei –
> Kikereküh! sie glaubten,
> Es wäre Hahnengeschrei.
>
> Die Kisten auf unserem Hofe
> Die tapezierten wir aus,
> Und wohnten drin beisammen,
> Und machten ein vornehmes Haus.
>
> Des Nachbars alte Katze
> Kam öfters zum Besuch;
> Wir machten ihr Bückling und Knickse
> Und Komplimente genug.
>
> Wir haben nach ihrem Befinden
> Besorglich und freundlich gefragt;
> Wir haben seitdem dasselbe
> Mancher alten Katze gesagt.
>
> Wir saßen auch oft und sprachen
> Vernünftig, wie alte Leut,
> Und klagten, wie alles besser
> Gewesen zu unserer Zeit;
>
> Wie Lieb und Treu und Glauben
> Verschwunden aus der Welt,
> Und wie so teuer der Kaffee,
> Und wie so rar das Geld! —

Vorbei sind die Kinderspiele,
Und alles rollt vorbei –
Das Geld und die Welt und die Zeiten,
Und Glauben und Lieb und Treu.

(B I, 126–7)

My child, we were both children,
Two children, little and gay;
We'd crawl into the hen house
And hide ourselves under the hay.

We crowed like cocks whenever
Somebody passed on the road –
'Cock-a-doodle-do!' They really
Thought that a cock had crowed.

We papered up the boxes
That round the yard were laid,
And there we lived together
In the splendid house we made.

The old cat of our neighbor's
Would come to visit there;
We received her with bows and curtsies
And compliments to spare.

'How *are* you?' we'd ask very kindly
As usual, time and again.
We've uttered the same polite murmurs
To many old cats since then.

We'd sit like oldsters exchanging
Nuggets of wisdom and truth,
Complaining how better the world was
In the good old days of our youth;

How love and faith and devotion
Were ready to disappear,
How money was getting scarcer,
And coffee was getting too dear! –

Gone are the games of childhood,
And everything's crumbled to dust –
The times, and the world, and money,
And faith and love and trust.

(D 92)

The refocusing occurs at two levels. First, we encounter children in the context of keeping livestock: 'Wir krochen ins Hühnerhäuschen, / Versteckten uns unter das Stroh'. The role-play and the essentially urban background that emerges later serve to emphasize the pastoral effects created by the children playing in the straw – and, of course, their relationship with the archetype of the child in the manger. But, secondly, this order of archetype and instantiation can be reversed: the Christmas world of the ox and the infant Jesus becomes contextualized as one moment in an extended recollection of childhood. Hide-and-seek, playing house in packing cases out in the yard, and inviting the neighbours' cat to tea are all parts of this reminiscence; and it is a world already made old by the games of children who 'klagten, wie alles besser/ Gewesen zu unserer Zeit'.

This familiarity with the way of the world gives *Heimkehr* XXXVII the quality of citation noted elsewhere. The poem quotes, and illustrates, the possibilities of Empsonian pastoral, of *multum in parvo*.[37] The simple story speaks a vast and complex truth – not primarily a truth about religion, but about the realm of faith to which childhood gives a name. The Wise Men are Christmas and Twelfth Night seen in a remote retrospect which, in the poem's opening line, reduces them to a mere title 'Die heilgen drei Könige aus Morgenland'. It is the context offered by the following poem which reveals this reminiscence as itself a reading, a citation of itself, musing on its possibilities and limitations. What is bafflingly unfocussed and open, in *Heimkehr* XXXVII, acquires from the vantage point of the following poem the double focus of its self-presentation. It is a text already being performed or read; in fact a reading would be a performance, and the major reader is Heine himself. His hand rests against his cheek, as Kraus had realized.

In *Lyrisches Intermezzo* LIX ('Es fällt ein Stern herunter') Heine foregrounds the problematic status of imagery, conceived as the fixed emblematics of personal experience, by organizing the text in a series of mutually exclusive formal patterns. In the Magi poem from *Heimkehr* a similar issue is dealt with, but with different rhetorical means. Here the text works through a triple structure in style and register. Pastoral contrasts of the great and the little are played out in contrasts of language: 'aus Morgenland' / 'in jedem Städtchen'; 'Die heilgen drei Könige' / 'Ihr lieben Buben und Mädchen'. The force of this pattern is constantly close to satire and *anti*-pastoral, working to uncover a false pietism. The second stanza then concentrates on disconnection and continued passage: 'wußten es nicht', 'zogen weiter'; but these effects serve to make the star shine out all the more brightly until it 'stund oben über, da das Kindlein war', as Luther's Bible says. 'Da sie den Stern sahen, wurden sie hoch erfreut. Und gingen in das Haus und fanden das Kindlein mit Maria . . .' (Matthew 2, 10–11a). By minute shifts of emphasis and tone, the final stanza gives way to the burlesque promised in the first. Its secular anti-pastoral undoes the festive magic with a single robust and mundane past participle – 'hineingegangen': the Christmas carol world is reread as 'Das Öchslein brüllte, das Kindlein schrie'.[38] These diminutives can no longer carry the burden of integration and universal reconciliation that the Epiphany 'in jedem Städtchen' had still borne. The caesura in the line, falling at the comma between the two unstressed syllables of an anapaest, makes for a very powerful sense of dissociation.

Perhaps thrown by this state of affairs – or perhaps because 'they rejoiced with exceeding great joy', as Luther tells us, more laconically: 'hoch erfreut' – the kings burst into song; the body of the poem, with its failures of integration (there is condescension in line 4) and its unanswered questions, reveals the kings in desperation – singing is a *pis-aller* rather than serene self-awareness. As a song itself, the poem moves towards reflexivity both because it wittily rereads the Gospel story, but also because of the edginess of its shifting registers. It is in itself already the object of reflection and citation. Once again we could put this down to an authorial irony – but such a move seems curiously pointless if it is designed to register the poem as the record of Harry Heine's alienation from the Christian celebrations of Christmas or the older poet's loss of faith in the spontaneity of a poetics derived from the habits and verbal gestures of folk poetry enshrined in the *Wunderhorn* anthology. What seems much more important is the effort undertaken by the poem to question the very categories of authenticity and sentiment.

The sequence of poems in *Heimkehr* XXXVII–XXXIX first appeared in 1826, although the second two poems of this group date from 1824 and were written to Heine's sister, as the MS dedication of XXXVIII indicates.[39] The sequence is hence doubly interesting since it gives some indication both of Heine's intertextual methods in the construction of sequences, and of the manipulation and *revocation* of autobiographical contexts.[40] Neither 'Mein Kind, wir waren Kinder' nor 'Das Herz ist mir bedrückt, und sehnlich/ Gedenke ich der alten Zeit' require any specific sense of familial or fraternal affection. Indeed much of *Buch der Lieder* encourages us to see the children as childhood sweethearts. It is the remoteness of that world which the third poem in the sequence takes up, by extending the lament of the second 'wie alles besser/ Gewesen' and that 'Alles rollt vorbei'. The retrospection and temporal framing implicit in XXXVII and developed in XXXVIII are reinforced, even explicitly reduplicated, in XXXIX. The result is a quite astonishing poem which mimes directness while challenging the terms of its own nostalgia.

Das Herz ist mir bedrückt, und sehnlich
Gedenke ich der alten Zeit;
Die Welt war damals noch so wöhnlich,
Und ruhig lebten hin die Leut.

Doch jetzt ist alles wie verschoben,
Das ist ein Drängen! eine Not!
Gestorben ist der Herrgott oben,
Und unten ist der Teufel tot.

Und alles schaut so grämlich trübe,
So krausverwirrt und morsch und kalt,
Und wäre nicht das bißchen Liebe,
So gäb es nirgends einen Halt.

(B 1, 127–8)

My heart is heavy – sad the present;
I think back to the olden days
When all the world was still so pleasant
And people went their peaceful ways.

Now, helter-skelter, elbows shove us,
Pressure and stress on every side!
Dead is the good Lord God above us,
And down below the devil's died.

Everything goes in churlish fashion,
A rotten, tangled, cold affair;
And but for a little love and passion
There'd be no surcease anywhere.

(D 93)

The second line of 'Das Herz ist mir bedrückt' gives particular prominence to the word 'ich', especially when it is read against the preceding poem, 'Mein Kind, wir waren Kinder', which operates with a first person plural; similarly, 'Alles rollt vorbei – / Das Geld und die Welt und die Zeiten' grounds the more generalized singular of 'der alten Zeit' in the third poem. What had been play-acting in the second poem, children's games aping adult habits of thought and speech, becomes a vivid and present sense of loss and nostalgia – a specific childhood memory (and Christmas and the Wise Men along with it) is grasped as 'olden days'. A further level of reflexivity has taken over, then, which in the second stanza can reach back to conceptualize the secularism of 'Die heilgen drei Könige'. And yet the security of a self-conscious nostalgia is disturbed lexically by the unusual adverb 'sehnlich' (longingly) and the even odder rhyme 'wöhnlich': what is lost is a habitable ('wohnlich') and perhaps still familiar ('gewöhnlich')

world. These are troubled formulations, but the greatest sense of disturbance appears at the end of the fourth line: 'Und ruhig lebten hin die Leut.'
The apocope 'die Leut' (abbreviating 'die Leute') is vernacular, and seems to
indicate another dimension of miming or ventriloquism. This unascribed
voice hints at idyllic conditions of village life which have now been destroyed
by the 'pressure and stress' of the present. But the idyll is overlaid with a
measurable degree of citation – the measure is the absent final *e* itself. This is
not just Heine *in propria persona*. 'Die Leut' becomes the marker of a whole
world which is now out of joint – dislocated and disorientated without God
or the devil to provide fixed coordinates. The insistent lament of the O in
rhyme and assonance in stanza 2 looks as though it might settle into the
unexceptional *Weltschmerz* of early nineteenth-century secularism, were it
not for the last stanza and its final turn. This too is deeply disturbed. Amid
the confusions, the 'bit of love' promises survival by recalling older values;
but then this phrase too, especially when contrasted with the modernisms
of the second line, is popular or vernacular and therefore, in some sense,
also a citation. Heine himself can scarcely utter the phrase authentically: it
is already a quotation in the very moment of writing.

The effect of this sequence in *Heimkehr* is to present, in the first instance,
a chronology of loss and progressive alienation: from the original enchantment of the Magi and Christmas, through a childhood miming of nostalgia
for that simplicity, to an adult nostalgia for that nostalgia in which vernacular immediacy has no more than rhetorical force. Here, no single element
in the series can securely retain authenticity. Quite precisely, in terms of
Kraus's analysis, the interior life is obliterated when supposed experience
(Christmas, 'die Leut', 'das bißchen Liebe') is grasped as already rhetorical,
as aestheticized, and so ornamental. But it is equally true that the contradictory frames and registers of these poems, like the differential structures
of 'Es fällt ein Stern herunter', put on show the discourses and mechanisms of self-transcription. Such poems seem to be assembled from the
linguistic odds and ends of a remembered authenticity. The constructive
principle that is at work in the *form* of the poem also governs the relations
between the different poems and through the cycles of *Buch der Lieder* as a
whole.

### DIE NORDSEE

The poems on the North Sea that conclude *Buch der Lieder* were the last
part of the book to be composed, in the two years before its publication,
and they present a curiously intractable conclusion, both in their own right

and in relation to the carefully managed cycles that go before them. Here Heine appears to embark ón a quite different project. Jeffrey Sammons remarks that they 'are unlike anything [he] ever wrote before; they have no models to speak of, and Heine never wrote anything like them again'.[41] This claim would need to be modified in the light of Heine's relationship to the poetry of Wilhelm Müller, ingeniously expounded by Michael Perraudin in his account of *Buch der Lieder*.[42] Nevertheless, *Die Nordsee* I and II certainly open up new territory, both thematically and formally.[43] The seascapes Heine devises are the first German poems on the subject and so present a new dimension in the development of nature poetry; and his unrhymed free verse provides a matching novelty in the versification.[44] Heine's trips to the island of Norderney in 1825 and 1826, which provide a context for the North Sea poems, suggest that they seize an unproblematic opportunity for autobiography, compared to the equivocations of what precedes them. Heine's letters to Moser and Varnhagen von Ense even speak of an 'autobiographical fragment', a 'fragment of my life'.[45] And the reputation of the roughly contemporaneous *Reisebilder* as transcriptions of personal observations and moods, as well as our generalized sense of their author, encourage a biographical reading at the close of *Buch der Lieder* as well. What is more, the main technical innovation in the two cycles of North Sea poems, their unrhymed irregular metre, sustains a sense of personal speech precisely because the verse seems so unregulated, promising a more direct and immediate self-expression than the closed and universalized form of the folksong-stanza earlier. The move towards rhapsodic and quasi-epic utterance retains its own traditions and precedents, however. There are reminiscences here of eighteenth-century experiments in a free hymnic style, and with the classical hexameter. Indeed, Heine's lineation often barely conceals perfectly adequate hexameters. On the other hand, Heine himself identified a new kind of 'travel verse' in free rhythms by Tieck and Ludwig Robert as a technical precedent.[46]

As a source for the new diction and themes of the poems, Manfred Windfuhr suggests that Voß's *Odyssey* translation provided the basic metrical model for the *Nordsee*.[47] Certainly a purist approach to the hexameter, like Voß's, generated a greater flexibility than Tieck's confessional verse, which often seems deliberately to avoid the natural pull of a metrical pulse. And Voß can also provide thematic parallels with Homer. However, Voß's presence in the North Sea poetry may have other dimensions. In his essay *Die Romantische Schule* (*The Romantic School*), Heine celebrates Voß's Protestant resilience and critical independence, which he traces by comparing his translations with those of A. W. Schlegel:

Where Herr Schlegel's translations are perhaps too soft, where his verses are sometimes like whipped cream, so that when you have taken them in your mouth you
don't know whether to chew them or drink them, Voß is as hard as stone, and you
must fear that you might break your jaw if you pronounce his verses. But what
marked out Voß so powerfully is the strength with which he struggled against every
difficulty . . . (B 3, 384)

The variations in metrical regulation which the free rhythms of *Die Nordsee*
bring about, and the impersonations of the final spondee (or its trochaic
substitute) in German hexameters ('gedankenbekümmert und einsam'
('troubled by thoughts and alone'), 'Schreiten über den wimmelnden
Marktplatz' ('striding over the populous market')), can give a similar sense
of weight and personal inflection. But the awkwardness of Voß's versification is also emblematic for Heine. This significance is most fully apparent in
his critical essays on German culture, thought and religion, *Zur Geschichte
der Religion und Philosophie* and *Die Romantische Schule*. Here two great
names typically mark out the German tradition of intellectual emancipation that Heine sketches: Luther and Lessing. When Voß is invoked as
a representative of German intellectual resistance to the irrationality and
Catholicism of the Romantic school, his importance is elucidated with
reference to Heine's other two critical heroes. In Heine's cultural history,
then, Voß is presented as the 'greatest citizen [Bürger] in German literature
after Lessing'(B 3, 382), who himself appears in Heine's account of German thought as Luther's greatest successor. Sure enough, the same trio of
intellectual heroes is completed in *Die Romantische Schule* when Voß and
Luther are linked by their common origins as peasants from Lower Sax-
ony. In *Die Bäder von Lucca* the same three authors are invoked in Heine's
polemic against the aristocratic hauteur of the classicizing poet August von
Platen's anti-Semitism, as well as his fashionable Catholic sympathies.[48]
And in this Italian *Reisebild* Heine even presents himself as next in line
to Luther, Lessing and Voß. The debates and public polemics launched
by or against Voß relate to his attack on Friedrich von Stolberg, who had
converted to Roman Catholicism. For Heine, Voß therefore represents a
kind of Lutheran earthiness, and the literary cause célèbre to which Heine
refers in his Italian travelogue and in the ideological essays of the early 1830s
was *contemporary* with the composition of *Buch der Lieder*.[49] In the later
essays, Heine associates Voß with a polemical style, like Luther's, that is
direct, even coarse, and virile ('derbkräftig', 'starkmännlich'). The presence
of Voß in the North Sea style hence signifies more than a technical resource
for versification. It also corresponds to Heine's own ironic rationalism and
his resistance to Romantic obfuscation and moodiness.

The protagonist of the *Nordsee* cycles is full of moody gestures as he meditates on lost love, the callousness of society, the indifference of nature, and the ineffectiveness of literature. His most typical condition is solitude: in the first cycle he sits 'engulfed in bleak thought and lonely' 'On the pale strand of ocean' ('Am blassen Meeresstrande, / Saß ich gedankenbekümmert und einsam', 'Abenddämmerung' ('Twilight')); or: 'And I sat on the shore and gazed at / The white dance of the billows' ('Und ich saß am Strand und schaute zu/ Dem weißen Tanz der Wellen', 'Erklärung' ('Declaration')); this solitary figure is repeatedly presented in terms of a consciousness challenging the power of nature – 'But I' or 'Yet I', raised, in 'Sonnenuntergang', to a universal condition of humanity ('But I, a human' ('Ich aber, der Mensch')). In the second cycle his posture becomes more supine: shipwrecked 'I lie on the seashore, / The bleak and barren seashore' ('. . . Lieg ich am Strande/ Am öden, kahlen Strande', from 'Der Schiffbrüchige' ('Shipwrecked')); the barrenness of the shore perfectly corresponds to the protagonist's own sterility, and the arrival of darkness perfects the pathos: 'The night yawned wide, / And long I sat in the darkness and wept' ('Und ich saß noch lange im Dunkeln und weinte', 'Gesang der Okeaniden' ('The Song of the Daughters of the Ocean')). If Kortländer is right and the seaside contemplatives of the *Homecoming* poem 'Wir saßen am Fischerhause' (*Heimkehr* VII: 'We sat by the fisherman's cabin') recall the foreground figures staring out to sea in so many paintings by Caspar David Friedrich, then Heine's solitaries in the *Nordsee* poems seem to be versions of the 'Monk by the Sea' facing the Sublime.[50]

The postures of this 'ich' figure in the poems are every bit as derivative as the worn-out poetic diction of earlier parts of *Buch der Lieder*: alongside the Homeric and hellenizing register that Heine has borrowed from Voß's *Odyssey*, he also returns to Byron's 'estranged heroes', particularly *Childe Harold*, for this mood of melancholy.[51] Perraudin suggests that the Hebridean 'blue-eyed northern child . . ./ The tempest-born in body and in mind' of Byron's *The Island* is also in play in the diction and imagery of 'Abenddämmerung'.[52] But elsewhere we also hear from a more familiar representative of Northern culture in the German literary repertoire. 'Ancient legends from Norway' together with 'Conjure-songs from the Edda, / And runic incantations' ('Uralte Sagen aus Norweg', 'Beschwörungslieder der Edda,/ Auch Runensprüche') appear in 'Night on the Beach' 'Die Nacht am Strande' ('Night on the Beach'));[53] in the 'Storm' ('Storm') of *Nordsee* I, 8, amid the notes of a bardic harp, a pale woman staring from her castle window over Scottish cliffs evokes an *Ossianic* world which returns with the 'woman of the Northland' ('ein Weib im Norden') in 'Der Schiffbrüchige'

(*Nordsee* II, 3). So while the poetic persona of the North Sea verse is full of high feeling and sentimental rhetoric, it is important to recognize that these poems too find ways to display the inadequacy of their grand gestures – even in the variety of their derivations.

In *Der Mann ohne Eigenschaften* (*The Man without Qualities*), Robert Musil identifies, with profound irony, an imperturbable use of the epic 'and' ('Ihr episch unerschütterliches "Und"'), and Heine registers a similar degree of absurdity through the texts of *Die Nordsee*.[54] His quizzical deployment of epic gestures is signalled by methods of burlesque and travesty. The 'dark stranger' ('der nächtige Fremdling') and Titanic lover of 'Die Nacht am Strande' may well bring back biblical times, in a rough paraphrase of Genesis 6.4:

> Die alte Zeit, wo die Götter des Himmels
> Niederstiegen zu Töchtern der Menschen,
> Und die Töchter der Menschen umarmten
> Und mit ihnen zeugten
> Zeptertragende Königsgeschlechter
> Und Helden . . .
>
> (B 1, 185);

> The days of old when the gods descended
> From heaven to the daughters of men,
> And embraced the daughters of men,
> And on them begot
> Scepter-wielding races of kings,
> And heroes
>
> (D 135)

but he still needs dosing with 'tea and rum' to deal with his immortal cough. This travesty is paralleled by the domesticity that overtakes Luna and Sol in the family conflict of 'Sonnenuntergang', the sunset poem in the first cycle of *Die Nordsee*, or Apollo alone in the parallel poem of the second cycle when he appears in a jacket of yellow flannel. (The ironic tension between the heroic and the domestic will return in much later poems in *Romanzero* such as 'An die Engel' ('To the Angels') or in the mundane aspiration of Achilles in 'Der Scheidende' ('Parting Word').) Alongside the diction and personalities of the *Odyssey* and his revived Byronic tone, Heine also leaves clues to his sources in a surprising range of authors. 'Die Götter Griechenlands' ('The Gods of Greece') is plainly a conscious rebuttal of Schiller's poem with the same title, but when the poet glimpses Zeus in the clouds – 'He holds his burnt-out lightning bolt, / Upon his face lie dolor and grief [Gram]' – the god's grief echoes the mortal sorrows of

Heine's shore-line wanderer, whose expression is itself derived from one of the earliest parodies of soulful irrationalism, Wieland's *Musarion*. Heine's 1820 poem 'Lieder 3' ('Songs 3') in the first section of *Buch der Lieder* – 'Ich wandelte unter den Bäumen / Mit meinem Gram allein' ('Under the trees' green ceiling / Alone with my grief, I wept' (D 24)) – unmistakably offers a truncated first-person version of the opening of Wieland's poem:

> In einem Hain, der einer Wildnis glich
> Und nah am Meer ein kleines Gut begrenzte,
> Ging Phanias mit seinem Gram und sich
> Allein umher . . .[55]

> Within a grove, much like a wilderness
> And bordering by the sea a small estate,
> Walked Phanias in grief all by himself
> Alone . . .

Solitary grief can be 'engulfed in bleak thought', as we have seen in 'Abenddämmerung', and beyond this slips into the sympathetic secularism of 'Die Götter Griechenlands' that begins to see the merits of antiquity against the foil of modern Christianity. The passion and pathos of the youth in the poem following this, 'Fragen' ('Questions'), provides an opportunity for Heine to withdraw even further from existential intensity towards a scepticism that anticipates the most radical doubts of his Lazarus poems twenty years later – where only 'a fool waits for an answer'.

The whole tendency of the *Nordsee* cycles parallels the shift of the heroic towards the domestic and even the convivial. The first step is the recognition that the high feelings engendered by the sea have no real correlatives in the natural world: the night simply *yawns* at the end of 'Gesang der Okeaniden'; the idyll at the end of 'Meeresstille' ('Calm at Sea') in the first cycle is shattered by the seagull spearing its basking prey, while the 'eternal stars' that come out at the end of 'Die Götter Griechenlands' care nothing for the demise of the the gods. The same unfeeling stars, 'festgenagelt, / Mit goldenen Nägeln' ('riveted fast / With golden rivets' (D 139)) represent the impotence of the protagonist's longing in 'Nachts in der Kajüte' ('At Night in the Cabin') – yet the counsel of the waves departs in burlesque from the classical advice of Sophocles that the best thing is never to have been born: 'Das beste wäre, du schliefest ein' – the best thing is to fall asleep in his cosy berth, gazing at the stars, which in its turn does indeed lead into another forlorn dream of happiness!

Calm seas and utopian prospects beckon but mislead: that is the clear message of the penultimate poem of the first cycle, 'Reinigung'

('Purification'), so the mysterious vision of Christ that follows it comes as a rather surprising moment of rhetorical closure. When it appeared in *Buch der Lieder* this poem's final part was suppressed – it had caused too much offence when the original conclusion to Heine's poem, published finally with the *Nordsee* travel picture, had denounced the language of piety as a self-serving sham, designed to achieve romantic advantage and professional preferment (see B 2, 187). The heavenly vision of 'Frieden' ('Peace') remains unquestioned until it is glimpsed again – through the bottom of a wine glass in Bremen's Ratskeller. In 'Im Hafen' ('In Port'), the penultimate poem of the second cycle, the vision of Christian self-abnegation that concludes the first cycle in 'Frieden' is echoed and countered. The safe haven of Christian faith (and therefore Heine's own baptism, as Briegleb notes)[56] is replaced by the rather different spirituality of alcohol. This inspiration opens up a world close to the Hebrew Bible – Bethel, Hebron, and the Jordan; and then vouchsafes a vision of angels, like Jacob's Ladder, as the poet ascends the stairs from the bar in the townhall cellars. These matched and contra- dictory visions, Christian and Jewish, self-denying and drunken, provide clues to a contested self-image, possible but not reliable constructions of a personality. In a parallel strategy, the biblical place-names match names from Greek myth (in 'Gewitter' from the second cycle, for instance) as rhetorical possibilities.

The reminiscences of the Hebrew Bible offer another opportunity for self-construction alongside the Homeric model of Odysseus (signally in 'Poseidon' in the first cycle, but in more general terms at the beginning of 'Im Hafen') and the Ossianic worlds of Scotland and Norway. This positioning of Heine's protagonist by reference to the Bible, Homer and Ossian renders him readily recognizable as another epigone of Goethe's Werther, who reflects his own states of mind in these two strains of epic poetry, while glimpsing a vision of the world of the biblical patriarchs in his encounters by the village well.[57] As has been noted, these resources in biblical and classical antiquity are joined in the protagonist's gesture of solitude and his underlying melancholy by the 'Byronic' Heine and *Childe Harold*, particularly its first canto (from which Heine translated a song in 1820). To this extent the poems of the *Nordsee* enact and confront the parade of 'subjectivity' in poetry more acutely than any of the earlier cycles: their models provide a montage of epochal gestures at subjectivity – ranging from the *Sturm und Drang*, through Classicism, to the high Romantic – in Goethe's Werther, Voß's *Odyssey*, and Byron. Once we see these literary possibilities in play in the poems of the *Nordsee*, the sense of authenticity promised by their spontaneous movement of free verse begins to look much less reliable. The careful occupation of a space between the literary and the autobiographical, which was evident in the unexpected temporal shifts of the verse preface to *Buch der Lieder*, continues to tantalize here.

Heine's return to a Byronic posture in the North Sea poems need not surprise us.[58] As the most emphatic and passionate case of Romantic self-presentation he needed to appear in the final catalogue of lyric possibilities. What is in play, more or less constantly through the poems of *Buch der Lieder*, is the larger public story which fragments of biography, anecdotes from a representative life are supposed to realize and so confirm. Experience is intelligible, it tells us, through the conventions of metaphor and of the lyric poem as a vehicle for private feeling. From its prefaces onward, the collection examines this principle in order to challenge and renew the practices of lyrical poetry.

Heine's linguistic and rhetorical turn continued to alarm perceptive readers. But he first made his mark with a new kind of travelogue. The free-wheeling style of his prose in the pictures of travel, which he developed through the 1820s up to the completion of *English Fragments* in 1830, continues to explore the playful and critical possibilities of a flexible literary persona, to the point of notoriety. To these virtuoso performances we now turn.

# CHAPTER 5

# In the diplomatic sense: reading Reisebilder

Throughout his life Heine liked to identify himself as the 'author of the Reisebilder', those 'travel pictures' that brought him his first public success, whether as fame or as notoriety – cardinally through the cheeky combination of wit and sentiment in his *Harzreise*. While it is possible to identify models for Heine's prose methods, both in the rationalistic, political travel writing of Georg Forster's *Ansichten vom Niederrhein* (*Views of the Lower Rhine*, 1791–94) and in the divagatory style of Laurence Sterne in *A Sentimental Journey*, Heine constantly develops his allusive methods independently and, in this way, generates a unique vehicle for cultural, social, and political critique. The pictures of travel Heine wrote between 1825 and 1830, and among which he subsequently included some earlier texts on Berlin, combine the freedoms of a fictionalized autobiography, the critical aims of the essay proper, and the cultural and topographical description of the places he visits. Here I consider, particularly in the works dealing with cities, the ways in which Heine's innovative style responds to aspects of the transition to modernity under conditions of censorship. If, on the one hand, the censor makes any form of direct political engagement difficult, Heine recognizes that other factors – economic and cultural changes – also play a part. The *Reisebilder* deal tactically and thematically with these conditions. Heine's style is a coruscating display of self-fashioning and feigned self-disclosure, capable in the texts on Italy in particular (*Die Reise von München nach Genua* (*The Journey from Munich to Genoa*), *Die Bäder von Lucca* and *Die Stadt Lucca* (*The City of Lucca*)) of grotesque satire, astonishing personal animus, and sustained social and political reflection. The present discussion focuses on earlier and later texts that address the question of direct or indirect communication, as an aspect of the original genre of which they are examples.

Heine's sustained innovation in the pictures of travel remains connected to the lyrical project we have considered in *Buch der Lieder*, and to the failures of affect that Heine puts on show in an exhausted poetic vocabulary.

The two North Sea cycles, which finally subject the postures of sentimental subjectivity to the scepticism of a modern critical sensibility, are closely connected to the *Reisebilder* through their prose complement, *Nordsee* III, which raises many of these issues.

## A MODERN STYLE

Heine visited the island of Norderney in 1825 and 1826, just as *Buch der Lieder* was reaching completion. The 'Reisebild' gives a rough shape to the impressions and reflections of a first-person author, and biographical assumptions are inevitable. After his initial account of the locals and their way of life come more general topics, triggered by the island experience: the contradictory and divided nature of contemporary consciousness ('Zerrissenheit'), in contrast to Goethe's characteristic form of perception as a 'naive' artist in Schiller's sense (see B 2, 221), and alongside him the historical grasp and significance of Napoleon, capable of another kind of immediate comprehension quite like Kant's 'intellectual intuition' (B 2, 234–5). Between these two poles of the North Sea prose, Goethe and Napoleon, Heine sets, apropos of the aristocratic clientele of Norderney, a discussion of the fragmented state of Germany. Fragmentation is also the theme of the 'motto' or epigraph for the work, which is given merely as a page reference to his friend Varnhagen von Ense's *Biographische Denkmale* (*Biographical Monuments*). The passage Heine refers to here notes the constraints and limitations imposed even on the greatest minds by the absence of German political or national unity. 'Even Frederick the Great and Luther,' Varnhagen observes, were unable to 'embrace the whole in a unified way' (B 2, 805). The sense of fragmentation announced in this passage provides the tacit theme of Heine's remarks on the character of Norderney's inhabitants, on the character and impact of the aristocratic tourists who visit the island, and within this context on the cultural and historical significance of two great contemporaries – Goethe and Napoleon.

The narrator of *Nordsee* III contrasts himself with the islanders and their less anguished lifestyle. Their shared experience and homogeneous beliefs guarantee a 'communal immediacy' (B 2, 213: 'die gemeinschaftliche Unmittelbarkeit'), sustaining their mutual communication. The bourgeois visitor, by contrast, suffers from an acute sense of isolation:

For essentially we live in spiritual and intellectual solitude; through a specific educational method or particular reading, chosen at random, each of us has received a particular personal orientation; each of us, behind an intellectual mask, thinks, feels and struggles differently from the others, and misunderstandings become so numerous and even in spacious houses life together becomes so difficult, and everywhere we are constrained, everywhere strangers [fremd], everywhere far from home [in der Fremde]. (B 2, 214)

The early part of the *Nordsee* prose develops this sense of individual alienation, in which the possibility of political emancipation is constantly accompanied by the most profound feelings of doubt. The processes of secularization, to which according to Heine the ancient certainties of the Roman Catholic Church have now succumbed, leave him divided between sympathy for what has been lost and the critical animus of Protestant rationalism. It is precisely this sense of inner division that is then identified as a cardinal 'image of the inner turmoil of modern thought' ('ein Bild von der Zerrissenheit der Denkweise unserer Zeit', B 2, 215). The characteristics of such modernity, as Heine perceives it, are a self divided in the very process of rationalization that goes with the secular, a loss of organic community, and the consequent isolation of the individual. His Norderney islanders stand on the brink of a new age, heralded by the novelty and innovation that come with their wealthy visitors: 'their old unity of sense and their simplicity is being disturbed by the prosperity of the local seaside resort' (B 2, 216). Exactly this loss of cultural coherence and continuity is evoked again in the discussion of Sir Walter Scott towards the end of *Nordsee* III, in connection with Scott's biography of Napoleon. Scott's 'elegiac lament' for Scotland's popular glory, lost to the depredations of foreign (i.e. English) custom, is seen to be no more than the symptom of a greater historic loss of nationality, which can be seen equally in German aristocracy and bourgeoisie alike. The failure of tradition is the result of nothing less than 'extensive, unattractive modernity' (B 2, 236: 'weite, unerfreuliche Modernität') that drives out the authority of aristocratic coats of arms along with the comfortable weight of bourgeois inheritance, and the faith and the faithful that have abandoned Catholic cathedral and rabbinical synagogue alike.[1]

This explicit context of modernity is introduced at the beginning of *Nordsee* III when Heine realizes that the forms of communication, available to the islanders as 'a single sound, a single facial expression, a single silent movement' (B 2, 214) within the framework of a community, are lost on the modern observer. In drawing attention to this gestural vocabulary and its social origins, Heine is also alerting the reader to the way in which other shared meanings have been lost in the process of modernity. Consequently we should also be alert to the possibility of new forms of communication. Here Goethe 'with his clear Greek eye' provides a model of objective description. Heine claims that Goethe's *Die Italienische Reise* (*Italian Journey*) can represent a land and its people 'in their true forms and their true colours' (B 2, 221). It will remain for later generations, he argues, to discover other meanings in what, for Goethe himself, remains naively unconscious. What is apparently objective is in fact full of implications.

As we have seen, the poetry of *Buch der Lieder* seems dedicated to an investigation of the way in which the vocabulary of lyrical subjectivity cannot any longer be securely deployed. There too the guarantees of linguistic affect have been cancelled. In the first of Heine's pictures of travel, and the one which achieved his first fame and notoriety, the *Harzreise* (*Harz Journey*), he demonstrates in a series of examples how the language of 'nature' and the assumptions of the pathetic fallacy have been corroded by utilitarianism, by the sheer currency of literary language, particularly in the 'educated' middle class of 'philistines', and by the growth of tourism – in this case around the Brocken mountain itself. Inherited values and meanings can still be recognized in the lives of simple folk, but they remain the objects of nostalgia for the modern traveller – unless he is vouchsafed the poetic insight to glimpse a fairy-tale 'Princess Ilse' in the Ilse valley, as Heine's narrator does during his final ascent of the Ilsenstein.[2]

The miners encountered in the course of the Harz journey, in Klausthal and Zellerfeld, take on the role that the fishing communities of Norderney will come to play in *Nordsee* III.

However quietly static the life of these people may seem, it is a truthful, living life all the same. The ancient trembling woman sitting by the stove, opposite the great cupboard, may well have been sitting there for a full quarter of a century, and her thought and feeling is without doubt closely interwoven with every corner of the stove and every single carving on the cupboard. And so the cupboard and stove are alive, for a human being has poured part of her soul into them. (B 2, 118)

At this point in his Harz narrative Heine moves on to describe the living significance of physical objects as they are experienced in the traditional fairy-tale, and relates this intensity of meaning to the pre-modern engagement of human and objective worlds in the pastoral simplicity of the mining community or of childhood. Such a profound, as it were un-alienated, life of the senses ('solch tiefes Anschauungsleben' (B 2, 119)) Heine paraphrases in terms of the same immediacy ('Unmittelbarkeit') he will find again on Norderney and in the forms of Goethe's self-expression (B 2, 213, 221). What is apparently direct and immediate in childhood and in the folk world of the miners or fishermen is understood as the 'pure gold of intuition' which the modern sensibility has 'effortfully changed into the paper money of book definitions' (B 2, 119). A little later, in *Die Reise von München nach Genua*, Heine himself will operate with a more abstract symbolism. The crucifix he describes there, propping up and also overgrown by a vine, has been taken to represent the opposition between the life-affirming force of Heine's own 'Hellenism', celebrating the sensuous Greek affirmation of the body, and the deadly asceticism of Christianity.[3]

The way in which immediacy of meaning and expression have been traded in for a bookish mediation of what is meant to be spontaneous is a recurrent issue in Heine's *Harzreise*. Just as in *Lyrisches Intermezzo* XXXVII of *Buch der Lieder*, where the middle-class strollers greet nature as if they have read Goethe's famous salutation in 'Mailied' once too often, so too the various tourists and travellers encountered on the Harz journey distort their direct apprehension of the natural world by the literary frame they impose on it. This literary deformation of experience reaches its climax in an encounter that ironically echoes the deeply human perception of the ancient cupboard ('Schrank') in Klausthal. During Heine's overnight stay on the summit of the Brocken, two students, under the excessive influence of alcohol and Ossian, mistake a wardrobe ('Kleiderschrank') for an open window, and, standing before it, address Night in tones of high melancholy. They have evidently been reading Goethe's *Werther* (who similarly recites long passages from the fake Celtic bard) and in all likelihood too many odes by Klopstock (mediator of Werther's passion for Lotte) into the bargain.[4] This episode is one of a number of aspects of the *Harzreise* that play on Heine's reception of Goethe. This Goethean subtext of the book can provide a striking example of the way Heine deals with the failure of immediacy in modern experience, by embracing patterns of mediation and indirection in order to recreate the community of meaning he had seen in the fishing community of Norderney. In the modern context, however, it is recreated for critical purposes.

The *Harzreise* breaks off and announces itself as a fragment before Heine's narrative of his real journey, in September 1824, reaches his notorious visit to Goethe in Weimar. The misplaced oratory of the two students on the Brocken amounts to a casual parody of the great man's first novel; and the entire project can be seen as an allusion to Goethe's own Harz journey in 1777 and to the enigmatic poem that recalls it, 'Harzreise im Winter' ('Harz Journey in Winter').[5] However, disappointed by the frailty of the elderly poet in 1824, as his letter to Rudolf Christiani of 16 May 1825 makes very plain, Heine establishes himself in explicit competition with his predecessor. When the visit was finally written up for public consumption in 1833, at the end of Book I of *Die Romantische Schule*, Heine admits to nothing but admiration for the Olympian figure he had encountered:

Even in great age Goethe's eye remained as divine as it had been in his youth. Time may have covered his head too with snow, but it could not make him bow. He held it high and proud, and if he stretched out his hand it was as if, with his finger, he could prescribe the path the stars were to take in the sky. Some have claimed to see a cold trait of egotism about his mouth; but this feature too is characteristic of the eternal gods, indeed of the father of the gods, great Jupiter himself, with whom I have already compared Goethe. (B 3, 405)[6]

By implication, however, Goethe's identification with Jupiter is already present in the *Harzreise*.

Heine organizes the material of his travel picture both geographically and through the alternation of day and night, of lived experience and emblematic dreams. The second of these recounts a version of 'the old fairy-tale of how a knight descends into a deep well where the loveliest princess has been paralysed in sleep by a magic spell'. In his attempt to liberate the princess, Heine the knight is assailed by an army of dwarves, who 'horribly wag their heads'. Heine goes on to explain: 'It was only as I struck out at them and the blood spurted out that I realized they were the bearded red thistle-heads that I had sliced off with my stick the day before on the country road' (B 2, 121).[7] To see how the fuller meaning of this passage is mediated – how Heine challenges the Olympian Goethe – it is necessary to note the detail of the German text: Heine notices 'daß es die rotblühenden, langbärtigen *Distelköpfe* waren, die ich den Tag vorher an der Landstraße mit dem Stocke abgeschlagen hatte' (my italics). The image of striking off thistle-heads explicitly recalls the opening lines of Goethe's famous poem on 'Prometheus' in which the Titan shouts to Zeus (Jupiter):

> Bedecke deinen Himmel, Zeus,
> Mit Wolkendunst,
> Und übe, dem Knaben gleich,
> Der Disteln köpft,
> An Eichen dich und Bergeshöhn . . .[8]

> Cover up your heaven, Zeus,
> With misty clouds
> And try your strength, just like a boy
> Slicing the heads off thistles,
> On oaks and mountain tops.

We should note that Zeus is the one like a boy hacking at thistles. Through an allusion to Goethe's poem, Heine identifies himself with the role attributed to Zeus by the Promethean speaker of the poem: for in the *Harzreise* Heine is the one who dreams of himself slicing at thistles; Goethe had been identified with the god, and tacitly Heine's narrator hence challenges the Olympian author of the poem. This complex trope had been prepared in the first of the dream sequences of the *Harzreise*. There, the narrator dreams he is back in the Law School at Göttingen University where Themis, the Titanic goddess of justice herself, beleaguered by the dry scholasticism of academic lawyers, finally cries out that she can hear 'the voice of dear Prometheus, bound by scornful power and silent force to the rock of his martyrdom' (B 2, 109–10). It seems more than likely that the figure of Prometheus here alludes emblematically to Napoleon, though Heine may also see himself as the spirit of freedom who cannot be liberated by the anachronistic discourse of German academic law, and from which he has fled into the other freedoms of the landscape.[9]

Because the force of gesture and speech within traditional communities have been lost to modernity, Heine devises the emblematic and allusive methods that we see at work in the episodes from the Harz journey considered here. Yet because the implications of 'a single sound, a single facial expression, a single silent movement' cannot any longer be assumed, Heine's *Reisebilder* repeatedly draw attention to the possibilities of reading and interpretation. In the Harz journey, the need for interpretative vigilance is expounded in relation to the theatre in Berlin. One of the students staying on the Brocken describes his recent trip to the city, concentrating on a restaurant and the gossip of the theatrical world. This cues Heine's narrator to offer extensive, scurrilous commentary on the significance of costume in a city so devoted to appearances. Finally, as the most difficult of the aesthetic practices under consideration, Heine explains 'the diplomatic significance of the ballet' (B 2, 147). According to this reading, when the dancer 'gradually rises to full expansion' (B 2, 148), for instance, he actually represents 'our excessively large friend in the east', Russia.[10]

Heine's anxieties about the likely response of the Prussian censors to this passage of satire were well founded.[11] Yet it is not the specific allusion to themes and issues in German and Prussian post-Napoleonic politics that is important here, so much as the possibility of allegorical reading that Heine is able to introduce. In a contrast that has been taken as representative of Heine's own writing, he exclaims: 'how great is the number of exoteric and how small the number of esoteric theatre-goers!' (B 2, 148). The esoteric audience must be alerted to the second order of significance from which the 'exoteric' outsiders are supposedly excluded. Such a community of reading can restore – for political purposes in modernity and for those in the know – the 'communal immediacy' of gesture celebrated among the fisher folk of Norderney.[12]

Heine's great 'pictures of travel' return to this possibility of 'diplomatic meaning' where what a casual listener or reader imagines has been said in reality neglects the text and its full implications. In the pseudo-autobiographical 'Reisebild' *Ideen. Das Buch Le Grand* (*Ideas: The Book of Le Grand*) Heine offers a different model from the allusive and allegorical pattern we have seen in the *Harzreise*. Between extravagant self-stylization and fictionalized autobiography in this text, Heine is able to generate a thematic structure organizing personal relationships and entanglements ('love'), the political freedom represented by the French Revolution of which Napoleon is the emblem and standard-bearer, and the difficulties encountered by an author working under conditions of censorship. Famously, these difficulties are summarized in the four words making up chapter 12 amid a welter of dashes that represent the censors' imagined excisions: 'The German censors – [etc.] idiots' (B 2, 283). This extremely *un*diplomatic style distracts from a sublinguistic or paralinguistic practice of communication that develops the allegorical implications that emerge in the *Harzreise*.

The possibility of another level or mode of communication appears at the very centre of the narrative in the figure of the drummer Le Grand, who is quartered with Heine's family during the Napoleonic occupation of Düsseldorf. Although they have no common language, Le Grand is able to 'drum' the history of the Revolution for young Heine's benefit, so that political communication is possible without direct discourse. Thus, although Heine's narrator has little or no French, drumming the rhythm of the 'Marseillaise' expresses 'liberté'; and the beat of the revolutionary song 'Ça ira, ça ira – les aristocrates à la lanterne' renders the violent 'égalité' that will simply string up the aristocracy (B 2, 271). Le Grand can articulate Heine's political satire by associating the idea of stupidity with the Dessau March and Germany itself with a rhythm transcribed as 'dum – dum – dum': dumb. The point is made by association. Such indirection is sketched for the reader in other terms, however: in contrast to the emblematic tropes of the *Harzreise*, in *Ideen. Das Buch Le Grand* Heine draws attention to an art of mnemonics and quotation. Heine's autobiographical narrator recalls the day when the Grand Duchy of Berg, where he grew up, was ceded to Napoleon, and the Elector departed (in fact to become King of Bavaria). After this abdication of power, the text records the arrival of French troops – but thereafter order is restored and school resumes. This return to normality allows Heine at the beginning of chapter 7 an apparently innocent segue into the regular curriculum, and he tells us what had to be learned by rote: 'the kings of Rome, dates, nouns ending in *im*, irregular verbs, Greek, Hebrew, geography, German language, mental arithmetic' (B 2, 266). In fact a very significant 'date' ('Jahreszahl') has just been passed, of course: so the dates memorized at school are less innocent than they might seem. Heine's technique for memorizing such numbers, he tells us, is to associate them in his memory with house numbers:

In those days if I thought of an acquaintance of mine I simultaneously recalled an historical fact, the date of which coincided with their house-number, so that I could easily remember it, whenever I thought of them, and for that reason an historical event always came to mind too whenever I caught sight of an acquaintance. (B 2, 266)

Memory allows for these metonymic moves, so that the most innocent-looking information can be the signal for an understanding that functions at a different level from direct statement. The drummer Le Grand himself, returning from the Russian Campaign, his drum intact, provides a model for this insistence on unspoken implications: 'He drummed now once again, just as before, yet without saying a word. If he was uncannily tight-lipped, his eyes spoke all the more eloquently' (B 2, 281).[13] The eloquence of the gaze lies precisely in what cannot be said.

The possibility of critique by implication is developed further when Heine explicitly expounds the virtues of quotation, in chapter 13. Addressing 'Madame', the imaginary interlocutrix who recurs in the text, the narrator defends his habit of digression, insisting that 'I write in a concentrated way, I avoid everything superfluous, often I even pass over what is necessary'. This omission clearly parallels the silence of Le Grand, so that the point or purpose of the text is understood as what is *not* said. In his wayward discipline of relevance, the narrator claims that an art of quotation has so far also been avoided, although 'quoting from old and new books is the chief pleasure of a young author, and a couple of extremely learned quotations is an ornament to the whole man'. He knows, he says, 'the trick of great minds who are good at picking the raisins out of buns and the quotations out of their lecture notes'; finally, the narrator adds, he could 'get a quotation-loan from my learned friends' (B 2, 284: 'eine Anleihe von Zitaten'). The gathering of quotations is elided with banking, so that quoted text takes on the force of a currency in circulation. Indeed, the narrator even lays claim to having invented the art of passing off forged quotations as genuine ones. In offering this casual commentary, Heine gives another indication to his esoteric readership of the techniques of allusion and association he is applying and of the need for vigilance and for an act of decipherment. But the idea of a quotation-loan takes up again the connection between experience, writing, and the economic context that had been invoked in the bookish paper money that robs the 'pure gold of intuition' of its immediacy in *Nordsee* III.

In order to ensure that the possibility of a potentially subversive art of quotation is properly recognized as part of his associative technique, Heine finally makes a proposal that links his reflections on quotation to the mnemonic programme outlined earlier: 'For the benefit of literature, I will not withhold another invention and will communicate it gratis: namely, I think it advisable to quote all obscure authors along with their house-number' (B 2, 284). The recollection of the function of house-numbers in the mnemonic strategy described earlier is a sufficient prompt to the reader to identify the single purpose of these patterns of implication and insinuation.

The development of a prose style based on the use of significant detail, isolated from its original contexts, like the art of quotation Heine describes here, gives some substance to Karl Kraus's critical remarks on the inauthenticity of his style, considered earlier. The elements of an allusive form appear to separate writing from its 'real' content. What should be instrumental in the appropriate description of the world becomes, in Kraus's terms, ornamental – at best the quirky evocation of a personality. Paradoxically, as we have seen, the methods of Heine's pictures of travel make explicit the exploitation of allegorical structures of which Kraus complains.

## APT SYMBOLS: BERLIN

Across the range of Heine's *Reisebilder* prose, the central intelligence is urban. This is explicit in the *Harzreise* with its pastoral appeal to the life and example of the shepherd boy, alongside the miners of Klausthal, but one could say that the whole sequence of the travel writing has a metropolitan frame. From the early 1820s onwards, Heine formed a sketchy plan for what he calls a 'metropolitan correspondence', developing the pseudo-epistolary form he exploits in the earliest travel writing, the *Briefe aus Berlin* (*Letters from Berlin* (1822)) and the essay *Über Polen* (*On Poland* (1823)). Until fairly recently these earlier travel writings were not printed in association with the *Reisebilder* proper, but relegated to a place among Heine's 'minor works'.[14] The text on Poland interrupted the Berlin reportage, and the final published form of the Berlin letters salvaged what was possible from what appeared originally in Heine's local newspaper, the *Rhein-westfälischer Anzeiger*. Yet the Berlin texts already lay the groundwork for the methods and tone of what is to come: so although Heine himself conceives of travel writing with a specifically urban focus as a new and *different* kind of 'Reisebild' in a letter to Moses Moser at the end of 1825, and dismisses the Berlin letters as 'padding' in the concluding text of the sequence of travel pictures, in fact the Berlin letters already demonstrate the development and significance of the techniques we have considered.[15]

Heine famously remarks that the defeat of Napoleon occasioned his Prussian nationality (B 6/1, 457),[16] and he remained something of a stranger in the Prussian capital. In the third of his *Briefe aus Berlin* he gleefully lists other young authors as 'not from Berlin' – and would clearly like to see himself aligned with them as a new talent in the city.[17] The tension between the city and the provinces is apparent in Heine's outsider position in the very first letter:

Don't think that I would forget our Westphalia so soon. September 1821 still lingers too well in my memory. The lovely valleys around Hagen, the friendly Overweg road in Unna, pleasant days in Hamm, splendid Fritz von B., you W., the antiquities in Soest, even the Paderborn Heath – I see it all vividly before me. (B 2, 9)

This introduction is designed to legitimate the letter form adopted and to guarantee its authenticity: the figures addressed really were the editors of the *Anzeiger*, but we can already recognize the tension between a modern urban world and a vague bond with nature that also displays its rootedness in German history:

I can still hear the ancient oak forests rustling around me and every leaf whispering: Here dwelt the ancient Saxons, the last to forfeit their beliefs and their German essence. I can still hear an ancient rock calling to me: Wanderer, stay, here Arminius conquered Varus. (B 2, 9)

The allusion to the story of Hermann's (Arminius') victory over the Roman legions seems to open the theme of patriotism, but beyond this sense of the allusion Heine is also implying the political issue of freedom – a further dimension of the tension between Berlin as the capital of Prussia, the evocation of Heine's Westphalian home and the German national idea embodied in Hermann. Within this set of tensions Heine registers the changing sense of national identity in the transition to modernity that he outlines again in *Nordsee* III. There is also a sense that Hermann's battle against Varus constitutes the first of a number of literary allusions to the work of the dramatist Heinrich von Kleist. His play *Die Hermannsschlacht* (*Hermann's Battle*) evokes the absence of German national unity through the figures of the prince of the Cherusces and his allies. The Arminius legend then returns in Heine's witty discussion of patriotism among German students compared with their Polish contemporaries:

You can see at once from their faces that no timid soul is lurking beneath their jerkins. Many of these Sarmatians could set an example of charm and noble behaviour to the sons of Hermann and [his wife] Thusnelda. (B 2, 15)

(Sarmatia, a lyrical term for Poland, was the ancient name for a region reaching from the Vistula and Danube to the Volga and the Caucasus; its nomadic inhabitants were famous for their banditry.) In Kleist's play, of course, Hermann's noble behaviour is seriously compromised by his strategy of black propaganda against the Romans; and Thusnelda comes off no better in the scene where she feeds a corrupt Roman legate to a wild bear! In this sense patriotism and by implication the beliefs of the ancient Saxons have little in common with a modern conception of the state. However, the reference to Prussian military pride provides a measure by which the current state of Berlin can be gauged:

Let us pause here for a moment and consider the great statue of the Great Elector. He is proudly seated on horseback, and slaves in fetters surround the plinth. It is a splendid bronze, and without doubt Berlin's greatest work of art. And it can be seen entirely free of charge because it stands in the middle of a bridge. (B 2, 10)

One element in this complicated piece of irony is the fact that the sculpture on the bridge can be seen for nothing. This remnant of a supposedly glorious past is not yet subject to the rule of money that dominates Heine's Berlin experiences. Berlin has achieved a certain degree of modernity, because it has very little history at all. Heine cites Madame de Staël in order to emphasize the historical dimension that the modern city lacks: 'Berlin, cette ville toute moderne, quelque belle qu'elle soit, ne fait pas une impression assez sérieuse; on n'y aperçoit point l'empreinte de l'histoire du pays . . .' (B 2, 19).[18] Berlin's relationship to the past, in its transition from a quasi-feudal order to modernity, is similarly stressed in another way in the first letter. Heine reaches the great thoroughfare of Unter den Linden and recalls there a cultural past:

I shiver when I think that Lessing may have stood on this spot. The favourite stroll of so many great men who lived in Berlin ran under the trees. 'Der große Fritz' walked here, this path was walked by – Him! But isn't the present splendid also? (B 2, 15)

As historical figures, Lessing and Frederick the Great go hand in hand, but the anonymous third man is ambiguous. The pronoun might simply repeat the supposed admiration for the king; but equally we are perhaps to understand here the Emperor Napoleon – also a figure of the heroic past who might have inaugurated a more liberal present. In this respect the reader is enabled to recognize that the present is not quite as splendid as the sarcastic author seems to make out: or it calls for an optimism of the will in the spirit of Gramsci.[19] Something about Berlin remains non-simultaneous, to use Ernst Bloch's phrase.[20] Heine's purpose in the Berlin letters is to decipher this ambiguity through the emblematic style he begins to develop. The city offers ready made the material for what he will describe in the *Harzreise* as 'diplomatic interpretation'.

The *Briefe aus Berlin* begin with an enigmatic motto:

> Seltsam! – Wenn ich der Dei von Tunis wäre,
> Schlüg ich bei so zweideut'gem Vorfall, Lärm.

> Strange! – If I were the Dey of Tunis,
> I would raise a commotion at such an ambiguous circumstance.

These lines come from a scene in Kleist's play *Prinz Friedrich von Homburg* (*The Prince of Homburg*) (act 5, scene 2) in which the Elector is surprised by the apparent rebellion of his niece's regiment under the leadership of Kottwitz, a figure of traditional loyalty to the Elector. What is important about this text for Heine is not merely the awkward question of public performances of Kleist's play, which is discussed later in the *Briefe aus Berlin*; he is drawn to the Elector's claim to be unlike the Dey. The quotation allows him, rather, to draw the *comparison* between this – and therefore any other – Prussian ruler and a proverbial despot.

The network of orientalism that threads its way through the text builds on this inaugural moment to indicate the double meanings in Berlin's 'ambiguous circumstances' – and to encourage the reading appropriate to them. Heine tells of a 'travelling orientalist', for instance, who visited the cathedral in the course of a city tour. The implication is that Berlin is the appropriate terrain for an oriental scholar because oriental conditions hold sway there. Schooled in Berlin itself as a pupil of Hegel, Heine might well be particularly sensitive to this diplomatic ambiguity in the course of the modern movement towards freedom.[21] After all, *Geist* is supposed to move from oriental despotism towards the freedom of the moral state. In the same way, even Goethe is seen as 'the Ali Pasha of our literature' (B 2, 63). The sound-track for this socio-political constellation is provided by Spontini, who wrote *Nurmahal, or the Rose Festival in Kashmir* for the marriage of Princess Alexandrine (B 2, 52). At the wedding even the Duke of Cumberland's coachman is seen in a livery that can bear comparison with

'Solomon in his glory' or 'Haroun al Raschid in state as a Caliph' (B 2, 49). The faux-naif gaze of his provincial origins permits Heine to offer the exotic ways of the city for political readings that open up the contradictions of modern life.

The start of the first letter introduces Heine's reflections on his own artistic method in the text. As a newspaper correspondent he recognizes that other publications limit his activities. On the face of it, however, anything seems possible when he asks 'What should I *not* write?' (B 2, 9) – at least until we identify the allusion to the Prussian censor![22] What he consciously and explicitly seeks to avoid is any kind of systematic approach ('Systematie'). Instead, the text is to be dominated by a free 'association of ideas' ('Ideenassoziation', B 2, 10).[23] As he develops this introduction to the problem of style, Heine indicates three areas in which the meaning of Berlin can be read as a modern city: food, art, and fashion. Jagor's invention of the truffle ice-cream represents the first of these; Spontini, the composer, 'appearing at the most recent ceremony for the award of decorations in a jacket and trousers of green velvet with golden stars' (B 2, 10), the second and third. Jagor is the owner of the 'Golden Sun' and along with figures such as Beyermann of the 'Café Royal' he comes to represent the consumer society of the capital: 'Jagor! A sun stands over this gateway to paradise. An apt symbol!' (B 2, 17). Between the free association of ideas and emblems of this kind Heine discovers in the emblematics of the city the fundamental structure of his journalistic style in this text. The objective account of people and monuments becomes the material of a political interpretation of the cityscape.

Heine returns to the question of technique at the beginning of his second letter:

It is true – I can be easily misunderstood. People don't observe the whole picture that I sketch, but the little figures I've drawn in to enliven it; and they may even think that I was particularly bothered about these figures. But you can paint a picture without figures, just as you can eat soup without salt. You can speak in a flowery way like our journalists. Whenever they talk about a great power in North Germany, everyone knows that they mean Prussia. I find it ridiculous. (B 2, 23)

What is seen and sketched has to be correctly understood: Heine's cynicism and his response to censorship are conjoined here. To speak so directly was not without risks:

At Schüppel's bookshop Kosmeli has published 'Harmless observations on a journey through part of Russia and Turkey' which are far from being harmless since this original mind sees things everywhere with his own eyes and freely and bluntly says what he has seen. (B 2, 40–1)

Kosmeli's Turkish travelogue provides another of the oriental allusions in the Berlin letters which we have been able to read as a reference to Prussian despotism through the clue provided by the motto from Kleist. Apposite symbols such as Jagor's golden sun provide a different clue to an understanding of Heine's symbolic codes. The apparently random notes and observations, gossip and anecdotes of life in the metropolis generate a context of meaning in Berlin that discloses the repressive politics of the post-Napoleonic world.[24]

### 'THE NAKED EARNESTNESS OF THINGS': LONDON

The conclusion of the third letter from Berlin attempts a comparison of England, France, and Germany on the basis of their respective styles in prose fiction. English style is realistic, says Heine, because the Englishman is always travelling; the French strike a note of easy sociability while respecting social values; but the poor German, with too little money to travel, is fundamentally asocial – and so must dream up an inner world of poetry and mysticism (B 2, 67–8). Six years later, as he brings the pictures of travel to a close with the *Englische Fragmente*, Heine returns to this national typology. Travelling up the Thames towards London (in 1827), Heine's conversation with another passenger contrasts a domestic view of political freedom – 'my house is my castle' (B 2, 534) – with French sociability and the dreamy interiority of the Germans – 'they are a speculative nation' (B 2, 535). English preferences for the domestic framework have significant consequences for Heine's model of communication. The privatization of political freedom he detects in England has brought about a reduction in the symbolic power of everyday events:

Even the fine, colourful uniform that proclaims a privileged military class among us [Germans], is far from being a mark of honour in England; just as an actor wipes off his make up after the performance, so too an English officer hastens to remove his red coat as soon as he is off duty . . . (B 2, 535)

Although Heine here uses the comparison to emphasize the Prussian caste-spirit, he also acknowledges the pure functionality of uniforms and other marks of social class. They lack animus or affect. As a result, the stereotyping techniques of the third Berlin letter are of limited use in the *Englische Fragmente*, but even here the attempt at interpretation also throws light on the significance of German cultural practices.

The levelling out of meaning in everyday life, registered in the case of military uniform, is closely associated with the principle of reproduction in commodity manufacture. Albrecht Betz was the first to identify the tripartite structure of the *Englische Fragmente*, and at the centre, 'like a jewel', rests 'the new "fetish" of the bourgeois world'.[25] But this degree of clarity is only gained after the event. Heine first encounters London with sheer astonishment – and this philosophical state of mind yields his first insight: 'Don't send philosophers to London, and certainly not a poet!'

I have seen the most astonishing thing that the world can afford to the astonished mind; I've seen it and I am still astonished – that stone forest of houses still stands rigid in my memory, and between them the thrusting river of living human faces . . . – I'm speaking of London. (B 2, 538)

Bernd Witte has written of the overwhelming 'natural' event of Heine's London visit as the foundation for his pessimistic view of the boundless productivity of English capitalism.[26] The natural metaphor of the stone forest at the start of the London fragment is also intended to bridge the steam-ship journey on the Thames and Heine's first impressions of the city. As twilight falls on the river, 'in the white veil of evening mist the outlines of objects fade, all that remains visible is a forest of masts rising tall and bare' (B 2, 537), and recalling the fact of British naval supremacy. Like the memories of a Westphalian landscape in the *Briefe aus Berlin*, the forest of houses and the river of humanity here evoke by contrast an unspoiled natural world before it is destroyed in the deformity of the nascent industrial city.

Heine experiences London as a mass society. The astonished German poet even experiences the statistical reality physically, as 'this damned jostling' (B 2, 539). But he also has a strong visual sense of intensive housing and the London fragment repeatedly describes terraces of houses. Heine reads this architectural effect as a sign of building speculation, responsive to the need for a home that is an Englishman's castle: in doing so he achieves an understanding of the way in which an economic infrastructure comes to determine the visual cityscape. For all that, however, the dwellings Heine describes are primarily middle-class if not even aristocratic. For the moment, the poverty of the workers or the underclass remains concealed.

The social and psychological effect of the capitalist form of the commodity is that Heine finds himself in a world of undifferentiated objects. Beyond the human meanings filling domestic objects among the Klausthal miners, and beyond the emblematic availability of Jagor's golden sun or the fashionable orientalism of Berlin, in London he encounters 'that naked earnestness of things, that colossal uniformity' that makes him plead 'do not send a poet to London' (B 2, 238). English objects and English conditions are anti-poetic and hostile to metaphor because they are marked by this naked earnestness ('dieser bare Ernst'). They are to be accepted simply as they are, without any symbolic reach.

The key terms that emerge here for Heine's London experience are uniformity and monotony. This levelling out even affects traditional views of national characteristics. The London stock-exchange, Heine notes, may still direct each nation to its appointed place on the floor, but the internationalization of Europe since the lifting of the continental blockade has obliterated old distinctions: 'The old characteristic stereotypes of the nations, such as we find in learned compendia and beer halls, are of no further use and only lead to melancholy errors' (B 2, 543). Just as Heine had recognized a loss of traditional, national communities of meaning under the pressure of 'an extensive modernity' in Walter Scott's elegies for a fading Scotland, so too in London the rapid development of the market has distorted traditional structures of meaning.

In stark contrast to this pattern of uniformity stand the beautiful objects and luxury goods in the shop windows. Each of these shines out in solitary perfection:

... because the Englishman delivers everything he manufactures in a completed state, and every luxury article, every 'astral' lamp and every boot, every tea-pot and every women's dress gleams in such a *finished* and inviting way ... (B 2, 541)

'Finished' appears in English in the original as a technical term for the perfection and material completeness of the commodity. What Heine calls 'the art of display' in the rest of this article had in fact caught his notice six years earlier in Berlin. There, in the Königsstraße, brilliantly illuminated goods in the shop windows 'almost blind us' (B 2, 11). It is not the urban experience of shopping or the brilliance of the displays that has changed the possible pattern of signification and diplomatic interpretation; what takes him by surprise is the perfection of form and workmanship in the glittering object, the luxury commodity, which is now available for purchase with money – and not simply to the order and patronage of aristocratic demand. These things simply cannot bear meanings in the same way.

Heine discerns the same loss of meaning in current political debates in England. Like many a continental intellectual, he is irritated by the discovery that the English rarely articulate a principle in their parliamentary debates – 'they discuss only the usefulness or the disadvantages of things, they present facts – some pro, others contra' (B 2, 583). The closeness of the English to reality that was invoked in the opening fragment of the text now becomes a single-minded utilitarianism that excludes interpretation.

Because things and facts stand for themselves and nothing else in the English context, the *Englische Fragmente* develop the technique of quotation projected in *Ideen. Das Buch Le Grand*, and exploited again in *Ludwig Börne*. Heine inserts extensive quotations at three points in the text. After a short introduction Fragment VII quotes Cobbett's essay from his *Weekly Political Register*, explaining the growth of the national debt as a consequence of the British victory over Napoleon. Heine defends the use of the quotation on the grounds of Cobbett's eloquence (B 2, 571). The translation of an account of Brougham as a parliamentary orator in Fragment VIII deals with his rhetorical skills in the House of Commons, as part of an account of current political discourse. When Heine lets representatives of England speak, it is hence part of his attempt to evaluate the possibility of political expression in this land of mere things in all their mute earnestness. Finally, in Fragment IX, a third example from English parliamentary debates provides a functioning form for Heine's own concerns: the parallel history ('Parallelgeschichte') that 'provides a bridge which Heine may cross from considerations of religious emancipation in Britain to another kind of emancipation on a larger stage: the freeing of nations from foreign rule' – though Britain itself generally abstained from such foreign interventions.[27] Heine demonstrates new possibilities for 'diplomatic interpretation' through the technique and range of political parable in Lord King's speech on Catholic emancipation to the House of Lords on 3 February 1825. In the fable, the Greeks are like the Catholic Irish and the Turks represent the British. The political implications of the parable can be assumed without the most awkward questions even being raised – personal sensibilities remain intact.

Heine's images of England provide their own 'parallel history' for the communication of his political concerns and critique. That is why the work and influence of Sir Walter Scott once again stands at the centre of his critical discussion of England. If Heine defends Scott against the complaint that 'he goes into too much detail, he creates his great figures merely by assembling a mass of small characteristics' (B 2, 549), he is simultaneously defending the free association of ideas in an assemblage of detail that constitutes his own method. More importantly Scott's work provides a site where two of Heine's concerns coincide. On the one hand he demonstrates the effects of commodity structure that bring literary practice closer to market forms; on the other, he provides a platform for a renewed interest in the revolutionary image of Napoleon. As we have seen, Heine's critique of Scott's talent in describing him as 'a millionaire whose whole fortune was in small change, and who has to drive up with three or four wagonloads of pennies and farthings whenever he has to pay over a large sum' (B 2, 549) explicitly relates literary method to aspects of the economy. The insight this yields seems to be that modern communication, bereft of the meanings still available in the Norderney communities of *Nordsee* III or among the miners of Klausthal in the *Harzreise*, is simply mechanical and superficial, and ultimately cynical. Heine's ironic defence of Scott (essentially that 'anyone can write a bad book') recognizes the collapse of his style under the pressure of economic necessity. The perception that 'a few red, blue and green words are scattered in vain into the colourless workaday discourse' (B 2, 551) is remarkably close to Kraus's attack on newspaper reporters who have to drag in 'a scrap of poetry' in their relentless pursuit of 'atmosphere': 'One sees green, the other sees yellow – they *all* see colours'.[28]

At another level, however, beyond the corruption of the aesthetic by the changing economy, the idea that Scott writes for money is morally and politically damning. Heine claims that Scott's plan for a biography of the Emperor was conceived simply to solve his own financial difficulties rather than to honour his obligations to his creditors.[29] That Heine *deliberately* pursues this coincidence of themes is, if anything, confirmed when S. S. Prawer comments, 'That Scott planned his biography before his bankruptcy clearly cuts no ice with this stern critic.'[30] According to Heine,

the Life of Napoleon came into being in hungry haste, in bankrupt enthusiasm, a book that was to be well paid for by the needs of a curious public in general, and of the English government in particular. (B 2, 549)

Scott has simply sold his rhetorical colours to reactionary powers. Heine, however, can call upon an alternative tradition in English literature. Swift's *Gulliver's Travels* provides another 'parallel history' through which the possibilities of a 'diplomatic meaning' can be opened up. Swift's satire finds a new application when the Lilliputians in particular are read as emblems of British small-mindedness towards Napoleon (Gulliver). In this parallel, a critical current from an earlier period and the political or moral symbols that are proper to it can be harnessed with unexpected relevance for the present; but that is because the 'land of freedom' Heine had greeted on his arrival in London is itself caught up in the contradictions of modernity.

England is both progressive and reactionary, and progress in trade and industry is no guarantee of liberalism in politics or law. Even its political institutions 'persist in a medieval condition, or rather in the condition of a fashionable Middle Ages' (B 2, 597). The English word 'fashionable' appears here in Heine's German, linking the traditionalism of the English constitutional monarchy and the absence of any social revolution in British history (ibid.) to the fashionable but superficial style of the luxury commodities he admires in the shops. Heine's critical reading of the city here attains an insight that will return in his account of the fashion for renaissance pastiche in the Paris of the 1840s. Recognizing the relevance of *Gulliver* and of the polite parallel talking of the House of Lords goes beyond the nod-and-a-wink of the mnemonics encouraged in *Ideas: The Book of Le Grand*. The London experience takes to new heights Heine's recognition that traditional meanings have been lost to modernity. Now even supposedly medieval practices are merely 'fashionable', and writing is threatened by economic necessity. In realizing this, Heine's last *Reisebild* faces up to the situation of writing in this new condition of *liberal* economic and political constraint by displaying the very methods that the English liberal economy has devised for itself. Like London, England as read by Heine becomes itself the instance of 'naked earnestness', undisguised, as it were unlayered, its own parallel.

PART II

*The real Heine*

# CHAPTER 6

# How to become a symbolist: Heine and the anthologies of Stefan George and Rudolf Borchardt

> reading backward . . . is always the way reading takes place: through our cultural formation.[1]

Heine's writing in *Buch der Lieder* and in the pictures of travel exploits the derivative and literary character of apparently biographical reference, and challenges his readers to attend to a deferred sense in an age when more naive communities of understanding have begun to disappear. By the end of the nineteenth century, however, he had achieved a broad popularity. Together with the iconoclasm of his poetics, this presented a major problem for the emerging modernist aesthetic. The form of his reception by twentieth-century authors in the symbolist tradition also makes it possible to identify those elements of his work which anticipate their own account of modernity. In influential anthologies, Stefan George and Rudolf Borchardt document the awkwardness with which Heine was read. Their critical and editorial handling of his poetry suggests ways in which his writing pointed towards aspects of symbolist poetics and also provides a context in which to examine *Atta Troll* as a poem that deals with the shift to modern sensibilities, as 'the last free woodland song of Romanticism', obsessed with modern styles.

## STEFAN GEORGE'S HEINE

Stefan George and Karl Wolfskehl first published their ground-breaking anthology *Das Jahrhundert Goethes* (*Goethe's Century*) in 1902. George's remarks in the preface to the first edition were widely influential, and clearly had a significant impact on Karl Kraus. While identifying Goethe as the dominant figure in nineteenth-century literature, George adds:

Yet we must in no way associate him (who can tolerate only Jean Paul as an opposite [als Gegensatz verträgt]) with another – least of all, as is unfortunately still done, with Schiller or Heine: the one the finest aesthetician, the other the first journalist, but both of them in this constellation of twelve more likely among the least than among the greatest.[2]

The dismissal of Schiller and Heine from any central place in the apostolic constellation of poets represented in the anthology is instructive. George claims that only Jean Paul can bear comparison with Goethe, presumably because Jean Paul is sufficiently unlike Goethe and sufficiently eccentric in his own right. In this company neither of the other canonical authors often mentioned in the same breath as Goethe is properly poetic at all. Schiller, however valuably, remains a theorist. In the description of Heine as a 'Tagesschreiber' the ephemeral political context of the work is stressed; by rendering in German the French word 'journalist' to produce this term, George also registers Heine's reputation as a hack. George's main point, it seems, is that Heine's position close to Goethe himself in the popular pantheon of German verse is undeserved. It comes as something of a surprise that Heine's journalistic powers are acknowledged in George's note at all. He speaks from his own devotion to aestheticism, and, as we have seen, his view is both transmitted and radicalized in the work of Karl Kraus.

However, George's selection from Heine's work is striking in other ways. Poems by Heine form a single sequence in *Das Jahrhundert Goethes*:

---

HEINE IN *DAS JAHRHUNDERT GOETHES*

*Buch der Lieder*

'Mir träumte einst von wildem Liebesglühn' ('Traumbilder I') ['I used to dream of passion, wild and free']

'An August Wilhelm Schlegel' (Nachlese zu den *Jungen Leiden*) ['To August Wilhelm Schlegel' (Supplement to *Youthful Sorrows*)]

'Es fällt ein Stern herunter' (*Lyrisches Intermezzo* LIX) ['A star is falling slowly']

'Am Kreuzweg wird begraben' (*Lyrisches Intermezzo* LXII) ['He's buried at the crossroad']

'Du bist wie eine Blume' (*Heimkehr* XLVII) ['O You are like a flower']

'Wo ich bin mich rings umdunkelt' (*Lyrisches Intermezzo* LXIII) ['Where I am dark shades benight me']

'Dämmernd liegt der Sommerabend' (*Heimkehr* LXXXV) ['Dusky summer evening lies']

'Nacht liegt auf den fremden Wegen' (*Heimkehr* LXXXVI) ['Night lies on strange roads before me']

'Abenddämmerung' ('Am blassen Meeresstrande' lines 1–12)
(*Die Nordsee* I, 2) ['Twilight' ('On the pale strand of ocean')]

'Aus den Himmelsaugen droben' ('Nachts in der Kajüte')
['Downward from the eyes of heaven' ('At Night in the Cabin')]

---

'Es träumte mir von einer weiten Heide' (both from *Die Nordsee*
I 7) ['I dreamt I saw a vast far-spreading wasteland']

*Neue Gedichte*

'Das gelbe Laub erzittert' ('Der scheidende Sommer': Nachlese 'zu einem
Kitty-Zyklus') ['The yellowing bower shivers' ('The parting summer': sup-
plement to 'Kitty')]
'Frühlingsfeier' ('Das ist des Frühlings traurige Lust') (*Romanzen* 2) ['Rite of
Spring' ('This is the sorrowful joy of spring!')]
'Es glänzt so schön die sinkende Sonne' (Nachlese 'zu einem Kitty-Zyklus')
['The setting sun flames out so brightly' (posthumous 'Kitty' poems)]
'Für die Mouche' lines 65–100 ('Zu Häupten aber meiner Ruhestätt']
('Nachgelesene Gedichte') ['For the Mouche'/('But at the casket's head
I now behold') (Posthumous poems)]

It is worth briefly describing the typographical and editorial effects of
George's anthology before proceeding to analyse the reading of Heine it
implies. Punctuation and capitalization in *Das Jahrhundert Goethes* conform
to George's own idiosyncratic system: capitals appear only at the beginnings
of lines; commas are replaced by his suspended stop. In this form, Heine
does not look like himself. The most radical intervention, however, is the
decision to cut texts. 'Abenddämmerung' breaks off at a point where Heine
has a comma, at the end of line 12; two passages from 'Nachts in der
Kajüte' are given out of context; and the version of 'Für die Mouche' ('For
the Mouche') gives nine stanzas from the middle of the poem, cutting the
opening contrasts between Greek notions of pleasure and the theophany
of Judah (B 6/1, 346) – the cardinal opposition between the materialism
of Greek culture and the Nazarenic spiritualism which Heine associates
with Judaism and Christianity. In this redaction, therefore, a dimension
fundamental to Heine's thought has been excised from his poem.

George's prefatory note indicates that the selection represents the small
range of work which can survive from one of the *smallest* talents 'in this
constellation'. Both the selection of poems and the radical editorial policy
applied to some of them indicate the aesthetic values at work in relation to
Heine's reception by George and Wolfskehl. It is striking that the choice
and sequence of the poems in the anthology more or less preserve the
chronology of Heine's work. George apparently acknowledges Heine's own
architectural ambitions in *Buch der Lieder* by beginning his selection with
Heine's own opening poem: 'I used to dream of passion wild and free' ('Mir
träumte einst von wildem Liebesglühn' ('Traumbilder I'). The flowers listed
in that poem will subsequently find their own correspondences in George's

work – not least in the hands of the angel from the Prelude to George's collection *Der Teppich des Lebens* (*The Tapestry of Life*); in its new context in George's pantheon, the poem itself comes to celebrate poetry as a record of loss: 'Long since they've flown and faded . . .' 'But you remain poor song' ('Verblichen und verweht sind längst die Träume . . .' 'Du bliebst, verwaistes Lied'). That is to say, Heine's act of memory, as an induction to the *Buch der Lieder* as a whole, is given a new task as the transcription of a poetic sense of absence, not unlike the pervasive sense of absence in the poetry of George's symbolist mentor Mallarmé: only the poem is left as an evocation of a dream of love. In this way the possibility of reference to the real world has become doubly remote. This is entirely congenial to George's own poetics of aesthetic autonomy, even if we recognize that he departs from the pure symbolist project himself, in a reversion to Parnassian ideals.[3]

The first of Heine's 'Dream Pictures' is a ghostly poem and in some ways a learned one. Because the poem survives its original generative impulse, it too is orphaned here ('verwaist') in relation to its context in *Buch der Lieder*, and therefore like a revenant; it is also curiously representative of George's and Wolfskehl's procedure in constructing their own sequence from Heine's poems. Because it retains its character as a prelude, even in George's anthology, 'Mir träumte einst . . .' still has a programmatic function. In Heine's own construction of his poetic persona, the title of the opening group of poems, 'Junge Leiden' ('Young Sorrows'), suggests, as we have seen, a poetry derived from a fantasy identification with Goethe's Werther; this self-stylization is followed by images of a more Gothic kind associated with figures such as Bürger, E. T. A. Hoffmann, and even Werner.[4] Isolated from Heine's strategies in his own collection, however, 'Mir träumte einst . . .' becomes a reflexive text:

> Mir träumte einst von wildem Liebesglühn,
> Von hübschen Locken, Myrten und Resede,
> Von süßen Lippen und von bittrer Rede,
> Von düstrer Lieder düstern Melodien.
>
> Verblichen und verweht sind längst die Träume,
> Verweht ist gar mein liebstes Traumgebild!
> Geblieben ist mir nur, was glutenwild
> Ich einst gegossen hab in weiche Reime.
>
> Du bliebst, verwaistes Lied! Verweh jetzt auch,
> Und such das Traumbild, das mir längst entschwunden,
> Und grüß es mir, wenn du es aufgefunden –
> Dem luftgen Schatten send ich luftgen Hauch.

(B 1, 20)

I used to dream of passion wild and free,
Of lovely tresses, myrtle, mignonette
Of lips so sweet and words so bitter yet,
Of doleful song in doleful melody.

Long since they've flown and faded – long the time!
Flown are the dreams, and images of dreams!
All that remains is what in burning streams
I poured so wildly into tender rhyme.

But you remain, poor song! Till night and death,
Go seek the dream I lost so long ago;
Oh, fly away, and finding, greet it so:
To airy shades I send an airy breath.

(D 10)

The implied autobiography of the original collection evaporates in George's selection to become a memory of a certain kind of poetic inspiration which exists, now, only in the fragments of its transcription: 'Du bliebst, verwaistes Lied! . . .' Poetry is defined as the very process of such evanescence: 'Verweh jetzt auch'. (The theme is recalled with the inclusion, as the third poem in the sequence, of 'Es fällt ein Stern herunter', where the vocabulary of evanescence is repeated when leaves and blossoms are blown away – 'Verweht ist Blatt und Blüt'.) In *Das Jahrhundert Goethes*, the experiential dimension of 'Mir träumte einst . . .' is foreshortened. More particularly, George's very procedure of selection 'orphans' ('verwaist') this poem, as it will isolate others later in the sequence.

This procedure of truncation or poetic ellipse is closely related to the general aesthetics of symbolism, from which the earlier work of Stefan George draws some of its most important inspiration, after his early encounter in Paris with Mallarmé and members of his circle. René Wellek has defined the decisive features of the properly *symbolist* symbol in comparative terms, and concludes that the general sense in which a symbol is a 'simple replacement' of the thing symbolized is conjoined in Symbolism itself with a suggestion of transcendent mystery.[5] There is an obvious line of descent for this poetic mystery, which certainly includes Baudelaire's idea of 'Correspondences' and the 'obscurity' of Mallarmé's syntax and diction, but it may even go back to Heine's more immediate friends and contemporaries in France, including his translator Nerval and Théophile Gautier. George's choice of poems from Heine emphasizes those features of his work which could be appropriated to fit George's own preferences. Eventually this reception produced a version of Heine's poetics congenial to the symbolist project. Haskell M. Block has shown how Nerval presents Heine's work in a version that renders his originally active representation of role and utterance as 'a state or mode of being'. Gautier himself confirmed this reading and anticipated the symbolist aesthetics of effect when he remarked that for Heine words did not designate objects, but rather evoked them ('Les mots pour lui ne désignent pas les objets, ils les évoquent').[6]

Wellek derives his understanding of symbolist poetics from the Prague formalist Mukařovsky. In this analysis, symbolism entails a reversal of 'the relation between the "thing" and the "image"'. Christine Brooke-Rose suggests 'the proper term is replaced altogether by the metaphor, without being mentioned at all'; so, in Bernard Weinberg's phrase, 'the symbol appears as a "truncated metaphor"'.[7] This process of truncation, we will see, is a characteristic of George's editorial approach as an anthologist. In stripping the work away from the life it had always been thought to reflect, George reinforces the split between poetic talent and moral character which had been the common currency of attacks on Heine. Without the context of the original cycles and sequences in *Buch der Lieder*, the poems by Heine presented in George's anthology seem impressionistic – as if they casually or opportunistically represent possible moods or emotions, without any real anchoring in the moral critique of a character. Yet in attempting to extract a version of the early Heine, in particular, that can satisfy the aesthetic readings of the fin de siècle, George's preferences curiously correspond to characteristic patterns in Heine's writing itself.

George's choice of 'Traumbilder I' to open his Heine sequence simultaneously recalls Heine's own structure in *Buch der Lieder*, and opens up Heine's text to symbolist reflexivity. It becomes a poem about the poetic recovery of an absent past. Thereafter, however, George's and Wolfskehl's anthology abandons Heine's sequence (even though the first nine of fifteen poems included are all taken from *Buch der Lieder*). 'Mir träumte einst' is followed by a sonnet to August Wilhelm Schlegel, one of two sonnets to Heine's mentor to be found among the *parerga* of *Buch der Lieder*. There were originally three poems to Schlegel, published in 1821 as a 'garland of sonnets'. It seems likely that George rescued this poem from oblivion after consulting Elster's edition of Heine's complete works (*Sämtliche Werke*, 1887–1890, reprinted 1893). The programmatic implications of its inclusion are every bit as clear as in the case of 'Traumbilder 1'. Heine's sequence of sonnets celebrates A. W. Schlegel's work in renewing German writing beyond the limits of what the *Buch der Lieder* sonnet calls the bogus muse ('Aftermuse', B 1, 65; D 45) – a grotesque figure of baroque courtliness caught in a state of eighteenth-century decadence. George might well feel attracted to this representation of cultural renewal, and particularly to the honorific Heine uses to address his teacher in this poem: 'mein hoher Meister' ('my lofty master'). Such a position of mastery nicely corresponds to what has been called George's fastidious 'aristocraticness'.[8] In this way Heine's poem can seem to anticipate in the figure of A. W. Schlegel the role of aesthetic leadership, which George took upon himself both within and beyond his famous circle, and the cultural transformation which he hoped to bring about. In 1821 Heine was describing his uncertainty about his own position:

> Der schlimmste Wurm: des Zweifels Dolchgedanken,
> Das schlimmste Gift: an eigner Kraft verzagen . . . (B 1, 222)

> The direst worm: the dagger thoughts of doubt,
> The direst poison: self-questioning despair. (D 164)

For *Das Jahrhundert Goethes* this can become a reflection of the crisis of modern poetry at the end of the nineteenth century and the beginning of the twentieth. There is perhaps even an anticipation of George's steely diction and versification. New shoots, Heine tells us, need support if they are to blossom in the garden of poetic enchantment:

> O mögst dus [das Reis] ferner noch so sorgsam warten,
> Daß es als Baum einst zieren kann den Garten
> Der schönen Fee, die dich zum Liebling wählte. (B 1, 222)

> Oh tend it still to let it [the sprig] grow and harden,
> Till as a tree full grown it grace the garden
> Of that fair nymph whose favourite you were. (D 164)

This sonnet is representative of a broadly symbolist poetics in one other way. As in 'Mir träumte einst . . .', the poem conjures up a memory of what is lost and perhaps unattainable. The last line – 'The flowers can speak and all the trees are singing' ('Die Blumen sprechen und die Bäume singen') – is identical to one spoken by Almansor to Zuleima, in Heine's play *Almansor*, which registers the changes that have overtaken both the garden in which they meet and his relationship with Zuleima.[9] Like the dematerialization that dominates in the first of the *Buch der Lieder* poems, the author's uncertainty gives way to an evocation of the possibilites of evocation. The memory of the nursery tale ('Von jenem Garten meine Amm erzählte:/ Dort lebt ein heimlich wundersüßes Klingen . . .': 'That garden – so my nursemaid would aver – / Is filled with magic sounds all sweetly ringing') survives only as the resonant possibility of mystery, hovering as the master's aesthetic project.

The sequence of poems that follows concentrates on Heine's evocation of mood. George includes three poems from near the end of *Lyrisches Intermezzo* (LIX, LXII, LXIII), punctuated by 'Du bist wie eine Blume' from *Heimkehr* (B 1, 130) ('O, you are like a flower', D 96). It is particularly appropriate that the first of these is 'Es fällt ein Stern herunter'. Because it equivocates about the status of its own diction and metaphorical force, this poem is ideally suited to give the same sense of suspended reference which seems so like symbolist 'absence'. Yet Heine is not a symbolist and could not be. Isolated from the autobiographical narrative of *Buch der Lieder* and its engagement with the rhetoric of anguished subjectivity, the poem can look like a familiar sketch of a mood.

There are clear formal reasons for the exclusion of *Lyrisches Intermezzo* LX: the rhyme scheme of its eight-line stanzas (alternating rhymes, followed by a couplet) is untypical, and the poem is insistently narrative. It is more striking that George does not include the laconic *Lyrisches Intermezzo* LXI ('Die Mitternacht war kalt und stumm', which initiates the final suicidal sequence in this part of Heine's book); the reasons are different but no less obvious. The failure of pathetic fallacy in this poem's foreshortened conclusion, underlined by Heine's insistent rhyme, simply contradicts the tone of high seriousness to which George's choice of poetry aspires.

> Die Mitternacht war kalt und stumm;
> Ich irrte klagend im Wald herum.
> Ich habe die Bäum aus dem Schlaf gerüttelt;
> Sie haben mitleidig die Köpfe geschüttelt.
>
> (B 1, 101)

> The midnight air was cold and still,
> Plaintive I wandered the wood at will.
> Out of their sleep I shook every tree;
> They waggled their heads in pity for me.
>
> (D 73)

Instead, the world of darkness and despair at the close of the *Intermezzo* is followed in George's anthology by moonlit evenings from the close of *Die Heimkehr*, where 'Dämmernd liegt der Sommerabend' (B 1, 148) ('Dusky summer evening lies', D 109) in particular repeats the breathless sense of a mood suspended in time.

These poems are followed by texts from the first *Nordsee* cycle. In 'Abenddämmerung' the sense of a mood glimpsed beyond time is imposed more vigorously. George prints only the first twelve lines of the poem, breaking off half-way through and abandoning the last twelve lines of

Heine's original second sentence and the interior monologue it implies. What is excised by this cut is the indication of social context and social class which Heine's boy who would squat on the steps by the front door provides ('Knabe/ . . . Auf den Treppensteinen der Haustür', B 1, 181), along with hints of a bewildered pubescent sexuality. The editorial process is less extreme in the two passages from 'Nachts in der Kajüte' that follow. However, without their context – a restless night at sea – the two texts lack both the obsessive repetition of Heine's star imagery and the ironic counterpoint which throws the poet's fantasies into relief.

Heine's experiments with unrhymed lines in regular rhythms in these *Nordsee* poems may have appealed to George because of the influence of *vers libre*. Bernhard Böschenstein has suggested that such lines are based on a kind of syntax which strips away the force of verbs and so elliptically foreshortens the sentence.[10] Such a sense of elliptical, dense utterance is enhanced by George's drastic editing, but Heine contributes to it himself by avoiding rhyme and emphasizing feminine endings.

George's choice of Heine's verse continues to prefer poems chosen from the uncollected or extra-cyclical and even posthumous poems. It would be fanciful to suggest that the *Neue Gedichte* poems included are suggestive of a year of the spirit like the one celebrated in George's own 'Jahr der Seele', and yet an interior and amorous seasonality emerges as the underlying theme of the last selection. George and Wolfskehl conclude with part of Heine's last poem, 'Für die Mouche', his nickname for his last great love, Elise Krinitz, who began visiting him in the final year of his life. The passage included begins at line 65 ('Zu Häupten aber meiner Ruhestätt' (B 6/1, 347); 'But at the casket's head . . .' (D 823)) and, over nine stanzas and hence with further omissions, presents the poet's dream conversation with the passion flower. A certain homage to Heine's private person is perhaps offered by the inclusion of at least part of his last poem. The earlier part of 'Für die Mouche', with its systematic contrasts between classical antiquity and the Old Testament, retains the discursive character of Heine's critical poetry. In terms of the aesthetic preferences and prejudices of the turn of the century, the wordless colloquy of the poet and flower readjusts and compensates for everything in Heine's work which might indeed seem too explicit.

> Wir sprachen nicht, jedoch mein Herz vernahm,
> Was du verschwiegen dachtest im Gemüte –
> Das ausgesprochene Wort ist ohne Scham,
> Das Schweigen ist der Liebe keusche Blüte.
>
> (B 6/1, 348)

We did not speak – my heart knew just the same
The thoughts unsaid that you were thinking of:
The word that's spoken is bereft of shame,
But silence is the pure chaste flower of love.

(D 824)

In a total sequence of fifteen poems George thinks nothing of decontextu-
alizing the texts of *Buch der Lieder*, editing down longer poems, or isolating
particular mood pieces in order to make them conform to standards of lyric
writing which seem alien to Heine's own instincts, but which also rescue
in his work a certain melancholia and a feeling of emotional and aesthetic
crisis to which the symbolist fin de siècle is much more sympathetic. The
survival of poems by Heine in *Das Jahrhundert Goethes* suggests also that he
retained some residual significance for George's aesthetic project. Friedrich
Gundolf's apologia for the Master, *George*, includes an account of Heine
in his discussion of George's times and poetic task which confirms Heine's
importance in this context. He is identified as the genius in whose language the historic break between a Goethean age and a time of decay and
decadence ('Zersetzung') was articulated.

[Heine] stimulated the powers of the old, dying world – now feverishly intense,
now slackened – and put them to the service of modernity, of the age itself [des
bloßen Zeitalters]. He put the magic of Goethe's linguistic heights to the test of
today's greed, and thereby turned a divine consecration into mere stimulation.
Thus he became he founder of journalism, of service to the day.[11]

Gundolf's identification of Heine with journalism, like his subsequent claim
to discover French 'salon chatter' among the elements of his style, indicates
the continuing influence of Karl Kraus on Heine reception – right down
to the famous shop-boy who loosened the bodice of the German language:
he made possible a priest's tone of voice for the shop-boy, poetry for the
orator, and unction for the banker ('Er hat dem Ladenschwengel den Ton
des Priesters ermöglicht, dem Redner die Lyrik, dem Bänker die Salbung').
Such Krausian point-scoring apart, it is because in Heine's poems fragments of transcendence survive in language to confront what Gundolf
calls progress, circulation, labour, the very age in itself ('der "Fortschritt",
der Verkehr, die Arbeit, das "Zeitalter" an sich')[12] that his work as a poet
becomes the very site of evanescence and absence. Heine may be the 'fate-
ful simplifier, blender and pusher' ('der verhängnisvolle Erleichterer, Ver-
mischer und Verschieber') of the German language, but he nevertheless
conserves the feverish energies of what was lost in the very moment of

its confrontation with the age, the 'Zeitalter', understood quite literally as the age *of time*. For that very reason he can provide a measure of George's task.

Neither the very brief preface to George's anthology nor Gundolf's apologia can provide the full aesthetic account which the editorial procedures of *Das Jahrhundert Goethes* require. A very similar approach is adopted, however, by one of George's successors in diction and 'aristocraticness'. Rudolf Borchardt's 1926 anthology *Ewiger Vorrat deutscher Poesie* (*Timeless Treasury of German Poetry*) makes Stefan George's importance quite clear. Borchardt explains that the older poet's work resists inclusion in anthologized form both typographically (because of its idiosyncratic punctuation) and in terms of any settled aesthetic judgement of its value. It is all of a piece, argues Borchardt: a consideration which certainly does *not* hold for Heine. According to *Ewiger Vorrat* George's work has fixed the standards by which the German tradition in lyric poetry can now be measured: 'George's standard has a retrospective effect; and so in this book, which does not visibly contain him, he is nevertheless contained as an invisible sum.' The heights attained by George's revival of the German lyric enable Borchardt and his readers to survey and to share 'this path through the ruins of modern German poetry' which the anthologist has had to traverse.[13] As Borchardt points out a little earlier in his 'Afterword', George had uniquely succeeded in breaking through the exhausted diction and forms, 'the stilted language and long since exhausted world of rhythms and strophic forms' which, he claims, had made such an unmitigated disaster of Hebbel's poetic efforts.[14] The failures of nineteenth-century poetry, seen from this vantage point beyond George's revolution, reach deep into the past. For the making of an anthology, this discovery of a fundamental weakness in the nineteenth-century tradition has shattering effects. Of Chamisso's poetry, for instance, nothing at all survives; and Borchardt can retrieve only 'shards from the most popular and most famous oeuvre of the whole century, Heine's'.[15] In Borchardt's view this was to be expected in Heine's case, because almost the whole of his work is marred by merely technical virtuosity and by the pursuit of an ideal that is little more than caricature.

The central terms of Borchardt's critique of Heine are deeply indebted to Kraus. Borchardt believes Heine's work can only be snatched from the general disaster as fragments and ruins because, ultimately, he was incapable of writing anything else. In spite of Heine's acknowledged gifts and his experience in the criticism of style, his work remains 'apish' ('äffisch') – by which Borchardt means it is both imitative and distorted. This is so for two reasons. First, Heine is said to be obsessed with effects and therefore with what is merely phenomenal in a poem. He consequently sets out to calculate how best to reproduce this effect on a supposed reader of his own work. Borchardt's phrase – 'calculierend verwirklichen': to realize by calculation – is reminiscent of the discussion that opens his reflections on the duties of the anthologist. He regards himself as the executor of a will, dealing with the inventory of 'a family fortune grown confused and morose in consequence of immense business affairs'.[16] The suggestion of calculation implies that Heine has collaborated with exactly those impulses which are most inimical to the survival of this heritage. It is precisely the conjunction of forces that Kraus had attacked as the short-cut from the counting house to the blue grotto:[17] rather than dealing in noumenal and transcendental absolutes, such poetry merely reproduces and, as it were, industrializes the effects of true inspiration, which can never be systematized or anticipated.

Borchardt recognizes the historical dilemma faced by a poet at the end of the period of art ('Kunstperiode') – Heine's own term for the aesthetic period that ended with Goethe's death: '. . . of course, all was fulfilled, everything had been said; now it could only be varied, treated individually, given greater density, summarized in epilogues, lamented in farewells'.[18] Heine succeeds in beginning such a task in 'the bitter-sweet, blithely confused opening lines' to which his inspiration leads him. Borchardt regards this gift as the prodigal generosity that fate saw fit to waste on Heine's ingratitude – for in Borchardt's view, he can never carry through the impulse of his brilliant openings.[19] Borchardt believes this is the result of Heine's miserliness with his true inner life in the poems; because he resists true autobiographical self-exposure, the reader ends up with an actor mugging at his audience in order to extort applause. The cost of such success, however, is the authenticity of the aesthetic work itself. Borchardt seems here to recall the theatrical imagery in poems such as *Heimkehr* XLIV ('Nun ist es Zeit' ('It's time I took good sense to heart')) and 'Sie erlischt' ('It Goes Out') from *Romanzero*. Theatre in this context represents the pursuit of the inauthentic, the staging of effects without real causes, which for the true lyric poet must reside in the density of an inner life given up to the world:

This poverty and this ungenerous meanness with his inner life – the only thing a poet has to give, and therefore not only to give but to give away, – condemns the whole immense mass of these verses, so extraordinarily artistic and immediately so striking for such a glittering talent, yet disappointing and embittering for their lack of any unselfconscious and loving nature.[20]

In order to present the truth of Heine's inspiration but also to excise the counterfeiting and calculation to which the poet abandons his work, Borchardt opts for George's editorial procedure – though Heine is not its only victim. Droste-Hülshoff and even Mörike are abridged, as is Hölderlin; and against all the evidence 'Hälfte des Lebens' is printed as a sketch for an ode.[21] In Borchardt's theoretical discussion, however, it is Heine who most signally justifies the principle. The anthologist's decisions approximate to the judgement of history:

In the face of such a decayed being, the Editor made himself into something like the assumed justice of history, and admitted Heine in the way that the chance of transmission, not entirely chance after all, has granted us even the greatest Greek poets: quotations from them that are preserved while the works themselves no longer exist, openings that go no further – and in Heine's work that only *seem* to go any further and form or conclude a poem, forming the gem of inspiration ('Einfall') with false stones and counterfeit gold into the appearance of a jewel.[22]

Borchardt sees his anthology as the instrument of a similar historical transmission and therefore of historical judgement. In fact Borchardt confuses the survival of Greek verse on fragments of papyrus or in mutilated codices with the way in which fragments of Greek philosophy survive because they have been quoted in an evaluative context; but Borchardt's intention is that Heine too will be judged by being cited in *Ewiger Vorrat*. The suggestion that the gem of a genuine, though brief, inspiration is dressed up in a false setting manages to give concrete form to Karl Kraus's perception that Heine was already his own impersonator, and that his work was a mosaic from which every imitator to follow him could remove a stone. Borchardt chooses to present only what seems authentic among these moments of poetic inspiration ('Einfälle').

Six poems from *Buch der Lieder* and *Neue Gedichte* are included. Borchardt's method as an anthologist is roughly chronological, though a certain degree of historical whimsy is evident when Gretchen's prayer from *Faust I* ('Ach neige') is included after a thirteenth-century 'Easter litany' apparently for thematic reasons.[23] Apart from poems by Goethe, only Eichendorff's 'Komm, Trost der Welt' is chronologically displaced in this way to appear after Grimmelshausen's 'Trost der Nacht'. According to a loose form of thematic grouping, Heine's poems appear dispersed among texts by other authors; and Borchardt gives them titles of his own devising.

---

HEINE IN *EWIGER VORRAT DEUTSCHER POESIE*

*Buch der Lieder*

['Melodie'] 'Nacht liegt auf den fremden Wegen' (*Heimkehr* LXXXVI) ['Night lies on strange roads . . .']

['Fragment'] 'Aus alten Märchen winkt es' (*Lyrisches Intermezzo* XLIII) ['From olden tales . . .']

['Lied'] 'Der Tod das ist die kühle Nacht' (*Heimkehr* LXXXVII) ['Ah, death is like the long cool night']

*Neue Gedichte*

['Phantasie'] 'Der junge Franziskaner sitzt' (*Romanzen* 4) ['The young Franciscan sits alone']

['Lied'] 'Es war ein alter König' (*Neuer Frühling* 29) ['There was an aged monarch']

['Fragment'] 'In meiner Erinnrung erblühen' (*Neuer Frühling* 30) ['Long faded memories . . .']

---

The first of the Heine texts included by Borchardt, 'Es war ein alter König' ('There was an aged monarch'), has been a popular anthology piece ever since. Borchardt uses the poem to manage a thematic shift from a series of texts, dominated by Platen and a rather metaphysical *Weltschmerz*, to a nostalgia ('Kennst du das alte Liedchen?') for what is ephemeral and subject to time. The truncation of Heine's poems in *Ewiger Vorrat* is in some cases more radical than in George's anthology: *Neuer Frühling (New Springtime)* XXX , to which Borchardt gives the title 'Fragment', appears in an extremely misleading form. This, the most radical of Borchardt's manipulations, also reveals his underlying poetic preferences:

> In meiner Erinnrung erblühen
> Die Bilder, die längst verwittert –
> Was ist in deiner Stimme,
> Das mich so tief erschüttert?
> Sag nicht, dass du mich liebst —
> (B 4, 312)

Long faded memories waken
I thought so long asleep –
What is it in your voice, dear,
That stirs my heart so deep?
Oh, do not say you love me
(D 324)

This is an extreme abbreviation. 'Aus alten Märchen winkt es' ('From olden tales . . .'), Borchardt's second 'Fragment' of Heine, at least survives with its major outline (the first and penultimate stanzas) intact.[24] The 'Fragment' 'In meiner Erinnrung erblühen' ('Long faded memories . . .') gives the quite false impression that the poem begins after some earlier part of the text which is now lost, and breaks off again after its meagre five lines. In fact the fragmentary character of the poem is entirely the effect of Borchardt's intervention. There is a certain parallel here to George's treatment of 'Traumbilder I'. Whatever is ironic and melancholic in Heine's poem is excised to leave a work evoking an epiphanic moment, instinct with other, lost memories. The reader might well ask who or what is represented in these lost images. Something in a voice has called them forth; and because this voice moves the speaker, there follows an injunction about declarations of love. The faded images are answered in the last stanza of Heine's original poem by 'faded roses' – mementos of old loves, perhaps even portraits or silhouettes of the women in question. In Borchardt's version, the opening is transformed into a sudden and thrilling inspiration which hints at the complexity of an erotic engagement, but leaves it caught up in mystery. The later 'Fragment' dismisses every element of expansion and repetition from Heine's evocation of a 'magical land' in *Lyrisches Intermezzo* XLIII, as well as the collapse of the poetic illusion with which Heine concludes. Borchardt thereby conforms to the poetic expectations of post-symbolist aesthetics by doing away with Heine's own discourse, the Byronic persona and argumentation of his poems, and leaving resonant symbolist symbols, shrouded in mystery.

In Adorno's account of Stefan George, a lecture originally broadcast on the Deutschlandfunk radio station in 1967, the symbolist aesthetic itself falls foul of time. For all his 'rigorous critique of the language material still capable of sustaining poetry after the collapse of the German linguistic tradition' ('rigorose Kritik des nach dem Zerfall der deutschen sprachlichen Tradition lyrisch noch tragfähigen sprachlichen Materials')[25] – a critique, that is, of what Gundolf had called 'the mere age' – George's timeless aspirations, no less than Heine's 'Lorelei', have been overtaken by 'Youth Movement hordes and their dreadful successors' – the Nazis. Survivals are rare, but not unheard of: 'At times, however, language itself really speaks from George, as if for the last time, in a way that others have only feigned'.[26] On equally rare occasions for George and Borchardt the same could be said for Heine too.

# CHAPTER 7

# The real Heine: Atta Troll and allegory

Everything that's baroque, everything sloppy, the unashamedly prosaic
character of these lines – is the very thing that is poetic.

(Alexander Jung)[1]

More than any other single text, *Atta Troll* is peculiarly representative of the
tensions at work in the poetry gathered together as Heine's *Neue Gedichte*.[2]
The prologue of the *Neuer Frühling* sequence, which opens the collection,
presents the poet dallying with amoretti and floral garlands while others
must fight in the great struggle of the times ('in dem großen Kampf der
Zeit', B 4, 298). Heine's constant assertion is that he has been 'a brave soldier
in humanity's war of emancipation', as he claims in *Die Reise von München
nach Genoa*, the first of the Italian *Reisebilder*. His second verse collection
works through this recognition of the political, pulling between the revived
lyricism of *Neuer Frühling*, the urban eroticism of the cycles on 'sundry
women' (*Verschiedene*), and the political engagement of the 'Zeitgedichte',
poems for the times. In different ways, all of these elements are present
in the comprehensive range of *Atta Troll*. On the other hand, the sense of
disruption in Heine's lyricism, which Borchardt identified in terms such as
'fragment' and 'ruins', is closely paralleled by Heine's own account of the
genesis of his great comic poem. His difficulties with its form point to a
serious struggle with changing styles and a fundamental engagement with
political aesthetics.

## AN INCOMPLETE PROJECT?

*Atta Troll. Ein Sommernachtstraum* was a long time in the making. Even
though Heine worked at it with unusual intensity, the 1846 preface has to
admit to a kind of defeat:

I nursed the aim of later publishing the whole in complete form, but this always
remained a good intention; and what happens with all great works of Germans,

such as Cologne's cathedral, Schelling's God, the Prussian constitution etc., also happened with *Atta Troll* – it was never finished. In this unfinished form, passably underpinned and rounded out only in outward appearance, I present it before the public today, in obedience to a pressure which certainly does not come from within. (B 4, 493; D, 419)

Heine's anxiety about the fragmentary nature of his poem when it reached its final form is in stark contrast to his confident assurances to prospective publishers four years earlier, in 1842. Cotta is told that the 'little comic epic . . . only needs a final polish' – though even at this stage the question of form is present. Heine thinks *Atta Troll* could do very well for Cotta's morning paper, the *Morgenblatt*, 'on account of its form – as a matter of fact, it consists of very short pieces, as in the *Cid*' (B 4, 985). This suggests that Heine was thinking of a serialization. His letter to Laube, who did eventually publish the first version of the poem in the *Zeitung für die Elegante Welt*, outlined a whole cultural-political programme of collaboration, as well as offering *Atta Troll* as 'the most significant thing I have written in verse'. The poem was to be an 'Evénement' for the reading public and certainly worth 10 Louis d'or to Laube's proprietor, and is clearly conceived by its author as part and parcel of a specifically political project of some urgency.[3] It is worth noting that at this stage Heine thinks the poem will be 'done and dusted and copied in my own hand [fix und fertig und eigenhändig abgeschrieben]' (HSA XXII, 37) in another week, after two weeks of final polishing. This may well be self-advertisement, but only a month later Heine wrote to Laube complaining of the difficulties he had encountered in completing the poem:

I took refuge in these alterations, as I sadly now cannot do one part of the poem that would be essential to round out the whole thing artistically, and nevertheless wanted to give you a rounded, makeshift whole. The knot that holds the whole plot together is missing – but the public won't notice. They only ever look at details. How right Goethe is when he says: 'if you're doing a piece, be sure it's done in pieces'. (HSA XXII, 43)

There is a sense in which Heine's concern about the artistic coherence of his work resulted from the circumstances of its publication. Laube was full of anxieties about the effects of Heine's frivolity, and the result was textual revision to the point of self-censorship: the 'tameness' of the journal that originally published *Atta Troll* and its editor's political anxieties imposed severe limitations.[4] In fact the failure of Laube's solidarity probably represented the greatest barrier to the satisfactory completion of the poem. Its political problems remained unresolved because they could not be sufficiently articulated. As a result Heine could find no aesthetic solution to the problem of the poem's coherence.

This view of *Atta Troll* depends on Heine's letters to Laube of 19 December 1842 and 11 February 1843.[5] However, alongside the political emasculation of the poem it is also possible to identify a purely literary difficulty. Heine himself addresses this aspect of the enterprise in the final canto of the poem: if *Atta Troll* really is the 'last free Romantic woodland song' ('vielleicht das letzte / Freie Waldlied der Romantik' (B 4, 570)), its relationship to Romanticism is uncertain and anachronistic. When he cites this famous phrase, in his *Geständnisse* in 1854, it is to place himself on the cusp of modernity:

I know it was 'the last free Romantic woodland song' and I am its last poet: with me the old lyrical school of the Germans has closed, while at the same time the new school, modern German poetry, was inaugurated by me. (B 6/1, 447)

From its earliest phase, the version of the poem printed as the so-called 'Laube-Druck' in his journal, the *Elegante Welt*, onwards, *Atta Troll* is marked by this moment of differentiation, between old and new kinds of writing.

This can be understood more clearly by tracing the origins of Heine's farewell greeting to Romanticism. It appears in the poem's dedication to Heine's friend Varnhagen von Ense, in the final canto, but in its earliest form it was not originally conceived for this last section of the poem, but rather as an alternative to part of Canto II – a passage to which Laube, ever sensitive to political censorship, had raised objections. But even that was not the earliest scene of the conflict between the last woodland song of Romanticism and the encroachments of a different time. In composing it, Heine drew on part of a much earlier draft of Canto III, in which this appeal to Romanticism is the precursor of a rejection of political ideology, as represented by the overtly political poets of the day.[6]

> Ach! es ist vielleicht das letzte
> Freie Waldlied der Romantik –
> In des Tages Brand- und Schlachtlärm
> Wird es kümmerlich verhallen!
>
> Andre Zeiten, andre Vögel!
> Andre Vögel, andre Lieder!
> Wie sie schnattern! Jene Gänse,
> Die gemästet mit Tendenzen!
>
> (B 4, 997)

> Ah! Perhaps it is the wildwood's
> Last free song of the Romantic!
> In today's wild din of battle
> It will die away in anguish.
>
> Other times and other birds!
> Other birds, and other songs!
> How they cackle, these fine geese,
> Fattened up with tendencies.
>
> (D 480)

In its earliest form, therefore, the politically 'tendentious' poems of Heine's contemporaries are presented as *texts of modernity*. Heine resists such *Tendenz* as part of his campaign against the ideological appropriation of art. However, the final location and revision of this text – in Canto XXVII – makes an altogether different kind of point. For all the poem's exuberance, Heine thinks his sympathetic friend Varnhagen will sense hesitancy and uncertainty:

> Trotz des Übermutes wirst du
> Hie und dort Verzagnis spüren.
>
> (B 4, 570)

> In despite of its high spirits
> Here and there you'll sense despondence.
>
> (D 480)

Secondly, in the final text of 1846, modernity is not merely the realm of day-to-day political struggle ('des Tages Brand- und Schlachtlärm') which intervenes in the poem's 'Waldeinsamkeit'; when Heine offers Varnhagen sounds 'from / days of dream now long forgotten' ('aus der längst verschollenen Traumzeit'), their consistency is interrupted by the play of 'modern trills and grace notes' ('moderne Triller'). If his letter to Laube of 20 November 1842 is to be believed, this too is an aspect of Heine's project in the poem which goes back to his earliest conceptions.[7] Heine writes:

In this second half, I have attempted to restore credibility to the old Romanticism, which they are trying to club to death at the moment; but not in the mellow tone of the earlier school, but rather in the cheekiest manner of modern humour, which can and must take all elements of the past into itself. (HSA XXII, 38–9)[8]

Across these different and chronologically distinct views of his poem, between 1842 and 1846, Heine seems to be making two kinds of claim. One is that *Atta Troll* was to have had a greater degree of coherence and aesthetic integration than it was possible for him to provide; the other is that some element of disruption – of broken form – was always integral to his conception.

Heine's uncertainty about the form of *Atta Troll* extends to the *captatio* which opens the 1846 preface. In finalizing *Atta Troll* with this 'Vorrede', Heine also lays claim to an underlying political and poetic theorem – namely that his representation of a distorted poetic does not detract from his reverence for the truth of art:

There are mirrors ground in so distorted a way that even an Apollo is necessarily reflected in them as a caricature of himself, and stirs us to laughter. But we are then laughing only at the distorted image, not at the god. (B 4, 495–6; D 421)

(There is perhaps a reminiscence of the 1839 preface to *Buch der Lieder* here; Apollo has been challenged, and blasphemy and hubris are only narrowly avoided.) Once again, Heine can be read as the herald of a symbolist aesthetic, in the sense that Apollo stands for poetry in some transcendental sense for which Heine's contemporaries and their obsession with 'Tendenzen' had no room.[9] The god's power exists only in that higher realm which can be indicated or gestured at, but which can no longer attain full expression in modern times. Apollo too is subject to the exile of the gods that Heine's work charted. Yet the citation of Apollo in the fairground mirror is not, in its context, unequivocal: Heine has been talking about 'the ideas that constitute humanity's precious achievement, and which I myself have fought and suffered for so much' (D 421, modified; B 4, 495). This leaves the reader with a crucial uncertainty once again: is the god intended as the emblem of poetry – or does he represent whatever is simply beautiful and admirable, such as the ideals of human freedom which, Heine's detractors believed, he had guyed in the poem?[10] The allegorical structure brought into play is not quite clear. And this is precisely the difficulty which the reader encounters at every turn in *Atta Troll*.

Of course, the poem clearly has a story to tell: the dancing bear Atta Troll makes his break for freedom in the Pyrenean spa-town of Cauterets, and addresses a number of appropriately emancipatory speeches to his offspring; a hunt for the escapee is launched and successfully concluded; and the poem ends with an epilogue describing Atta Troll's final resting place as a bearskin rug in Paris. This tale achieves the continuity of a sequence (of events) – but that in itself does not take the poem very far towards any projected coherence. In his letter to Laube of 7 November 1842, Heine had promised 'contemporary allusions a-plenty' and 'mockery of contemporary ideas', and so the poem's reach as a piece of satire can be extended by allegorical readings. In this respect *Atta Troll* has two obvious points of contemporary reference. One is the ideological potpourri which is satirized in the bear's speeches. The other is emphasized by Heine himself when he speaks of *so-called* political poetry: the muses had been called upon 'to enter the service of the fatherland – say as army canteen girls of freedom or as washerwomen of Christian-Germanic nationhood'.[11] This alternative bridges a certain political divide: it is not only the early political poets of the 1840s such as Herwegh or Hoffmann von Fallersleben whom Heine has in view, but also liberal-nationalist authors like Max Schneckenburger and Nikolaus Becker who distinguished themselves with works like 'Die Wacht am Rhein' during the 'Rhine crisis' of 1840.[12] Hence the terms set out in the preface make no distinction between *Vormärz* radicals on the left and liberal patriots. In fact the 'washerwomen of Christian-Germanic nationhood' ('Wäscherinnen der christlich-germanischen Nationalität'(B 4, 494)) are reminiscent of Heine's other portmanteau description of the state of play in German culture after the defeat of Napoleon in *Die Romantische Schule*:

When German patriotism and German nationhood finally achieved total victory, what also triumphed definitively was the popular Germanic-Christian Romantic school – 'neo-German-religious-patriotic art'. (B 3, 380)

The range of Heine's targets – from the poets of political *Tendenz* to the post-Napoleonic Romantic backlash (of which Tieck is Heine's favourite representative) – seems dangerously broad. Indeed, one influential modern critic has written that 'the political premises of *Atta Troll* border on nonsense';[13] and more recently that, read by the standards of the 'animal fable', 'the ideological message gets completely tangled up in contradictions that cannot be resolved dialectically'.[14] In sum, then, this case for ideological confusion asserts that even in a context of literary satire, it is hard to see how the critique of Freiligrath's poem 'Der Mohrenfürst' ('The Moorish Prince'), whose doubtful similes are pilloried throughout *Atta Troll*, and, on a different level, of Herwegh can be successfully married to the attack on the Romantics suggested by the washerwomen of the preface.

In his letter to Laube of 20 October 1842, Heine claims to write in some sense in defence of 'the old Romanticism that they are trying to club to death.' On this view, his work reinstates the old Romantic manner, not as mere repetition but as a modernization or 'bringing up to date'. By the time he comes to write the preface, however, in 1846, Heine himself has taken a rod to the Romantic past:

I wrote [*Atta Troll*] for my own pleasure and enjoyment, in the capricious dreamlike manner of the Romantic school in which I had passed the pleasantest years of my youth, finally giving the schoolmaster a thrashing. (B 4, 495; D, 421)

Years later, when the poet reflects autobiographically on the shape of his own career in his *Geständnisse*, it is to claim his mock epic as a last celebration of the Romantic impulse – a 'swansong of the waning age', as he wrote to Varnhagen in 1846 (HSA XXII, 281).

This apparent resolution is rendered more awkward by the range of distinct literary-political positions which *Atta Troll* might be said to represent allegorically at various points. The uneasy hesitation between contemporary allusions and 'the thousand-year reign of Romanticism' ('das tausendjährige Reich der Romantik' (HSA XXII, 181)) remains. Recent commentators have preferred to emphasize the reference to the political poetry associated with various brands of liberal politics before 1848. Indeed, the sheer brilliance of Heine's fable offers both a corrective to the earnest rhetoric of *Tendenz* and a model for a different style of political engagement.[15] The object of the satire may then be extended from the purely literary context to the partisan divisions of German emancipatory thought, some of which are reflected in the confusions of the bear's demagogic oratory. On the one hand, writes Manfred Windfuhr, *Atta Troll* is

in favour of unity and equality, particularly of the latter in fact, on the other he favours gymnastics à la Turnvater Jahn and Maßmann, unwavering loyalty and strict belief in God . . . This mixture is intended to represent the supposedly progressive ideologies in Germany. The confusion is a precise image of the world of political thought at the time to the east of the Rhine.[16]

Windfuhr's proposal is comprehensive. Any incoherence can plausibly represent the confusions of real political debate. But *Atta Troll* becomes a peculiarly blunt instrument of such a critique: the poem's satirical reach becomes overextended because it allegorizes too much! Heine seems to have seen this possibility when he responds, in a letter of February 1843, to his mother's queries about the new poem:

You ask me about *Atta Troll*; he might have picked up a bit of colour from an emancipation Jew, but between you and me I only had in mind the satire of human liberalism ideas in general. You see, I am answering your question. (HSA XXII, 51)

Heine, we know from *Deutschland. Ein Wintermärchen* (Canto XX), did not always answer his mother's awkward questions so readily; and this cosy anodyne is almost a direct inversion of his claim in the preface to have defended 'those ideas that are a precious achievement of humanity'. Ultimately, the suggestion that *Atta Troll* is allegorically all of a piece seems to distract from the consciously fragmentary quality of the poem, which

Heine made little effort to conceal – not least because he felt confident that his public would not notice the inadequacy.

Against this sense of a large allegorical pattern which will never quite settle into complete focus because its targets are too many and too varied, it is possible to set the strategy of the poem as a serial production and as an exercise in parody. Heine stresses the intermittent and fractured result of his method, in recommending *Atta Troll* to Cotta for the *Morgenblatt* (B 4, 985). Admitting to his poem's inconsistency and its reliance on a kind of 'collage' effect, in his letter to Laube he is subsequently optimistic about the likely reception of the piece in the spirit of Goethe's advice from the 'Prelude' of *Faust*.

The fragmentary nature of the poem also reflects what is known of Heine's habits of composition. He says of himself: 'People talk about inspiration and the like – I work like a goldsmith making a chain – one little link after another – each joined to the next.'[17] Ernst Weidl's description of the process of writing which can be discerned in the MS evidence confirms this serial and additive procedure: 'Tiny interchangeable linguistic elements are experimentally put together in constantly different combinations, varied and thus polished up.'[18] Indeed the art of aesthetic arrangement displayed by the construction of *Buch der Lieder* parallels Heine's description of the *Harzreise* as 'Lappenwerk' or patchwork, in letters to Moser and Merckel.[19] Weidl summarizes this process of montage: 'Heine's skilled artifice depends on the combination of the most subtle obsession with detail and a sophisticated calculation of the organization of all the parts within the context of the whole.'[20]

## PARODY

If, in Heine's own eyes, unifying organization seems to be wanting in *Atta Troll*, the poem undoubtedly provides a case of his obsession with detail. This is so because of the strategy of parody which dominates in the poem. In this respect, the leading allusion to Freiligrath's 'Der Mohrenfürst' ('The Moorish Prince'), which is parodied throughout the poem, is a significant measure of its general character. The motto to *Atta Troll* pinpoints the central reference:

> Aus dem schimmernden, weißen Zelte hervor
> Tritt der scharlachgerüstete fürstliche Mohr;
> So tritt aus schimmernder Wolken Tor
> Der Mond, der verfinsterte, dunkle hervor.
>
> (B 4, 492)

From the white-gleaming tent steps, straight and sure,
All armed for battle, the princely Moor:
So too from the cloudbanks' dark contour
Comes the moon, eclipsed and now obscure.

(D 419)

The precise terms of this passage recur in the poem on only a few occasions. In Canto I (69–72) the 'Moorish Prince' appears as a figure of exile. The bear is like him because he too remembers happier days of freedom in his youth. Heine comes closest to the passage cited in the motto when he rewrites it at the beginning of Canto IX:

> Wie die scharlachrote Zunge,
> Die ein schwarzer Freiligräthscher
> Mohrenfürst verhöhnend grimmig
> Aus dem düstern Maul hervorstreckt:
>
> Also tritt der Mond aus dunkelm
> Wolkenhimmel . . .
>
> (B 4, 516)

> Like a tongue of burning scarlet
> That a black-skinned Freiligrathian
> Moorish prince with jeering fury
> Might stick out from lips of shadow –
>
> So the reddish moon emerges
> From the darkling cloudbanks.
>
> (D 437)

Here Heine reverses the function of the metaphor that had amused him in the source text. It is no longer the dark moon which serves to image the emergence of the moorish Prince from his tent; instead his tongue stuck out 'with jeering fury' provides a metaphor for the moon. Obviously this is not making any kind of point about the political poetry of *Tendenz*. Instead it draws attention to the inadequacy of Freiligrath's technique *as a poet*. This incoherence is underlined at the very end of Canto XXVI (effectively the end of the poem before the epilogue to Varnhagen):

> Hab mir schon ein rundes Bäuchlein
> Angemästet. Aus dem Hemde
> Schaut's hervor, wie'n schwarzer Mond,
> Der aus weißen Wolken tritt.
>
> (B 4, 568)

> 'See, I've fattened up this rounded
> Little belly. It's protruding

> From the shirt like a black moon
> Peering out of whitish cloudbanks.'
>
> (D 479)

Freiligrath himself does not venture as far as a 'black moon', of course; Heine extrapolates it from the confused simile of his source. Freiligrath's work is not simply judged for its sentimentality and forced exoticism – though these judgements *are* made, especially in Canto XXVI. Fundamentally, however, it is the strains in metaphorical language itself which are stressed. This is perhaps the point of *Atta Troll*'s ironic query in Canto V:

> Singen nicht die Nachtigallen?
> Ist der Freiligrath kein Dichter?
>
> (B 4, 508)

> 'Do not nightingales make singers?
> Isn't Freiligrath a poet?'
>
> (D 431)

In Canto XI of *Deutschland. Ein Wintermärchen*, Heine draws attention to another aspect of Freiligrath's craft as a poet when he writes that, had Hermann not won the battle of the Teutoburger Wald against Varus's legions

> Der Freiligrath dichtete ohne Reim,
> Wie weiland Flaccus Horatius.
>
> (B 4, 601)

> And Freiligrath would write unrhymed verse
> As once did the great Horatius.
>
> (D 502)

But as things have turned out:

> In Reimen dichtet Freiligrath,
> Ist kein Horaz geworden.
>
> (B 4, 602)

> Freiligrath writes in rhyming verse –
> He hasn't become a Horace.
>
> (D 503)

The original poem, 'Der Mohrenfürst', provides a fine example of this aspect of Freilgrath's art when rhyme seems the best reason for believing that in Africa, on the banks of the Niger, the Prince could have hunted the lion and tiger! The Moor's claim in Canto XXVI that he is finally surrounded by the flora and fauna of his homeland, including the lion and tiger, suggests that Heine had noticed this slip. Through his parody, the local detail of the source text becomes the brief focus for the allusions he had promised.

Each of these details sets in play a host of resonances, but none of them provides a settled point of reference in terms of which the poem can be unequivocally decoded. Canto VIII finds Atta Troll in the bosom of his family. He is well into his stride denouncing the corruptions of humanity, and he turns to a denunciation of progressive philosophers of religion – the 'atheists' Feuerbach and Bauer. Against this the bear sets his own understanding of the divine:

> Selbst das kleinste Silberläuschen,
> Das im Bart des greisen Pilgers
> Teilnimmt an der Erdenwallfahrt,
> Singt des Ewgen Lobgesang!
>
> Droben in dem Sternenzelte,
> Auf dem goldnen Herrscherstuhle,
> Weltregierend, majestätisch,
> Sitzt ein kolossaler Eisbär.
>
> (B 4, 515)

> 'Even the smallest lice that nestle
> In the beard of hoary pilgrims
> And thus share their holy journey–
> They too sing eternal praises!
>
> 'In the starry tent above us,
> On the golden throne of lordship,
> Ruling all the world, majestic,
> Sits a polar bear, a titan.'
>
> (D 436)

The appearance here of the 'starry tent' directs the reader to Schiller's 'Ode to Joy' – 'Brüder – überm Sternenzelt / Muß ein lieber Vater wohnen' ('beyond the starry tent / there must dwell a loving father').[21] Once this allusion is recognized, the anomalous 'silvery louse' in the pilgrim's beard offers itself for scrutiny. Schiller was not the only poet to have hymned the cosmic harmony; and Klopstock's 'Frühlingswürmchen,/ Das grünlichgolden neben mir spielt' ('Springtime grub, / playing near me, green and gold') in 'Die Frühlingsfeyer'('Spring Festival')[22] provides a possible point of reference – not a source, necessarily, but a context for the diction which is being guyed by Atta Troll's rhapsody. (Indeed, it has been claimed that, earlier in the same passage, Heine has the saccharine nature-piety of the later Romantics in his sights too.)²³ Heine's major polemical point – about anthropomorphism in theological accounts of the universe – has nothing in particular to say about Schiller's poem, or Klopstock's, or for that matter Brentano's childlike hymn 'Kein Tierlein ist auf Erden' ('No tiny creature on the earth'). The allusions remind us of the part played by a certain range of vocabulary in theological and homiletic writing, but it is the montage of parodies that gives rise to the absurdity. The artifice of Heine's strategy of local parody and the complexity of his combinatory procedures make *Atta Troll* an enigmatic poem, often in need of scholarly elucidation. And yet such scholarship leaves the central problem of the avoidance of full allegory in the poem unresolved.

The theological strand of the text re-emerges in Canto XXIII, shortly before Atta Troll's capture and death. He describes to his children a dream he has had of heaven:

> Selig blinzelnd in die Höhe,
> Sah ich in des Baumes Wipfel
> Etwa sieben kleine Bärchen,
> Die dort auf und nieder rutschten.
>
> Zarte zierliche Geschöpfe,
> Deren Pelz von rosenroter
> Farbe war und an den Schultern
> Seidig flockte wie zwei Flüglein.
>
> Ja, wie seidne Flüglein hatten
> Diese rosenroten Bärchen,
> Und mit überirdisch feinen
> Flötenstimmen sangen sie.
>
> (B 4, 561)

> 'Blissfully I blinked my eyes up
> To the treetop where I saw them –
> Seven little playful bearlets
> Sliding up and down the branches,
>
> 'Gentle, graceful little creatures
> With a pelt of rosy-reddish
> Color, and, upon their shoulders,
> Silken tufts like two new winglets.
>
> 'Yes, those rosy-reddish bearlets
> Did have things like silken winglets,
> And they sang with thin, unearthly
> Voices like the sound of flutes!'
>
> (D 473)

There seems little doubt that Heine has here combined the familiar image of Jacob's Ladder from Genesis 27, the traditional association of the seven Pleiades with the Great Bear, and a much more obscure allusion to Hoffmann's tale *Der goldne Topf (The Golden Pot)*. When its hero Anselmus first glimpses the magic snake Serpentina with whom he falls in love, we read:

But at that moment a trio of crystal bells seemed to peal out above his head; he looked up and saw three little snakes, gleaming in green and gold, coiled round the branches and stretching their heads towards the evening sun.[24]

In *Die Romantische Schule*, Book II, (B 3, 440) Hoffmann's coarse and unromantic effects are used as a foil for the delicacy of Novalis; and a little later he is compared unfavourably with Arnim as an author of ghost stories. But neither this critical context in Heine's work nor Heine's reliance on Hoffmann's *Doppelgänger* motif in *Buch der Lieder* explains the purpose of this casual parody.

The details are precise: the direction of the gaze, the insistence on arithmetic exactness, the sense of colour, the musicality of the effect, and even the doubtful diminutives are all present. Perhaps Atta Troll himself is supposed to have read Hoffmann and to be like those who had read him in his own time – in Heine's description, 'people whose nerves were too strong or too weak to be affected by gentle harmonies' (B 3, 440). The reader's successful recognition of a source text in the allusion of parody is no real help in any attempt to interpret the poem by decoding it. In this way, parody and its sense of the localized detail (of style, theme, or imagery) resists the larger claims of allegorical reading. What we may be tempted to think of as a web of allusions is more like a series of highly localized distractions. The local is the focal, as the site of a parodic emptying of meaning from the cited texts. It is, of course, the sentimentality of Freiligrath's poem that irritates Heine, but his own writing draws attention in detail to the failures of lyrical language and of the whole discourse that goes with it; *Atta Troll* can only digress through an accumulation of gratuitous exempla.

### DIGRESSION

The fundamental structure in which Heine's parody-allusions present themselves is that of interruption and a recurrent breaking-off. The casualness of his tone distracts from the regularity of these digressions, in a manner which has suggested comparison with Sterne. At the centre of *Atta Troll* Heine places a sequence of such apparent digressions – including digressions from digressions – from his central narrative of the pursuit of the bear: they form part of the narrator's mountain walk with the zombie Laskaro as they search for Atta Troll. The first is an encounter with village children ending in the words of their round dance – 'Giroflino, Giroflette'; then comes the atmospheric description of the 'Cagots' and their miserable lives as social pariahs of the Pyrenees; and finally Canto XVI relates the narrator's conversation with the Pyrenean snow:

> Schaust du diese Bergesgipfel
> Aus der Fern, so strahlen sie,
> Wie geschmückt mit Gold und Purpur,
> Fürstlich stolz im Sonnenglanze.
>
> Aber in der Nähe schwindet
> Diese Pracht, und wie bei andern
> Irdischen Erhabenheiten
> Täuschten dich die Lichteffekte.
>
> Was dir Gold und Purpur dünkte,
> Ach das ist nur eitel Schnee,
> Eitel Schnee, der blöd und kläglich
> In der Einsamkeit sich langweilt.
>
> (B 4, 532)

> When you see these distant summits
> From a distance, they lie gleaming
> As if decked with gold and purple,
> Proud and splendid in the sunlight.
>
> But when viewed from near, the glory
> Fades away upon the vision:
> Just like other earthly grandeurs,
> You're deceived by light effects.
>
> What you thought was gold and purple
> Is, alas, no more than snow –
> Merely snowbanks, dull and doleful,
> Hanging on in solitude.
>
> (D 450)

The passage is rightly famous because it apparently provides a clue to Heine's general method. Klaus Briegleb emphasizes the importance of such close inspection: 'the writer describes what he experiences if he observes celebrity at close quarters, and on the basis of a comparison of the way things sound in language with the proximity of experience a critique of reality is developed'.[25]

The distant observation of the snow as one feature in the sublime landscape gives way, on closer inspection, to a disenchanted recognition of reality – 'no more than snow'. The conversation that ensues rejects the possibility of pathetic fallacy – because the aspirations attributed to the snow are debunked by the poet's more down-to-earth assessment of the way of the world. The idea entertained by the snow – that a dew-drop might become a pearl – is a traditional conceit; but even here parody of detail is present in an allusion to the first poem in the Parables from Goethe's *West-östlicher Diwan* (*Western-Eastern Divan*).[26] However, it is important to recognize that Goethe's presence is not confined to the career prospects of the snow. He is also present at the very beginning of the Canto. Here Heine draws on the opening of Goethe's elegy 'Euphrosyne':

> Auch von des höchsten Gebirgs beeisten zackigen Gipfeln
> Schwindet Purpur und Glanz scheidender Sonne hinweg.

> Even from the highest mountains' icy jagged peaks
> Purple and glory of the departing sun fades.

The lexical details of Heine's opening stanza – 'Bergesgipfel', 'Purpur', 'Sonnenglanze' – bear a clear resemblance to Goethe's dramatic introit; but the specificity of the reference is fixed by the further development of the narrative in Goethe's ghostly conversation with the shade of the recently deceased actress Christiane Becker, and by the centrality in the elegy of the notions of deception, disappointment, and disenchantment ('Täuschung'/ 'Enttäuschung').[27] Heine, in describing his narrator's walk in the mountains, cannot resist the literary model of Goethe's journey through Switzerland in 1797 and *his* colloquy with an imaginary presence.

These Goethean allusions in Heine's text are important because they undercut any sense we may have of mood or of moral reflection in this Canto. (Even the extent of the Goethean subtext is doubtful: is the hawk or vulture ('Geier') of line 44 related to the 'Geier' at the beginning of ('Harzreise in Winter') with its hope that the poem may hover like a bird of prey ('Dem Geier gleich')? Has Goethe's poetics been similarly shot out of the air? Brummack has identified in Canto XXII a paraphrase of Goethe's 'image of the ethical and religious beggar's coat' in Heine's response to the Swabian school of poets, which gives these moralists also a part in *Atta Troll*'s complex make-up – and Goethe a hand in the bear's Wittelsbach epitaph in Canto XXIV!)[28] It is not only the allusion to a succession of Goethe's poems which has been abrupt; our sense of a subjective mood, safely anchored in the personality of the author, has been disrupted as well.

There is a double uncertainty. At any moment of 'mood' – such as the 'Cagots' Canto or here in Heine's 'Schnee-Kaput' ('Snow Chapter') – the guarantee of emotional authenticity may be unexpectedly withdrawn; its text may unmask itself as borrowed glory; or its unity may be disrupted by the insistent need to pursue the narrative. Yet, as we have seen, the twists and turns of the story, although they seem to invite allegorical decipherment, resist unitary interpretation. Small wonder, then, that the final Canto addressed to Varnhagen von Ense begins by citing a response to Ariosto's *Orlando Furioso*:

> Wo des Himmels, Meister Ludwig,
> Habt Ihr all das tolle Zeug
> Aufgegabelt? . . .
>
> (B 4, 569)

> 'Where in heaven, Ludovico,
> Did you get to fish up all this
> Crazy stuff?'
>
> (D 479)

The regularity of the 'modern trills' which tumble and play through the course of a text which seems to present familiar ground ('. . . some modern trills and grace notes / Flicker through the olden music' (D 480)) means that everything is now patchy, systematically incoherent.

### VIRTUOSITY AND PERSONALITY

One of the most important effects of the 'incidental' literary allusions which pepper the text of *Atta Troll* is a sense of spontaneity and anarchic originality. The meaning of any localized parody remains personal and private. This is the point that Heine seems to be making in the preface when he cheerfully insists that he wrote the poem for his own pleasure and enjoyment (B 4, 495). This 'pointlessness' is trailed as a poetic programme at the beginning of Canto III:

> phantastisch
> Zwecklos ist mein Lied!
> (B 4, 501)

> Full of fancy
> Aimless is my song.
> (D 426);

but an earlier version of the same text identifies its strategy as a move against the allegorization inherent in the poetry of *Tendenz*:

Traum der Sommernacht, phantastisch
Zwecklos ist mein Lied! Ja, zwecklos
Wie das Leben, wie die Liebe!
Wittert nicht darin Tendenzen –

Atta Troll ist kein Vertreter
Von dickhäutig deutscher Volkskraft,
Und er greift nicht allegorisch
Mit der Tatze in die Zeit ein –
                        (B 4, 989–90)[29]

Summer night's dream, full of fancy,
Aimless is my song. Yes, aimless
As is love, as life is aimless!
Don't go hunting ideology –

Atta Troll does not speak for
Thick-skinned German national forces,
Nor yet does he, as an allegory,
Get his paws on current history.

Heine's final version of this programme skips the gesture towards his aesthetic opponents. His poem is now grandly

. . . zwecklos
Wie die Liebe, wie das Leben,
Wie der Schöpfer samt der Schöpfung!
                        (B 4, 501)

. . . aimless
As is love, as life is aimless,
As Creator and creation.
                        (D 426)

This solution reverts to principles that Heine had identified in *Die Romantische Schule* when describing the debate between the Schillerian and Goethean schools of thought: Goethe's supporters, he notes,

. . . remarked with a smile that the Goethean heroes could hardly be represented as moral, but that this promotion of morality that people demanded of Goethe's works was in no way the purpose of art: for as in the order of creation itself there were no purposes.[30]

Heine's appeal in *Atta Troll* Canto III to Goethean heterocosmism – to art as an independent other world (B 3, 393) aligns him with the principles of what he himself called the period of art that coincided with Goethe's lifetime. But while he clearly distances himself in this way, even in the form of satire, from the moral demands of political *Tendenz*, the independence of the work of art (*Atta Troll*) is limited to the originality and spontaneity of its authorship, as quirks of personality, nonce allusions, a kind of private joke. Avoiding alliances with 'thick-skinned' German nationalism as well as the allegorical methods of ideological poetry means treading a very narrow line. The poem's preference for a Goethean art-for-art's-sake does not espouse the foundation of art's autonomy in density of poetic vision and intensity of experience, however. As we have seen, the Cantos of 'mood' (XIII–XVI or even XVII) are undermined by their limited relevance to the narrative and by their repeated disclosure of the literary (and therefore *in*authentic) origins of these supposedly genuine impressions of mood and affect.

This is certainly the effect of Cantos XIII and XVI. In the first of these *Stimmungsbilder*, crossing the dark Lac de Gobe in night and silence promotes melancholy associations with crossing the Styx to the Underworld; but the note of personal engagement comes from the rejection of these possibilities – 'No, I'm not yet dead and done with . . .' (D 446) – and from brief flirtation with the ferryman's nieces. Similarly, the snow dialogue of Canto XVI gives a sense of individuality by rejecting traditional tropes and Goethean models. In each case the withdrawal of expected intensity and a kind of evaporation of moral seriousness becomes in itself the mark of individual temperament. In the intervening Cantos XIV and XV, on the other hand, Heine's strategy is rather different. XIV begins with a 'mood' very like the opening of XVI, though under a more positive sign. The marriage game of the children, and the bear-hunter's cod autobiography that follows, are interrupted by the Giroflino dance of the children, and by the hint of devilry in the narrator's person. Yet here we encounter a kind of suspension of positions and an avoidance of any rhetoric of closure: the echoes that pursue the narrator as he climbs down into the valley image the absence of conclusion which the reader too senses.

In a parallel, but actually different, way the 'Cagots' Canto leaves the reader with little sense of perspective; the end hesitates between the moral critique of social and religious prejudice and a sort of blank objectivity:

> Und ich küßte auch sein Kind,
> Das, am Busen seines Weibes
> Angeklammert, gierig saugte;
> Einer kranken Spinne glich es.
>
> (B 4, 532)

> And I also kissed his infant
> That lay clasped to his wife's bosom
> Sucking avidly for nurture;
> It looked like a sickly spider.
>
> (D 450)

The extent to which, in these instances, the authority of a 'point of view' has been withdrawn is parallel in its force to the concentration, elsewhere in the poem, on the tight focus of relatively unmotivated parody. The astonishing admission in the preface to the French translation of *Atta Troll* that it has no apparent subject – 'un poème qui n'a pas de sujet bien palpable'[31] – leaves only, as Heine goes on to say, 'the arabesques and allusions of which the fable is merely the pretext' ('les arabesques, les allusions dont cette fable n'est que le prétexte'). The fable (with the moral and satirical expectations it arouses) is merely a pretext for this play of reference but it does not provide the resulting work with anything resembling a unitary logic.

It would be possible to read Heine's French phrase 'qui n'a pas de sujet bien palpable' in the stronger sense that *Atta Troll* lacked any authorizing subjectivity. But such a 'death of the author' would be too extreme a reading. Certainly, the I-persona of the poem drifts from the amused sophisticate who is reminded by Mumma's dancing of la Grand' Chaumière in Mont Parnasse to the Hunter who accompanies Laskaro as fellow Argonaut. Nevertheless Heine himself offers aesthetic programmes in Canto III; and he is securely present as 'ich' from the end of Canto II (49–56), where Juliette's Parisian *nostalgie de la boue* marks the distance of an urban sensibility in the face of Romantic sublimity.[32] That altered taste dominates the opening stanzas of Canto I, and particularly the dramatization of a wild landscape in which is found 'das elegante / Cauterets': what the enjambement has not said, in addition to the precise register of the loan-word, is filled out by the careful observation of beautiful women on the balconies of the small town. This urban and urbane presence is only rarely identifiable in the course of the poem.

Heine's wryness in fragments of parody is constantly dissipated by the pursuit of relevance, that is by the effort to locate the fleeting focus of ironic digressions in the stability of an allegorical framework. (Hoffmann's *Der goldene Topf*, for instance, has to stand in for Heine's critique of Romantic excess.) Nevertheless, a sphere of personal accountability apparently emerges exactly after the hesitancy of the central cantos (on the Lac de Gobe, with the Giroflino children, among the Cagots, and in the snow canto). The Hunter speaking in the first person gives his account of the Wild Hunt. This narrative maintains the level of arcane scholarship which underlies the parodies elsewhere in poem. Yet, even in the procession of the Wild Hunt, fixed categories of interpretation cannot hold their ground. While Goethe and Shakespeare stand as great creative personalities, the first group of women following them are part mythical-medieval and part urban Parisian. The grisettes come dressed up like actresses:[33] 'Parodistisch

hinterdrein / Auf Schindmähren, magern Klappern' (B 4, 540) ('Like a
parody behind them, / Mounted on their skinny dobbins' (D 456)). The
effect of these shifting perspectives, even within the individual canto, is to
resist unitary interpretation of the varying levels of meaning at which these
figures operate. (Heine considers such a possibility himself in Canto XI,
where he describes the figure of a Spanish beggar and conjectures that he is
perhaps a symbol of intellectual commerce between France and Spain (B
4, 521).)

It is the achievement of this urban *anti*-sublime to demonstrate that the
world of Romantic nature imagery simply will not function any longer.
After 1840 metaphors of this kind may well be all too susceptible to ideological exploitation, by the party around the Prussian crown prince and
its mystic-organicist view of the state in which *everything* would be nature.
The frame of *Atta Troll* scotches that kind of sentiment, from Juliette's
Parisian laughter in Canto I to her bearskin rug in XXV:

> Juliette hat im Busen
> Kein Gemüt, sie ist Französin . . .
>                    (B 4, 499)
>
> Juliet's French, she has no feelings
> In her bosom . . .
>                    (D 424)

Seen from Paris, the posturing of German national sentiment ('Gemüt')
absurdly fails to face up to the challenges of modern experience. But – and
this seems important – the speaking *I* of *Atta Troll* does not provide any
systematic counter-position. Doctrinal formulation is explicitly rejected
by the aesthetic claims to be fanciful and aimless in Canto III. Instead, a
number of alternative ways of writing converge. *Atta Troll* strings together
the pointes of allusion and parody; yet their extreme local focus puts the
reader at the mercy of individual taste, of individuality. When this individuality offers to open out into 'Gemüt' – mood or feelings – its discourse
turns back into citation or becomes oddly unfocussed, and somehow held
in suspension; and in Canto XX, with its dream of fair women, it does
both.

In the last resort, then, the coherence of *Atta Troll* can only be located in
the person of 'Heine' the poet himself. But 'Heine' is the name for a rather
complex authorial presence. He recedes in the deferral that does not quite
identify the spa visitor in Cauterets (who, according to Canto XXV, has
often stood barefoot on the pelt of Atta Troll) with the poet of *l'art pour
l'art* in Canto III, the Hunter who accompanies Laskaro the zombie, or the

ironic, and therefore 'real' Heine who writes to his friend Varnhagen in the final canto.

What frustrates the reader is the constant display of critical temperament without any corresponding positive commitments. Alexander Jung's review of the first published version of the poem in 1843 called *Atta Troll* 'the ruin of a ruined poet' precisely because, in spite of all its rejection of mood, 'here and there the style of the genre picture and the cheerful sensuality of the old Heine still flashes out' – and Jung is clearly thinking of the treacherously moody middle cantos (B 6/2, 677). Even a more sympathetic reviewer looked forward to 'many more, even less "tendentious" poetic productions'.[34] Heine's prismatic authorship, dispersed between poet, 'I', and Hunter, declines to take up an authorial position.

In this, of course, he could not be less like his hero. Atta Troll is bursting with opinions to which he gives the full authority of his age and worldly experience. As a result, the bear is celebrated in the Wittelsbach Valhalla after his death not for the views he holds but for *the very fact that he holds them*:

> Atta Troll, Tendenzbär; sittlich
> Religiös; als Gatte brünstig;
> Durch Verführtsein von dem Zeitgeist,
> Waldursprünglich Sanskülotte;
>
> Sehr schlecht tanzend, doch Gesinnung
> Tragend in der zottgen Hochbrust;
> Manchmal auch gestunken habend;
> Kein Talent, doch ein Charakter.
>
> (B 4, 563)

> 'Atta Troll: bear with a cause.
> Moral, pious. Ardent husband.
> Led astray by our Zeitgeist,
> Primitive sans-culotte of the forest.
>
> 'Dancing: bad. But strong opinions
> Borne within his shaggy bosom.
> Sometimes also stinking strongly.
> Talent, none; but character, yes!'
>
> (D 475)

It was the reverse of this antithesis that Heine had suffered in much of the criticism he faced. He insists on the point in the preface to *Atta Troll*: 'In those days talent was a very unfortunate gift, for it meant you were suspected of a lack of character' (B 4, 494); the terms of this populist critique are rigid, but Heine is able to open them up to scrutiny by the introduction of his own term – 'Stil'. Style measures talent and reflects character, but the freedom of style and the reality of poetic licence break up, in the first instance if not in the last resort, the biological-materialist determinism of *talent*. Writing itself becomes possible as a form of intervention – and that had been the substance of Heine's very personal argument with Ludwig Börne all along.

# CHAPTER 8

# *Ventriloquism in* Ludwig Börne: eine Denkschrift

Whether at the most intimate 'personal' moments . . . or strolling insignificantly in the street – precisely when remaining 'what he really is' – the author is always masked and middle, always *inter* and *inter*, mediating and vanishing, the reader launched.[1]

## AN EXEMPLARY DISAGREEMENT

What almost scuppered Heine's reputation and compromised the popularity of *Atta Troll* was the memoir he published about a former acquaintance and long-term adversary, Ludwig Börne. This book has retained a kind of notoriety, but it has scarcely been one of Heine's most readily accessible works. *Atta Troll'*s playful satire on the inflexibility of radical and conservative politics seems to conceal the acrid and intimate reality of the *Denkschrift*, a work that takes up some of the central concerns of the satire. After a period of friendship and sympathy, however cautious, between 1827 and 1831, the relationship between Heine and Ludwig Börne, the two leading writers on the left, became increasingly strained.[2] No one seems to have anticipated the virulence with which Heine finally settled his account with Börne in his 1840 biography. As Thomas Mann recognized, however, *Ludwig Börne: eine Denkschrift* was not simply a personal invective. He makes remarkable claims for Heine's achievement.

As a writer and universal psychologist he never surpassed the achievement of this book, nor was he ever more far-sighted – particularly in the interpolated *Briefe aus Helgoland*. His psychology of the Nazarene type anticipates Nietzsche. His profound insight into the opposition of spirit ('Geist') and art (and not merely of morality and art), his question whether the harmonious combination of the two elements, spiritualism and Hellenism, might not be the task of European civilization as a whole, anticipates Ibsen and more than him. And incidentally this book contains the most brilliant German prose before Nietzsche.[3]

Mann makes his preference for *Ludwig Börne* part of a declaration of modernism, marked by the names of Ibsen and Nietzsche. Alongside the psychological schema of Nazarene spiritualism and Hellene materialism, Mann also stresses the sheer quality of Heine's writing. It is all the more surprising, therefore, that this most brilliant work of German prose before Nietzsche has only rarely been available in recent times outside the various collected and selected editions. The critic Hans Mayer included it in a selection of Heine's critical prose writings in 1971, presented as 'contributions to the German ideology' and clearly appealing by its very title to a marxisant readership emerging in the wake of the events of May 1968.[4] More recently, for the bicentenary of the birth of Ludwig Börne, the poet and essayist Hans Magnus Enzensberger published a 'collection of texts and other material, without commentary' under the title *Ein deutsches Zerwürfnis* (*A German Quarrel*), which includes all the available documents, both public and private, of the tense and difficult relationship between Heine and Börne.

Enzensberger's editorial note makes clear that he regards the conflict between the two writers as fundamental to any understanding of modern German literature. He claims it is the most momentous literary controversy in the language; and the purpose of his anthology is not the complete documentation of subsequent discussions ('such a collection of material would not fall under my interests'), but rather the recognition that the debate between Heine and Börne continued well into the twentieth century and Enzensberger's own career – not among critics or historians of literature in the media or the academy, but among writers themselves: 'It has been writers who have sustained the great conflict right into the present' (*DZ* 365–6). The full purport of Enzensberger's gathering of texts remains enigmatic. Lothar Jordan has traced similarities between Enzensberger's oeuvre and Heine's, and draws a particularly striking parallel between Enzensberger's argument with Peter Weiss on 'political solidarity' and the conflict between Heine and Börne.[5] There seem to be two issues for which their feud is clearly exemplary. First, until very recently the status, in Germany, of the writer as an *intellectual* has often been conceived in terms of conflict with the political establishment. Enzensberger's 1988 newspaper essay for *Die Zeit* 'Macht und Geist: ein deutsches Indianerspiel' ('Power and Intellect: a German Game of Cowboys and Indians'), celebrates the triumph of the written text over the venal attacks of political hacks by reference to Heine: 'The opponents of a certain Hamburg Jew now only turn up in the footnotes to his writings, which are on sale in every station bookshop.'[6] A couple of years earlier, as we have noted, Jürgen Habermas had made Heine a paradigmatic figure in his *Merkur* essay 'Heinrich Heine and the Role of the Intellectual in Germany'.[7] Secondly, and within this general context of critical and oppositional literature, Enzensberger proposes the conflict between Heine and Börne as a type of the rift that still divides German writing on the left. Enzensberger does not specify the terms of this conflict, but includes in his anthology part of Martin Walser's essay 'Heines Tränen' ('Heine's Tears') in which the 'Heine-factor' is defined as 'the permeability of the linguistic membrane to personal existence, which he conquered' (*DZ* 360).[8] This personal disclosure through language is nevertheless achieved in a context which Walser's essay defines as ironic:

> This disguise that can be recognized as disguise isn't some fad of Heine's . . . it's his literary achievement, and the method he had to develop because he couldn't trust himself just to assert anything without proving it by all kinds of personal statements and simultaneously limiting his assertion, often enough to the point of revoking it. (*DZ* 359)

The identification of personal statements – or, more precisely, admissions of personal engagement – recalls a famous passage in Book 5 of *Ludwig Börne* in which Heine speaks of 'this constant assertion of my personality' ('dieses beständige Konstatieren meiner Persönlichkeit'); and it is the quality of this self-revelation in the *Denkschrift* that caused its original notoriety and, now, causes its difficulty. The 'Columbus-like discovery' of the presence of the writer, on Walser's reading, does not presuppose any security of identity. Rather, such an author is exposed and at risk. By such means, however, a remorseless self-assessment leads to very precise political judgements.

## SCANDAL, IDEOLOGY, OR AESTHETICS?

On its first publication the *Denkschrift* of Börne did not seem to testify to sound judgement, political or otherwise. Friedrich Engels's response can stand for many others: he regarded Heine as an apostate and his book as 'the most despicable thing ever written in the German language' (*DZ* 303; B 4, 696). Marx, at least, seems to have taken a contrary view, though his review of *Ludwig Börne* has proved to be untraceable – if indeed it was ever written.[9] There can be little doubt that Heine was planning to whip up a controversy with the book, even if the title under which it originally appeared ('Heinrich Heine über Ludwig Börne', placing Heine *above* his opponent) and which aroused the anger of Börne's supporters because of its apparent arrogance, was the artefact of his publisher Campe. Yet Campe himself wrote to Heine on 21 August 1840, immediately after the publication of the *Denkschrift*, in anger and desperation: he accused him of being out of touch with the German situation, and with having – inadvertently, we must assume – wounded the German public in the most tender part of its consciousness.

Everyone sees in Börne not the writer, but a martyr for German freedom, and in this way he has a claim to being canonized in the calendar of saints in spite of you and your drummer-boy, which will draw down the full weight of German fury on your head. . .

Do you understand your error? How do you intend to set things to rights – how could you do it?! There are suicides among human beings who voluntarily turn their backs on life. But on literature? That *is* a novelty . . . (*DZ* 275; HSA 25, 277)

The miscalculations attributed to one of Campe's star authors are as puzzling as Campe's complaints about the new book are belated: in July of that year, while the *Denkschrift* was still in the press, he had written, 'The book should be treated like an explosion'! (*DZ* 111; HSA XXV, 265) By August, just like any other publisher with a difficult author, Campe hoped that this particular disaster could be made good by the rapid composition of a successful novel ('a brilliant new publication, a novel for instance', HSA XXV, 278). But the publisher is in no doubt about the cause of the disaster. Heine, isolated in Paris, had simply failed to gauge Börne's moral authority with the German public. The great man's death, of a lung infection in the Paris influenza epidemic of 1837, may have been banal; but by now he had become a 'martyr of German freedom'. There is every reason to agree with Jeffrey Sammons's assessment that '*Börne* is the strangest book Heine ever wrote, and one of the most complex'.[10]

The relations between the authors and their publisher had been difficult in the preceding years, and Heine's anxiety about Börne's place in Campe's publishing programme leaves its own mark of professional jealousy in the *Memorial*. But the focus of what Campe regards as literary suicide is the failure to measure the tone of moral seriousness that Börne's death required: as Campe wrote to Heine a week earlier, 'He is dead and can't defend himself' (*DZ* 272). The gibe about Börne as a merely jealous 'drummer-boy' ('Tambour-Maître', B 4, 94) is sufficient indication of Heine's frivolity in relation to this national saint presumptive. Although he defends himself over the supposed arrogance of Campe's title (and stresses repeatedly towards the end of the work that it is designed neither as apologia nor as critique), *Ludwig Börne* provides ample evidence of its author's lack of piety towards the dead revolutionary. Even the account of Börne's death is laced with covert allusions to his hypochondria and to his practice of a quack cold-water cure. In this way the narrative of death and Heine's ironies are set in very close proximity to one another (B 4, 100f.), and it is hard to see how he could seriously have expected any other kind of response. Even among Heine's allies, readers who recognized both the book's humour and its depth were still alarmed by the inevitable consequences of attacking a dead national hero. August Lewald wrote on 14 September 1840: 'The coarse common folk don't understand that it would have been ruthless if you had published this book while Börne was alive and would have wounded him' (*DZ* 285–6; HSA XXV, 283). This probably puts too mild a construction on Heine's motives; in many respects the *Memorial* itself suggests that his long silence in the face of Börne's attacks expressed his contempt rather than any concern for the feelings of his adversary. What is important, however, is the puzzlement felt by many of Heine's friends about a work that was anyway bound to be controversial. The parts in Book 1 dealing with Börne's relationship to Jeanette Strauß (née Wohl) and, in Book 4, with his establishment of a *ménage à trois* in the Strauß household in particular were unavoidably scandalous.

When challenged by his friend Laube, who was to have been the dedicatee of the work, Heine's response clearly indicates that his own concerns were quite different. But his strategy remains a puzzle. Laube's earliest memoir of Heine, dated 1846, claims that the manuscript was in his possession for weeks on end in the second half of 1839. He remonstrated with Heine about the ideological risks his book would run, and read out to him the most dangerous passages. And Heine apparently replied, with Wildean bravura, 'But isn't it beautifully expressed?' (*DZ* 102);[11] the same tone survives in Laube's later memoirs:

With a smile he handed me the manuscript and was astonished by my shock. I was against it for a thousand reasons. First, for strategic reasons in the sense of the liberal army in operation. Why uncover and widen this rift among liberal forces?! (*DZ* 103)

Heine's smile as he hands over his work in this account (dated 1868) is a smile of technical mastery, and even Laube's *final* attempt to record the scene, in 1875, retains the same inflection:

In the course of the year, as is well known, he wrote the book nonetheless and triumphantly brought the manuscript with the words: Read and try to stay in charge of your senses. It is extraordinary. I did remain in charge of my senses and called the book empty and merely irritating. (*DZ* 106)

In this version Heine does not even take note of Laube's advice, offered in the earlier memoirs, that the book should include an ideological 'mountain' as a substantial alternative to Börne's political position. But there is other evidence to suggest that, in spite of minor variations, the gist of Laube's story is true. In a letter to him, just after publication, Heine himself recalls the discussion of the 'mountain' which has not saved him from the political manoeuvrings of his opponents, and particularly Karl Gutzkow; he adds:

Joking aside, my *Börne* is a very good book – yesterday evening I read two-thirds of the Gutzkow *Börne* – God knows it had the same effect on my brain as a narcotic draught. I slept soundly all night through. It is boring beyond measure. (*DZ* 288)

'Joking aside': the better book easily disqualifies its rival, Gutzkow's *Life*, and the aesthetic thereby disqualifies the tedious political correctness which the moral tone of Börne's commemoration was thought to demand. Heine is convinced in all these cases of his own achievement, and the frivolity of his (non-)self-defence repeats the style of the book itself. Although there is some evidence that he was shaken by it, Heine does his best *not* to take the criticism of his *Denkschrift* seriously.[12] He adopts instead a strategy of asides and distractions, a focus on the apparently tangential – because at bottom a certain kind of seriousness was the very thing that his facetiousness and wit were designed to combat.

Campe had sensed that the German public had been wounded where it was most sensitive, 'in its innocent opinion'. And this seems to hint that Heine's Börne book cannot be read innocently – that it is a work of (and for) careful reflection and calculation.[13] After the July Revolution, when Heine moved to Paris, he had done his best to keep at arm's length the German republicans living there in exile. His resistance to their conspiratorial goings-on is extremely complex, but as he presents it, it begins with an intolerable experience of men in smoke-filled rooms:

Imagine my shock: when I attended one of the popular gatherings I've just mentioned in Paris, I found all these national saviours with tobacco pipes in their gobs, and the whole room was so full of evil-smelling tobacco smoke that it went straight to my chest, so that it would have been flatly impossible for me to say a single word . . . (B 4, 75)

Heine's allergic response to tobacco smoke is parallel to his famous repugnance at the thought of shaking hands with the 'Volk':

Thus, e.g. you have stoutly to shake hands with all the audience, all these 'brethren and neighbours'. It may be meant metaphorically when Börne claims that, in the event that a king ever shook his hand, he would hold it in the fire to purify it; but it's absolutely not figurative but meant quite literally, that if the people shook my hand I would wash it afterwards. (B 4, 75)

Yet the account of the German refugees gathered around Börne, in Book 3 of the *Denkschrift*, is evidence neither of Heine's bourgeois sensitivities nor of his monarchist pretensions. It is not the calloused hands of the working class he avoids but the *form* of this revolutionary grouping. Indeed, later in Book 5, Heine returns to the image and offers his hand to the dead Börne, but on his own terms: 'It was never tainted by shaking hands with the mob, any more than by the filthy gold of the people's enemies' (B 4, 132). Heine sees that the egalitarianism of Börne's 'brethren and neighbours' is the result of a political abstraction imposed by a kind of ethical terrorism, and leads only to what has been called 'jejune association',[14] hungry for legitimation. This is what Börne craves in his 'multifarious study of newspapers'. Heine paints a colourful picture of the German revolutionaries in exile, desperate for evidence that the current of history is running their way: '"Here, read it for yourself, here in black and white"' (B 4, 64) in the 'apocalyptic messages ['Hiobsposten'] . . . heaped together from the most unreliable papers' (B 4, 98). But another possible source of legitimacy for Börne's political stance might be found in Heine himself and his public status as a writer.

Heine's suspicions of such political organizations are paralleled by his doubts in relation to the very unequal practice of democracy ('Volksherrschaft') in America. He cites the case of American blacks as evidence of the failures of an egalitarianism installed by 'a precipitate and immediately formalized popular emancipation'.[15] Even Gutzkow's *Life of Börne* recognizes the hot-house activism of the Paris émigrés as feverish association ('Associationsfieber') and notes that Heine 'was appalled by this mass fraternization' (*DZ* 260). Some of the same uncertainty survives in his anxiety about the advent of communism;[16] but in the 1830s and in the *Memorial* Heine manoeuvres to maintain his independence as a writer. Although he was drawn into supporting the revolutionary Free Press Union formed among the German émigrés in May 1832, he complained well before this happened that his name was being used as a political lure ('Lockvogel', HSA 21, 31), as the publisher J. F. von Cotta reported:[17]

I hear he is irritated that his name is always put alongside Börne's, to be paraded as an advertisement for all kind of free thinking. Heine is supposed to have said very wittily that, if his name is always going to be packed up with Börne's, he would at least like a lot of cotton laid in between. (*DZ* 41; Werner/Houben I, 260)

The methods Heine adopted to place such a layer of insulation between himself and Börne's activists often look like an avoidance of politics altogether. Shortly before the conclusion of Book 5 of the *Denkschrift*, Heine quotes several pages from Börne, critical of himself and of his essays *Französische Zustände* (*Conditions in France*). This passage from Börne's *Briefe aus Paris* (*Letters from Paris*, dated 25 February 1833, and originally published in 1834) describes Heine caught between the opposing forces of aristocrats and democrats, attempting to hold some impossible middle ground: 'but poor Heine has two backs, he fears the blows of the aristocrats and the blows of the democrats, and to avoid both he must go forwards and backwards at one and the same time' (B 4, 136). The battle lines confronting each other here are drawn from the old guard of Prussian authoritarianism and Metternich's restoration, on the one hand, and the liberal (bourgeois) opposition of whatever hue, on the other. In broad terms, it is the latest phase in the crisis of state and civil society that began with the emergence of a sphere of public opinion ('Öffentlichkeit') around the middle of the eighteenth century and continued in the bureaucratic reforms which followed towards its end. Börne identifies Heine's position as doubly exposed, but also as deeply paradoxical: his avoidance of 'politics', of the ground marked out by the readily recognizable terms of the conflict, makes his political stance seem contradictory – at once progressive and regressive. It is *unaccountable*.

## MORAL AUTHORITY AND POLITICAL AUTHORSHIP

Heine had good reason to see himself as positioned obliquely in relation to this conflict of interests; he makes it clear that in his view Börne would do better to find a tangential position also. While one of the reasons Heine gives for avoiding his antagonist is Börne's 'constant tub-thumping . . . nothing but political grumbling' (B 4, 98), on the occasion when according to Heine Börne invaded his apartment in the middle of the night to hold forth, Heine successfully interrupts the bar-room orator with what appears to be a joke: 'I believe he could have carried on speaking like this without a pause until the next morning, if after a long silence I had not burst out "Are you the beadle?"' (B 4, 100).

The beadle ('Gemeinde-Versorger', literally the community provisioner) was an official in the Jewish community whose job it was to ensure a quorum of adult males for Divine Service in the synagogue; the idiom indicates that the person addressed in this way is a busybody. In its context, however, Heine's remark is doubly effective. While making fun of the idea that he is drumming up support, it also returns Börne squarely to his marginal position, as a Jew, in relation to the stable oppositions of the central political conflict between aristocrat and democrat – just as the treatment of blacks in America gave the racist lie to the claims of democracy; the anecdote further suggests that the political community, which Börne supplies ('Versorger') ideologically, is also marginal.

Heine defines his own absence from the field of positions in which Börne believes all political discourse is located as an indifference ('Gleich-gültigkeit') that he affects, and which for Börne immediately becomes an indifferent*ism* ('Indifferentismus', B 4, 98). The avoidance of a 'position' must itself become a position. But Heine's side-stepping of the issues pro-moted by Börne and his supporters as ethical (i.e. in terms of virtue – 'Tugend') had long been a source of irritation. From the earliest period of Heine's stay in Paris, Börne's letters to Jeanette Wohl complain that Heine will not take himself seriously, that he lacks principle, that the only thing that interests him about the truth is its beauty.[18] The *Denkschrift*, and later *Atta Troll*, face these criticisms of Heine's political ethics in terms of the opposition between 'character' and 'talent'; but the strategy Heine adopts in the Börne book in order to negotiate his oblique position in relation to Börne's sectarianism and 'terroristical expectorations' (B 4, 64) is a sustained discussion of literary *style*.[19]

In some respects the success of Heine's 'obliquity' is all too complete. The shift from issues of moral authority to qualities of authorship is not lost even on very critical contemporary reviewers. Jakob Kaufmann's article in the *Zeitung für die elegante Welt* suggests that it was only gradually possible to take stock of the scandal represented by the appearance of the *Denkschrift*:[20] 'The new literature has met with a misfortune the grave significance of which will only be recognized on account of its painful aftermath' (*DZ* 279). And he is simultaneously aware of and puzzled by Heine's critical emphasis:

Like a small-minded reviewer, Heine may count the spots of rust on the Titanic sword of Börne's style; he may intimate that only a master of metrical forms can also be a master of prose; he may grant Börne only wit that sometimes becomes humour; all of this is perhaps the honest opinion of his narcissistic soul; and in the end, what did it matter to B[örne] whether anyone praised his style or criticized it. He was above the vanity of the literati. (*DZ* 280; cf. B 4, 689)

The project of the *Denkschrift*, as it is read here, merely confirms the pusillanimity of Heine's criticisms and his self-regarding conclusions, yet it apparently has no real bearing on Börne and his status at all. When the reviewer asks later in the article 'Whatever possessed Heine to write this ill-fated book?' his question seems heartfelt and echoes Laube's worry that the liberal camp would be split unnecessarily. Heine's intentions, in terms of style, or structure, or argument in the *Denkschrift* remain profoundly obscure because they escape the categories of ethical indignation and universal aspiration that Börne's model – his Titanic sword – sets out to impose.

## INCIDENTAL WRITING

The presentation of the figure of Börne in the *Denkschrift* is constantly interrupted. The book begins conventionally enough with a childhood memory of seeing the great man in Frankfurt, but the expository tone (which is already ironic when Börne's very gait is described as revealing 'something secure, definite, *characterful*' (B 4, 10, my emphasis)) soon gives way to a different tone. Heine turns from his ostensible theme to make other, apparently casual remarks. A key word for this procedure is 'incidental' ('beiläufig'), as in the broadening of his theme which Heine introduces in the following way: 'Prose nowadays, as I should like to remark in passing ('beiläufig'), has not been created without much effort, consideration, contradiction and difficulty' (B 4, 11). This instance of the incidental occurs in a passage which itself appears to move away from Börne's reputation to a discussion of what might also seem incidental – the relationship of his journalism to the history of style. The anecdotal and associative move shifts the focus of the opening of the *Denkschrift* from Börne's stature as a critic (which the first paragraphs have gently guyed) to the activity of writing as such. In this way, by abandoning the rhetoric appropriate to his own text, as a posthumous celebration or even an extended obituary, Heine can resist and examine the authority which, he recognizes, Börne transferred from theatre criticism to criticism of politics, but without necessarily arrogating the same authority to himself. The Börne book remains neither an apologia nor a critique, but instead contests the authority of a style.

The casual or incidental quality of Heine's writing itself stands in a parodic relation to what Heine calls Börne's 'jumps' and 'jumping from one subject to another' (B 4, 62, 63). In Book 3, Heine ascribes this feature of Börne's conversation (which the *Denkschrift* regularly and wittily impersonates) to 'moody madness' (B 4, 63) – that is, to a real mania – rather than to 'mad moods' that might pass as quickly as they come. What is involuntary for one writer becomes a *calculation* of style for the other; but in this too Heine challenges Börne on the terrain of his own authorship, where individual commitments to political causes cannot self-evidently find an adequate formulation in forms of public expression, and 'speak as we feel' is not the most reliable political slogan.

In the conflict between Heine and Börne big questions about the nature of writing and the status of the writer are crucially at stake. Heine's project in this very radical book is to find an effective way of writing that does not depend on personal commitment and breast-beating pathos. In this sense it is possible to identify here an 'agon of authorship' of the kind defined by Gillian Rose: 'Facetious form not "grand narrative" sustains this double agon of authorship, which seeks to examine authority without arrogating it, to suspend the ethical and not abolish it.'[21]

In the course of *Ludwig Börne: eine Denkschrift* Heine deploys a remarkable range of techniques in order to avoid the seriousness enjoined by association with Börne. But their contest as authors need not be understood too hastily as a strategy of the marginalized. Michael Werner has suggested that the competition between the two writers in the years in which they both lived in Paris was real enough. Their supposed joint leadership of the Young Germany movement in fact put Heine and Börne in competition for journalistic territory. Börne was the originator of a rhetorical style which Heine had adapted for himself. Ironic and subjective, it was designed to engender political insight by contriving unexpected conjunctions of material.[22] Even the technique of casual comment ('Beiläufigkeit') in the *Denkschrift* could be seen as turning such methods against their originator, but in the interests of undermining the political imperatives of the German patriots in Paris and the ideological gridlock they imposed. Hence, even when Heine registers his disagreement, he nevertheless operates tactically to avoid being forced to declare himself either for or against the republicans – as he says, he has neglected 'the former out of conviction and the latter out of prudence'.[23] There were real ideological grounds for the split between Heine and Börne too. Werner suggests that Börne described Heine as furiously rococo ('furieusement rococo')[24] because he saw in Heine's equivocation a parallel to the eighteenth-century materialist and atheist views that could readily be adopted by the *grande bourgeoisie* to bolster their own self-enrichment. Heine saw in Börne a spokesman for the unholy alliance between socialist egalitarianism and Catholic fundamentalism. (That conjunction was represented for Heine by the priest and popular writer La Mennais, who was translated into German by Börne.) Heine offered resistance on both fronts. He sees in this association a consequence of Börne's naturally spiritual and puritanical bent:

In his later period Börne even turned to historic Christianity, he almost sank in Catholicism, he fraternized with the priest Lamennais and once, when he made a public statement about a disciple of Goethe's, a pantheist of the blithe observance, he adopted the most repulsive mendicant tone [Kapuzinerton]. (B 4, 18)[25]

The pantheist of the blithe observance ('von der heitern Observanz') is, of course, Heine himself. In resisting both the religious foundations and egalitarianism of the doctrine embraced by Börne, Heine reconstructs as a *psychological* conflict the argument about materialism and the ambiguity of its usefulness to different class-positions. He sketches the timeless struggle between two kinds of personality – the Nazarene and the Hellene. A psychological predisposition ('Naturell') determines the Nazarene antipathy to Hellenic vitality, sensuality, and the joyous pursuit of pleasure. Börne's opposition to Goethe (and, by implication, to Heine) is the result of this innate drive (B 4, 17–19). In the case of the Hellene personality, however, Heine equivocates: his term refers to 'a tendency of mind and point of view both innate and *acquired*' (B 4, 18, my emphasis). Such a cast of mind is learned behaviour as well as the result of an inherited disposition. Within the Nazarene ethic, Börne's political passion is not in doubt:

His subsequent political exaltation was founded on the stark asceticism, on the thirst for martyrdom that is generally found among republicans, which they call republican virtue and which is so very like the early Christians' addiction to the Passion. (B 4, 18)

Heine's point would be that the supposedly emancipatory ideology, which masquerades as moral *passion* and republican *virtue*, in fact remains contestable. His own strategies of writing and of critique cannot be checked by a moral decisionism that claims to find an absolute grounding in the personality. Heine will argue something very similar about the supposed relationship between 'character' and commitment. 'Talent' – the aesthetic – re-opens questions that seem closed.

CONFLICTS OF INTEREST

Nevertheless what is at stake is not only ideological. There is also a simple material basis for Heine's opposition to Börne, and one that the latter recognized perfectly well. Only weeks after their first meeting in Paris, Börne claimed, in a letter of 13 October 1831, that Heine 'is afraid of my competition' (B 4, 744). For financial reasons, Heine needed a French audience – and gained one through his contacts with the St Simonians, with the literary circles of Paris, and by collaborating with French journals and publishers, including Eugène Renduel, who initiated a French edition of his work.[26] In the context of the *Denkschrift*, however, Heine senses he must face sharp competition from Börne on home ground, in the programme of their German publisher Campe.

In the account of their Frankfurt meeting in 1827, the first after Heine had glimpsed Börne as a child, the talk rapidly turns to publishers:

Our conversation began with Cotta and Campe, and when, after some customary complaints, I admitted the good qualities of the latter, Börne confided that he was pregnant with the publication of his complete writings, and would make a note of Campe for this project. (B 4, 13)

This sounds like a recommendation.[27] The possibility that Heine did recommend his competitor is confirmed by Campe's comment in a letter to Heine on 28 December 1831: 'You introduced Börne. He has returned his verdict on you. Now are you happy?'[28] But the possessive designation of Campe in the *Denkschrift* as 'publisher of the "Reisebilder"' (B 4, 14) suggests Heine's own sensitivity on the matter. Certainly, as the years went by, Heine increasingly suspected that Börne's *Briefe aus Paris* were receiving preferential treatment from Campe.[29]

This straightforward struggle for pride of place in Campe's enterprise is the most direct ground for the growing conflict between the two writers. Heine elaborates their competing claims in a number of ways. In Book 3 he claims to desire popular influence as an orator ('Volksredner'), like Börne, and not as a Petrarchan poet. This admission is offered as a surprise to the reader ('an admission . . . that you weren't expecting' (B 4, 74)): after all, the purpose of the attacks mounted on Heine by Börne and his school had been to reduce him, precisely, to mere poetry:

. . . they denied me any character at all, and only allowed any validity to the poet. Yes, I received my political discharge, so to speak, and was as it were transferred in retirement to Parnassus. (B 4, 129)

When Heine claims to aspire to oratory, however, it is important to recognize that the example he cites – 'like Demosthenes I sometimes declaimed on the solitary sea-shore when the wind and the waves roared and howled' (B 4, 74) – conceals an allusion to the 'Nordsee' cycles from the end of *Buch der Lieder*. As we shall see, the fluency with which Heine cites other texts, his own as well as Börne's, in the course of the *Denkschrift* is an important part of his strategy of indirection, of the oblique.[30] Nevertheless, he is also able to be perfectly direct in his assessment of the conflict. In Book 4,

Börne's allergic responses are simply put down to what looks like professional jealousy: '. . . all his hostility was ultimately nothing other than the little jealousy felt by the little Tambour-Maître towards the great Drum-Major' (B 4, 94). If Börne is a little drummer-boy, Heine is the drum major; and the allusion is to the Napoleonic drum-major of *Das Buch Le Grand*. He is reappropriated by Heine in the 'Zeitgedichte' ('Poems for the Times') of his *Neue Gedichte* as 'Der Tambourmajor' ('The Drum Major') – 'he flourished his baton on parade' (D 395; B 4, 416) – while in its full account the *Denkschrift* shows how Robespierre is recapitulated by Börne. Evidently the political too was a significant part of their contest.

## QUESTIONS OF STYLE

The issue of authorship which underlies the material, personal, and – so the claims to Demosthenian oratory indicate – political contest between Heine and Börne is presented in two ways, as the strategy of the *Denkschrift* opens in Book 1. Rahel Levin-Varnhagen's remarks on Börne's style come as an unexpected distraction from Heine's exposition of his earliest encounters with his antagonist. Karl August Varnhagen is recalled recommending essays by Börne, and Rahel's mysterious smile lends weight to his proposal. What she has to say is less easily understood: 'Rahel also commented on his style, in words that anyone unfamiliar with her language would badly misconstrue; she said: Börne cannot write, any more than I or Jean Paul can' (B 4, 11).[31] The readily misunderstood remark has a double weight. Heine, of course, does want to suggest that Börne could not write, and he will go on to criticize his style in some detail. But beyond this, Rahel's enigmatic judgement of Börne's inability 'to write' allows Heine to launch a discussion of style which is absolutely central to the work as a whole, in its argument and structure.

Börne and Rahel Varnhagen are among those who write 'in a certain intoxication of spirit', Heine explains, but only Rahel appreciates the other kind of style, which gives plastic and objective form to thought and feeling. The reference to this sort of writing, associated above all with Goethe, sets Heine's own sense of Börne's style within a general renewal of contemporary prose promoted and discussed in Rahel Varnhagen's salon.[32] Both her sympathy for Börne's spontaneous way of writing and the context of the salon, as the space in which these judgements were encouraged, also indicate Börne's failure to appreciate the difficulty of direct speech. As we noted earlier, racial difference (in the deflating 'Are you the beadle?')

can undermine the apparent universality of Börne's political discourse. By associating him with Rahel Varnhagen – who lamented 'that I simply cannot drag myself free of the constant and constantly renewed misfortune of my false birth'[33] – Heine emphasizes once again the marginality of their positions – as woman, as Jew, as exile.

The unfamiliarity of Rahel's language, cited by Heine, marks the way in which she resolved the difficulty presented by her structural exclusion from the operation of civil society:[34]

She was able to see the instability arising from the conjunction of freedom and lack of freedom within civil society – contracts and their contradictions – from the extraordinary position of being simultaneously excluded from that civil society yet hostess to the birth of the modern, bureaucratic, 'nation'-state.[35]

Heine recognized in her person and in her work as a writer common aspirations and an uncertain common project. Her 'familiar, enigmatically melancholy smile' (B 4, 53) is the sign of her persistence in a language of intimation and gesture which will defeat subsequent exegesis:

We – we understood each other through a mere glance, we looked at each other and knew what was taking place inside us – this language of the eyes will soon be lost, and the written monuments we leave behind [unsere hinterlassenen Schriftmäler], e.g. Rahel's letters, will be simply indecipherable hieroglyphs for those born later, – this I know . . . (to Varnhagen von Ense, 5 February 1840, B 4, 753)

After her death, Heine celebrates a mode of indirection that guaranteed an alternative but nevertheless shared understanding. This has been identified with the theme of secrecy and self-censorship;[36] but a style of communication modelled on Rahel's leaves the text indecipherable, hovering, and digressive.[37] The very 'genre' of her writing as published posthumously by August Varnhagen, the *letter itself*, becomes the instrument of this other, suspended 'public sphere' or 'Öffentlichkeit'.

It was not only through literature that Rahel seemed to be informed about Börne, and as I recall, she assured me on this occasion that letters existed, which Börne had once addressed to a beloved person, in which his high and passionate mind was expressed even more splendidly than in his published essays. (B 4, 11)

This correspondent was Henriette Herz; and Rahel's remarks, drawing on knowledge that goes beyond the literary, suggest the alternative, semi-public sphere, created by the circulation of private letters beyond their immediate recipients.[38] The role of Jeanette Wohl as the original addressee of Börne's *Briefe aus Paris* (as another 'beloved person') recalls, later in the *Denkschrift*, this parallel public domain, which Börne's polemics have abandoned.

Heine repeatedly confronts the political radicalism of his rival's ethical principles with the scandalous individuality of Börne's private life, particularly his relationship to Madame Wohl.

Madame Wohl exercised a great influence on Börne at that time, perhaps the greatest of all. Mention has already been made of this ambiguous lady in these pages, and one did not know what form of address her relationship to Börne entitled her to: was she his mistress or simply his spouse? For a long time their closest friends were firm and rigid in their assertion that Madame Wohl had been secretly married to him, and that one fine day she would present her compliments as Frau Doctor Börne. Others believed that only Platonic love reigned between them, as it once did between Maestro Francesco and Madonna Laura, and they certainly found great similarities between Petrarch's sonnets and Börne's Paris letters. These, as a matter of fact, were not addressed to some airy figure of the imagination but rather to Madame Wohl. There is no doubt that this contributed to their value, by giving them a particular physiognomy and the element of individuality that no amount of artifice can imitate. (B 4, 95)

This sort of writing made *Ludwig Börne* scandalous even to Heine's supporters – and indeed to Jeanette Wohl herself. Such direct and improper suggestions insist on the individual case. Ultimately they led to Heine's duel with Mme Wohl's husband, Salomon Strauß. The reference to Petrarch returns the scandal to its other foundation, the contest between the poet of *Buch der Lieder* and the popular political 'orator' which had been in play (in reverse) in Book 3 (B 4, 74). Although he repeats the anecdotes with relish, Heine's purpose in retailing the old gossip about Börne and Jeanette Wohl is not simply to challenge the morality of the man who had condemned his own lack of 'character'. Rather, he undermines the moral categories in which such judgements are formulated, substituting instead a set of arguments about effective style, as he does here. Personalizing the argument breaks the rules of a political discourse which claims to be universal, and scandal goes some way to unmasking the hypocrisy of such politics – and perhaps the inadequacy of its cynicism.

After the departure from Paris of two fellow republican émigrés (Garnier and Wolfrum), Börne 'appeared immediately and in person [unmittelbar persönlich] among the Paris revolutionaries', Heine tells us: 'he no longer exercised control through the agents of his will, but in his own name' (B 4, 93). Wolfrum, Heine has just explained, died under an assumed name (literally, under an alien name: 'unter fremdem Namen') so there is a bitter irony in his acknowledgement of Börne's direct and personal form of address. Yet the removal of intermediaries is the key to his behaviour. Heine wants to show that, in the current circumstances, it is just not possible to conduct political argument as a frontal attack. Börne mistakes the political terrain when he forces private faces to appear in public places. Just as he could well do without the mediating 'agents' Wolfrum and Garnier, so too he thought he could happily dispense with the secret agents of 'the other side': he would rather write their reports on his movements himself – "'... for I have to make all these trips anyway. Perhaps I could make a living by acting as my own spy'" (B 4, 95). Heine appears to acknowledge the virtues of directness, at least as a matter of style in Börne's *Briefe aus Paris*, but in the same moment devastatingly uncovers the immediate (unmediated) truth about Börne as nothing less than scandalous: impropriety, jealousy, resentment, self-deception, and hypocrisy. To this denunciation of the republican scandal that goes by the name of Ludwig Börne, the humane description of the death of Wolfrum under his assumed name ('unter fremdem Namen') stands in the starkest possible contrast (B 4, 92–3).

With enormous virtuosity, Heine deploys a whole range of destabilizing effects against such Jacobin directness. The step that makes his brilliant display possible is the realization that the question of style is not incidental. It comes to dominate thematically in the first Book of the *Denkschrift*, and Börne's rhetoric in *Briefe aus Paris* is finally dispatched in Book 3:

... the former police clerk from Frankfurt am Main now plunged into a sansculotterie in thought and expression of a kind never experienced in Germany before. Heavens! What terrifying syntax! What treasonable verbs! What anti-monarchist accusatives! What imperatives! What illegal question marks! What metaphors – the merest shadow of them would entitle you to twenty years' imprisonment. (B 4, 66–67)

Heine's attack cuts both ways. He finds Börne's treasonable verbs and illegal question marks unreflected, innocent of serious political calculation; but they are also ludicrous and badly written. 'Entsetzliche Wortfügungen' (which I translate as 'terrifying syntax') are terrible *as* grammatical or lexical constructions, and not only as assertions of power. Even in this instance Heine indicates in his analysis of Börne's style that there is a deeply personal component in its motivation, which nevertheless cannot be accounted for by the direct form of Börne's rhetoric. Heine measures a change in his opponent's writing. The former 'police clerk' ('Polizeiaktuar') lost his professional position – and so changed his style – when the emancipation of the Jews was withdrawn by the Frankfurt senate after the fall of Napoleon, in 1815. Börne's radical vocabulary replaces a habit of self-censorship in 'the man who always retained in his style something of the narrow-minded and conformist habits of the bourgeoisie in a "free" German city' (B 4, 66). The closure of a *carrière ouverte aux talents*, Heine suggests, drove Börne towards the style of a sansculotte. As in the case of the blacks of America, this suppressed context tacitly reminds the reader that the mere articulation of principles does not in itself constitute a position in the state or in civil society, nor does it guarantee the universal authority which an individual might attempt arrogate to himself.

The most extended discussion of the relationship between style and character appears in the last Book of the *Denkschrift*. Here Heine suggests that 'The principle that an author's character can be identified from his style is not necessarily correct' (B 4, 130). Ever since their earliest encounters in Paris, Börne (and his supporters) constantly complained of Heine's weakness of character and lack of principle: 'he has no beliefs'; 'how can anyone ever believe a man who believes nothing himself?' (*DZ* 16, 48). It seems likely, however, that the meditation on character and style in the *Denkschrift* is prompted by an earlier text written by Börne himself. The idea of a match between character and style is derived from Buffon's adage 'le style, c'est l'homme même' – the style is the man himself;[39] and Börne had already published his reflections on the limits of Buffon's claim in his 'Observations on Language and Style', an essay of 1824.[40] Here good style is essentially represented as a distraction from the political imperatives which can only be properly expressed as content, principle, in short as *character*. Börne's remarks are a sophisticated satire on the notion that fine style can and should occupy authors in times of political repression: when there is no scope for the moral critique of tyranny, mere style can be practised and improved by translation: 'I practised further, and in this way little by little I translated almost the whole of Horace. And now they lie there, the poor odes and satires, and I don't know what to do with them.'[41] The figure of Horace stands in here for the proverbial cowardice of poets. Heine himself calls the Roman poet 'that smooth roué' (B 4, 157) in his *Don Quixote* essay, and the attack on Platen in *Die Bäder von Lucca* associates the supposed moral decadence of its victim with the imitation of Horatian odes (among other genres). This is no more than the common ground of a traditional exegesis of Horace's 'speedy flight' from battle in *Odes* II, 7; however, Börne's 1824 'Observations' already deprecate style as 'a talent that can be developed through industry';[42] and so the opposition of talent and character, which becomes the focus for Heine's sharpest attack, is already a factor in Börne's thought. Everything in the *Denkschrift* is designed to undermine this apparently self-evident moral position.

## CHARACTER

Heine offers the following definition of 'Charakter':

Character is what someone has who lives and acts within the particular circles of a particular life-view, and as it were identifies himself with it, and never finds himself contradicting it either in thought or in feeling. In the case of very distinguished minds that tower above their age, the masses can therefore never know whether they possess character or not . . . Less gifted people, whose more superficial and narrower life-view is more readily plumbed and assessed, and who have proclaimed their life's programme, as it were, in the public arena once and for all and in popular language – the honoured public can always get hold of such people in context. It possesses a criterion for each of their actions, taking pleasure meanwhile in its own intelligence just like finding the answer to a guessing game, and joyfully announces: *that* is a character! (B 4, 130)

There is a personal edge to this account – since Börne claimed he always checked any new publication against his previous writings to insure that no new or contradictory opinion had crept in unnoticed. But, more generally, Heine's careful use of what seem to be two neologisms ('as it were identifies himself with it' ('gleichsam mit derselben identifiziert'), 'their life's programme, as it were' ('gleichsam ihr Lebensprogramm')) registers a shift in public awareness according to which character must be identified with a publicly defined ethical programme. Those with lesser gifts are reduced without remainder to their views, and so they are solved like a riddling word-game of the time ('Charade'). The match between principles and actions or statements engenders a joyous q.e.d.

Heine rejects the opposition of character and talent by introducing a different term. Just as the scandalous disclosures relating to Börne and Jeanette Wohl ultimately challenge Börne on the very margin between life and literature, so too in the discourse of the *Denkschrift* the ethical universal of character is challenged by the 'real' – and singular – Heine, who refuses to be reduced to any identification with ethical programmes.

However, if this constant assertion of my personality is, on the one hand, the most appropriate means to promote an independent judgement on the part of the reader, I also believe, on the other hand, that I have a particular duty to emphasize my own person in this book because, through the confluence of the most heterogeneous circumstances, whenever either Börne's friends or enemies discussed him, they never ceased to expatiate more or less kindly or maliciously on my own writings and doings. (B 4, 128)

What Heine calls the conjunction of the most heterogeneous circumstances was in fact the consistent attempt by Börne's party to exploit Heine's reputation as a writer for one position or another in the argument between the aristocratic restoration and republican democracy. Heine refuses the terms of these possible alignments, and foregrounds instead 'the constant assertion of his personality'. In the sphere of public discussion (and book reviews – 'Besprechungen'!) there had been a *de facto* confusion of two lives and oeuvres;[43] the political commitment of identification and 'solidarity' had been demanded and imposed. Heine hesitates before such coercion and then makes his hesitation itself a form of resistance. In the long run, this withdrawal from the terrain of given political positions and their life-programmes is designed to emancipate his readers, who must arrive at a judgement for themselves ('Selbsturteil').

Börne's position has to assume an immediate continuity between writing and ideology. He takes it for granted that *Französische Maler* (*French Painters*) is evidence of Heine's 'indifferentism towards the sacred cause of humanity' (B 4, 99). But Heine distinguishes two kinds of style: the psychosomatically constrained, subjective expressivity of his adversary, and the free ('objective') manipulation demonstrated by his own work. The link between style and commitment may be

applicable in the great mass of authors whose pen is guided in writing only by momentary inspiration and who obey the word more than they command it. Among artists this principle is inadmissible for they are masters of the word, manipulate it for whatever purpose, imprint it by their own volition, write objectively, and their character is not betrayed in their style. (B 4, 130)

The momentary inspiration that guides the mass of authors recalls the discussion in Book 1 of the sympathy felt by Rahel Varnhagen for Börne's *spontaneity*. As against this, Heine claims for himself a mastery of the word. His phrase – 'Meister des Wortes' – is clarified by an earlier passage, in Book 4, when Heine complains of the difficulty of responding to journalistic writing (whether anonymous or not) which needs his name to lend itself legitimacy. He must then face the dilemma that, whether he argues back or not, his name will have been exploited. Odysseus' treatment of Thersites seems to offer a preferable model:

Indeed it was an instructive example you gave us, Son of Laertes, patient royal sufferer, Odysseus! You, the Master of the Word, who exceed all mortals in the art of oratory. There was no one to whom you would not return answer, and your speech was as willing as it was victorious. A slimy Thersites was the only one on whom you would waste no words, such a man you thought unworthy of reply, and when he reviles you, you thrash him without a word. (B 4, 107)

The context of these remarks has been identified as the series of attacks mounted against Heine in the press by Ludwig Wihl (and Karl Gutzkow), as a result of the *Schwabenspiegel* ('Mirror for Swabians') affair. In 1838 Heine's intention to publish the emancipatory verse of the *Verschiedene* cycles ('Sundry Women') was frustrated by the criticism of the Swabian moralist poets, and by his former ally Gutzkow.[44] However, the Homeric model is equally significant in the *Denkschrift*. Heine had – he hoped – thrashed Börne by maintaining his public silence (and the participle 'schweigend', translated here as 'without a word', could be read in an instrumental sense, to mean 'you thrashed him by being silent'). More broadly he claimed for himself the same mastery of the word attributed to wily Odysseus.

This is the first appearance of a recurrent image, which associates Odysseus' patient endurance in suffering ('Dulder') with his fluent and cunning speech. In *Lutetia*, it is usually King Louis-Philippe who appears in this Homeric comparison: 'Or is such a lust for war merely a warlike ruse of the divine sufferer Odysseus?' (B 5, 307) Later, the king is said to be like Odysseus 'the patient and inventive sufferer' (B 5, 330) and finally, in a variant reading of *Lutetia* I, article XVIII in the *Augsburger Allgemeine Zeitung*, Odysseus is praised for having avoided fighting 'if he could make do with the diplomacy of speech' (B 5, 1005). Odysseus is celebrated for his ruses, for his inventiveness, and for the substitution of diplomatic talk for direct conflict. These qualities – imagination, cunning, and diplomatic language – all provide the strategic means by which Heine's 'mastery of the word' could resist Börne's moral immediacy as a judge of character.

### VENTRILOQUISM

Between the account in Book 1 of Heine's encounter with Börne in Frankfurt and the continuation of their conversations in Paris, culminating in Heine's comic account of Börne's enthusiasm for the 'Hambach Festival', Heine inserted as Book 2 a series of letters he claims to have written while in Heligoland, reflecting his mood before and after news reached him of the July Revolution in Paris. (In fact these 'letters' are of a later date, and are designed to celebrate July 1830 as a renewal of the revolution and Heine's insight into its significance.) The Cuxhafen letter at the end of Book 2 of the *Denkschrift* provides a clue to the cunning of Heine's construction in the Börne book as a whole. The sea passage which will take Heine's narrative from holidaying in Heligoland to revolutionary Paris is a rough crossing: 'Even the sea, like other persons, rewards my love with trouble and torture' (B 4, 56). Like other parts of the Heligoland letters, this allusion is obscure. The other persons who cause hardship and torment may well include Börne, of course, as well as the traditional objects of Heine's unrequited love; but the hostility of the sea seems more immediately to recall the anger of Poseidon and the vicissitudes of Odysseus on his journey home. In the event, the context will itself provide an instance of Odysseus' 'military cunning' – and so of Heine's strategy.

The noise of the storm becomes a cacophony of voices: 'they howl bad, incomprehensible verses . . . and whistle the most uncanny follies in my ear with their stupid falsetto voices' (B 4, 56) – until sea-sickness leads finally to the internalization of one such voice, and Heine imagines he has become a whale with the prophet Jonah in his belly. The Cuxhafen letter then includes a long passage attributed to the prophet and presented as a form of ventriloquism: 'Thus more or less my ventriloquist preached' (B 4, 57). This text derives only minimally from the biblical precedent (in Jonah 3, 4) but there are arguably echoes of texts by Börne,[45] as well as more general similarities both with the earliest of the *Briefe aus Paris* in which Börne describes his journey to Paris, and with the prophetic and denunciatory style which often supervenes in the conversational style of his letters. Later Heine is dismissive of this manner: 'He was as bad a prophet about others as he was about himself' (B 4, 77); and in the Cuxhafen letter too the prophet is ultimately vomited up and spat out – as if the transition from the earlier friendly relations between the two authors and their more troubled time in Paris were marked by a physical regurgitation of what had previously been absorbed.

The double focus permitted by the model of ventriloquism is sustained by the close parallels which Heine projects between his own biography and Börne's career.[46] For instance, it has been shown that the views on love and maturity ascribed to Börne in Book 1 (B 4, 20) are actually derived from the autobiographical fragment by Heine known as 'Love in Youth and in Age' (DHA 11, 194).[47] As Koopmann remarks, in *Ludwig Börne: eine Denkschrift* 'Heine puts these thoughts, as is often the case with his synthetic procedure, into Börne's mouth'. Heine's assimilation of his own point of view to what is ascribed to Börne gives a stronger sense to the need to expel this Jonah from his belly, at the close of the 'Letters from Heligoland', but also plays on the supposed identification of the two as a double-act leading the Young Germany movement – of which we have seen him complain elsewhere.[48]

The source and status of the conversations with Börne reported by Heine have always been controversial, and earlier in Book 1 Heine has been caught putting words into Börne's mouth in a more extended and substantial way.

Börne, Heine recalls, takes the well known anecdote (from Thiers's *Histoire de la révolution française*) of Napoleon smashing a piece of porcelain (in his impatience at the snail's pace maintained by Austrian diplomats).[49] This story becomes an occasion to ruminate on the danger of domestication presented, for radical politicians, by fragile material possessions:

> You have no notion, dearest Heine, how one is kept in check by the possession of beautiful porcelain. You see me for example. Once I was so wild when I had little baggage and no porcelain at all. With possessions, particularly with fragile possessions, come fear and servitude. (B 4, 15)

However, these reflections are in turn derived from an autobiographical passage from the paralipomena to Heine's *Die Bäder von Lucca*.[50] The fact that the text from the Italian *Reisebild* was suppressed means that this ventriloquism was, at best, a private joke rather than a polemical move. Yet the pattern of citation involved reflects Heine's consistent practice of recycling material as well as his constant reworking of individual passages or even phrases, and indicates the recurrent structure of the *Denkschrift*. Indeed, an even more complicated process of textual origination has been suggested, for it may be that the *Denkschrift* here reflects the text of Heine's unpublished memoirs of their earliest meetings in Frankfurt, when Börne did perhaps say something of this sort – which Heine subsequently appropriated for *Die Bäder von Lucca* in 1828/9 (see B 4, 778). Hence, the words attributed to Börne's reading of Thiers's history in fact draw on an unpublished passage from *Die Bäder von Lucca*, which may in turn reflect an original exchange between the two men. How is this 'mingling and inter-involvement of the two positions', which is indeed 'one of the oddities of the work', to be understood?[51]

The Cuxhafen letter presents a model for the uncertainty of such a writing-process via the ventriloquism of Jonah. This model is given its most substantial realization in the pattern of quotation that appears in the last three books of the *Denkschrift*. Book 3 is historically very precise. Heine repeatedly dates his encounters with Börne and his work: 'in the autumn of 1831', 'Börne wrote this on 20 March 1831' (B 4, 61, 77; cf. 80–1, where Heine is quick to specify the original reference of Börne's remarks). Heine's detailed chronology clearly confirms the derivation of the Börne material from some earlier memoir; more importantly it bears out Heine's own claims with regard to his method:

> As I have already said, I am delivering neither an apologia nor a critique of the man with whom these pages are concerned. I am drawing his picture with a precise indication of the place and time he sat for me. (B 4, 128)

The technique described here is painterly, and Heine openly acknowledges the circumstances of the portrait. In the Epistle Dedicatory to *Lutetia* he goes on to describe the documentary process with the more objective image of the 'honest daguerreotype' (B 5, 239). In *Ludwig Börne*, however, the documentary impulse still depends on quotation. In this first, very limited sense Heine can be said to ventriloquize Börne by lending him voice: '"The republic" – I'll let the man finish, while skipping many curlicues and digressions – "the republic must be achieved"' (B 4, 62). At the end of this diatribe, Heine attributes the divagations of Börne's talk to his multifarious reading of newspapers, as we have seen (B 4, 64): so that Börne, in turn, is giving voice to the political discourse of a complex political liberalism. In this way the attribution of fixed positions is undermined by a multiplication of voices, very like the voices of the storm and the prophet Jonah in the Cuxhafen letter.

The ventriloquisms of this strategy, rather than harmonizing an authoritative polyphonic structure, continuously destabilize the faith in authority ('Autoritätsglauben') which had guaranteed the position of writers in an earlier social order: 'The kings depart, and the last poets go with them. "The poet should go with the king" – these words may well now fall prey to a quite different meaning. Without faith in authority no great poet can arise either' (B 4, 141). Instead, shifting substitutions and citations leave ready distinctions suspended. The problem of textual authority, raised by Heine's willingness to exploit quotations and to reroute his own views through the mouths of others, is particularly acute in its occluded form in Book 3: Heine's account of *Börne's* polemical remarks on Friedrich von Raumer reveals extremely close verbal parallels to his *own* discussion of Raumer in the preface to *Französische Zustände*. Where Heine's preface has: 'He is a thoroughly peaceable man who calmly stands in line [ein friedlebiger Mann, der ruhig Queue macht]' (B 3, 96), the Börne of the *Denkschrift* reveals that this characteristic of Raumer's patience is borrowed from the latter's own published letters: '[such tireless mobility alongside such tireless force] clearly emerges in the letters where the poor dog himself explains on every page how he calmly stood in line outside the Paris theatres [vor den Pariser Theatern ruhig Queue machte] . . .' (B 4, 64–5).[52] The *Denkschrift* erodes the authority of its claims to authenticity by putting Raumer's words into Börne's mouth, words that turn out to be Heine's paraphrase in the preface to *Französische Zustände*. In this way Heine's writing withdraws the authority of any personal adversarial position to generate instead these feints and allusions.

In Books 4 and 5 the impersonation of Börne in reconstructions of his conversation is extended by direct quotation: Book 4 cites the passage concerning the editor of the *politisches Wochenblatt,* Karl Ernst Jarcke, directly from Börne's *Briefe aus Paris* (26 November 1832); in its turn, this quotation duly includes a paragraph from Jarcke's article to which Börne is replying. Book 5 opens with Heine's self-quotation 'from my book "de l'Allemagne"' (by which he means *Zur Geschichte der Religion und Philosophie*) and subsequently cites a long passage attacking Heine's *Französische Zustände* which includes allusions to Articles VI and IX from Heine's essays.[53] Börne's text on Jarcke is presented as part of a defence of Börne's patriotism, launched rather earlier: 'Indeed, he was not merely a good writer, but also a great patriot' (B 4, 110); but Heine contextualizes the passage from *Letters from Paris* with the old racial argument against Börne's claims to represent national liberalism. His reflection on Börne's Jewish ancestry in 'the people of the Spirit' (B 4, 119) ends with a scurrilous allusion to Hegel:

Nature, Hegel once said to me, is very strange. The same instruments that she employs for the most sublime purposes, she also uses for the vilest tasks, for example that member to which the highest mission, the reproduction of humanity is entrusted, also serves to – (B 4, 119)

Heine's Hegel story, with its vulgar punch-line, refuses Börne's tone of moral seriousness. It is frivolity of this kind that makes possible the apparently incidental ('beiläufig'), oblique movement of Heine's writing. In this context the joke about the dishonoured member enables him to bring together the fate of 'Israel', the Jews as simultaneously victims of anti-Semitism and 'people of the Spirit', and the prospects for political emancipation in Germany. The two problems, he suggests, have a single solution – the arrival of the earthly Messiah.

This sequence of ideas, exploring parallels between the marginalization of the Jews and the need for democratic institutions in Germany, anticipates Marx's arguments in *Zur Judenfrage* (*On the Jewish Question*) and the key role played by apparently marginal groups in the 'Economic and Philosophical Manuscripts'.[54] Heine's argument comes to rest, however, in the splendid Hassidic narrative of the Messiah, held in golden chains, that brings Book 4 to a close. The purpose of the chains is explained 'with a sly look and a deep sigh' (B 4, 120) by the great Rabbi of Krakow, Manasse ben Naphtali. The Messiah must be restrained because 'the time has not yet come' (B 4, 121) for the liberation of his people from their sufferings. Heine is not only sketching a theory of the revolutionary 'moment' here. His suggestion of necessary restraint in the pursuit of human emancipation confronts Börne's headlong but unrealistic activism with a broader view of history; and through Heine's facetiousness he also mounts an attack on the claims to moral authenticity that sustained Börne's hostility in life, and fired the severity of his disciples after his death. To all this Heine gave the name Nazarene.

VIRTUOSO FRIVOLITY

This ethics is presented in *Ludwig Börne* as an inward-looking resentment, which anticipates Nietzsche's 'psychology of *ressentiment*' in *Zur Genealogie der Moral* (*Genealogy of Morals*):[55] not only the envy Börne demonstrates for Heine confirms this psychology; he is repeatedly seen as peevish, bad-tempered ('verdrießlich', B 4, 9), and hostile – Heine speaks of 'the cutting mistrust that lurked in all his features' (B 4, 61). Heine recognizes all too clearly the profound resignation that draws Börne into the arid community of the German exiles in Paris with its false sense of solidarity, summarized as 'the banal manners of a demagogue of the lowest kind':

> ... he pulled his cap down over his ears and refused to see or hear anything more, and hurled himself into the howling abyss ... That is a recourse that always remains to us when we have once arrived at those hopeless lands where all flowers have withered, and where the body is weary and the soul peevish ... (B 4, 76)

The rigidity of this Nazarene ethic mistakes even a bargaining position for moral high ground: 'From time to time, however, it happens that people lose themselves in their role, and cunning playfulness becomes tediously serious' (B 4, 112). It is this mistake that leads Börne, according to Heine, to the compounded hypocrisies of his relationship with Jeanette Wohl (B 4, 97) alongside the promotion of republican virtue. In particular here, Heine's attack is directed at the overhasty alliance between republicans and the 'Catholic' socialism represented by La Mennais. But the general point also holds, that Börne has settled for an authoritarian, 'pietistic' resolution of political tensions which need to be kept in suspension and 'cunning play' in a 'becalmed period of peace such as the present' (B 4, 91).[56] 'Cunning playfulness' indicates the critical intelligence that will continue to recognize the repeated (dis)guises taken on by conflicting forces, while playing them or outplaying them at their own game.

Heine's brilliantly comic accounts of two patriotic gatherings of students and other activists give ample evidence of these illusions and self-deceptions. The liberal 'Hambacher Fest' (1832) in Book 4 and the nationalist 'Wartburgfest' (1817) in Book 3 were both 'mountain festivals' ('Bergfeier') and so susceptible to the tone in Börne's 'propaganda' (B 4, 72) that goes with sermonizing on the Mount ('Bergpredigerton' (B 4, 73)).[57] The older, jingoistic nationalism of the Wartburg will retain its liberal Hambach guise until the morning after its revolutionary success – but no longer, Heine warns: thereafter all differences will be resolved by the guillotine (B 4, 90). But the *Denkschrift* is in no doubt about the difficulty of resisting the ethical foreshortening occasioned by the Nazarene mentality, only too readily at home, by implication, among present-day nationalists.

Heine's whole technique as an author is designed to resist the enticements of precipitate alliances, and the sectarian splitting that shadowed them, as he tells us, in the German republican movement (B 4, 90). The disguises of his cunning playfulness revel in the style of distraction, deferral, and the apparently incidental. The instrument of this style is its willingness to pursue or to float repeated figurations which do *not* 'solve the riddle' in a secure commitment of character. Perhaps more clearly than any other work before *Lutetia*, *Ludwig Börne* allows compositional technique to override the linearity of narrative. It seems likely that the process of integrating material from an unknown original memoir source with later additions enabled Heine's collage methods to generate a pattern of coherences based on leitmotifs. In this sense the endings of each of the five books of the *Denkschrift* orchestrate a theme of apocalyptic or revolutionary secrecy, another 'ruse of reason'.[58] Yet any consistent attempt to decode such figures would be mistaken.

The recurrence of the cry 'Pan is dead' in the Heligoland letters, for instance, remains resistant to full interpretation – 'not explicable without remainder', Klaus Briegleb notes gravely. To take an even more extended sequence, there is clearly some kind of link between Börne's certainty, in Book 1, that he will be able to break his porcelain fetters ('Porzellanfesseln') and smash his gilded tea-pot ('vergoldete Teekanne') and the Hassidic tale of the Messiah restrained by golden chains from saving his people ('seine Hände seien gefesselt mit goldenen Ketten') at the end of Book 4. (At one level, the implication is that the failure ('restraint') of Börne's revolutionary intentions has been providential.) Yet with the self-quotation from *Zur Geschichte der Religion und Philosophie*, which opens Book 5, the image of porcelain returns. Such figural combinations suspend the 'meaning' of the image, if we take it to be a withdrawal from progressive politics in Biedermeier Germany, by leaving open the possibility of revolutionary delay as the simultaneous alternative. In the 'becalmed' condition of the restoration that choice cannot be made. The closure which might have been possible once, in an age that believed in authority, is rescinded in modern post-revolutionary times. As the dream recorded in the Heligoland letter of 10 August reveals, heaven stands empty 'as in houses where a bankruptcy

or a death has occurred' (B 4, 55). Heine's comic brilliance recognizes the
condition of the times, but rejects Börne's republican rush to judgment,
at least until the time is right. For the present, there is little ground for
optimism, but there are plenty of grounds for wry irony.

The only figure that can hold the common ground for Heine and Börne
as the shared space of their writing is that of exile. For all his exasperation,
Heine retains a remarkable generosity towards the great writer and patriot;
and their common experience of writing as extraterritorial re-echoes from
the moment in their fictional stroll when they hear Psalm 137 intoned in
the Frankfurt ghetto:

What is that song? I asked my companion. 'It is a good song,' the latter replied
with a surly laugh, 'a lyrical masterpiece that could hardly find its equal in this
year's poetic anthology . . . Perhaps you know it in the German translation: We
sat by the rivers of Babylon, our harps were hung on the weeping willows, etc.
A splendid poem! – and old Rabbi Chayim sings it very well with his tremulous,
ruined voice;' (B 4, 22)

Börne's surly laugh asserts his superiority to the lapsed Jew Heine, and
perhaps also to the traditional Judaism of the ghetto. Heine's deep sense
of exile, in Börne and himself, returns and frames the *Denkschrift* in the
acknowledgement of Paris as Babylon and the city of the damned in Book 5:
by day Heine walks, 'corpulent and laughing, through the glittering streets
of Babylon', but as evening falls 'the melancholy harps' of exile sound in
his heart (B 4, 125; compare 141). After Börne's death, and after the most
explicit condemnation of the barren utilitarianism of the 'modern puritans'
(B 4, 141), Heine's text finally follows the last German nightingale and the
last classical nymph as they go into exile. His writing, conversely, is *their* last
resort – the final defence against self-styled republican repression. Heine's
scandalously aesthetic talents, in the *Memorial*, hold open the options which
Nazarene characters – whatever their political hue – would rather close
down.

# PART III

## Parisian writing

# CHAPTER 9

# *Scheherazade's snapshots:* Lutetia

I have already written down a large part that is new, I might almost
say added it creatively (which remains just between ourselves) . . .

(12 August 1852)

I am conscious that in my book *Lutetia*, which consists almost exclusively of facts, I have not communicated a single fact without tested
witnesses and guarantees.

(17 August 1855)[1]

## POLITICS AND FASHION

In the early 1840s Heine returned to writing about Parisian politics and
culture in a series of reports for the *Augsburger Allgemeine Zeitung*. It was
a field in which he had worked a decade earlier. *Französische Maler* had
described paintings in the Salon of 1831; and *Französische Zustände* presented
the leading personalities and parties in Paris after the July Revolution, in
a context which increasingly aspires to social and historical generality.[2]
By comparison, *Lutetia* often seems weighed down with detail: this later
journalism stays close to the political events of the day – Guizot's ministry,
the position of the King, and the condition of the urban proletariat – but
also records personal impressions of the culture and economy, and even
individual encounters with prominent figures of the time. The combination
of historical and personal material in *Lutetia* appears to justify Karl Kraus's
complaints about Heine's legacy to modern 'impressionistic journalism'. In
his scorn for the Insel Verlag's description of the Paris prose as the 'still vital
achievement of modern journalism',[3] Kraus quotes Heine's letter to Campe
of 7 March 1854, describing *Lutetia* as a 'chrestomathy of prose' (i.e. like
an anthology of selected passages used by students of a foreign language)
which will be 'very beneficial in the formation of a style for popular topics'
(B 5, 958).

Kraus thinks that the modern journalism initiated by Heine's work is responsible for a reduction of historical events to the lowest common denominator of personal response; and because this generates a kind of writing that can fit anything and everything, experience itself is rendered interchangeable – like any other commodity on the market. The real world becomes no more than a function of the journalist's impressions: facts are merely local colour. In his own retrospective commentary on *Lutetia*, Heine concedes that the form of the fact is used to clothe subjective opinion; but in other ways his whole method undermines the stability of 'objective facts'.

Considerations of style were particularly important when Heine returned to the material. Between 1852 and 1854 he re-edited and in some cases rewrote the published and unpublished texts of the 1840s to yield the sixty-one articles in *Lutetia*. He had reworked his earlier Paris journalism for the *Französische Zustände* volume in the same way. This editorial process was conceived, in part at least, as a restitution of what had been damaged by censorship when his work had been originally prepared for publication in the *Augsburger Allgemeine*. The repeated theme of Heine's Epistle Dedicatory and of the preface to the French translation is the recovery of good style and the reconstruction and clarification of his own methods. However, the editorial construction of *Lutetia* also presents Heine's writing in a complex temporal perspective. *Lutetia* appeared in 1854 and in French translation, as *Lutèce*, in 1855. Considering the Paris texts from this point more than a decade after their original composition, Heine is anxious to defend his own reputation. The collected journalism is restored to his authorship from the anonymity of its original publication in the newspaper, and Heine puts his name to it. However, *Lutetia* also emerges in a changed political context. Its reappearance in the Second Empire tacitly underlines and confirms Heine's uneasiness about the stability of the Orleanist settlement and his recognition of the threat presented both by 'communist' movements and by Bonapartist memories: the one spectre resolutely defeated by Louis Napoleon's coup d'état, the other embodied by him as Napoleon III.

Marx's *18th Brumaire of Louis Bonaparte* (1852), famously, demonstrates that great events and characters in world history repeat themselves, so that Napoleon Bonaparte's coup against the Directory on 18 Brumaire of revolutionary year VIII is recapitulated (as farce) by Louis Napoleon on 2 December 1851.[4] Heine anticipates this modern understanding of historical imagery. Rather than defining it (as Marx does) as a compulsive conjuring of the past, however, he recognizes that historical or cultural moments are not fixed functions in the representation of social or political formations.

Rather, they are constantly appropriated, reappropriated, and revalued. Heine shows a society in which almost any event or object can be manipulated for ideological purposes. He records how the augurs of the Bourse can interpret every smile and frown on the face of Baron Rothschild (B 5, 354). In the unreliable calm of the 'juste milieu', the politics of the centre created after the accession of King Louis Philippe, the objectivity of the real world has become saturated with signs, symbols and emblems. Heine responds to this condition both with a demonstration of its effects, and with a style that mimics its structure. In *Ludwig Börne: eine Denkschrift*, Heine's ventriloquism and its complex framework of quotation, self-quotation and oblique quotation insist on mediation, against any kind of authoritarian closure. *Lutetia* recognizes the struggle for allegorical and emblematic control and achieves its critique by emphasizing and even indulging the ambiguity of cultural symbols and the allegories they set in play.

Heine observes the various attempts to harness significance for conflicting causes against the background of a long history. *Lutetia* – Lutetia Parisorum – is a Roman name for Paris, from Book VI of Caesar's *Gallic War* (DHA XIII/1, 469). Heine came up with the title for his last Paris book, in a letter of 20 May 1854, quite late in the negotiations with his publisher. Campe was pleased with his proposal. It seemed to him to offer the reader prospects of old Paris. The excavations of ancient Paris begun in 1844 and, perhaps, the discoveries made during the early years of Haussmann's building boom in the 1850s may have stimulated this archaeological perspective. Paris-*Lutetia*, the modern city that still reveals the lineaments of an ancient one, is a space in which a classical tradition, of empire as well as republicanism, is being contested. In the passage from antiquity to modernity the meaning of the past must be continually reassessed. Recalling the time of Caesar's history, Heine cites the warlike passions 'that have been blazing and seething so tempestuously among the French since the time of the Gauls' (B 5, 408), only to recognize that these fires are long extinguished. The burial of Napoleon's remains after their return to Paris serves only to mark the end of an heroic age:

The Emperor is dead. With him died the last hero in the old style and the new philistine world can breathe again, as if released from a glittering monster. Over his grave a bourgeois industrial world [eine industrielle Bürgerzeit] is rising, which admires quite different heroes, virtuous Lafayette, for instance, or James Watt the cotton spinner. (B 5, 409)

What remains of the *grande armée* is little more than a Roman satire ('römisches Spottlied') on Napoleon, the dead victor of French history.

In this period of transition, the funeral of Napoleon has special historical significance. The Emperor represents the extension and the limitation of the idea of popular revolution: in *Nordsee* III (the prose travel-picture in the sequence) Heine identified 'the heroic youth of France' as a hero of epic proportions, 'the beautiful hero who dies young' (B 2, 239), but the idea that called this hero into battle has finally failed:

> Napoleon . . . was not capable of opposing Europe's surge forwards with the magic of the idea that could produce armies out of thin air; he no longer had the strength to break the fetters with which he himself had kept that idea in chains . . . (B 5, 347)

Napoleon's appropriation of the revolutionary idea robs it of its appeal, and others will be beneficiaries of its legacy; yet the Emperor remains the ambiguous symbol of revolutionary power and of its imperial exhaustion. Paris is hence the archaeological site of a power-struggle, the constant attempt to occupy the classical memory for republican or autocratic interests.

Reference to antecedents in antiquity was a standard manoeuvre in Bonapartist propaganda. Heine conforms to the same pattern in *Die Romantische Schule*, where Napoleon appears as 'the great classicist, as classical as Alexander and Caesar' (B 3, 380).[5] In the day-to-day politics of the July Monarchy this struggle for the past is played out between a number of different parties: supporters of the constitutional monarch, the Bourbon legitimists, republicans, and communists. But Heine also recognizes various attempts to lay claim to revolutionary and imperial traditions through the subordination and exploitation of the cultural and economic life of the city.

Heine had remarked years earlier, apropos of the fortification of Paris: 'Hence we perhaps attain to the great movements of politics through the medium of architecture' (B 3, 81). In an extended meditation on the political significance of the ways in which a city marks its history (Article XXXVIII), he points out that the 'communist' threat to Napoleon's memory, enshrined in the Vendôme column, affects both the imperial architecture of Napoleon's mausoleum and the survival of epic poetry itself (B 5, 382). The national poem, typically in Virgil's *Aeneid*, is achieved under the protection of an imperial patron. Because of the ideological bond between political formation and aesthetic form, which Heine will seek to analyse for the case of the juste milieu, the overthrow of an empire or a throne has direct cultural consequences. Significant political change will entail a loss of meaning in art and even the destruction of the art forms that such polities have appropriated.

There are other claimants to the legacy of the classical tradition and to political significance, however: Article LVII (5 May 1843) determines a further displacement of political issues by aesthetic and financial matters.

Real politics has now retired to its mansion on the Boulevard des Capucins. Meanwhile industrial and artistic questions are the order of the day, and the argument now is whether sugar cane or sugar beet should be favoured; whether it is better to hand over the northern railway to a private company or to develop it entirely at the expense of the state; whether the success of 'Lucretia' will get the classical system in poetry back on its feet again: the names mentioned most frequently at the moment are Rothschild and Ponsard. (B 5, 447–8)

At a time when international politics, represented by the ministry of foreign affairs in the Boulevard des Capucins, has been supplanted by domestic issues, Heine's list of burning issues is sweetly even-handed: sugar, the 'Chemin de fer du nord', and neo-classicism. Yet none of the apparently discrete items in this heady mixture is insignificant. Politics withdraws to the ministry of foreign affairs – and questions of railway finance and sugar production stand in for the larger issues of free trade and national transport which were central to the Orleanist venture.[6] Alongside these indices, a small neo-classical revival also figures as an event worthy of mention in the same breath as Rothschild himself. The banker had a controlling interest in the railway, and his patronage, we are told, has also spoken for the classical canon from Homer to Racine and Goethe, 'dead poets the lot of them' (B 5, 452).[7] Rothschild succeeds earlier aristocratic patrons in Versailles or Weimar, so that their authors are inherited, along with the tradition of antiquity ('Homer') that they represent. In a more literal sense, Ponsard's success with *Lucretia* looks set to restore the fortunes of French classicism after the failure of Victor Hugo's Romantic play *Les Burgraves*, which had served up 'the dregs of our Romantic cookery, versified sauerkraut'. But if classicism is restored, it is not clear whether it will reinstate the style of the Revolution, of Robespierre and St Just – or the style of the Empire.

Heine is impatient with bad imitations of German Romantic posturing. He argues that a kind of classical continuity *is* maintained in spite of all Victor Hugo's medievalism. Hugo's disastrous play allowed the new money-aristocracy to retain in a modernized form the boredom meted out to the ancien régime at the Comédie-Française. Yet they must still endure 'the mouldy scum of that ancient sleeping draught [die moderige Hefe des antiken Schlaftrunks]' (B 5, 434) as well. As a passage in the original article points out, Ponsard's play 'puts the dusty old debates about the classical and the Romantic back on the agenda, a conflict that is getting positively boring for the German observer' (B 5, 1018). The aesthetic argument is old hat, but the meaning of the classical draws on a variety of instances – from antiquity, through seventeenth-century theatre ('the ancient sleeping draught') and, in painting, David's 'dry and academic imitation of Greek sculpture' (B 5, 376), to the stoicism of Guizot's 'ancient equanimity [antike Unerschütterlichkeit]' (B 5, 375). According to the 'Retrospective clarification' that Heine added to his discussion of corruption in Guizot's administration in 1854, the classical theme of his personality was explicitly acknowledged when German scholars praised Guizot in Pindaric odes faithfully imitating even the prosody of antiquity (B 5, 472).

However, there is one particularly dominant form in which the July Monarchy rehearses its classical aspirations. The imitation of Renaissance interiors and Renaissance 'design' in the 1830s and 1840s indicates a special affinity:

Does our present time [Jetztzeit] perceive an elective affinity with that period, which, thirsting for a fresh and vital draught, looked for that rejuvenating spring, just like us, in the past? I do not know, but the time of François I and the companions of his taste exercises an almost ghastly magic on our imaginations, like the memory of circumstances we lived though in a dream; and then there is an uncommonly original charm about the way that age was able to digest a rediscovered antiquity. What we see here is not, as in the School of David, a dry and academic imitation of Greek sculpture but rather a fluent melding of Greek art with Christian spirituality. In the art styles and lifestyles [Kunst- und Lebensgestaltungen] that owe their existence to the marriage of the most heterogeneous elements, there is such sweet, melancholy wit, such an ironic kiss of reconciliation, radiant high spirits, an elegant terror, which we find uncannily compelling – we know not how. (B 5, 375)

In an article for the *Augsburger Zeitung* describing the glittering success of Meyerbeer's *Huguenots* (B 5, 142) in 1836, Heine had gone on to celebrate the Rothschild *palais* as the most famous instance of the new Renaissance style, uniting 'everything the sixteenth century could think up and that the nineteenth century could pay for'. Far from establishing timeless standards, democratic or imperial, such Renaissance pastiche is a negotiable commodity like any other. Heine's commentary in *Lutetia* brings a subtle analysis to bear on this Renaissance style and on the psychology of fashion in general. François I is credited with having brought Renaissance architecture from Italy to France. The present is haunted by the 'ghastly magic' of the period, like the memory of something in a dream. Heine indicates here that there may be an *unconscious* bond between changes in public taste, expressed in fashionability, and the political and ideological framework in which they occur. The window-shopper or flâneur is drawn to the Renaissance-style

items on display in the Rue Vivienne or the Boulevards (B 5, 375) by a spell
that is beyond full conscious control. The compulsion driving these devo-
tees of style is uncanny because Renaissance pastiche provides an *appropriate*
objective correlative for social forces which cannot be readily sensed in any
other way. This is the significance of Heine's final phrase, 'we know not
how'.[8]

Heine's account of a marriage of these heterogeneous elements is a specific
reference to the way in which early French Renaissance architecture grafted
Italian ornament and classical orders on to essentially Gothic structures.
The melancholy wit and the ironic kiss of reconciliation bear witness to
this false combination. Heine deciphers its elements as Hellenic materialism
and Christian spiritualism: as in *Die Romantische Schule,* classical antiquity
represents the emancipation of the flesh, while spiritualism mortifies the
flesh in the revived medievalism of the Romantic movement (B 3, 361–
71). These are the forces that reappear in the apparent compromise of the
July Monarchy and its juste milieu, the balancing act between democratic
emancipation and autocratic control. Melancholy and irony are the ways in
which self-consciousness recognizes the falsehood of these claims to balance
out contradictory powers, or to recover the force of a sixteenth-century
resolution in the nineteenth-century version of its superficial 'style'. The
apparently random facts of fashion and public taste have been coerced by
the ideological strategies and weaknesses of the social formation.

POLITICAL HERMENEUTICS

Heine's reflections on fashion and style appear in an article that takes its
cue from the shop-windows of Paris, just before Christmas 1841:

Now that the New Year is approaching, the day of gifts, the shops here are outdoing
one another with the most varied displays. The sight of them provides the idle
flâneur with the most pleasant pastime; if his brain is not entirely empty, then
thoughts may even occur to him from time to time, as he looks at the colourful
wealth of artistic luxury items behind the shining windows – and perhaps casts on
eye over the members of the public standing next to him. (B 5, 373)

The flâneur of this window-shopping stroll has been taken as the representative figure of Heine's own style in *Lutetia.*[9] Such writing would
be observant, fluent, and critical without being fixed in any theoretical
framework. A *flânant* style would continue to suspend the finality of its
judgement just as the ventriloquist frameworks of *Ludwig Börne* reject any
ultimately closed intellectual commitment. Walter Benjamin's discussion

of the flâneur in relation to Baudelaire's modernity has given this figure a special critical currency. However, Heine himself offers another image for his journalism as a style of continuous procrastination: he writes as *Scheherazade*. Article XIX returns to the possibility of war between France and England in their struggle for influence in the Near East: Thiers, Heine conjectures, has unleashed the demon of war like a genie from a bottle. This Arabian Nights image sets the tone, and Heine's article ends:

> The post is about to go, and like the Sultana Scheherazade we interrupt our tale, promising the rest tomorrow [vertröstend auf Morgen], when on account of the many inserted episodes we shall equally provide no conclusion, however. (B 5, 316)

Scheherazade must extend her narrative and defer closure if she is to avoid execution: in an obvious and important way she therefore represents Heine as a writer. Scheherazade is threatened by the authority of the Sultan Schariar, while for Heine the threat appears in the form of the Bavarian state censorship exercised on his Augsburg publisher; Heine too avoids settled positions and conclusions in favour of a narrative of continuous interruption. There is still a reminiscence of the Arabian Nights when, in the French preface of 1855, he confesses to creating fictional friends to speak on his behalf and admits to operating with parables:

> That is why my letters contain many little tales and arabesques the symbolism of which not everyone understands and which could appear to the coarse gawper as trading in small-minded anecdotes or even as mere gossip [kleinliche Anekdotenkrämerei oder gar als Commerage]. (B 5, 230–1)[10]

The extended decorative line of the arabesque corresponds to the endless narrative of Scheherazade. To an untutored eye, Heine believes, he will appear to deal only in anecdote and gossip – and the way he puts this ('erscheinen konnte' / 'ont pu paraître' suggest 'could and did appear') indicates a willingness to provide the occasion for misunderstanding; but the French preface is extremely direct about *Lutetia*'s methods of ideological disguise. The coarse and untrained reader is to be gulled into taking the narrative at its face value, as a rehearsal of facts. This exclusively objective registration of Parisian life is presented as the technique most appropriate to the traditions and aspirations of the paper, the *Augsburger Allgemeine Zeitung*:

> Familiar with the traditions of the Allg. Ztg., I knew for instance that it had always set itself the task not only of bringing all the facts of the time as quickly as possible to the public's attention, but also of registering them in full, as it were in a world-archive. (B 5, 230)

Archival writing seems merely to itemize and register data, and Heine claims that his critical method 'clothes in the form of fact' both events and his own opinion of them. For this reason a symbolic meaning is brought into play ('Symbolik'/ 'le sens symbolique', B 5, 230/222) though it is never specifically elucidated at any stage. The effect of this apparent limitation of relevance or resonance, through the emphasis on the factual, is closely parallel to the breakdown of metaphor that characterizes Heine's poetics from the *Buch der Lieder* to *Atta Troll*; and the use of a quiet symbolism here echoes the patterns discerned as 'parallel history' in *Englische Fragmente*. Drawing back – or even withdrawing altogether – from the allegorical significance of his reportage is now seen as an ideological manoeuvre, enabling political insinuation without the stability of an obvious *parti pris*. Instead the details of life, on the streets of Paris as well as in the chamber of deputies, 'speak for themselves'.

Such a neutral presentation of the world reflects contemporary perception. In a wry and lengthy account of Horace Vernet's painting of Judah and Tamar in the salon of 1843, Heine first considers the morality of the story in Genesis 38 and the new authenticity in French representations of the Near East after the conquest of Algiers, before finally getting to work on Judah's realistic camel in the picture:

Here a German painter would perhaps have emphasized the form of the camel's head, the meaningful [das Sinnige], the primordial, yes the Old Testament aspects. But this Frenchman has simply painted a camel the way God made it, a superficial camel without a single symbolic hair, which stretches its head over Judah's shoulder and observes the dubious business with the greatest indifference. This indifference is a feature of the picture under discussion and in this regard as well it bears the imprint of our age. (B 5, 484)

Vernet's superficial camel, indifferent to its own significance, has no point to make beyond its own real existence.[11] In representing the camel the painter has no axe to grind, and his neutrality reflects the objectivity to which Heine lays claim in a further figure for his own writing: the daguerreotype. As we have seen, Helmut Heißenbüttel cited the analogy with this early form of photograph in order to claim Heine as an objective 'linguistic documentarist'. The parallel Heine draws between his own work and a kind of photographic realism is found in the Epistle Dedicatory to Prince Pückler-Muskau. Heine claims that he intended only to provide a picture of the age itself:

An honest daguerreotype must render a fly just as well as it renders the proudest horse, and my reports are a daguerreotype history book in which each day gave its own likeness, and through the conjunction of such pictures the artist's ordering spirit has produced a work in which what is represented documents its veracity in itself. (B 5, 239)

Anything and everything might find itself represented in such images, and Heine admits to his own role in selecting and ordering the elements of his picture-book history. It is true that elsewhere Heine can be critical of the authenticity of the daguerreotype. In the *Geständnisse*, for instance, when he attacks Protestant communities in Europe and the United States that model themselves too rigorously on Old Testament principles, he suggests that they lack real colour and vitality, like a monochrome photograph: 'as if daguerreotyped – the contours are anxiously correct, but it is all grey on grey, lacking the sunny lustre of colour in the Promised Land' (B 6/1, 486). In the *Aufzeichnungen* (*Sketches*, notes and parerga drawn from his papers) Heine even suggests that the daguerreotype is evidence of the fact that art has nothing to do with nature (B 6/1, 665). This critical line emphasizes the challenge that the new technology represented and Heine's continuing reflection on the documentary possibilities of his own methods.

However, his attempts to describe the practices of his own writing in theoretical terms, both here and in the French preface, are uneasy and ambiguous. Heine's daguerreotype somehow manages to authenticate its faithfulness as a representation by virtue of what it represents. And yet, like Vernet's camel in Article LIX, the objects represented have no significance beyond themselves. Heine presents his photographic realism as the form in which non-political topics appear. The subtitle of *Lutetia* ('Reports on politics, art and national life') gives these sketches of art, the academy, and popular life a subordinate position in the reportage, designed to enliven 'gloomy reports' in the field of politics. In the Preface, however, the form of fact, which is very close to the daguerreotype as self-authenticating truth, is revealed as the disguise under which Heine records his personal views, and hence can smuggle a political truth, past the vigilance of the censor and the sensitivity of the *Augsburger Allgemeine*, into the harbour of public opinion (B 5, 230). In the same metaphor, the 'freebooter' Heine admits to sailing under flags of convenience, flags 'with emblems which were not exactly the proper expression of my convictions'. And from these uncertain emblematics it is a short step to the esoteric symbolism of the narrative arabesques which emulate Scheherazade's endless story.

The daguerreotype, the emblem, and 'le sens symbolique' of the preface hint at, but also withhold, the possibility of a general decipherment. Even if Jeffrey Sammons is right to insist that *Lutetia* is a creative work and 'not a reliable historical document, a scripture, or a cryptogram that we need to decode in order to discover its secret message',[12] there are clear indications that Heine understood his work in terms of Scheherazade's narrative of infinite postponement and Daguerre's technology of immediate authenticity – and it is Heine who devises, for his critique of the symbolism at work in the July Monarchy, this strategy of open secrecy in which the everyday factitious world is swept up into the practice of a political hermeneutics. The esoteric reader he had invoked in the pictures of travel is still required.

Heine's writing in *Lutetia* regularly depends on the identification of a particular event or object offered to the reader for interpretation, as a prospective allegorization of the real world.[13] In the French preface, Heine himself describes his political insinuations as deploying the methods of parable (B 5, 230); and Article XVIII suggests that a 'parabolic hint' ('parabolische Andeutung', B 5, 313) can be risked in relation to a topic otherwise too delicate for discussion. Parable hence seems to provide a further general term for the method of *Lutetia*. In all of these terms, except the daguerreotype, personal political judgement is held in abeyance and the emblem or symbol seems to have a life of its own.

There are some instances, however, in which the space between metaphor and judgement is greatly reduced. The obelisk of Luxor is the most famous example of such direct symbolism. It is constantly associated with Guizot and the question of the stability of his government:

> Will Guizot last? Holy God, in this part of the world nothing lasts for long, everything wobbles, even the obelisk of Luxor! This is no hyperbole but the literal truth. For several months now the talk has been that the obelisk is not firm on its pedestal, that at times it rocks from side to side . . . it is always bad if the public harbours doubts about the firmness of things; their best support disappears along with belief in their permanence. Will they last? I believe at any rate that they will hold to the end of the next session, the obelisk and Guizot alike, who displays a certain similarity to the former – e.g. that he is not in the proper place. (B 5, 380)[14]

A precarious greatness, with the suggestion of an alien imposition of power, is established here and immediately decoded: 'the obelisk and Guizot alike'. Heine's ambiguous German has no real English equivalent. He leaves it initially unclear: does he mean 'Will the obelisk last?' or 'Will Guizot last?' by the pronominal 'Wird er sich halten?' The very phrase 'Wird sich Guizot halten' becomes a leitmotif in *Lutetia* associated with the obelisk, so that in Article LII the minister's inactivity ('he holds himself as still as marble') appears to be modelled on the stillness of the Egyptian monument. Ultimately, in Article LVIII, Guizot's survival in a period of ministerial crisis

appears without reference to the obelisk, and yet the context – of falling tow-
ers, falling weather-vanes, and storm winds unleashed by Russian shamans
on the Neva – makes it clear that the figuration of political instability is still
recalled in the assertion that 'Guizot will last for some considerable time
yet' (B 5, 457).[15]

Even in the case of the obelisk of Luxor and its signification as the
stability – or lack of it – of Guizot's ministry, the context of the object,
both in the real world and in the text of Heine's Paris book, is of great
importance. The obelisk stands in the Place de la Concorde, known in
1841 as the Place Louis Quinze – the square in which Louis XVI had been
executed. It stands therefore in 'the most modern square in the world, the
square where the modern age really began', surrounded

> by the exclusively theatrical architecture of modern times, sculptures in rococo taste,
> fountains with gilded naiads, allegorical statues of French rivers, whose pedestal
> holds the caretaker's office, in the centre between the Arc de Triomphe, the Tuileries,
> and the Chambre des Députés . . . (B 5, 381)

This location gives contemporary meaning to a monument which, strictly,
should have no meaning at all. Transposed from its place at the entrance to
the temple in Luxor, it stands mysteriously itself in its 'livery of hieroglyphs';
but it is surrounded by modern architecture, which is designed to have
meaning via the allegories of the Rivers of France done in the rococo taste
of the ancien régime. Such buildings are only ever a theatricalized façade,
given some minimum utility by the lodge for a concierge built into the
pedestal of the statue. The obelisk throws into relief the modern buildings
around it. Because they have meanings, their substance as buildings is split
off from the significance they carry. Finally the position of the obelisk
between the Napoleonic Arc de Triomphe, the Orleanist Tuileries and the
bourgeois-democratic Chambre makes it an appropriate emblem of the
positioning of Guizot's ministry in the juste milieu.[16] The real question of
its physical stability is much less important than the development of this
association with Guizot through the successive articles in which the 'Will
it (he) last?' theme recurs.

## UNSTABLE IMAGERY

In important ways Heine recognizes that mere facts and little tales ('His-
torietten') are always open to appropriation and interpretation. In a report
on the concert season, in Article XXXIII, he had recorded the fact that one
of the German virtuosi in Paris announced himself on his visiting card as

'ami de Beethoven'. Two years later, he returns to this case (in Article LVI) and admits that he had never actually seen such a card:

I did not invent the story but perhaps believed it with too much readiness – given that with everything in the world, more depends on plausibility than on truth itself. The former demonstrates that the man was thought capable of such folly, and provides us with a measure of his true nature [Wesen], while the true fact in itself can only be an accident, without any characteristic significance. (B 5, 447)

The item of gossip turns out to be important not because of its truth but because of its plausibility. 'Facts' become the site of active interpretation, and are already located in public discourse. Heine is unusually aware of the way in which facts or, for that matter, gossip can be exploited, one way or another, in an ideological act of appropriation.

The reference to dealing in malicious tittle-tattle ('Anekdotenkrämerei') in the French preface acknowledges an insight developed in Article XXV. If the anecdotal had been unmasked in *Buch der Lieder* as symptomatic of the bourgeois agenda of individuation and private experience, in *Lutetia* anecdotes are recognized as politically labile in the *public* world they occupy. Article XXV announces the publication of Louis Blanc's history of the July Revolution, *Histoire de dix ans.* Heine presents not a review, but an account of the author in the context of left politics in Paris so that readers can recognize the political orientation of Blanc's history. He is identified as the heir of Robespierre and representative of a 'Spartan' egalitarianism which would destroy greatness and all its works. This aligns him with the 'communist' left, and his book on the July Revolution makes public a number of 'new and wicked anecdotes' which delight the republican party because their butt is the ruling bourgeoisie and its citizen king; for the same reason, however,

For the legitimists . . . the book is true caviar, for the author, who spares the legitimists themselves, derides their bourgeois conquerors and slings poisonous mud at the royal mantle of Louis Philippe. Are the stories that Blanc tells about him true or false? (B 5, 328)

Blanc's tales of the bourgeoisie can be used by the anti-royalist camp just as readily as by the ultra-royalist supporters of the Bourbons. Anecdotes may stand in for a larger agenda, but their valency can change dramatically according to the context in which they appear.

Heine retells from Blanc the story of a letter Louis-Philippe, then Duke of Orléans, supposedly wrote when Charles X wished to appoint him Lieutenant General of France. Dupin, who promoted the Orleanist cause, encouraged him to refuse the King's offer outright, and drafted a letter couched in strong terms; Louis-Philippe, however, resorted to the ruse of wishing to show Dupin's draft to his wife before signing it, and thus succeeded in substituting his own letter of loyal acceptance, which he sealed in Dupin's envelope without him noticing.

In Heine's reading, the scenario of this purloined letter is deeply resonant. If republican interests, and presumably Louis Blanc's 'communist' sympathizers, see in the story evidence of Louis-Philippe's servility, and if the Bourbon legitimists interpret the scene as proof of Louis Philippe's betrayal, Heine celebrates instead the duke's artistry, cunning, and finesse in hastening Charles's abdication: 'But only the envelope was the same, the nimble-fingered artist had substituted a quite humble document for Dupin's crude and blatant letter' (B 5, 329). Historically, Louis-Philippe did not in fact respond to Charles's belated appointment until after he had received his letter of abdication.[17] Ten years after the July Days, the fiction is more important than any historical truth, however; and Heine leaves open another reading of the anecdote. The future bourgeois monarch served his own interest, and thereby eased the process of constitutional change. Furthermore, as an artist, Louis-Philippe can represent Heine himself, so that the substituted letter figures as his own method of addressing a message under a cover to which he can make no personal claim, but which presents him as doing one thing when in fact he is doing another.[18] The envelope must be opened on reaching its destination, but not before time.

Two aspects of political or ideological symbolism are involved. In daily life, both in state ritual or political debate and in the streets and arcades of Paris, the ways in which the July Monarchy comes to be represented are unstable; its repertoire of politically or culturally meaningful images is subject to cynical appropriation – sometimes by contradictory forces. Heine traces and replicates this volatile symbolism through the fragmentary narratives and the patchwork of factual observation in his 'picture-book' history. Buildings and monuments, personalities, and visual images of the early 1840s can all become strategic emblems in the playfulness of his writing. Context indicates their fuller meanings without ever fixing the symbol or representation in any strict allegorical equivalence. The real world presents itself with photographic immediacy, but its sheer facticity postpones the completion of decipherment, like Scheherazade's tales.

In some of Heine's street scenes the metonymic shift of emphasis is fairly transparent, for all that. His description, in Article IV, of the pamphlets and books read by workers in the Faubourg Saint-Marceau, and of the songs he heard sung there, indicate the growth of a popular socialism which thrives on the memory of 1789. The patter of proverbial remarks attributed to Sancho Panza at the start of the article does nothing to conceal the dangerous theme of nascent communism that is addressed, but it very effectively masks the degree of seriousness with which it is approached. Similarly towards the end of the same article Heine includes a joke about the Catholic devotions of the legitimists: '"the good Lord has many visitors" . . . "they are bidding farewell"' (B 5, 254). This can conceal neither the implication of cynicism in the churchgoers nor Heine's own scepticism; but the tone is lightened, even though a further threat to the July Monarchy is under discussion.

The larger threat to Louis-Philippe comes from the republican and communist left, in Heine's view. Article L, one of the most celebrated 'real allegories' in *Lutetia*, discovers an image of the proletarian danger to the July Monarchy in the rats believed to infest the plaster elephant standing in the Place de la Bastille. The elephant had been a trial model for an elephant fountain planned for the square by Napoleon, and described in *Französische Maler* as giving 'a fair representation of the conscious strength and mighty reason of the people' (B 3, 80). Only the plaster model of this project survived; at a later stage it was to have become a monument to the July Revolution itself. Article L decodes the plaster elephant very directly: the municipal council has decided not to destroy it for fear of the rats which may be living inside it (and which might spread, after its destruction, to the working-class suburbs of Saint-Antoine and Saint-Marceau); in the same way,

How much they would like to tear down Louis Philippe, that great wise elephant, but they fear His Majesty the sovereign King of the Rats, the thousand-headed monster, which would then come to power . . . (B 5, 413)

The monarchy is hence a bulwark for the bourgeoisie against the tide of proletarian unrest. In Article XXXIV the same role had been attributed to Guizot, whose real business is said to be the maintenance of bourgeois rule. What Heine does not elaborate in the case of the plaster elephant in the Place de la Bastille is the significance of the historical transmission of one and the same monument from Napoleonic origins to the juste milieu. Yet the way in which an historical symbol can be occupied by successive ideologies could hardly be clearer.

In other cases, however, the significant image is much less readable. Article XVII deals briefly with the effects of the war-scare in July 1840 after the four-power convention was agreed in London, and with Palmerston's foreign policy in regard to the Eastern Question; the article particularly discusses reports in the French press concerning the Damascus pogroms.

Heine conjectures that French readers believe accounts of the Jewish ritual murder of a capuchin priest not because the French are anti-Semitic but because their natural scepticism leads them to think ill of any religion. The final paragraph of the article apparently illustrates French scepticism at a popular level:

How strangely gullibility is linked among the common people of France with the greatest scepticism, I commented a few evenings ago in the Place de la Bourse, where a fellow had posted himself with a large telescope and would show you the moon for two sous. Meanwhile he was telling the gawping onlookers how big the moon is, so many thousand square miles, how there were mountains on it, and rivers, how many thousand miles away from the Earth it is, and other remarkable things, which irresistibly drove an old porter who was walking by with his wife to spend two sous and have a look at the moon. His dear better half, however, resisted with rationalistic passion and advised him to save his two sous for tobacco: it was all superstition, she said, everything people said about the moon, its mountains and rivers and its inhuman size, it was all made up to separate a fool and his money. (B 5, 309–10)

This scene provides a complicated embodiment of scepticism and credulity, as the author promises. The telescope stands in, as a stock image, for Galileo's struggle against the dogma of the Catholic Church. However, the lunar landscape which it reveals is subject, in turn, to the scepticism of the porter's wife. While other onlookers are taken in by talk of the moon's mountains and rivers, and of its true distance from the Earth, she regards scientific discoveries as superstition, invented with the express intention of extracting her husband's cash. Her doubt includes the imaginary rivers as well as the real lunar mountains and the moon's true dimensions. Her discovery is that even such scientific views of nature can be marketed.

A final point is left unstated. The telescope is set up in the Place de la Bourse, and Article XVII begins by describing the closure of the stock exchange in response to bad news on the diplomatic front. Prices are depressed, and trading has been interrupted. Heine rounds off his text by returning to the Bourse in his final paragraph, where the porter's wife demonstrates the same doubt about investment as the exchange itself. Tobacco will make a better buy for her husband's two sous, and trading is difficult at more than one level.

Heine's use of images drawn from the *realia* of the Paris streets, the salons and concert rooms, or the Chambre des Députés, relies for its effect on the active reading of context. In some cases delayed connections in a pattern of informal cross-referencing give the immediate details of a report or description a range of meaning far beyond its realism. Ironically, this is particularly true of the representation which Heine had used to designate *mere* objective realism: Horace Vernet's camel. The first part of the appraisal of 'Judah and Tamar' settles on the camel the imprint of the modern age. Vernet is said to have demonstrated a contemporary tolerance and objectivity towards the Bible, which provides the themes for a number of his pictures:

In this manner he painted Judith, Rebecca at the Well, Abraham and Hagar, and so too he painted Judah and Tamar, a splendid painting, which because of its locally styled frame [wegen seiner lokalartigen Auffassung] would make a very fitting altar-piece for the new Parisian church of Our Lady of Loretto, in the Lorettes quarter. (B 5, 484)

The suggestion that the picture should be exhibited in Notre Dame de Lorette ('im Lorettenquartier') should awaken our suspicions. In Article IV Heine had described this church as a focal point for fashionable Catholic devotion in the juste milieu, particularly among Bourbon legitimists (B 5, 254). In some way Vernet's painting, camel included, is the emblem in which religion and politics are configured. The picture represents the scene from Genesis 38 when Tamar, Judah's daughter-in-law, seduces him because he has failed to give her his third son as husband in place of the first two, Er and Onan, who have both died after being married to her. The analogy Heine devises is hence, first of all, narrative: Tamar disguises herself as a temple prostitute in order to draw Judah into the dubious negotiations which are so calmly observed by the camel; the new church dedicated to Our Lady of Loretto is in a red-light district where local prostitutes are called Lorettes, after the church; hence the painting of Tamar as a temple prostitute, busy at her trade, would be specially appropriate. However, it has also been suggested that the term 'lorettes' was specially used for the mistresses kept by bankers in the 9th arrondissement.[19] Heine's allusion to other biblical paintings by Vernet perhaps indicates the same point: Judith, Rebecca at the well, and Abraham with Hagar are all, in one way or another, connected with marriage, fidelity, or sexual power. Wealth and its corruption are therefore doubly present in the pseudo-ecclesiastical context Heine proposes for Vernet's painting. Judah represents wealth and power misused, as it is by the fashionable worshippers at Notre Dame de Lorette; and Parisian prostitutes serve in the temple of the god of the juste milieu: 'For money is the god of our age and Rothschild [the banker] is his prophet' (B 5, 355).

The witness of all this is the camel – 'without a single symbolic hair', we should recall. However, in Article LVII, dated 5 May 1843, two days earlier, the camel puts in another appearance; indeed, as originally published in the *Augsburger Allgemeine*, the review of the paintings in the 1843 Salon had formed the final part of the same article.[20] After considering the parallels between the patronage of Rothschild's money-aristocracy and that of Louis XIV, Heine moves on to consider the happiness of the rich in this life. But he immediately recalls Christ's saying that it is easier for a camel to go through the eye of a needle than for a rich man to enter the kingdom of heaven. Heine styles Christ as 'the divine communist' in this context, so that when the whole matter of the moral divide between rich and poor is summed up as 'the great camel question', the reader is expected to hear echoes of 'the great bread question' articulated in Saint-Just's slogan 'le pain est le droit du peuple' (B 3, 570). However unsymbolic Vernet's camel may appear to be, Heine's deferred connection makes it, in its context, the rebus of corrupt wealth in the juste milieu. His re-editing of the articles for *Lutetia* splits his original text and separates the allegorical emblem from the context of its decipherment. In this way Heine achieves the postponement and episodic dispersal he identifies with Scheherazade's narrative – and avoids the suppression that his tacit critical conclusion might provoke.

The camel can only achieve this richly allusive status as an emblem if images in general are scrutinized with unusual care for their political resonances. A series of articles (XXXV, XXXVII, and XXXVIII) present engravings as a popular means of access to important contemporary paintings. In each article the print of one or more paintings, which have recently been published, is moralized. Paintings carry emblematic meanings, but as monochrome etchings they also circulate much more widely. By addressing this published form Heine recognizes the entry of images from painting into public awareness and the growing sensitivity to images promoted by such commercial exploitation. It is no longer the artist alone who reveals the temperament of the age or its neuroses. Fashion and market trends provide the symptoms of a new political psychopathology.[21] In the first of these articles Heine describes an encounter with Victor Cousin, the academician, philosopher, and government minister. In the midst of the diplomatic crisis of the Eastern Question, Cousin is found standing outside a shop on the Boulevard des Italiens, admiring prints of works by the German artist Friedrich Overbeck. The 'quiet and pious heads of saints' in these pictures become figures of a peace now lost, and hence, by means of an allegorical inversion, of German hostility towards France during the so-called Rhine crisis, when German nationalists were convinced the French were about to seize the Rhine. (The same moment is invoked in the conversation with the Rhine in *Deutschland. Ein Wintermärchen*, Canto 5.) As Cousin and Heine are presented walking on, arm in arm, they in their turn are moralized as figures of reconciliation.

In Article XXXVII, Heine's account of Léopold Robert's painting 'Les Pêcheurs' ('The Fishermen') elaborates both the details of the print and his own view of the artist much more fully. To the extent that the fishermen of the title represent 'vassals of poverty' (B 5, 377) and citizens of want, they join the other representations of the working class in *Lutetia* as an emblem of communism. Heine explicitly compares this last painting by Robert, who had committed suicide shortly after its completion, with his earlier painting of reapers. Its summery landscape and happy peasants are replaced by the winter harbour of Chioggia and its poverty. Heine recalls seeing 'Les Pêcheurs' for the first time when it was shown for the benefit of the poor and in memory of the artist. Returning to his own memories of his death, Heine conjectures that Robert committed suicide for aesthetic reasons – 'he died of a lacuna in his capacity for artistic representation' (B 5, 379). This provides a new account of the distinction between historical painting and genre painting. In an earlier essay on Robert in *Französische Maler*, Heine suggests that historical painting, based on biblical or mythological as well as literally historical subjects, had traditionally given expression to a 'profound thought' (B 3, 52); genre painting on the other hand had presented themes from popular life which permitted picturesque local colour. Heine had claimed that Robert's work defeated the distinction between the immediacy of genre and the intellectual seriousness mediated by historical paintings. Robert's peasants are seen as the focus of immense vitality, so that 'Les Moissoneurs', as described in *Französische Maler*, becomes ideological – a Saint Simonian celebration of the body (B 3, 54–6) – and hence attains the dignity of historical painting through the representation of a profound thought.

In *Lutetia*, however, Robert's oeuvre is finally dismissed as genre painting. The artist has been made desperate by his inability to emulate Raphael and Michelangelo. In Heine's view 'Les Pêcheurs' is merely composed from finely executed details, but therefore lacks unity (B 5, 379) and higher harmony. The same accumulation of detail and its relation to a significant structure is in its turn a problem for Heine's reconstruction of his Paris journalism. Like the anecdote of Louis-Philippe's letter to Charles X, the blurring of the distinction between history and genre, and its subsequent restoration in the *Lutetia* article provide an important commentary on Heine's own handling of 'generic' material. If Robert's last picture lacks the unity of a profound idea, it is because for him the scene of poverty *cannot* be read as the emblem of an historical force. Heine recognizes its deeper significance and so closes his *Lutetia* essay as it had begun, with the proletarian poor and their growing political importance. The immediacy of genre is the staple of Heine's street scenes, but he opens these finely executed details to the structural coherence of a possible allegorization. Robert's failure is to be Heine's success: his tableaux and *transpositions d'art* are drawn very concretely from the daily life of Paris and its fashions, but invite and imply historical understanding.

This loose allegorical reading of fashion and the *Zeitgeist* achieves enormous analytical power in Heine's discussion of Delaroche in Article XXXVIII. A number of the paintings described in Heine's account of the Salon of 1831 had become popular as engravings in the 1840s. Heine first considers the success of Delaroche's new portrait of Napoleon, based on the Emperor's death mask as well as on previously unknown images and private communications from those who had known him. This work, however, is dismissed in exactly the same terms as Robert: 'I have already indicated the main issue: the eclectic procedure, which promotes a certain superficial truth but does not allow any profound essential thought to emerge' (B 5, 383). This 'superficial truth' is the mark of contemporary taste and perception; but the accumulation of authentic details from various sources does not produce the intellectual substance of history painting. As a detail in Heine's tableau of Paris, however, it speaks of the synthetic nostalgia of the bourgeois monarchy for the lost glories of the past, but also of the passing of the revolutionary impulse. The image of a dead emperor introduces a whole series of regicidal engravings after Delaroche – of Charles I in prison, of Cromwell contemplating the body of King Charles, of the princes in the Tower, and of Lady Jane Grey, as well as those of men condemned to death for defending a king (Stafford) or for attempting the overthrow of autocracy (Richelieu with Cinq-Mars and de Thou). Like Louis Blanc's *Histoire de dix ans*, Delaroche's images can be appropriated both by the sentimental nostalgia of aristocratic Bourbon legitimists and by the triumphant bourgeoisie – they all buy them.

Heine's repeated references to the firm of Goupil and Rittner, who market the best-selling prints, and indeed his coinage of the phrase 'engraving hit of the season' ('Kupferstich-Löwe der Saison', B 5, 376) emphasize the commercial context in which Delaroche's images achieve their widespread currency. Goupil was one of the first gallerists to create an art market in Paris.[22] The peroration of Article XXXVIII identifies the complex relations between the mode of reproduction for a popular market, the representation of historical change, and the complacency of its ideological reduction to cheap sentimentality; such images are:

The favourites of the bourgeoisie, the decent, worthy citizenry who regard the surmounting of difficulties as the highest task of art, who confuse the gruesome and the tragic, and enjoy the edification they receive from the sight of fallen greatness – in the sweet knowledge that they are safe from such catastrophes in the modest darkness of a modest arrière-boutique in the Rue Saint Denis. (B 5, 384)

This back shop ('arrière-boutique') recalls the bourgeois state boutique ('bürgerliche Staatsboutique') which represents the July Monarchy in XXXIV (B 5, 366), and the grocery specializing in spices from the variant text of Article I:

If [the French] had chosen any old spice merchant in the Rue Saint Denis as king, he would have acted exactly like Louis Philippe in the same circumstances, and similarly sacrificed all national and state interests to the interests of his person and his household. (B 5, 993)

In *Französische Zustände* (B 3, 127) Louis-Philippe stands for the whole July Monarchy as 'la boutique incarnée', the *shop incarnate*. The context of the article as a whole invites a more elaborate reading: the sentiment of bourgeois taste fails to recognize the social forces that can still overthrow monarchs, bourgeois monarchs included, along with their money-aristocracies. Heine opens this article with his Guizot topos, contemplating the fall of greatness in the instability of the obelisk of Luxor. Guizot's portrait too had appeared in the windows of Goupil and Rittner (B 5, 326). The threat by association (because the gallery specializes in the fall of kings, as it were) may be small, but historical images are profoundly destabilized. There can be no absolute claim to the meaning of Delaroche's Charles I from Bourbon supporters, Orleanists, republicans or 'communists'. Because such images are labile, they become the *site* of political differences. (We shall see Heine himself deploying the political ambiguity of the memory of Charles I in a remarkable poem from *Romanzero*.) Heine above all realizes that where the economic and the aesthetic meet, and art enters the commodity market, its claim to stable significance is replaced by conflicting readings which may not even recognize or know of each other.

## CHAINING THE GHOSTS

Karl Kraus's polemic in 'Heine und die Folgen' is fired by his anxieties about commodity production invading the primal sphere of art. Far from capitulating to this trivialization of experience, it is now possible to see that Heine provides the ground for a critique of modern culture. He acknowledges the greater liberalism of the French press, the logic of its argumentation, and the clarity of its political language in comparison with German journalism; and yet he also identifies the essential limitations of modern press freedom:

It is . . . usually the capitalists or industrialists of some other kind who put up the money to found a paper. In doing so they speculate on the circulation the sheet will find, provided it has understood how to gain a reputation as the organ of a particular party . . . (B 5, 281)

Capital investment in newspapers, expressed as the political alignment that guarantees a market sector, is a far more dangerous constraint than the red pencil of the German political censor. French journalists must simply write to order – 'just as it said in the instructions [ganz so . . . wie die Consigne lautete]' (B 5, 281). Such control of the press by its capitalist investors is still a censorship of political content.

   In the sphere of musical performance, however, Heine sees a form that parallels the bourgeois state: 'For some time now we have had peace and quiet, at least as far as the députés and those who play fortepiano are concerned' (B 5, 297). The piano becomes the special emblem of bourgeois hegemony: while the ruling class may aspire to the form of classical tragedy that had represented the ancien régime, 'Pianoforte is the name of the instrument of torture with which high society is particularly tormented and punished for all its usurpations' (B 5, 435). Heine's analysis of the fad for playing and listening to the piano in the early 1840s combines personal sensitivity, social sarcasm, and a striking grasp of cultural sociology. Complaining that 'the everlasting piano-playing' is interminable, and that his English neighbours are practising a brilliant work for two left hands, Heine registers the level of sheer public noise in Paris. (His letters 'Über die Februarrevolution' ('On the February Revolution, 1848') similarly record the deafening effect of 'constant drumming, shooting, and Marseillaise' (B 5, 207).) However, the piano comes to represent the temper of the age:

The way this piano-playing has got out of hand and particularly the triumphal processions of the piano virtuosos are characteristic of our time and bear most authentic witness to the victory of the realm of machinery over the mind [Geist]. (B 5, 435)

The victory of the machine in the cultural sphere reflects the growing control of society as a whole by industrial interests: Rothschild and his financial aristocracy 'will soon constitute not so much the committee of oversight for the Railway Society, as the committee of oversight for our whole civil society' (B 5, 450). This economic imperative even finds expression in the various publicity campaigns launched by or on behalf of the piano virtuosi who arrive in droves (Heine says 'like grass-hoppers') each winter. To have been reviewed in Paris at all will guarantee their success elsewhere in Europe – which is why the dust of the publisher Moritz Schlesinger's boots is said to be visible on their laurels (B 5, 436). Towering above them all is Liszt, but even he initiates purely economic change in the performance of music by presenting solo concerts (B 5, 358).

Heine regards the enormous popularity of the concert season as symptomatic of a much broader shift in Parisian culture. Article XXXIII, commenting on the Salon painting of 1841, registers a crisis in painting, sculpture, and architecture in the July Monarchy. The apparent success of these, it now seems, had been artificial – 'its pinions were only externally attached, and its enforced flight was followed by the most lamentable fall' (B 5, 356): the Icarean flight of art now reveals its superficiality. The point is made in different terms by the theatricality Heine discerns in the 'allegorical' modern architecture surrounding the obelisk of Luxor, and especially in the popularity of Renaissance pastiche after 1830. Such forms have been utilized for a retro style because their original meanings are lost. Instead they are commoditized, appropriated, and occupied – much as the pedestal of the Allegory of the Rivers of France on the Place Louis XV is occupied by its concierge office.

Music presents a particularly acute case of this evaporation of reference. In order to draw out the contrast between Rossini's *Stabat Mater* and Mendelssohn's *Paul* (of all things), Heine recalls a Petertide procession he had witnessed in Sète, in which children played the roles of bishops and members of religious orders, as well as the figures of the Passion. Such an immediate expression of conviction is 'no imitation in the historical grand manner' (B 5, 397), which he identifies with Prussian religious hypocrisy. Rossini's *Stabat Mater*, it is claimed, expresses the same childlike faith: 'he had no need to construct the spirit of Christendom academically first, much less to write a slavish copy of Handel or Johann Sebastian Bach' (B 5, 398). Such impersonation, however, has been Mendelssohn's recourse; and even though Rossini is called on as a positive model for religious music, there is even a suggestion that, though his memories of childhood faith are more productive, Rossini's work is not wholly authentic either.

Music is the form in which art progressively loses its grip on materiality:

in the end, even the sense of colour is extinguished, which is surely always bound up with particular drawings; and intensified spirituality, the realm of abstract thought, takes hold of sounds and notes in order to express a babbling effusiveness [eine lallende Überschwenglichkeit], which is perhaps none other than the dissolution of the whole material world: music is perhaps art's final word, just as death is life's final word. (B 5, 357)

In this Hegelian aesthetic, the substantial meaning of the symbolic order disappears. Liszt playing Beethoven seems to Heine the non plus ultra of such a process of spiritualization: Beethoven drives music 'towards the acoustic agony of the phenomenal world, towards that annihilation of nature that fills me with horror' (B 5, 358). Beethoven destroys nature by contributing to the progressive elimination of reference to anything outside the work of art. This is what Heine calls the spiritualization ('Vergeistigung', B 5, 356) of music; and the crisis of representation it involves is borne out for Heine by Beethoven's deafness: in the end he hears only the memories of sound, 'phantoms of sounds long faded'.

These ghosts of long-forgotten sounds are the most extreme case of the haunted condition Heine describes in Paris. The return of Napoleon's mortal remains conjures its own revolutionary spectres, 'ghosts of Anno 89' (B 5, 299). Heine recognizes the great continuity between the Revolutions of 1789 and 1830 when he asserts that 'the Revolution is still one and the same' (B 5, 319). The revolutionary moment both extends itself and *repeats* itself: ghosts of the Revolution are joined, therefore, by ghosts of the ancien régime. Article XXXIX correctly observes the continued presence of aristocrats among the deputies of the Chambre (B 5, 386). Shades of the past constantly reappear to haunt the single moment of Revolution that is simultaneously a period of transition ('Übergangsperiode', B 5, 346); and this accounts for the popularity of the song from the stage version of Bürger's 'Lenore': 'Hurrah! les morts vont vite – mon amour, crains tu les morts?' (B 5, 299, 'Hurrah! The dead come quickly – my love do you fear the dead?'). It is a symptom of the possession of this time by forces not entirely of the present.

The continuous revolutionary time underlies and sustains the emblematic and symbolic world of the July Monarchy, leaving symbols and emblems open to appropriation by its many conflicting ideological forces. Heine has two responses. First, he allows his own writing of the 1840s to accumulate meanings in the additive form of the *archive*, as his reference to the *Augsburger Allgemeine* as a 'world archive' indicates. This accumulative principle, which enables Heine to smuggle his contraband into the haven of public consciousness, is never as secure as it seems. The historian Mignet provides a model of the archivist's activity. In Article XXXV Heine describes a session of the Academy of Moral and Political Sciences in which Mignet delivered a memorial address after the death of one of the leading figures in the Revolution. The historian speaks with 'the voice . . . of the real director of Clio's archives' (B 5, 369). The muse of history may have unequivocal judgements on such matters, but Mignet must formulate his view with diplomatic care:

The circumstances of the day must be considered with intelligent deference whenever the recent past is discussed. It is an alarming task to describe the storm we have survived while we still have not reached harbour. (B 5, 369)

The image of safely reaching harbour is parallel to the freebooter of the French preface, which designates Heine's own attention to the immediate situation in dealing with the recent past. While Mignet may claim that modern conditions ('moderne Zustände') have achieved a sure foundation, Heine reads the threat in Thiers's smile as he listens to the lecture in the Academy. More than ever, modern conditions call for wise circumspection.

However, Heine also offers a glimpse of a second model for his own contemporary historiography in *Lutetia*: not Mignet's archive but Diderot's *Encyclopédie*. Diderot first appears, in the 'Addendum 1833' of *Französische Maler*, to represent what is progressive and critical in modern art (B 3, 75); and readers have often found Heine's work reminiscent of Diderot, both intellectually and stylistically. Alexander Jung's contemporary review of *Zur Geschichte der Religion und Philosophie* recalled *Le Neveu de Rameau* (B 3, 927, 931), and a possible source for *Die Bäder von Lucca* may be *Jacques le fataliste.*[23] More substantially, the conception of Heine's series of Salon volumes, designed to accommodate the critical work written in Paris but not published in book form, clearly derives from Diderot's Salons.[24] *Lutetia* hints at a further parallel.

The first part of the text 'Communism, Philosophy and the Clergy', which appears in the appendix to *Lutetia*, deals with the work of Pierre Leroux and Victor Cousin. Compared to Cousin's philosophical eclecticism, which confines itself to the metaphysical realm, Leroux's *Encyclopédie universelle* is greeted as 'a worthy continuation of his predecessor . . . that colossal pamphlet in thirty quarto volumes, in which Diderot summarized his century's knowledge' (B 5, 498). Heine had been on friendly terms with Leroux, and in many respects his development from Saint Simonianism to socialism is similar to Heine's own path. Heine too extends the encyclopedia to resume the knowledge of the age. In the divagations of his style, however, it is the *Encyclopédie's* trick of deferred critique that is suggestive for Heine's writing.

Diderot's own definition of 'Encyclopédie' – 'ce mot signifie enchaînement de connaissances' – gives some indication of the interplay possible within an apparently formal (alphabetical) arrangement. By the repetitions of his figurative discourse, Heine manages the same kind of 'enchaînement' across his own texts, within the formal chronology of the calendar. The obelisk of Luxor, Vernet's camel, the piano virtuosi of the Paris season, or Napoleon's ashes can all take on subversive significance. As in Diderot, 'a straight-faced article could be undermined by an insidious cross-reference to some other article', in order to avoid censorship – and the 'Encyclopédie' article admits as much.[25] Heine improvises this echo effect[26] of his writing to mimic the symbolic revenants ('les morts vont vite'), the return of the repressed in the July Monarchy.

### WRITING *POSTE RESTANTE*

Heine also sees that these repetitions have their limits. 'The second act is the European, the world revolution, the single combat of the dispossessed against the aristocracy of possession' (B 5, 406): ultimately, Heine believes, the gathering forces of the impoverished urban proletariat will abolish national and religious conflict to achieve unequivocal happiness. But that is not the end of the story. Article XLVI goes on to imagine a post-revolutionary *third* act in the global drama in which a final struggle establishes 'only One Shepherd and One Flock . . . , a free shepherd with an iron crook and an equally shorn, equally bleating human flock!' (B 5, 406–7).[27] It may even be that Marx's ill-remembered citation of Hegel at the beginning of *The 18th Brumaire* is mixed up with the two acts of Heine's revolutionary spectacular. The third act envisaged here is at once authoritarian and strictly egalitarian. By associating the evangelical imagery of the one fold and the one shepherd with the apocalyptic rod of iron, Heine recalls the dangers of socialism's flirtation, in figures such as La Mennais, with religious doctrines that he regards as innately authoritarian. Such a conjunction of 'spiritualism' and moral rigorism is very close to the core of his polemic with Börne.

The prospect of a 'communist' equality also puts an end to the play of figures in which Heine's own writing subsists, as a critique. Article XXVIII describes an untimely and therefore brief triumph of the proletariat as a misfortune 'as, in their foolish frenzy of equality, they destroy everything beautiful and sublime on this earth and specifically unleash their iconoclastic fury on art and science' (B 5, 337). The French preface to *Lutetia* returns to these sombre iconoclasts ('ces sombres iconoclastes'/ 'jene dunklen Ikonoklasten', B 5, 224/232) who will use pages from the *Buch der Lieder* for a bag of coffee or a twist of snuff. The world of imagery is broken, and the instability of signification – in the juste milieu – finally settles down into the transparency of need, use-value, and unequivocal social justice.

Such a settlement is for the future, however. Heine sends his book about Paris into the world with a personal guarantee of its authorship.

Travellers who visit places memorable through art or because of historical association often inscribe their respective names on interior or exterior walls, more or less
legibly, depending on the kind of writing materials they have at their command.
(B 5, 234)

Heine's Epistle Dedicatory to his friend and fellow author Prince Pückler-
Muskau appears to offer another limitation to the unstable play of emblems
and symbols. In the French preface, he announces his intention to publish
under his own name letters and reports that had first appeared without a
byline. Their author had been identified only by the anonymous ciphers
added for purposes of payment by the Augsburg newspaper's accounts
department (B 5, 228). Here he adds the authentication of his own name –
like the initials carved on some monument by passing tourists.

In this chaos of inscriptions our attention is suddenly drawn to two names, carved
next to one another; the date and the year stand underneath, and an oval encircles
names and date which is intended to represent a wreath of oak or laurel. (B 5, 235)

Although the signature does not stand alone, it can stand out in 'this
chaos of inscriptions' by being coupled with – witnessed by – another
famous name; by bearing a date; and by being surrounded by oak leaves,
to indicate military or political victory, or laurel to distinguish the triumph
of artistry. In this case, Heine tells us, the garland linking his name with
his friend's is the text of *Lutetia* itself, a triumph of his art and of political
strategy. Heine, as it were, leaves his mark on Paris. And he insists on the
authenticity of the date, and of the encounter with an old comrade-in-
arms, by invoking their common reputation as travellers: 'yes, travellers
were we both, on this earthly globe, that was our earthly speciality' (B 5,
235). The German word for travellers, 'Reisende', once again cites Heine's
stock in trade as 'Author of the Reisebilder', his earliest success. Lastly, the
model of the objective daguerreotype guarantees historical authenticity and
accuracy in the text that is to follow. The signature is authentic, the dates
are authentic, and the text is 'photographically' accurate. Heine is confident
that imagery can be avoided: 'To speak without images [unbildlich], the
present volume consists for the most part of daily reports, which I had
printed some time ago in the Augsburg *Allgemeine Zeitung*' (B 5, 235).
After the 1848 Revolution, and then more intensively under Napoleon III,
the destabilizing and subversive activity of *Lutetia* can come to rest in
Heine's book, his personal, biographical measure of Parisian life, in direct
communication with its dedicatee.

Pückler-Muskau is the fitting reader: 'The Master to whom I dedicate
this book understands the craft' (B 5, 235), the writer's craft. The Prince's

reading will be matched and appropriate to Heine's writing, yet this strict circle of writing and conformable reading is not quite closed. Pückler-Muskau is not in place: 'Where am I to address my book? Where is he? Where does he abide, or rather where is he galloping, where is he trotting?' (B 5, 239). Pückler's travels unleash a torrent of exotic names and places, from Prussia and Poland to Arabia and Ethiopia; from the long-legged Hut-Hut and the miraculous bird Simurgh, to the Queen of Sheba and Lady Hester Stanhope, English traveller in the Middle East who thought Heine the 'chief of [the] sect of polytheists'.[28] This flight of fancy illustrating Pückler-Muskau's literary genre becomes the annotation of Heine's real life, the more so for reusing, in the bird 'Hudhud' and the miraculous Simurgh, the fauna of his own preface to *Französische Zustände* of 1832 (B 3, 103). The self-quotation, right down to the casting of Metternich as 'old Simurgh, the Dean of diplomats, the ex-vizier of so many pre-Adamitic sultans', draws life and work into extravagant figuration once again.

In Heine's letters 'On the February Revolution, 1848' Scheherazade had been silenced:

In her tales Scheherazade risked many a bizarre impertinence, many all too peculiar leaps, and the sleep-drunk Sultan quite calmly put up with the most blatant infringements of plausibility; yet if the inventive lady had ventured truly to tell the tale of the last three weeks, the daily events of the recent past, Sultan Schariar would surely have leapt from his bed with impatience . . . (B 5, 213–4)

In the course of the events of 1848, across Europe, Heine goes on, 'truth has laid aside the garment of plausibility'. In his letter to Pückler-Muskau, Scheherazade begins her tales afresh, and fantasizes the disappearance of Heine's dedicatee – who may therefore never read his Epistle Dedicatory: 'Where is he now? In the Occident or the Orient? . . . Must I address my book to Kyritz [near Potsdam] or to Timbuktu, *poste restante?*' (B 5, 241). The absent dedicatee, the elusive reader Pückler, represents other readers: he has already represented ex-vizier Metternich's readership, who, to Heine's delight, had found tearful consolation in his *Buch der Lieder*. Now the correspondence from Paris becomes an open letter, awaiting and risking – in the *poste restante* – many subsequent, more or less attentive readers, for whom an elective affinity with Heine's contemporary moment, his 'Jetztzeit', would give new life to his emblems – Karl Kraus and Walter Benjamin among them.[29]

# CHAPTER 10

# Mathilde's interruption: archetypes of modernity in Heine's later poetry

> . . . but he did not find archetypes of modernity.
>
> (Adorno)

'Die Wunde Heine', Adorno's centenary radio-talk for 1956, tries to fix Heine's historical position by way of a comparison with Baudelaire. By being subjected to the processes of reproduction in the literary sphere, Heine had been brought into direct contact with the most modern currents of the nineteenth century – 'Heine, like Baudelaire, looms large in the modernism of the nineteenth century';[1] but while Baudelaire heroically extracts a dream and an image from the increasingly corrosive experience of modernity, transfiguring the loss of all images itself into an image, Heine apparently, in his own historical moment, was unable to develop sufficient resistance to the development of capitalism. He applies techniques of industrial reproduction to an inherited repertoire of Romantic archetypes, but the other modernity – the modernity of the city – is reserved for Baudelaire.

Adorno's notion of such archetypes almost certainly derives from his knowledge of Benjamin's *Arcades* (*Passagen*) project from the 1930s. To a very large extent Adorno and Benjamin were unfamiliar with the corpus of Heine's work beyond *Buch der Lieder*. The *Arcades* indicates that Benjamin had begun to consider Heine mainly because of Baudelaire's sympathetic interest in him.[2] In 1935 Adorno suggested Heine might be expected to provide further evidence of the process of commoditization.[3] And Adorno made one further suggestion by sending a couple of stanzas from the *Romanzero* poem 'Jehuda ben Halevy' because they allude to a number of issues of central concern to Benjamin:

> Der Jehuda ben Halevy,
> Meinte sie, der sei hinlänglich
> Ehrenvoll bewahrt in einem
> Schönen Futteral von Pappe

Mit chinesisch eleganten
Arabesken, wie die hübschen
Bonbonnieren von Marquis
Im Passage Panorama.

(B 6/1, 149)[4]

And Jehuda ben Halevy,
In her view, would have been honoured
Quite enough by being kept in
Any pretty box of cardboard

With some very swanky Chinese
Arabesques to decorate it,
Like a bonbon box from Marquis
In the Passage Panorama.

(D 671)

Benjamin's reply is both excited and curiously aggrieved. Adorno would never have *found* these lines, he suggests, had he not been guided by Benjamin's work on the Paris arcades and (we might further conjecture) by the themes of his 1935 sketch.[5] For it is not only Heine's familiarity with the *Passage des panoramas* which is important here, but also the sweet-box from Marquis's shop in that arcade which might appropriately hold Halevi's poems.[6] In 'Jehuda ben Halevy' Heine's wife complains that the jewel box which had contained the gems and pearls of King Darius and which, when it passed into his possession, Alexander had used to hold manuscripts of Homer, should be sold for cash if it ever came into Heine's possession. As far as she is concerned, an ornate cardboard box, like Marquis's, would be good enough for Halevi's works. These lines take on a peculiar resonance in the light of Benjamin's remarks on 'Louis Philippe or the Interior'.[7] As will become clear, the reduction of art to the status of a modern commodity in the course of its historical reception is among the central concerns of Heine's late verse. The *chinoiserie* of Marquis's sweet-box traces out the lineaments of Halevi's poetry seen, through Mathilde's modern eyes, as no more than a piece of oriental exoticism.

## TRADITION AND MODERNITY

Heine's later poetry has been widely recognized as innovatory and at times strange and incommensurable.[8] *Romanzero*, the collection which Heine believed would form the third great pillar of his reputation, is divided into three unequal parts: 'Historien' ('Tales'), 'Lamentationen' ('Lamentations'), and 'Hebräische Melodien' ('Hebrew Melodies'). 'Jehuda ben Halevy' is the middle poem of the three making up the third of these.[9] Heine's letter to Campe of 28 August 1851 suggests that he had misgivings about the poem not unlike those associated with the composition of *Atta Troll*:[10]

I shall give only a brief preface, even though I would have so many things to say on the author's behalf. The poem entitled 'Disputation' was written in great haste after your departure. The one preceding it is actually a mere fragment – I lacked the leisure to polish and complete it . . . The shortcomings that such hastiness produces in a book are not noticed by the mass of readers, but they are no less present for all that and sometimes torment the author's conscience. (B 6/2, 15–16)

Given that the 'Hebräische Melodien' were the last poems to be completed, his complaint that he was short of time is probably no less than the truth, but the similarity of Heine's excuses here, and of his remarks about the insensitivity of the audience, to the correspondence with Campe and Laube in connection with *Atta Troll* suggest a common motivation. What is at stake once again is the unity of the poem and the plausibility of Heine's intention to complete it.

Along with 'Der Apollogott' ('The God Apollo') and 'Der Dichter Firdusi' ('The Poet Firdausi'), 'Jehuda ben Halevy' is one of the great poems of *Romanzero* dealing with the fate of poets and poetry. At the end of its first part Heine makes the scant regard he appears to show for his audience the privilege of true genius:

> Solchen Dichter von der Gnade
> Gottes nennen wir Genie:
> Unverantwortlicher König
> Des Gedankenreiches ist er.
>
> Nur dem Gotte steht er Rede,
> Nicht dem Volke – In der Kunst,
> Wie im Leben, kann das Volk
> Töten uns, doch niemals richten. –
> (B 6/1, 135)

> Any poet who possesses
> This, God's grace, we call a genius:
> Monarch in the realm of thought, he
> Is responsible to no man.
>
> He accounts to God, God only,
> Not the people; both in art
> And in life, the people can
> Kill us but can never judge us.
> (D 659)

This conclusion is reached at the end of a meditation on the early life of the great Jewish poet, prompted by a reminiscence of the opening of Psalm 137. Among the shadowy figures conjured by the lament for Jerusalem is Halevi. He thus becomes visible within a certain tradition, both religious and poetic, whose voices are heard singing psalms ('Psalmodierend, Männerstimmen') (B 6/1, 130), 750 years after Halevi's birth. The first part of the poem goes on to tell how, touched by the primal language of the Torah and Talmud, and especially by the poetic power of the Halacha or Babylonian Talmud, Halevi's poetry became a pillar of fire to the Diaspora. The second part of the poem returns to the great elegy of Psalm 137. Heine's narrator identifies himself with this old song that 'moans and hums like a kettle':

> Lange schon, jahrtausendlange
> Kochts in mir. Ein dunkles Wehe!
> Und die Zeit leckt meine Wunde,
> Wie der Hund die Schwären Hiobs.
>
> Dank dir, Hund, für deinen Speichel –
> Doch das kann nur kühlend lindern –
> Heilen kann mich nur der Tod,
> Aber, ach, ich bin unsterblich.
>
> (B 6/1, 135–6)
>
> Long it has been seething in me –
> For a thousand years. Black sorrow!
> And my wounds are licked by time
> Just as Job's dogs licked his boils.
>
> Dog, I thank you for your spittle,
> But its coolness merely soothes me –
> Only death can really heal me,
> But, alas, I am immortal!
>
> (D 660)

There is an important and difficult temporal dislocation involved in this positioning of Heine's narrator. He speaks within the tradition of dereliction which includes Job and the Babylonian exiles of the psalm, and yet unmistakably defines himself in relation to his own mortal sickness and to history as a repetition of suffering. A modern Jewish poet in Paris sees himself as the Jew of history, perhaps as the Wandering Jew. Both timeless and yet subject to time, the specific substance of this tradition is grasped by the modern poet in his own time as a 'Spleen', which is also a revolutionary animus cited from the end of Psalm 137:

Tolle Sud! Der Deckel springt –
Heil dem Manne, dessen Hand
Deine junge Brut ergreifet
Und zerschmettert an der Felswand.

Gott sei Dank! die Sud verdampfet
In dem Kessel, der allmählich
Ganz verstummt. Es weicht mein Spleen,
Mein westöstlich dunkler Spleen –

(B 6/1, 136)

Seething mad! The lid blows off –
Hail to him, the man 'that taketh
All thy little ones and dasheth
This young brood against the stones.'

God be thanked! The steam is cooling
In the kettle, which now slowly
Quiets down. My spleen subsides,
That black Western-Eastern spleen –

(D 660)

Time that licks the narrator's wounds identifies him with the long history of human suffering, in a trajectory that will lead to a moment of revenge, with its implication of a turning of the tables after an event of revolutionary violence.[11] Yet the poem does not fully represent this utopian possibility. Its preoccupations are with the huge European literary tradition in which Halevi and his modern avatar Heinrich Heine are situated.

The twelfth-century Spanish poet is placed in the company of the troubadours of Provence and of Petrarch, but Jehuda dispenses with the distant beloved of Courtly Love and declares instead his poetic longing for Jerusalem and its ruins.[12] In its turn Halevi's nostalgia is compared to the inexplicable desire of the troubadour Geoffroy Rudèl for Melisande of Tripoli. Throughout the movement of the second section, this is accomplished via a number of digressions: the elegy of the psalm leads to 'Heine's' 'black Western-Eastern spleen', which seems consciously to counter Goethe's orientalism in the *West-östlicher Diwan* and unconsciously to anticipate a key term in Baudelaire's account of Parisian modernity. Thence the poem returns to Jehuda Halevi, whose nostalgia for Jerusalem is set against the traditions of Courtly Love, only to be confirmed in its essential relation to that tradition by the similarity of Halevi's death at the feet of his beloved Jerusalem to the death of Geoffroy at the feet of Melisande.

At the same time the poem exquisitely recalls the opening of the Book of Lamentations and the cry for Jerusalem:

> Sie, die volkreich heilge Stadt
> Ist zur Wüstenei geworden,
> Wo Waldteufel, Werwolf, Schakal
> Ihr verruchtes Wesen treiben –
>
> (B 6/1, 139)

> She the crowded holy city,
> Has become a desolation
> Where wood demons, werewolves, jackals
> Carry on their vile existence –
>
> (D 662)

This metrical paraphrase renders Luther's 'Wie liegt die Stadt so wüste, die voll Volks war?' of Lamentations 1, 1 ('How doth the city sit solitary that was full of people!'). The subsequent references to jackals, snakes and birds of the night have an Old Testament resonance: the jackal in Lamentations 5, 18 and, among the night birds, the derelict owl of Psalm 6, 2. The overall effect of this is to place Halevi *and Heine* in a tradition of lament – to which the immediately previous book of *Romanzero* has borne witness.[13] The references and allusions open a temporal perspective which the remaining parts of the poem will extend in an extreme way to establish an encounter with the demands of modern civilization. The third section of the poem develops a digression which bridges the time of Halevi and Heine's own time, the one leading the 'caravan of pain' of Israel's exile, the other 'crippled in torment' ('krüppelelend') as his Jewish successor in modern Paris.

The vehicle employed to achieve this link is, to say the least, implausible: Heine describes a highly ornate casket looted by Alexander from Darius at the battle of Arbela.

> Dieses Kästchen, selbst ein Kleinod
> Unschätzbaren Wertes, diente
> Zur Bewahrung von Kleinodien,
> Des Monarchen Leibjuwelen.
>
> (B 6/1, 142)

> Now, this chest, itself a treasure
> Of inestimable value,
> Served to hold the monarch's treasures,
> All his precious body jewels.
>
> (D 664)

The poem recounts that Alexander had subsequently used this jewel case to hold the manuscripts of 'ambrosial Homer' (B 6/1, 144; D 666), and placed it by his bed so that memories of Homeric heroes might fill his dreams. Heine has an alternative proposal. Were he in possession of the casket, he would place in it the poems 'of our rabbi':

> Des Jehuda ben Halevy
> Festgesänge, Klagelieder,
> Die Ghaselen, Reisebilder
> Seiner Wallfahrt – alles ließ' ich
>
> Von dem Besten Zophar schreiben
> Auf der reinsten Pergamenthaut,
> Und ich legte diese Handschrift
> In das kleine goldne Kästchen.
>                     (B 6/1, 145)
>
> All Jehuda ben Halevy's
> Festal songs and lamentations,
> The ghazals and travel pictures
> Of his pilgrimage – I'd have it
>
> All engrossed on purest parchment
> By the greatest scribe that's living,
> And I'd place this manuscript in
> That same golden little casket.
>                     (D 667, modified)

By means of an unmistakable self-reference, the famous author of the *Reisebilder* imagines here a time in which he is the recipient and beneficiary of the tradition of Halevi, enshrined in Darius' jewel-box; and the allusion to his own literary output makes it clear that this tradition is also maintained in Heine's *own* 'pilgrimage'. In his preference for Halevi, Heine articulates a change of traditions. The casket had previously contained the works of Homer, representing for Heine the sunny and sensual world of Greek antiquity and his own Hellenic principle; and Heine imagines himself in Dionysian terms, crowned with vine-leaves and drawn by panthers. Darius' casket comes therefore to represent, figuratively and imaginatively, the *vehicle* of these traditions; but they have to be sustained by the transcription which writes them again for the present, just as the practised scribe ('Zophar' from Hebrew *sofer)* must transcribe the holy texts. The box, which has contained or might (again) contain the relics of the great traditions of Greek and Hebrew poetry, hence comes to figure as Heine's own writing, which also 'holds' this tradition.

However, literary tradition and its continuities do not provide the main instance of cultural transmission in 'Jehuda ben Halevy'. In Part III Heine pursues the extremely digressive history of the artefacts contained in the jewel casket of Darius. Among these treasures plundered by Alexander, the poem concentrates on the pearls which pass by gift, sale or inheritance from Thais of Corinth via Cleopatra and the Catholic Kings of Spain, to the wife of Baron Salomon Rothschild in Paris. These world-famous pearls (B 6/1, 146) are poor stuff, the poem tells us, when compared to the pearls of Halevi's lament for Jerusalem:

> Perlentränen, die verbunden
> Durch des Reimes goldnen Faden,
> Aus der Dichtkunst güldnen Schmiede
> Als ein Lied hervorgegangen.
>
> (B 6/1, 147)

> Pearly teardrops, strung together
> By a golden thread of verses,
> Made into a song by labors
> In the poet's golden forge.
>
> (D 668)

This identification of the pearls which the casket of Darius had contained and the poetry of Jehuda Halevi, which, according to the narrator's conjecture, it *might* contain, provides the highly attenuated logic which holds together the ostensible theme of the poem and the elaborate digression of Part III. Part IV begins by appearing to raise this very anxiety – that the third section of the poem has abandoned any attempt at coherence:

> Meine Frau ist nicht zufrieden
> Mit dem vorigen Kapitel . . .
>
> (B 6/1, 149)

> My good wife's dissatisfaction
> With the chapter just concluded . . .
>
> (D 670)

In fact, Heine's wife has other things on her mind, but the digressions that have supervened in Part III will be the first point of reference for most puzzled readers. This section of the poem successfully completes the *vita* of the poet-saint Jehuda Halevi by describing his death in Jerusalem at the hands of a Saracen and his reception into heaven to the strains of 'Lecho Daudi Likras Kalle', which Heine believes is Jehuda's own Sabbath hymn. But the digressions of the narrative threaten to frustrate the telling of his story. In an important sense, the interruptions to the poet's biography as told in the poem *parallel* the provenance of Baroness Rothschild's pearls. The metaphor presenting Jehuda Halevi's writing as pearly tears ('Perlentränen') insists that the central issue is the process of transmission in the reception and renewal of his work, and indeed that at its core are the tears shed by humanity through the ages.

However, the intervention from 'meine Frau' at the opening of Part IV is guided by a different consideration. She is alarmed by the idea that her husband might *not* immediately sell the casket of Darius for cash in order to buy her a cashmere shawl. This repeats the earlier reference to Heine's financial worries (B 6/1, 145; D 667), but more importantly stresses a factor already apparent in the dispersal of Darius' state jewels. Increasingly, the process that begins with Alexander's gifts (to his army, his mother, and even to his old teacher 'and the world's rump-thumper', Aristotle) comes to be dominated by the cash-nexus.[14] The same power is also evident, we have to reflect, in the encounter with tradition worked out at the end of *Romanzero*.

Mathilde's query and the fact that she has never even heard of Jehuda Halevi set off a recapitulation of the question of tradition traced out in the logic of the poem – but the sequence of the narrative continues to be subverted by digressions. Heine first attributes his wife's ignorance of Halevi to the inadequacy of Parisian girls' schools (including the one she had been to) and sketches a history of Jewish poetry in Spain. His assessment of Gabirol and ibn Ezra alongside Halevi is derived from 'Alcharisi':

> Alcharisi – der, ich wette,
> Dir nicht minder unbekannt ist,
> Ob er gleich, französ'scher Witzbold,
> Den Hariri überwitzelt
>
> Im Gebiete der Makame,
> Und ein Voltairianer war . . .
>
> (B 6/1, 151)

> Alcharisi – who no doubt you
> Also do not know although he
> Was a Gallic wag who out-wagged
> The *Makamat* of Hariri
>
> And in this department shone as
> A Voltairean . . .
>
> (D 672)

Once again, Heine is himself implied by this citation. The Arabic form of the 'Makamat', developed by the poet al-Hariri, deploys parody and allusion for critical effects; and al-Charisi had written a verse history of his antecedents in this form, just as Heine's narrative now repeats the action of retrospection in the witty form of his Spanish trochees. Yet in the very moment of re-establishing the continuity of the tradition and the supremacy of Jehuda Halevi, Heine interrupts his poem again with a digressive and fantastical account of ibn Ezra's travels.[15]

In the uncertainties and disappointments of ibn Ezra's life Heine recognizes the fate of poets as constant victims of ill fortune. Even Apollo, the father of all poets, suffered such a fate when he lost Daphne to her laurel bush and so became 'the divine Schlemiel'. The Jewish nickname for those who are dogged by bad luck begins a further digression on the etymology of the word made famous by Adelbert von Chamisso's tale *Peter Schlemihls wundersame Geschichte* (*The Strange Tale of Peter Schlemihl*). Chamisso and his book's Jewish dedicatee, Julius Eduard Hitzig, are dragged into the poem as expert witnesses.[16] A retelling of the tale of zealous Phinehas follows. In Numbers 25 he kills a man who had brought a Midianite woman into the camp of the Israelites. According to Heine's account Phinehas killed the wrong man, and 'Schlemihl Ben Zuri Schadday' died instead of the guilty Zimri. Acknowledging this universal ill fortune of poets, the poem ends with the story of the third of the Jewish poets of Spain, Gabirol. He is murdered by an envious moor, whose guilt is revealed by the sweetness of the figs borne on the tree under which he has buried the poet's body. (Heine's own poems are the sweet fruit of a suppressed tradition.) Under torture, the moor confesses his crime:

> Darauf riß man auch den Baum
> Mit den Wurzeln aus dem Boden,
> Und zum Vorschein kam die Leiche
> Des erschlagenen Gabirol.
>
> Diese ward mit Pomp bestattet
> Und betrauert von den Brüdern;
> An demselben Tage henkte
> Man den Mohren zu Corduba.
>
> (B 6/1, 158)

> Thereupon they tore the fig tree,
> Roots and all, up from the soil,
> And Gabirol's murdered body
> Was discovered to the light.
>
> With all pomp they reinterred him,
> And his brethren stood in mourning,
> On the selfsame day the moor was
> Hanged upon Cordova's gallows.
>
> (D 677)

At this point the work breaks off, but it is not at all clear how such a fragment could have been completed.[17] The pomp of the poet's funeral extends the celebration of his fame in life – a fame to which the poem itself now significantly contributes. As has been noted in other contexts already, a further element of self-reference is also apparent in this fantasy of posthumous glory: envious neighbours get their comeuppance, just like, Heine may have hoped, his supposedly treacherous cousin Carl, who, Heine believed, threatened to withhold the continuation of the allowance he had received from his uncle after Salomon Heine's death in 1844.[18] The digressive pattern of the poem has made it more or less impossible to return to the eponymous hero; but in the end all paths will lead back to the author, the modern instance of a line descended variously from Apollo, Psalm 137, and 'Schlemihl ben Zuri Schadday'.

Heine's poem has by now offered an alternative tradition – another kind of continuity. The transmission of the substance of tradition which the earlier parts of the poem enact is now shadowed by the inheritance of the Schlemihl. Heine marks the parallel by a characteristic repetition. In Part I, Halevi's life in the tradition of Psalm 137 opens with the phrase 'Jahre kommen und verfließen'; here in Part IV the Schlemihl-digression too ends with this phrase:

> Jahre kommen und vergehen –
> Drei Jahrtausende verflossen,
> Seit gestorben unser Ahnherr,
> Herr Schlemihl ben Zuri Schadday.
>
> Längst ist auch der Pinhas tot –
> Doch sein Speer hat sich erhalten,
> Und wir hören ihn beständig
> Über unsre Häupter schwirren.
> (B 6/1, 156)

> Years come round and years pass onward –
> Full three thousand years have fleeted
> Since the death of our forebear,
> Herr Schlemihl ben Zuri-shaddai.
>
> Phinehas is long dead also –
> But his spear is ever with us,
> And we constantly can hear it
> Swishing round above our heads.
> (D 675–6)

Phinehas ('Pinhas') and his spear come to represent here all those, like Ludwig Börne and his German republicans, whose zeal and puritanism set out to destroy the happy and the sensual, the witty and the frivolous that are the poet's privilege. The constant disturbances of tradition and cultural transmission are hence bridged by the other history, that of authoritarian repression. The exile of the Jewish poet Heinrich Heine, in Paris and in his protracted final illness, becomes the ultimate figure of a tradition of dereliction *and* heroic survival.

The tradition, displayed in 'Jehuda ben Halevy' through the mythical figures of Apollo, the Schlemihl, Jeremiah and the Babylonian exile, ekes out a threadbare existence in modern Paris. But the verses which had caught Adorno's attention present a different kind of threat or attenuation. Mathilde suggests that Darius' plundered casket, were it to come into her husband's possession, had much better be sold – since a cardboard box like Marquis's *bonbonnière* will suffice to hold the works of Halevi; but the status of the work handed on in tradition and worthy of preservation in the casket changes radically. The chinoiserie of the 'pretty box of cardboard' (D 670; B 6/1, 149) reveals it as the decorative and merely functional substitute for the original casket, which might have *treasured* the auratic texts of the past. We have seen that Heine's poem struggles to recall an almost forgotten tradition (the Jewish poets of twelfth-century Spain) in its historical context of Courtly Love, and then relates the *modern* poem's own lament for the makers to the other tradition, of dereliction, in which Halevi stands. In modernity the tradition runs out of steam. Its continuities have been disrupted by the failures of pedagogy and the enervation of narrative. Heine's tumbling anecdotes can remember what the memory of tradition was like, but in the modern moment of the present the form taken by a full realization of such memory is that of exhaustion.

The vehicle for this process is the mimed form of the Spanish romance. In the context of *Romanzero*, however, this form becomes more significant. Heine says in his 'Postscript' that he chose the title because the tone of the romance dominated in the poems (B 6/1, 180), but it is nevertheless clear that the proposal for the title in fact came from Heine's publisher. Campe promoted the new collection with enormous energy – and great success. Indeed, his efforts led him to a significant innovation in the history of the book-trade: the illustrated dust-jacket in which the book was issued;[19] the title too played a significant role in this commercial promotion because the romance as a genre (and even the single word of the title) had been immensely successful for publishers right across Europe ever since the mid 1840s.[20] In this context, Mathilde's suggestion about Marquis's *bonbonnières* seems to recognize the *commercial* appropriation of the poetic tradition.

In the first book of *Romanzero*, 'Historien', 'Der Dichter Firdusi' illustrates another encroachment of cash values into the sphere of the artist of tradition. Ferdausi wrote a history of the ancient kings of Persia, and cherished the memory of Iran's ancient Parsee religion. But the Shah, instead of paying him for this poetic labour in gold coin as he seemed to have promised, sends silver. The Shah's promise is conceived less as a 'unit price' – a thoman per line – than as an appropriate but not expressly *calculated* reward for the poet's skill. Ferdausi needs the money:

> Der Poet riß auf die Säcke
> Hastig, um am lang entbehrten
> Goldesanblick sich zu laben
>              (B 6/1, 50)

> Then the poet quickly opened
> Both the bags, to feast his eyes on
> All the gold he long had needed
>              (D 595)

– but instead of being an equal gesture rewarding his genius, the Shah's calculation makes of it a negotiable price. That is the point of Ferdausi's reaction: he divides the silver between the three men who have served him most recently: the Shah's messengers and the bath attendant. This restores the money to the status it should originally have had, in an act of gratitude and generosity. Ferdausi's greatest scorn is reserved for the Shah's unworthy exploitation of an ambiguity based on the fact there is only one name for the coin of the realm, whether of silver or gold. In the face of this false equivalence, the poet withdraws; and the generous gifts of the repentant Shah do not reach him before his impoverished death. Ferdausi's practice of memory and tradition cannot survive in an age when the uniqueness of greatness is subject to money's law of equivalences.

The relevance of Ferdausi's fate to Heine's own circumstances is not hard to see. The relationship between poet and patron, as in many other poems from the last period of Heine's work, stands for the breakdown in his relationship with his publisher, Campe, between 1848 and 1851, and also for the financial anxieties caused by the death of his uncle. Heine himself is profoundly affected by the process in which lyrical greatness is measured by monetary values. (Brecht's poems 'Schlechte Zeit für Lyrik' ('Bad Times for Poetry') and 'Lied der preiswerten Lyriker' ('Song of the Cut-price Poets') take up the same chorus.) However, the structure of 'Der Dichter Firdusi', as well as the substance of its narrative, repeats the lesson of exhaustion which is apparent when 'Jehuda ben Halevy' peters out. The line of the narrative is, in one sense, unrelieved. Ferdausi's epic emerges in a moment when the history of Persia's ancient kings has run aground on the reign of a Shah who has substituted meanness and trickery for generosity. When the poet takes up his 'Wanderstab' and sets off into exile, it is poetry itself which has departed. The ancient unity of poet and king cannot be recovered, no matter how generous any subsequent act of restitution may be – and there is every reason to think that the Shah would like to restore the poet to his old standing:

> Firdusi? – rief der Fürst betreten –
> Wo ist er? Wie geht es dem großen Poeten?
>
> (B 6/1, 52)

> 'Firdausi?' Upset, the king was staring:
> 'How is our noble poet faring?'
>
> (D 596)

But the Shah's reawakened generosity fails to reach the poet before his death. The tale unfolds in a relentless linearity: as the caravan of unimaginable wealth reaches Ferdausi's place of exile, the poet's body is carried out for burial.

In another sense, however, the unrelenting declension of the poem is played off against its variety. Each of its three parts is cast in a different form: the opening section deals with the composition of Ferdausi's most famous work, the *Schach Nameh* (*Book of the Kings*) in unrhymed trochaic four-line stanzas, which adopt an appropriate range of images for the Persian subject. Against this grand orientalizing manner, the second part of the poem sets a conversational tone in which the poet Ferdausi speaks in his own interest ('Hätt er menschlich ordinär/ Nicht gehalten was versprochen . . .' ('"If he had, like other men / failed to keep a promise, merely"')) and in *abba*-rhymed four-liners. Finally, the third part completes the narrative in iambic couplets, demonstrating, from time to time, Heine's notorious wit as a rhymster: 'Zins' (interest) rhymes with 'Provinz' (province), 'Kamele' (camel) variously with 'erwähle', 'Befehle', and 'Kehle' (choose; commands; throat); and 'Karawane' (caravan) with 'Führerfahne' (leader's flag). Only the four-beat rhythm remains consistent amid this burgeoning variety, but it has moved from the oriental mimicry of the first section to a *Verserzählung* (narrative poem) form close to *Knittelvers* in the third, which both looks back to Wieland in the eighteenth century and forward to Wilhelm Busch later in the nineteenth. Such formal variations demonstrate a virtuoso control of form and tone, and measure *Heine's* credentials as a poet. His retelling of an old tale, presented as oriental pastiche, as travesty, and in the demotic speech attributed to Ferdausi, reveals the *modern* gaze turned on the remote past. Heine the modern is apparent in the irony that recognizes the familiarity of the Shah's meanness and Ferdausi's fate. The sheer variety of ironic forms, however, threatens to slip into an infinite series.[21] Only a random interruption – the end of this particular narrative – apparently avoids the implied principle of proliferation.

Mathilde's intervention in Part IV of 'Jehuda ben Halevy' puts an end to these apparently endless variations by distracting the narrative with its own real-time context in Paris. Her interruption is significant in two ways: in offering to substitute packaging for an ancient artefact she demonstrates that the principle of 'the exchange of equivalent values' is incompatible with tradition.[22] More generally, her utterance draws attention to the discrepancy between the heroic world of the figures of tradition and the disenchanted truth of the everyday.

### THE MODERN CITY

The progress of the secular, charted in the decline of Ferdausi and the desacralization of art in 'Jehuda ben Halevy', is seen most clearly in 'Der Apollogott'. The god is first glimpsed in the context of a Romantic ballad in which a young nun observes his passage down the Rhine in the company of the Muses: far from being the *Apollon mousagetes* of classical myth, this exiled divinity is no more than the secularized figure of a popular street song. The young nun pursues her idol, only to be told that Phoebus is now identified as the cantor of the German synagogue in Amsterdam, Rabbi *Faibisch*. A *Jewish* Apollo most fully expresses the reality of the exile experience: the exiled god is Heine's contemporary – indeed, he has become identical with Heine, Jewish poet of and in exile.[23] In this way, 'The God Apollo' parallels the structure of 'Jehuda ben Halevy' in settling the exhausted legacy of the great tradition on its own author: the encounter of modernity with its predecessors in antiquity and history – Apollo and the muses, Jehuda, Ferdausi – is articulated as the constant meeting of the mythical with the personal and historical in the figure of Heine himself.[24]

The provisional end of a classical tradition is twice marked as *urban*. In the second poem of 'Der Apollogott', ancient Greece and modern Paris are elided:

> Ich bin der Gott der Musika,
> Verehrt in allen Landen;
> Mein Tempel hat in Grächa,
> Auf Mont-Parnaß gestanden

Auf Mont-Parnaß in Gräcia
Da hab ich oft gesessen
Am holden Quell Kastalia,
Im Schatten der Zypressen.
(B 6/1, 32f)

I am the god of music, I,
Beloved by lads and lasses,
My temple under Grecian sky
Stood on Mount Parnassus.

I often sat in times gone by
Upon Parnassus mountain
Where cypress shades and shimmers vie
Beside Castalia's fountain.
(D 581)

The insistent '-a' rhymes of this text, remarkably represented by Hal Draper's '-i' equivalents, sustained over eight stanzas, indicate parody and travesty.[25] Yet 'Mont-Parnaß in Gräcia' is not exactly a modernization of Mount Parnassus, but nor is it simply a joking allusion to Montparnasse in Paris: it indicates a point at which it is possible to see what the tradition of Parnassian Apollo and the Muses has now been reduced to, for it has come to rest in the theatres and bars of modern Paris; similarly, the discovery that 'Faibisch' Apollo gathered his muses from an Amsterdam 'Spielhuis' makes the moment of the advent of modernity specific in the nineteenth century city. (It is worth recalling that Büchner had dwelt on the coincidence of classical republican aspirations and low-life sensuality in *Danton's Death*, twenty years earlier.)

If 'Der Apollogott' and 'Jehuda ben Halevy', in their different ways, argue that the final resting place of an exhausted tradition is the modern city, the poem preceding 'Der Apollogott' provides the historical data of the emergence of this secular modernity. 'Pomare' takes the most significant possible place in the sequence of the 'Historien'. All of the preceding poems have recalled the defeat and discomfiture of aristocrats and monarchs. (This is even true of the satire on Gautier's Parnassian celebration of Countess Marie Kalergis, 'Der weiße Elefant'.) 'Pomare' interrupts and redefines this theme by presenting a vaudeville dancer who has named herself after the queen of Tahiti. The poems appearing under her name mark the point at which modern Paris, and therefore a modern polity, emerges in the historical series which has just concluded with poems on King Charles I ('Karl I') and Marie Antoinette, both of them victims of revolutionary execution.

'Karl I' presents an extremely sophisticated use of the traditional historical ballad. Its reference to the ballad tradition makes possible a contemporary political critique of great flexibility. While appearing to *rehearse* the popular form, with the reminiscences of a feudal-aristocratic society appropriate to the genre, Heine's poem opens up the generic text to contemporary reference.[26] 'Karl I' requires a double reading: in the terms given by its first publication, in 1847, it meditates on a moment before the decisive act of regicide. Read in this way, the ballad projects both the anxieties of a feudal social order aware of the growth of forces that will ultimately overthrow it, and the ideological 'lullaby' which is specifically designed to prevent those forces from recognizing their own strength. *After* 1848, however, the ballad evokes not so much aristocratic fears of proletarian overthrow, as the acknowledgement that democratic aspirations have come to nothing. The merely chronological parallel between 1649 and 1847–9 provides the groundwork for a complex argument about literature (the ballad as a popular form), ideology (the maintenance of feudal order in Germany), and revolutionary change. The twin impulses which provide the poem's energy are pre-revolutionary aspiration coupled with the anxiety and, ultimately, the pessimism of radical politics about realistic prospects for change. It is this pessimism which is finally resolved into post-revolutionary disappointment. The argument of the poem hence remains historical. By looking back to Charles I it remembers what was possible and how the ballads and lullabies of feudalism could resist that possibility. On the other hand, by reflecting the disappointment of radical aspirations after 1848, it can also remember revolutionary hope – but only to make it the measure of a *deferred* modernity. This is what modern readers sense as the element of pastiche in 'Karl I', miming a form it has shown is fossilized while acknowledging that its own ironies may be self-defeating.[27]

'Marie Antoinette', with its recollection of antecedents in the 'ghost ballad', functions in a similar way[28]. The ghosts of the dead queen and her courtiers are, quite literally, the spirits of the *ancien régime* which haunt the scenes of their former ceremonial splendour. In an act of archaeological interpretation, Heine points out the political meanings attached to the Tuileries. However, the poem does more than warn against the political dangers implicit in monarchist aspirations. Its grotesque heroine, daughter of Maria Theresia and grand-daughter of German Kaisers ('deutscher Cäsaren'), can do *no more* than haunt the present:

> Sie muß jetzt spuken ohne Frisur
> Und ohne Kopf, im Kreise
> Von unfrisierten Edelfraun,
> Die kopflos gleicherweise.
>
> (B 6/1, 27)

> She has to go haunting uncoiffured
> And headless, before the eyes
> Of noble dames who, just like her,
> Lack hair-do and head likewise.
>
> (D 576)

The rules of the royal *lever* are now fundamentally ludicrous. Heine's sense of the ridiculous extends and even over-extends his description of the 'empty posing' of court ceremonial, 'Ein leeres Gespreize, ganz wie sonst'. Ultimately the scene of royal pretension is finished off rhetorically by the sheer vulgarity of the modern world:

> Die Oberhofmeisterin steht dabei,
> Sie fächert die Brust, die weiße,
> Und in Ermangelung eines Kopfs
> Lächelt sie mit dem Steiße.
>
> (B 6/1, 28)

> The Mistress of the Robe stands by
> Fanning her breast with care,
> And since she's lacking in a head,
> She smiles with her derrière.
>
> (D 577)

What is coarse about this is designed as a direct confrontation of the rather circumstantial vocabulary of the poem, the Gallicisms and archaisms of Heine's parody of ceremony. This ritual of the past may haunt the present as a threat of renewed feudal monarchy, but the sheer vulgarity of the smiling arse is the symbol of a powerful and popular secularism that traditional aristocracy simply cannot survive.

'Karl I' and 'Marie Antoinette' provide the decisive context for 'Pomare' in relation to the aristocratic theme of the earlier parts of the 'Historien' and its political secularization. The images of a monarchy deposed are now realized in the strictly *metaphorical* sense of Pomare's claims to be a queen. Her travesty of royalty provides an index of secular modernity, in the very moment at which Paris fully appears in *Romanzero*. The dense meanings of the two preceding poems, with their intricate negotiation of the relation of past and present in radical memory and the transmission of power, invite a similarly vigilant reading of 'Pomare': if the dancer's name reveals kingship as at best metaphorical, in the second poem of the series her dance recalls a beheading. Salome's dance before Herod, which Pomare evokes, refers, in the context of Parisian politics after the July Revolution, to the Saint Simonian triumph of the flesh over the Baptist's asceticism, as well as recalling the guillotining of 'Marie Antoinette'. However, there is a wider pattern in the poem's handling of an antiquated institution. The modern gaze turned on the past can only cite it as myth. Heine's poems on 'König David' ('King David') and 'Das goldne Kalb' ('The Golden Calf') later in the 'Historien' repeat this movement of secularization: the dance around the golden calf of Exodus is only intelligible as the glorification of capital in modern Paris, just as the patriarchal King David can only be quoted as evidence of the cynicism of autocracy.

Pomare's cancan, the revolutionary dance, establishes the political meanings of her popularity, but the remaining poems of the sequence present a different destiny. In the first instance, Pomare is lured by her new-found wealth to behave with the disdain of the *ancien régime*; however, her success as a latter-day Salome is overwhelmed by her career as a courtesan, in poem III, by her death and, in the last poem, by her funeral. In one sense the montage, in 'Pomare', of poems which had previously appeared separately offers no more than a realistic reconstruction of the Parisian milieu in which a dancer might well accept the role of mistress, only to become a common prostitute dying in penury. The circumstances of her burial –

> Keinen Pfaffen hört' man singen,
> Keine Glocke klagte schwer;
> Hinter deiner Bahre gingen
> Nur dein Hund und dein Friseur.
> (B 6/1, 31)

> No hymn from your priest-confessor,
> No sad bells tolled on the ear;
> Only your dog and your hairdresser
> Followed close behind your bier.
> (D 579)

– marvellously anticipate Heine's own 'Gedächtnisfeier' (commemoration service), in the second book of *Romanzero*, when neither a Requiem Mass nor the Jewish Kaddish is to be said; at the same time, this meagre ceremony exemplifies the desacralization of life and death by the everyday, figured here by the dog and hairdresser. In 'Pomare', therefore, Heine could be said to fulfil one of Adorno's fundamental requirements by way of the archetypes of modernity; for he presents the extent to which human beings are themselves transformed into mere commodities.[29]

In the classical case of such reification, Baudelaire's 'Une Charogne', the dead prostitute ('Her legs spread out like a lecherous whore') is presented as entirely physical, a being reduced merely to its constituent parts:

> Le soleil rayonnait sur cette pourriture,
> Comme afin de la cuire à point,
> Et de rendre au centuple à la grande Nature
> Tout ce qu'ensemble elle avait joint.
>
> The sun on this rottenness focussed its rays
> To cook the cadaver till done,
> And render to Nature a hundredfold gift
> Of all she'd united in one.[30]

The comparison with Heine's procedure is instructive. He too presents the dead body of the dancer-prostitute as a merely physical object; but instead of allowing the cadaver to return to nature, Pomare is the necessary commodity of the medical school anatomy-class: which is not to say that the medical school is ultimately any different from the knackers.

> Und der Carabin mit schmierig
> Plumper Hand und lernbegierig
> Deinen schönen Leib zerfetzt,
> Anatomisch ihn zersetzt –
> Deine Rosse trifft nicht minder
> einst zu Montfaucon der Schinder.
>
> (B 6/1, 30)

> And some clumsy dirty-handed
> Student slashes, as commanded,
> At your body fair and still
> For his anatomic drill –
> And your steeds will end ill-starred
> One day in a knacker's yard.
>
> (D 579)

In the whole movement of 'Pomare' Heine constantly provides a social context for his critique of the commodity as it is given institutional status in theatre or vaudeville, prostitution and anatomical dissection. But the *form* of this third poem should not escape our attention either. The contexts of the commodity appear, here, in trochaic couplets. Pomare's fate emerges in a vernacular form reminiscent, once again, of *Knittelvers*, and hence appears as the most everyday event. Perhaps these lines should recall popular *Bänkelsang*, in a devalued and disenchanted moral judgement of the way of *all* flesh. The knackers of Montfaucon (as the pseudo-comic rhyme on 'nicht minder' and 'Schinder' indicates) put a stop to the proliferating couplets of the third poem, but they cannot provide a closure that is not ironic.

There is another important way in which 'Pomare' provides a key to the forms in which Heine derives archetypes for the Parisian modernity which dominates in this poem. In the last section, he considers the traditional sources of consolation – a good death and Christian burial. But this 'funeral celebration' is bare and impoverished, conducted without benefit of clergy and theologically hollow:

> Arme Königin des Spottes,
> Mit dem Diadem von Kot,
> Bist gerettet jetzt durch Gottes
> Ewge Güte, du bist tot.
>
> Wie die Mutter, so der Vater
> Hat Barmherzigkeit geübt,
> Und ich glaube, dieses tat er,
> Weil auch du so viel geliebt.
>
> (B 6/1, 31)

> Ah poor queen of mocking faces,
> Crown of mud upon your head,
> Now you're saved by the good graces
> Of the Lord, for you are dead.
>
> As your mother, so the Father
> Showed you mercy from above;
> This, I think, he did the rather
> Since you too gave so much love.
>
> (D 580)

The fluency of Heine's verse contains great complexity and ambivalence. Pomare is not rich but rather the *poor* queen of scorn, and it is unclear whether she is 'queen of scorn' because she dispensed her mockery to others or because she is the object of a social contempt which is now all her realm. Ultimately the queen of derision is defined by her laughable pretensions, on the stage where she began. The rhyme of 'Spottes' (derision, scorn) with the enjambement of 'durch Gottes / Ewge Güte' (literally 'through God's eternal goodness') indicates a comic turn, but only in preparation for the theological bathos of 'you are dead'. Salvation is reduced here, finally, to death itself, which is at least preferable to the ministrations of the medical students in the previous poem. But even this is capped by the final stanza's blasphemous citation of Jesus' saying in Luke 7, 47: 'Her sins, which are many, are forgiven; for she loved much' ('Ihr sind viele Sünden vergeben, denn sie hat viel geliebt'). Pomare's death comes about because she has 'loved' so much, with the implication that its cause was venereal disease. Such is the mercy of God the Father.

When Pomare dies in her poor old mother's garret the resources of sentiment are demonstrably exhausted. This old woman looks back to the poverty of 'Das ist ein schlechtes Wetter' ('This surely is dreadful weather' in the *Buch der Lieder*); the parallel between God the Father and Pomare's mother in the final stanza ('Wie die Mutter, so der Vater') remains uneasy because the pastoral effects of the contrast between divine love and maternal human care, which it sketches as the transcendent realized in the domestic, are undone by the context of theatrical sleaze, betrayal and sheer poverty. In Heine's modernity, the residual *memento mori* which concludes Baudelaire's 'Une charogne' ('– Et pourtant vous serez semblable à cette ordure') is not possible. Modern Paris sours the very material of moral consolation.[31]

EVERYDAY LIFE

The city appears in 'Pomare' in its most public forms: the vaudeville theatres, the public streets and parks, and finally the cemetery. This Paris leaves an intermittent trace through Heine's later poetry from the 'Sundry Women' sequences of *Neue Gedichte* and the Jardin des Plantes in *Atta Troll* to the poems of 1853 and 1854. Just as Apollo acknowledges the imperative of the quotidian, so too Heine's lyrics of Parisian life accede to the dominance of the everyday. One of Heine's best-known poems, already referred to, the 'Gedächtnisfeier' ('Commemoration Service') in the 'Lazarus' cycle of the second book of *Romanzero*, rejects even the formalities of funeral ceremonial and yearsmind in favour of an everyday mourning. Heine's wife Mathilde visits the cemetery in Montmartre 'when the weather is fine and mild', and, however moved she may be, the poem ends with a wonderful note of realism:

> Keine Messe wird man singen,
> Keinen Kadosch wird man sagen,
> Nichts gesagt und nichts gesungen
> Wird an meinen Sterbetagen.
>
> Doch vielleicht an solchem Tage,
> Wenn das Wetter schön und milde,
> Geht spazieren auf Montmartre
> Mit Paulinen Frau Mathilde.
>
> Mit dem Kranz von Immortellen
> Kommt sie mir das Grab zu schmücken,

Und sie seufzet: Pauvre homme!
Feuchte Wehmut in den Blicken.

Leider wohn ich viel zu hoch,
Und ich habe meiner Süßen
Keinen Stuhl hier anzubieten;
Ach! sie schwankt mit müden Füßen.

Süßes, dickes Kind, du darfst
Nicht zu Fuß nach Hause gehen;
An dem Barrieregitter
Siehst du die Fiaker stehen.

(B 6/1, 113)

Not a mass will be sung for me,
Not a *Kaddish* will be said,
None will say or sing a service
On the day that I lie dead.

But on some such day it may be,
If good weather is foreseen,
Ma'am Mathilde will go strolling
On Montmartre with Pauline.

She will come to deck my grave with
*Immortelles*, and say with sighs:
'*Pauvre homme!*' and wipe a teardrop
Of damp sorrow from her eyes.

But, alas, I shall be living
Too high up – there'll be no seat
I can offer to my darling
As she sways on weary feet.

Oh you sweet and chubby child, you
Must not walk home all the way;
You'll see coaches standing ready
At the barrier gate that day.

(D 644)

The cabs wait at the city boundary marked by Louis-Philippe's fortifications: Heine's poem moves from the secular impulse of its opening to ready acquiescence in the ordinary realities of Paris at its close.

'Gedächtnisfeier' works its way towards this unemphatic last line via a careful management of the resources of irony. The familiar trochaic tetrameters of the first stanza in fact present a much grander rhythmic movement, focussed on the words 'Messe', 'Kadosch', and the repetition of 'nichts'; this gains a strong sense of cadence from the enjambement of 'gesungen / Wird'

leading to the rhyme. The 'Doch' of stanza 2, introducing the uncere-
monious celebration of the anniversaries of Heine's death, therefore, also
introduces a tripping counter-rhythm which echoes the good spirits of his
wife and her friend Pauline Rogue as they set out for Montmartre on a fine
day. The third stanza distances itself from the emotion of the occasion by
including a French phrase, so that the less than silent final /e/ of 'homme'
becomes comically over-stressed by its position in the German metrical
scheme. The emergence of the poem into French at this point has been
prepared by the earlier appearance of Montmartre and of the 'immortelles'
of Mathilde's wreath. French is also the language of the everyday, set in
contrast to the ritual Hebrew of the kaddish and the implied Latin of the
Requiem Mass. The stanza wryly acknowledges the limits of Mathilde's –
perhaps sentimental – 'Feuchte Wehmut' ('damp sorrow'), but it does not
undermine its sincerity; and the final stanzas continue to hold this hint of
irony in check. The notorious rhyme and assonance on 'meiner Süßen' /
'mit müden Füßen' (for my sweet / with weary feet) does not step beyond
the bounds of realism. Mathilde, overweight, must take a cab; and with a
final French word the poem comes to rest, apparently as reconciled to its
urban setting as T. S. Eliot's 'lonely cab-horse' in the 'Preludes'.

Yet this recognition of the day-to-day plainness of city life, formally
echoing the rejection of ceremony announced at the start, excludes any
satisfactory tone of closure just as much as it does any emotional afflatus.
Such an uneasy balance is characteristic.[32] Heroic gestures, for instance,
are demonstrably inappropriate. In 'Zwei Ritter' ('Two Knights') they
are unmasked as evidence of the bad faith of self-deluded Polish patriots. Crapülinski and Waschlapski are down-at heel survivors who, like
Herwegh in 'Der Ex-Lebendige' ('The Ex-Living Man') and Dingelst-
edt in 'Der Ex-Nachtwächter' ('The Ex-Night Watchman') among Heine's
'Lamentations', must come to an accommodation with the slackening of
energy and resolve which is also the everyday. Conversely, in Heine's domestic poems about his concern for his wife, such as 'An die Engel' in the
*Romanzero* 'Lazarus' cycle or 'Ich war, o Lamm, als Hirt bestellt' ('I was,
my lamb, your shepherd here') from the uncollected poems, the high style
and high feeling of religious rhetoric is ironically undone by the particularity of the case: in 'An die Engel' the mythological grandeur of 'dread
Thanatos', with its associated language of 'Schattenreich' ('the realm of the
shades') and the classicizing syntax of the line 'Wird Witwe sie und Waise
sein' is challenged by the rhymes on Mathilde ('eurem Ebenbilde', 'Huld
und Milde') which conclude the last two stanzas. It would be inappropriate
to describe this effect as bathos. There is real sentiment in the way the poem

names Heine's wife, but her *ordinariness* is the focus of attention rather than the older language of myth or of a prayer to the guardian angels.

The interruption of tradition and of narrative which Mathilde's intervention brings about in 'Jehuda ben Halevy' is recapitulated whenever banal daily life takes over from poetic imagery and diction. Within the severe constraints of Heine's sickroom and 'mattress grave', it is often *sound* alone which comes to signify the dystopia of the everyday. 'Frau Sorge' ('Dame Care') focuses on the squeaking lid of the snuff-box used by the nurse who sits with Heine, and in the final stanza on the noise of her blowing her nose, which *interrupts* his reverie.

> An meinem Bett in der Winternacht
> Als Wärterin die Sorge wacht.
> Sie trägt eine weiße Unterjack,
> Ein schwarzes Mützchen, und schnupft Tabak.
>
> > Die Dose knarrt so gräßlich,
> > Die Alte nickt so häßlich.
> >
> > (B 6/1, 115)

> Beside my bed this winter night
> Old Care keeps watch, a nurse in white;
> Her cap is black; she sits and rocks
> And snuffs tobacco from a box.
>
> > The box-lid squeak is grating;
> > The ugly old dame's waiting.
> >
> > (D 645)

This poem takes up themes and diction from the motto poem of the second book of *Romanzero*, the 'Lamentations', and from 'Rückschau' ('Looking Backward'), the second of the 'Lazarus' poems. Its central figure, 'Frau Sorge', is named in such a way as to recall *Care*, the last and most persistent of the four grey women in Goethe's *Faust Part II*. There may even be a more extensive Faustian subtext. Goethe's Sorge is an appropriate sickroom-attendant for Heine: she is sister to death and heralds his coming; indeed, the sound associated with Frau Sorge's snuff-box also announces her arrival in *Faust*.[33] She puts in an appearance elsewhere in Heine's work. In 'Rückschau' the poet had been oppressed 'by black cares' ('bedrängt von schwarzen Sorgen', B 6/1, 106), so that when a similar dark woman blinds him with her kiss in the second of the additional 'Lazarus' poems in *Gedichte 1853 & 1854* (*Poems 1853 & 1854*) ('die schwarze Frau . . . küßte mir blind die Augen' (B 6/1, 202)), there is a reminiscence of the moment when Sorge blinds Faust in Goethe's drama. This blinding goes hand in hand, for Faust, with his disenchantment and the foreswearing of magical powers which must precede his full imaginative recognition of a wholly human world and its incessant and heroic activity, reclaiming land from the sea to achieve independent human community. But in poem after poem Heine shows the failure of this utopia. Modernity for him is an experience of standstill.

### MODERNITY AND CONTINUITY

Everyday life is indicated by images of banality and articulated by strategies of non-closure, often working against the emotional or rhetorical force of poetic diction. The subject himself, in poems of extraordinary *finality*, is presented in anti-heroic terms of exhaustion and emptiness. 'Sie erlischt', poem 18 in the *Romanzero* 'Lazarus' cycle and 'Der Scheidende' ('Parting Word' in Draper's version; literally 'the departing one') define Heine's sickness and prospective death as the exhaustion of the poetic.

Modernity understood as the supervention of the everyday is presented in 'Sie erlischt' as an *empty theatre*:

> Der Vorhang fällt, das Stück ist aus,
> Und Herrn und Damen gehn nach Haus.
> Ob Ihnen auch das Stück gefallen?
> Ich glaub ich hörte Beifall schallen.
> Ein hochverehrtes Publikum
> Beklatschte dankbar seinen Dichter.
> Jetzt aber ist das Haus so stumm,
> Und sind verschwunden Lust und Lichter.
>
> Doch horch! ein schollernd schnöder Klang
> Ertönt unfern der öden Bühne; –
> Vielleicht daß eine Saite sprang
> An einer alten Violine.
> Verdrießlich rascheln im Parterr
> Etwelche Ratten hin und her,
> Und alles riecht nach ranzgem Öle.
> Die letzte Lampe ächzt und zischt
> Verzweiflungsvoll und sie erlischt.
> Das arme Licht war meine Seele.
>
> (B 6/1, 119)

> The curtain falls, the play is through,
> The gentlefolk go home on cue.
> And did they like the play, I wonder?
> I think I heard the *Bravos* thunder.
> A much respected public clapped

Its thanks to the poet for the play.
But now the house is silence-wrapped,
Laughter and lights have dimmed away.

But hark, a sound rings dull and thin
From somewhere near the empty stage:
Perhaps a string has snapped within
A violin decayed with age.
Some rats are scurrying here and there
Rustling around the dim parterre,
A rancid reek from every hole.
The last lamp sputters low in doubt,
It groans despair, and it goes out.
That last poor light was my own soul.

                                  (D 648)

The image of the final curtain was sufficiently powerful for Heine to repeat
the opening line of this poem within the different poetic development of
'Der Scheidende' (B 6/1, 349–50).[34] There, the departing audience provides
a prospect of domestic pleasures preferable even to an heroic death. In 'Sie
erlischt' what dominates is the emptiness of the theatre. The sensitivity
to sound which was apparent in the squeaking of Dame Care's snuff-box
produces the positively Chekhovian effect of the snapping violin string;
but that noise, both uncanny and vulgar ('schnöd'), is succeeded by the
'groaning' and 'hissing' oil-lamp of the soul.[35] These noises suggest a later
archetype: the irritated solitude of the domestic interior in Baudelaire's
*Spleen* poem 'Pluviôse irrité contre la ville entière' in *Les Fleurs du Mal*.

L'âme d'un vieux poète erre dans la gouttière
Avec la triste voix d'un fantôme frileux.
Le bourdon se lamente, et la bûche enfumée
Accompagne en fausset la pendule enrhumée, . . .

Some poet's phantom roams the gutter-spouts
Moaning and whimpering like a freezing soul.
A great bell wails – within the smoking log
Pipes in falsetto to a wheezing clock . . .[36]

Baudelaire's interior is dominated by the sight of his mangy cat and the
reminiscences of malicious gossip and old love-affairs. Heine, on the other
hand, is constantly accompanied by his anxieties about Mathilde's future
and by his own inescapable illness. In the empty auditorium the extinction
of the soul leaves an uncanny and anxious space, populated by scurrying
rats. Survival, in this group of poems, can only be unheroic, and the shade
of Achilles is right. Yet vestiges of a moralizing interpretation of the fact of

death remain: even in this darkened theatre, the phrase 'That last poor light was my own soul' ('Das arme Licht war meine Seele') retains the pathos of individuality, prepared in the fine adverbial extension of 'ächzt und zischt' ('groans and hisses') beyond the line-end in 'Verzweiflungsvoll' ('full of doubt') at the beginning of the previous line.[37] Ultimately even this pathos can be withdrawn.

In Heine's later poetry his remarkable craftsmanship manipulates versification in the direction of prose. In poem 8 of the additional 'Lazarus' cycle in *Gedichte 1853 & 1854* ('Zum Lazarus' ('To Lazarus')) for example, Heine (probably) meditates on the letter of sympathy written by his cousin Therese after her belated visit to Paris in 1853. Although the poem begins in high style with its 'lightning flash that lit up bright / The night's abyss' (D 713), the prose rhythm that follows allows normal syntax, carried across the line-end, to render the line break almost inoperative: 'your letter revealed how deep my misfortune is' – 'Er [dein Brief] zeigte blendend hell, wie tief / Mein Unglück ist, wie tief entsetzlich' (B 6/1, 206).

Alternatively, *excessive* rhyme withdraws the legitimacy of the poetic, as in the earlier poem 6 from the same group of amatory reminiscences in the supplementary Lazarus cycle:

> Du warst ein blondes Jungfräulein, so artig,
> So niedlich und so kühl – vergebens harrt ich
> Der Stunde, wo dein Herze sich erschlösse
> Und sich daraus Begeisterung ergösse –
>
> Begeisterung für jene hohen Dinge,
> Die zwar Verstand und Prosa achten gringe,
> Für die jedoch die Edlen, Schönen, Guten
> Auf dieser Erde schwärmen, leiden, bluten.
>
> (B 6/1, 204f.)

> You were a blonde young lady, well behaved,
> So proper and so cool – in vain I craved
> The hour when your heart unclosed, revealing
> Its depths of inspiration and high feeling –
>
> High feeling for those lofty sentiments
> Too often scorned by prosy common sense,
> Which yet the best and noblest men we know
> Give all their dreams and suffering here below.
>
> (D 712)

The excessive rhymes ('artig'/'harrt ich', 'Dinge'/'gringe'), the circumstantial rhyming subjunctives of the first stanza ('erschlösse', 'ergösse'), the metrically necessary but grammatically redundant -e on 'Herze', the parallel lists at the end of the second stanza, together with the explicit contrast with prosaic understanding and the consistent dominance of prose syntax (in stanza 1) mean that, cumulatively, the opening of this poem does more than challenge recognizable poetic diction. In what follows, of course, cliché is the main target, until the poem climaxes in sarcasm:

> Als wie ein Mädchenbild gemalt von Netscher;
> Ein Herzchen im Korsett wie'n kleiner Gletscher.
> (B 6/1, 205)

> Just like a girl conceived by Netscher's art –
> Beneath your stays, a glacier for a heart.
> (D 712)

Even here the additive structure of the couplets weakens the sense of closure proffered by the extreme rhyme on a proper name.

In such poems verse-technique is deployed to *dramatize* non-closure. The everyday presents itself as the 'normal' continuity of the mattress-grave, as the unexceptional pleasures of an 'homme moyen sensuel', as the ordinary demands of domesticity. In two important cases, the possibility of closure is disturbed in a different way: 'Disputation', the poem which concludes the 'Hebräische Melodien' in *Romanzero*, and 'Für die Mouche' ('I dreamed a dream upon a summer night'), the poem generally regarded as Heine's last. In each case, the poem abandons an exhausted 'irony' in which dialectical tension has been reduced to a banal repetition of blank contradictions – between Jew and Christian, between Hellenic pleasure and Mosaic asceticism. To awake from an endless series of contradictions returns the dissatisfied visionary to the everyday – of the grimly empty theatre and the domesticity of the humblest living philistine in Stuttgart – 'Stukkert on Neckar', home of Swabian pietism and the Swabian moral poets ('Der kleinste lebendige Philister / Zu Stukkert am Neckar' (B 6/1, 350)). The boredom of the unresolved controversy or the ennui of bourgeois daily life are experiences of temporal continuity in which even death itself fails to constitute an *event*.

### MODERNITY AT A STANDSTILL

In the famous 'Nachwort' to *Romanzero* Heine offers a final image of the *empty* continuity of modernity as he sets out to bid a tearful farewell to his readers. To avoid such sentimentality he reminds them of the prospect of renewed acquaintance in the afterlife where, he is convinced, he will

continue to write and his audience to read. His guarantor for this conviction is Swedenborg. The point of this reference to Swedenborg might
be understood as part and parcel of Heine's return to belief in a personal
God; however quizzical his poetic investigations of the figures of Lazarus
and Job may be, the evocation of the Prodigal Son returning to the Father
after 'a long time tending swine with the Hegelians' (B 6/1, 182; D 695)
carries conviction.[38] There are also strong signs, however, that Swedenborg
serves a different purpose in a context that is at least light-hearted and even
anti-theological.

Heine's attention appears to have been drawn to Swedenborg by Eduard
von Fichte, who understood his appearance in the 'Postscript' as evidence
of Heine's determination to *rid* himself of philosophical arguments for the
survival of the soul. Heine's own letter to I. H. Fichte about the 'Postscript'
gives the same impression. His appropriation of Swedenborg smacks of
opportunism: 'In a book I am publishing at this very moment in Hamburg
I could turn what you said about Swedenborg to very good account.'[39]
Beyond any personal theological quest, Heine's account of his revised religious understanding is presented as a negotiation of social and political
debates. His need for a divinity with the intentional and even physical
attributes of a *personal* God is *dated* to 1848. According to the 'Postscript',
the failure of Heine's health (and wealth) occasioning the revision of his
religious scepticism happened in May, while in his autobiography, the
*Geständnisse* (B 6/1, 475), the date is *February*. This discrepancy is instructive. The promise of an afterlife emerges in the historical moment of a
workers' revolt, the ludicrous hesitations of the Provisional Government
of 1848;[40] and the 'after' of this afterlife clearly points towards the failure
of the June Days and the suppression of revolt by a bourgeois republican
regime. Against this 'atheist' bourgeois republic (itself shortly to become
Louis Bonaparte's Second Empire), Heine reasserts his democratic credentials, his belief in a personal God, and even a continued devotion to the
pagan gods of his earlier work.

All this needs to be borne in mind if Heine's use of Swedenborg is to be
understood. The failure of the ancient gods, figured as the amputation of
the Venus de Milo, bonds them to Heine's own physical debility: though he
must bid Venus farewell, he has foresworn nothing; and, as we have seen,
the secularization and even judaization of Apollo in his exile from Greece
makes his condition *coincide with* Heine's own. The experience of present
reality is suffused with the transmission of the past, and in an imaginative
leap tradition is enlivened at the very moment of its destruction. This had
been the fundamental structure of *Romanzero*. Heine's most immediate

personal reality is his own interminable dying: 'I am dying so slowly that it is becoming positively boring for me as much as for my friends,' he remarks (B 6/1, 180; cf. D 693); and his moribund continuance figures in the poems as a domestic status quo.

The supplementary 'Lazarus' cycle in the *Gedichte 1853 & 1854* twice presents his condition as an immobilized continuity. The third poem very precisely sets out two temporal frames. The first is the time of the present as stasis:

> Wie langsam kriechet sie dahin,
> Die Zeit, die schauderhafte Schnecke!
> Ich aber, ganz bewegungslos
> Bleib ich hier auf demselben Flecke.
>
> (B 6/1, 202)

> How slowly time, the dreadful snail,
> Comes crawling with its sluggish pace!
> But I, who cannot stir at all,
> Am fixed here in the selfsame place.
>
> (D 710)

The poem goes on to describe the author's condition as a kind of death ('Perhaps I have been long since dead'), haunted in his dreams by the phantoms of pagan divinities. The only place in which these two temporalities – of contemporary stasis and historical haunting – can be brought together is in the action of the poem itself:

> Die schaurig süßen Orgia,
> Das nächtlich tolle Geistertreiben,
> Sucht des Poeten Leichenhand
> Manchmal am Morgen aufzuschreiben.
>
> (B 6/1, 202)

> These dread, sweet orgies of the night,
> Mad revels of a spectral play –
> Often the poet's lifeless hand
> Will try to write them down next day.
>
> (D 710)

This double time, held in the structure of the poem, is the mark of the great poems of *Romanzero* as well as the *Gedichte 1853 & 1854*; it looks back to *Atta Troll* and the Wild Hunt, forward to 'Für die Mouche'. Heine finds no scope for heroic gestures in dreaming and registering what has been lost. In the Lazarus poem the poet's corpse-like hand only *attempts* to record his dreams. The alternative is provided by poem 11 in the second Lazarus sequence, in which, like the Greenlanders at the end of the *Romanzero* 'Postscript', who reject a Christian heaven that has no place for their seals, Heine renounces the joys of the afterlife for the continuity of a bourgeois domesticity: 'beside my wife in statu quo!' (B 6/1, 208; D 715).[41]

Heine's 'Postscript' to *Romanzero* reveals that his paralysis *also* coincides with the condition of modernity. But while his immobilization can be projected as the continuity of domestic bliss, the afterlife cited from Swedenborg defines its own paralysis in rigid fossilization ('fossile Erstarrung' (B 6/1, 185)) as an endless repetition of the same: in Heaven the majority of history's famous personalities 'remained unchanged and occupy themselves with the same things they did before; they remained static' ('stationär') (D 697)); on the rare occasions when some of the great and good have changed, this can only confirm the unchallenged way of the world. In Swedenborg's afterlife nothing changes, and even the corruption of saints (Antony and Susanna) or the moral conversion of the sexually perverse (Lot's daughters) simply reflect, Heine argues, the bad continuity of life after 1848. Beyond the walls of his sick-room, outside the mattress grave, Heine senses with growing anxiety the rapacious modernity which has been unleashed in Paris, not merely, as Benjamin's Baudelaire book has it, the capital of the nineteenth century, but 'the world capital of light' ('die leuchtende Hauptstadt der Welt' (D 703)) evoked in 'Babylonian Anxieties' ('Babylonische Sorgen' (B 6/1, 193)). In spite of all this activity, the Second Republic and the Second Empire spell only political inertia.

AFTER 1848

Heine's sensitivity to Mathilde's interruption, the contemporary distraction, sounds a familiar note of warning in relation to the modernizing and secularizing forces which the 'Tales' of *Romanzero* record. Mathilde interrupts an already disjointed and meandering narrative to insist that, like anything else, the casket of Darius – and the process of tradition which it represents – has its price. A parallel anxiety is evident in the French preface to *Lutetia*, when Heine contemplates the sombre iconoclasts of the communist movement who herald a time when pages from *Das Buch der Lieder* are used for a bag of coffee or a twist of snuff (B 5, 232). In the late poetry he recognizes all too clearly the consequences, for poetry and for the articulation of experience, of social forms dominated by the commodity – though, on Cook's reading, he also believed that his poetry still had the resources to mount a resistance.[42] Unlike Walter Benjamin, Heine derives the baleful condition of modernity from the political failure of 1848 rather than from economic and socio-psychological factors structuring the experience of time.[43] Against the homogeneity of this political afterlife, projected as Swedenborg's vision of heaven in the *Romanzero* 'Postscript', Heine pits all the resources of tradition, classical and above all Jewish, renewed and revitalized in the work of the poems themselves and of his own activity as poet. It is an unequal struggle. In their engagements with cultural and political history, held prismatically in his own experience of exile, Heine can register the condition – and claims – of modernity after 1848, even if the position is hopeless, a position already 'lost / In Freedom's war' ('verlorner Posten in dem Freiheitskriege' (B 6/1, 120; D 649)).

This famous phrase opens the last of the Lazarus poems in *Romanzero*, a poem which Heine originally intended to call 'Verlorner Schildwacht' ('Lost Sentry'); its final French title, 'Enfant perdu', is largely unexplained. It has been suggested that Heine was already thinking of a French translation of his original title as 'Sentinelle perdue',[44] but the retrospective character of the poem suggests the child we should think of is the one who wanted to have been born on New Year's Eve 1799, and thus to be biographically in the vanguard of nineteenth-century modernity. Heine's emancipatory project 'in freedom's war' was overtaken by another modernity, after 1830 in the July Monarchy and again after 1848. As its scans the fate of tradition, his late poetry engages with the claims of this modernity so that, in the great poems, through the paralysis of his own experience, and in imaginative self-identification with poets of the past, a whole history becomes legible.

Walter Benjamin could hardly have asked for more.[45]

# PART IV

# Epilogue

# CHAPTER II

# The tribe of Harry: Heine and contemporary poetry

In this final chapter I shall ask how some contemporary poets have read Heine, as they take up and extend his poetic practice. The investigation takes its cue from English poetry and the *tribe of Ben* celebrated by Ben Jonson in his 'Epistle to one who would be sealed of the tribe of Ben'. For the poet's followers, membership of the tribe (who were also known as the Sons of Ben) came to signify a certain set of aesthetic commitments, to convivial wit and to the plain style – and, in the poem that commemorates their solidarity, to a certain degree of resistance to 'the animated porcelain of the court'.[1] For a number of reasons a *tribe* of Harry Heine provides an appropriate term with which to assess Heine's poetic posterity. The *Romanzero* poem 'Jehuda ben Halevy' shows the extent to which the fate of poetry, in its transmission to subsequent generations, is an important question for Heine himself. Just as Heine's reverence, in that poem, for the Jewish poets of medieval Spain amounts to a self-definition as their modern avatar, so too among contemporary poets Heine will prove to be more than a formal model for modern appropriation. Secondly, the notion of a *tribe of Harry* raises the question of filiation in relation to Heine's reception in the twentieth century. Karl Kraus's polemic 'Heine and the Consequences' raised the question of his influence and of the consequences, for the status of literature and literary language, of sustained imitation by contemporaries. Because Heine's style was itself derivative, Kraus argued, it can be infinitely replicated by 'successors' who in fact anticipate their supposed model: 'This is an original that loses the very thing that it suggested to others. And can something be an original when its imitators improve on it?'[2] This reverses the usual order of precedence from originality to imitation, or from source to influence. The priority of successor over predecessor, as Kraus understands it, means that Heine's work actually destroys the possibility of tradition. He has allowed the repetitive, reified structures of the commodity to gain access to the inner sanctum of the aesthetic.

The response of the 'writing expert', as Kraus called himself, is so allergic that the rights and wrongs of his case are scarcely relevant; yet, as J. L. Sammons pointed out over a decade ago, the effects of Kraus's essay are still very much alive in the critical and scholarly community.[3] Kraus clearly is right, however, to see Heine as in some sense tangential to the main lines of development in the German lyric. Many of the strongest poets writing in German after 1945 have claimed a different line of descent. Hölderlin, the Romantics, and then Rilke have been the dominant influences in a poetry which has characteristically aspired to the sublime. In his *Journal* Brecht identifies the fracture between this 'pontifical line' and its profane counterpart derived from Heine:

that splendid unity, so full of contradiction, collapsed immediately after goethe; HEINE taking the wholly secular line, HÖLDERLIN the wholly pontifical. of these the former saw the dissipation of language, because naturalness can only be achieved by small infringements of the formal rules. on top of that [wittiness] is always a fairly irresponsible affair, and the effect that a poet achieves by being epigrammatic absolves him from all obligation to strive for poetic effects, his expression becomes more or less schematic, all tension between the words disappears, and the choice of words grows careless: by poetic standards that is, for lyric poetry has its own substitute for wit. the writer stands for nothing but himself.[4]

Brecht's own anxieties about the representative nature of poetry are apparent here in his reflections from exile. The poets he next mentions in the *Journal* as members of the pontifical and profane lines are George and Kraus himself; and this may be sufficient indication that Brecht's analysis here is also guided by Kraus's essay in setting so much store by the creative tension in lyrical language and by the preservation of form.

For some, the force of the profane line has been exhausted. Heiner Müller, in his response to the award of the 1985 Büchner prize (*I Am a Nigger* (*Ich bin ein Neger*)), announced that 'Heine the Wound' in German culture, originally identified by Adorno in 1956, had healed over. It had left a scar, he conceded; but the continuing wound in literature was now uniquely Büchner. This sense of exhaustion is also apparent in a short text by Thomas Brasch simply called 'Heine':

> Aus seinen Mündern
> fallen Schatten
> in seinen Haaren
> nisten Ratten
> hinter den Augen
> stürzen Wände
> es wachsen Algen
> um seine Hände.

Jetzt bricht der Fluß
die letzten Dämme
und trägt zum Meer
die schweren Stämme.
In seinen Liedern
wird es still
weil er für keinen
nicht mehr singen will.[5]

From his mouths
fall shadows
in his hair
nest rats
behind his eyes
walls collapse
algae grow
around his hands.
Now the river breaks
the last dams
and carries to the sea
the heavy tree-trunks.
In his songs
it grows quiet
because he won't sing
any more for no one

Brasch's poem transparently conflates Heine with the figure of Ophelia from Georg Heym's poem of that name – itself modelled on Rimbaud's 'Ophélie':

Im Haar ein Nest von jungen Wasserratten
Und die beringten Hände auf der Flut
Wie Flossen . . .[6]

In her hair a nest of young water rats
And her ring-laden hands upon the flood
Like fins . . .

The timber floating off to the sea is reminiscent of Ophelia's last journey, in Heym's poem, towards an apocalyptic horizon of time; and the collapsing dams appear both in Heym's poem and in another important early Expressionist text, van Hoddis's 'Weltende' ('End of the World'). Brasch's point seems to be that, seen across the great divide of early Expressionism, Heine's poetic personality has lost authority. Where Heym's Ophelia dreams of a crimson kiss ('von eines Kusses Karmoisin') and sees the final sun setting in her brain, Brasch's Heine can only imagine the emancipation, provided by collapsing walls, which had once been a firm article of belief. However much the double negative of the close may seem to equivocate, and the 'mouths' of Heine's various styles continue to cast shadows, Brasch's main insight seems to be that Heine's songs have fallen silent as he is finally overtaken by the river of time.

For all that, there have been *allusions* to Heine among other contemporary writers, sometimes in unlikely places. John Felstiner suggests that the line 'Dein goldenes Haar Margarethe' ('Your golden hair, Margareta') in Paul Celan's 'Todesfuge' ('Death Fugue') reminds us of the Lorelei combing her golden hair in Heine's poem.[7] The siren turns up again in the title poem of Ursula Krechel's first collection *Nach Mainz!* (*Off to Mainz!*). In this poem, 'Angela Davies, the Virgin Mary and I' escape from maternity hospital on hearing that there is to be a new division of Germany between a capitalist north and socialist south. Swimming down the Rhine 'to Mainz' they gain the assistance of a passing boatman:

> . . . Am Loreleifelsen treffen wir
> tatsächlich einen Fischer in seinem Nachen.
> Er rudert gemächlich damit er sich unterhalten kann.
> Später bittet er uns in seinen Kahn.
> Besonders Maria weckt sein Interesse.
> Sie gleiche einer bestimmten Person aufs Haar.[8]

> At the Lorelei rock we encounter
> for real a fisherman in his skiff.
> He rows gently so that he can chat.
> Later he invites us into his boat.
> Mary in particular arouses his interest.
> She's the spitting image of a certain person.

The German pun (literally, 'she resembled a certain person to a hair') achieved at the blonde Virgin's expense is no more than a casual notion, the local colour of a conversational poem, or perhaps even the *de rigueur* allusion to Germany's socialist poet in a text which tried to reimagine the partition of Germany before 1989 as its own act of ideological commitment.

It is probably this stereotypical political role that Alfred Andersch felt he had to invoke in relation to Hans Magnus Enzensberger's second collection, *landessprache* (*national language*): 'There is no comparison for the emergence of Hans Magnus Enzensberger on the stage of German intellectual life other than the memory of Heinrich Heine.'[9] Here, Heine provides the only possible point of reference for an original volume of poetry with political edge. Enzensberger's own styles and methods are more characteristically derived from Brecht, however, and perhaps even from Schiller's philosophical poems. Andersch alludes to Heine, not because of any precise derivation of style, form, or diction, but because by the late 1950s, and in the context of the West German restoration and the Cold War, Heine had been reduced to his representative role as the poet of the left, irrespective of the particular linguistic effects or poetic 'themes' which might provide some concrete measure of his influence.

For a succession of post-war poets, however, Heine's political reputation is more than a convenient cliché, because their own verse is closer to the profane line. Quite apart from the cynicism and studied awkwardness to which Heine subjects the poetry of romantic love in *Buch der Lieder*, his resistance to versions of the Sublime can be found in the parody of Klopstock and Ossian in the *Harzreise* episode of the tired and emotional students who become trapped in a wardrobe, as well as in the Captain's question 'Doctor, what the devil's got into you?' at the end of 'Seegespenst' ('Sea Apparition') from the *Buch der Lieder* 'Nordsee' cycle. Such profanity sets a tone which eventually settles in the threadbare secularism of 'Der Apollogott' in *Romanzero*. This is the Heine who nourishes the cynical and deflating effects in early Expressionist poets such as van Hoddis and Lichtenstein. Among contemporary writers, Wolf Biermann's memories of Heine in Paris provide a telling instance of this anti-poetic tone in 'Auf dem Friedhof am Montmartre' ('In the cemetery in Montmartre'):[10]

> Auf dem Friedhof am Montmartre
> Weint sich aus der Winterhimmel
> Und ich spring mit dünnen Schuhen
> Über Pfützen, darin schwimmen
> Kippen, die sich langsam öffnen
> Kötel von Pariser Hunden
> Und so hatt' ich nasse Füße
> Als ich Heines Grab gefunden.
> Unter weißem Marmor frieren
> Im Exil seine Gebeine
> Mit ihm liegt da Frau Mathilde
> Und so friert er nicht alleine.
> Doch sie heißt nicht mehr Mathilde
> Eingemeißelt in dem Steine
> Steht da groß sein großer Name
> Und darunter bloß: FRAU HEINE
>
> Und im Kriege, als die Deutschen
> An das Hakenkreuz die Seine-
> Stadt genagelt hatten, störte
> Sie der Name HENRI HEINE!

Und ich weiß nicht wie, ich weiß nur
Das: er wurde weggemacht
Und wurd wieder angeschrieben
Von Franzosen manche Nacht.

Auf dem Friedhof am Montmartre
Weint sich aus der Winterhimmel
Und ich spring mit dünnen Schuhen
Über Pfützen, darin schwimmen
Kippen, die sich langsam öffnen
Kötel von Pariser Hunden
Und ich hatte nasse Füße
Als ich Heines Grab gefunden.

At the Montmartre cemetery
The winter sky weeps to a close
And in thin shoes I jump
Over puddles – floating in them
Fag ends slowly dissolving
Turds of Paris dogs
So I had wet feet
when I found Heine's grave.
Under the white marble
His bones freeze in exile
With him lies Madame Mathilde
So he doesn't freeze alone
Now she's not called Mathilde any longer
Engraved on the stone
Stands his great name
And beneath it just Mrs Heine

And in the war when the Germans
Had nailed the city on the Seine
To the swastika, they were disturbed
By the name of Henri Heine!
And I don't know how, I just know
This: it was removed
And written back again
By Frenchmen many a night.
At the Montmartre cemetery
The winter sky weeps to a close
And in thin shoes I jump
Over puddles – floating in them
Fag ends slowly dissolving
Turds of Paris dogs
So I had wet feet
when I found Heine's grave.

The poem does double duty in recalling both the refusal of memorial acts in Heine's own poem about a visit to his grave, 'Gedächnisfeier' ('Commemoration'), and Biermann's visit to the cemetery. The obliteration of Jewish memory, including the name of Heine, was the cultural equivalent of the Nazis' 'final solution'. In Heine's poem, his wife 'sways on weary feet' up to Montmartre on a mild day. Biermann, on the other hand, pays his respects in the rain, and gets wet feet for his pains – the stress of 'Und so hatt' ich nasse Füße' is in explicit contrast to Mathilde's weary feet ('mit müden Füßen') in Heine's poem.

Biermann's text acknowledges its debt to Heine in a number of other ways. He retains Heine's characteristic trochaic metre; yet where Heine is carefully distant and neutral in his allusions to the everyday world of cabs and the 'barrier gate', Biermann's account of modern Paris is more naturalistic, with its puddles, decaying cigarette-ends and dog-turds. Where Heine makes a French word ('Pauvre homme') comically take its proper syllabic stress at the end of a German line, Biermann trumps his model by making the Seine rhyme *in French* with the name of the poet carved on the grave: Henri Heine. This *French* pronunciation of his name is particularly appropriate since it speaks for the defence of the poet by French patriots against Nazi barbarism, and perhaps reminds us of Heine's amusement that in French 'Henri Heine' is all too readily elided, via 'Enrienne' as 'un rien' – a mere nothing – in his *Memoiren* (B 6/1, 588). The repetition of the opening verse at the end of the poem provides the closure required by Biermann the chansonnier, but it cannot avoid the pathos to which Heine's original poem sets strict limits. In 'By an open fire in Paris' ('Kaminfeuer in Paris'),[11] which ostensibly deals with an evening spent with Parisian friends, Biermann recalls Heine's political isolation in exile via a paraphrase of the poems 'Anno 1839' and 'Nachtgedanken' from the *Neue Gedichte*, but then faces a similar difficulty:

> Ich trank mein' Wein und hörte zu
> Und dachte an Deutschland dabei.
>
> Ja, ich dachte an Deutschland in der Nacht
> und stocherte in der Asche.
> Doch wer behauptet, ich hätte geweint
> Der lügt sich was in der Tasche.
>
> I drank my wine and listened
> While I thought of Germany.
>
> Yes I thought of Germany in the night
> And poked around in the ashes.

But anyone who claims that I had cried
Is making the whole thing up.

'Nachtgedanken' (B 4, 432–3) ('Thinking of Germany in the Night' (D 407)) and 'Anno 1839' (B4, 379–80) ('O Germany, my love afar, / I weep when memories of you start!' (D 369)), the poems Biermann alludes to, balance homesickness, acute political anxiety, and self-irony. What is striking is that Biermann's poems do more than quote or commemorate Heine: in each case the possibility of a continuing creative relation is sketched in the context of a changed and changing political history. The visit to Heine's grave in Montmartre is *already* marked by the active attempts of a barbaric regime to obliterate all traces of a Jewish and liberal poet. Biermann's writing in these poems quotes or impersonates Heine, who, like François Villon in Biermann's 'Ballade', becomes an historical model and point of reference. It is equally striking that the erased name is restored in the Montmartre poem by a French patriot: at this point the significance of Biermann's relation to Paris as the city of Heine's exile becomes transparent. For Biermann, as for other writers on the left after 1968, countries beyond Germany's borders seemed to offer a haven of real socialist traditions alien to their homeland; and in the prefatory material to the volume of his collected poems and songs which Biermann published shortly after losing his GDR citizenship the solidarity of the Italian Communist Party (PCI) and the songs of the Italian workers' movement are celebrated with a parallel sentimentality.[12]

Heine's exile and the solidarity of French socialists during the Occupation give expression to Biermann's own multiple sense of exile. In the autobiographical note which concludes the collection bleakly entitled *Nachlaß I* (*Literary Remains*) he describes his exclusion from the GDR: 'At the age of 16 Wolf Biermann voluntarily left the city of his birth, he went to his homeland, the GDR. 24 years later he was driven from Germany into exile in Germany.'[13] The loss of GDR citizenship leaves Biermann exiled within his own land, caught between the two existing German states, but he also speaks to the predicament of a left intelligentsia which saw no prospects for the liberal version of socialism it had espoused. The comradeship of other European communist parties, and particularly the PCI, is no more than a measure of their experience of loss.[14] In this way Heine the practising poet readily disappears behind a further emblematic significance, figuring the exile of socialist aspirations. In such poetry Biermann avoids isolation by seeking out noble or heroic precursors, among whom Heine is the most important.

Heine comes to represent a rather different predicament in the work of another distinguished poet from the GDR. Günter Kunert contributed a sequence of Heine poems to the journal *Neue deutsche Literatur* (*New German Literature*) for the 175th anniversary of Heine's bith in 1972. These were reprinted with a brief commentary by the author in the catalogue of the 1997 Düsseldorf centenary exhibition, '*Ich Narr des Glücks*' (*'I, Fortune's fool'*).[15] As Kunert explains, Heine serves here as a mask behind which it was possible to mount an attack on the GDR itself, though some allusions, such as that to Heine's claim to be 'buiding a mountain' ('Ich baue am Berg') in his Börne book, seem to lack any specific point. Kunert is at his best here where he impersonates Heine's rhyming and tone. More recently, the title of his 1990 collection *Fremd daheim* (*At Home and Out of Place*) suggests a mood similar to Biermann's. The collection includes a sequence of poems entitled 'In Heines Sinn' ('In Heine's Sense'). They continue the catastrophist tone which has become Kunert's stock in trade, and Heine is required here to sound out the angry theology of his 'Zum Lazarus' poems from the *Gedichte 1853 & 1854*. Kunert's 'Ratschlag in Heines Sinn' ('Advice in Heine's Spirit') offers this guidance:

> Die Augen zu. Die Ohren taub.
> Kein Wort zuviel. Vor allem glaub
> der stillen Güte jener Macht,
> die über deinem Haupte wacht,
> das ständig es von Leere voll
> und weiterhin so bleiben soll:[16]

> Eyes closed. Ears deaf
> Not a word too many. Above all believe
> In the quiet goodness of that power
> That watches over your head
> That it may be full of emptiness
> And should remain so, on and on.

It may be that this is intended to echo

> Also fragen wir beständig,
> Bis man uns mit einer Handvoll
> Erde endlich stopft die Mäuler –
> Aber ist das eine Antwort?
>                         (B 6/1, 202)

> Thus we ask and keep on asking,
> Till a handful of cold clay
> Stops our mouths at last securely–
> But pray tell, is that an answer?
>                         (D 709)

from the end of 'Laß die heilgen Parabolen' (B 6/1, 201) ('Drop those holy parables' (D 709)) in the *Lazarus* supplement of the *1853 & 1854* collection;

on the whole, however, the versification here recalls Wilhelm Busch, the comic moralist of the late nineteenth century, more than Heine. Later in the sequence, the poem 'Titanic-Gedenkblatt' ('Titanic Memorandum') owes, one suspects, as much to Hans Magnus Enzensberger's epic of dysfunctional human progress, *Der Untergang der Titanic* (*The Sinking of the Titanic*), as it does to anything in Heine – at least, so it seems until a certain 'Melusine' appears:

> . . . Melusine
> du treibst an mir vorbei
> die Augen offen ganz schwarz
> Nachtblick
> dunkler als diese Tiefe
> wenn der Scheinwerfer wieder
> erlischt. Und ich weiß nicht
> ob du überhaupt noch lebst
> bevor dein Körper fischleicht
> verschwimmt nahebei.

> Melusina
> you drift past me
> your eyes open quite black
> night sight
> darker than these depths
> when the search light goes out
> again. And I don't know
> whether your even alive
> before you're body, light as a fish,
> slips into the murk near at hand.

The searchlight recalls those who left the GDR by swimming. The water nymph and the recollection of death by drowning are focussed by the 'ich weiß nicht' ('I know not') tag of Heine's 'Lorelei' – 'I do not know what it means . . .' (D 76), probably the best-known trademark line in Heine's poetry. Here it becomes the forgotten foil for Kunert's meditation on greater catastrophes. For all his claims to a greater affinity with a Jewish predecessor, however, Kunert's relation to Heine remains conceptual. Little in his practice, diction or poetic posture substantiates his work as being 'in Heine's sense'.

For such emulation we must turn to the maverick virtuoso of German lyric poetry since the 1950s, Peter Rühmkorf:

> Die Loreley entblößt ihr Haar
> Am umgekippten Rheine . . .
> Ich schwebe graziös in Lebensgefahr
> Grad zwischen Freund Hein und Freund Heine.[17]

> The Loreley lets down her hair
> Just next to the polluted Rhine
> I hover with grace in mortal danger
> Right between Old Jack and Old Harry.

Rühmkorf's poem 'Hochseil' ('High Wire') from his collected poems of 1975, *Wer Lyrik schreibt ist verrückt* (*Anyone Who Writes Poetry Is Mad*) is one of two texts that declare an interest in Heine's continuing significance: the other is explicitly entitled 'Heinrich-Heine-Gedenklied' ('Memorial song for Heinrich Heine').[18] We should first note a broader sense in which for Rühmkorf, as for Biermann, Heine is exemplary. Heine's oeuvre as a whole is a model for the characteristic range of work which many leading writers of this generation have undertaken. In Rühmkorf's case it comprises poetry, polemical essays, political fairy-tales (*Märchen*), autobiography, the pursuit of popular forms and the revival of folk-legend. Nor would it be difficult to recognize in this pattern and variety of writing the work of Hans Magnus Enzensberger.

In Rühmkorf's case, Heine also stands for the split personality that expresses itself through what he and his friend Werner Riegel defined as 'schizography': the simultaneous commitment to 'the soul of the poet' and 'the soul of political community' ('des politischen Gemeinschaftswesens'); to sensuous individualism and to collective engagement. Asked in an interview whether this was an original position, Rühmkorf replied:

No, it's an old contradiction – in these climes it was particularly brought to notice by Heinrich Heine. The poet thirsts for unlimited freedom of individual development, and the communal political man preaches equality and justice.[19]

This productive tension has driven Rühmkorf's work from early in his career; but his recently published diaries develop another relation to Heine. Among the fragments of poems in progress or *in statu nascendi* which run through the diary entries and which Rühmkorf calls 'Leuchtquanten' ('Light-quanta'), the following lines appear on 23 December 1989:

> Weil, du weißt in der Eile doch gar nicht,
> was du der Menschheit noch mit auf dem Weg geben sollst –
> Eine Handvoll Erde?[20]

> Because in your haste you just don't know
> What you should send mankind on its way with –
> a handful of earth?

We are back with the 'Lazarus' poem 'Laß die heilgen Parabolen'; but it is not merely a moral position which is offered. The diary records a meeting with Professor Manfred Schneider from Essen 'who has written so winningly about Heine's melancholies'.[21] Such melancholia has political origins, and Heine's remark in 1848 'Of the events of the time I say nothing', quoted in Rühmkorf's *TABU* at the end of December 1989, confirms the diarist's anguished response to the events of the *Wende* and the collapse of the GDR during the previous two months. In such a context Heine has become once again an exemplary figure, and identification with him confirms the melancholic personal agenda of what is rapidly becoming Rühmkorf's own late work.

Heine's poetry and Heine's life provide a poetic resource and a way of defining a career. 'Suppentopf und Guillotine'('Soup-pot and Guillotine'), Rühmkorf's lecture in response to the award of the Heine-Medal by the city of Düsseldorf, concentrates on the possibilities of a psychological decoding of Heine's relationship to his mother as a model for subsequent 'women figures';[22] and it is striking that in a personal anthology Rühmkorf edited, Heine is represented by a passage from the *Memoiren*.[23] Furthermore Heine's relationship to his mother clearly provides a mirror for Rühmkorf's own maternal bonding ('Mutterbindung').[24] The 'Gedenklied für Heinrich Heine' ('Memorial Song for Heinrich Heine') from the early collection *Irdisches Vergnügen in g* (*Earthly Pleasure in g[ravity]*), whose title parodies the Enlightenment poet Barthold Heinrich Brockes's *Earthly Pleasure in God*, is therefore a multiple homage.

> Ting – Tang – Tellerlein,
> durch Schaden wird man schlau;
> ich bin der Sohn des Huckebein
> und Leda, seiner Frau.
>
> Ich bin der Kohl- und bin der Kolk-,
> der Rabe schwarz wie Priem:
> ich liebe das gemeine Volk
> und halte mich fern von ihm.
>
> Hier hat der Himmel keine Freud,
> die Freude hat kein Licht,
> das Licht ist dreimal durchgeseiht,
> eh man's veröffentlicht.
>
> Was schafft ein einziges Vaterland
> nur soviel Dunkelheit?!
> Ich hüt mein Kopf mit Denkproviant
> für noch viel schlimmere Zeit.
>
> Und geb mich wie ihr alle glaubt
> auf dem Papier –:

als trüg ein aufgeklärtes Haupt
sich leichter hier.[25]

Ting – Tang – little dish
once bitten and you're wise
I am the son of Huckebein
and Leda his lady wife

I am the coke- and I am the croak-
the raven, as black as baccy
I love them, all the common folk,
and keep well away from them

Here heaven has no joy,
joy has no light,
the light gets sieved three times over
before they'll publish it.

How can a single fatherland
produce so much darkness?
I load my head with food for thought
and yet worse times to come.

And yield myself, as you all think,
on paper
as if an enlightened head
weighed less heavily there.

The poem encodes its author's own paternity as the son of 'the teacher
Elisabeth R. and a travelling puppeteer H.W. (the name is known to the
author) . . .'[26] both through the mythical and literary figures of Leda and
Hans Huckebein, the unlucky raven (from Wilhelm Busch), and through
the act of memory implied by the title. The four-line rhymed stanza declares
its derivation from Heine's manipulation of the Romantic folksong stanza;
but in these 'Monomanic Songs' the traditional form has clearly had more
than a brush with the diction of other later poets, including the Brecht of
the *Hauspostille* (*Book of Household Devotions*) and Gottfried Benn, from
early Expressionism to his 'static' poems. Rühmkorf has himself provided
or, perhaps more precisely, *avoided* an authorial interpretation of this text.
He identifies the poem broadly as a case of the 'schizographic' writing he
described programmatically in the late 1950s:

It is to be understood: with forethought two masters are being served and
a song is sung with forked tongue; here verses make ambiguous half-light their
guiding principle, and particular psychological ambivalences attempt to present
themselves in mixed aesthetic effects, grating tones and interference.[27]

To serve two masters by speaking 'with forked tongue' allows the poet's division between affect and intellect to give expression to political tensions of the real world by constantly questioning the status of lyrical writing. What might seem to be merely personal and associative is revealed as symptomatic of much larger contexts. In this way the very act of recollecting Heine in the poem provides a grand measure of the *contemporary* situation of poetry.

The opening of the poem presents a children's rhyme which Rühmkorf claims is authentic. In this way the poem allies itself with a popular folk tradition of the kind represented in Rühmkorf's anthology *Über das Volksvermögen*[28] (an ambiguous title: 'On the Power of the People' / 'On the National Wealth') and explored in Heine's essays on the significance of folk superstition in *Elementargeister* (*Elemental Spirits*, B 3, 643–703) as well as in many of his more Gothic ballads and poems; the nursery rhyme is joined by a second popular genre, a proverb, distorted to repeat a self-description from the first of Rühmkorf's three 'self-portraits':[29] 'durch Schaden schlau geworden' – literally 'grown wise through harm'. The proverbial principle is now 'once bitten, twice *sly*': both because 'schlau werden' (to become sly) is a low register equivalent of 'klug werden' (to become wise, hence to be the wiser), and because in a world of mediatized censorship *cunning* has become one of the great Heinesque virtues. The truth of Rühmkorf's insight points to Heine's sliding identification with the cunning Odysseus and the patient Louis-Philippe, 'the patient majesty' ('der königliche Dulder'). More specifically, in recalling Heine's complex game of hide-and-seek with the censor, the poem seeks in its own terms to give expression to what otherwise remains unspoken.

Hans Huckebein, the unlucky crow, brings a new poetic presence to the text; not only Heine but also Wilhelm Busch can provide a further model for the experience of damage, even for the poet whose other line of descent comes through the classicism of a Greek myth, Leda, via the blasphemy of substituting Hans Huckebein for Zeus's swan. (Rühmkorf, fathered by a travelling puppeteer, relishes his own illegitimacy.) This double ancestry in the classical and the popular subsequently makes itself felt in the second stanza's revision of Horace: 'Odi profanum volgus et arceo' reads here as 'I love them, all the common folk, and keep well away from them'. This in turn comes both to summarize Heine's anxieties about the prospects for poetry under the aegis of the communist interest, 'the dark iconoclasts' of the French preface to *Lutetia*; but also to parody the implausibility of a common front being mounted by poetry and political egalitarianism. We are reminded that Heine was enough of an aristocrat of the spirit to admit in *Ludwig Börne: eine Denkschrift*: 'it is absolutely not figurative, but meant quite literally that, if the people were to shake my hand, I would wash it afterwards' (B 4, 75). The alliance between the working class and West German writers and intellectuals which became a dominant theme of the student movement ten years later is identified here as one of the difficulties inherited by contemporaries from Heine's problematic artistry in the 1840s.

The allusions of Rühmkorf's poem are often out of the way. In 1959 the two German states, existing in parallel, might well make the idea of a single fatherland ('Ein *einziges* Vaterland') a source of obscurity – not least in relation to the political appropriation of Heinrich Heine by Western liberalism and GDR communists. At the end of a list of negatives (no joy, no light) there is still the prospect of threefold censorship (perhaps by the Western occupying authorities or by the three political parties of the Federal Republic) before publication can be permitted. Rühmkorf as Heine's modern successor can take his cue from Heine's strategy of smuggling critical ideas past the censors under the guise of wit or realism. This intellectual contraband ('Gedankenschmuggel') is celebrated in *Deutschland. Ein Wintermärchen* and *Ludwig Börne*, and as we have seen, it is one of Heine's tactics in *Lutetia* to sail under false colours. Where it succeeds, poets can overwinter into an even worse future:

> Die Contrebande, die mit mir reist,
> Die hab ich im Kopfe stecken.
>
> (B 4, 579)

> I take contraband along with me
> But it's in my head it's hiding.
>
> (D 485)

The poem concludes by challenging assumptions about the apparent facility of a literary talent that formulates its moods and ideas in a complex play of artistry and intellect. (Rühmkorf has commented more recently: 'No offence, but in these parts artistry [Artistik] is a foreign word, and as we know, contempt for foreign words is the beginning of xenophobia.')[30] Rühmkorf's final stanza insists on our expectation, as readers, that the printed text 'on the page' gives secure access to the author's views as a liberal heir of the Enlightenment ('ein aufgklärtes Haupt'). Yet the principles of artistry and intellectual smuggling make such a personal point of reference increasingly difficult. Rühmkorf's poetological essay 'Einfallskunde' ('A Doctrine of Notions') returns to the question:

If a lyric poet says *I*, the idea might get about that Mr So-and-so was talking about himself. The first person singular, artfully or effortfully wrapped in the garment of poetry, provides sufficient and often sufficiently justified grounds for misrecognition: after all, what is at stake here is a changeling personality, half sprung from nature, half enveloped in a costume, and when people tread on a shadow's train, it is sometimes the real man who is startled.[31]

Such constant play with the ambiguity of public status and private emotion or private commitment was a central feature of Heine's literary persona, cultivated as an autobiographical truth behind the feints and impersonations that guard his privacy. Rühmkorf's work has developed successive techniques to avoid mere 'self-expression'. In his earliest verse and journalism, multiple pseudonyms cover his tracks. Of these Leslie Meier survived longest and the long-dead Leo Doletzki is the most recent ghostly manifestation.[32] Early poems such as 'Running Wild in What's Uncertain' ('Wildernd im Ungewissen') and, in particular, the uncollected poems in *Heiße Lyrik* (*Hot Poetry*)[33] develop a kind of counter-persona through parodies of Gottfried Benn. This technique is further developed in wry and often satirical self-identificatory 'variations' on poems of Klopstock, Hölderlin, Eichendorff, and Claudius. Finally, in the solidarity of translation, especially of Walther von der Vogelweide but recently of the Swedish poet Carl Michael Bellmann,[34] Rühmkorf explores the possibilities of a multiple personality.

This contemporary practice of a schizographic poetry extends the modernist principle of pseudonymity in texts which are simultaneously confessional, conceptual, *and* political interventions. Read against Rühmkorf's methods, the bare but inescapable parodies of *Buch der Lieder*, the affective and atmospheric uncertainties of the *Atta Troll* allegory, and *Romanzero*'s complex recognition of tradition in discontinuity can be understood as the risky attempt to find a place for poetry amid the disenchantments of modern times. It is appropriate therefore that Rühmkorf invokes Heine in a poem celebrating this vital risk: 'High Wire' ('Hochseil') and its circus imagery takes up, in literal terms, the high view of public artistry which marks Rühmkorf's whole career:

> Wir turnen in höchsten Höhen herum
> selbstredend und selbstreimend,
> von einem I n d i v i d u u m
> aus nichts als Worten träumend
>
> Was uns bewegt – warum? wozu? –
> den Teppich zu verlassen?
> Ein nie erforschtes Who-is-who
> im Sturzflug zu erfassen.

Wer von so hoch zu Boden blickt,
der sieht nur Verarmtes/Verirrtes.
Ich sage: wer Lyrik schreibt ist verrückt,
wer sie für wahr nimmt, wird es.

Ich spiel mit meinem Astralleib Klavier,
v i e r f ü ß i g – vierzigzehig –
Ganz unten am Boden gelten wir
für nicht mehr ganz zurechnungsfähig.

Die Loreley entblößt ihr Haar
am umgekippten Rheine . . .
Ich schwebe grazös in Lebensgefahr
Grad zwischen Freund Hein und Freund Heine.[35]

We do our acrobatic turns in the highest region
self-evident and self-rhyming,
of an *individual* made only
of words we're always dreaming.

What moves us to – the why and wherefore? –
abandon the circus mat?
To compose from scratch our own Who's Who
and risk it will all fall flat.

Just look back to the ground from so high up,
you'll see what's impoverished and astray.
I say: whoever writes poems is crazy,
if you take them for gospel, you will be.

With my astral body I play the piano,
*four-footed* – forty-toed –
Right down on the ground we count
as no longer completely responsible.

The Loreley lets down her hair
Just next to the polluted Rhine
I hover with grace in mortal danger
Right between Old Jack and Old Harry.

The circus floor-cloth ('Teppich') sets Rühmkorf in relation to Rilke's *saltimbanques* in the fifth *Duino Elegy*:

auf dem verzehrten, von ihrem ewigen
Aufsprung dünneren Teppich, diesem verlorenen
Teppich im Weltall.[36]

on the threadbare carpet, thinned by their everlasting
leaping up, this forlorn carpet / lost in the universe.

Rühmkorf's paraphrase only serves to reinforce the anti-sublime tension between the flight of artistry and the inescapable ground of the ironic. The poem ends in a similar refusal of sublimity. The Lorelei's Rhine is polluted, and the high-wire artist can avoid his own post-Romantic fate through the balancing act of the poem.

Rühmkorf retraces the autobiographical expectations that Heine's poetry simultaneously stages and avoids – in the sense that the truth of *Buch der Lieder*, for instance, will always evade us. An individual can be dreamed into existence through words alone because the lyrical poem generates the internal harmonies of rhyme (as 'selbstreimend') but also because it can seem *self-evident* that the lyric speaks *of a self* (in the double sense of '*selbst*redend', both in its dictionary sense of 'obvious' and literally 'self-speaking'). Its high-wire act is constantly under threat, its central performer tortured by the prospect of failure. It is largely in late poems (such as 'Sie erlischt' in the *Romanzero* 'Lazarus' cycle) that Heine provides a model here; but the poet who 'hovers . . . in mortal danger / right between Old Jack and Old Harry' combines huge self-regard with the endless risk of his *salto mortale*: vanity on the stage of *vanitas*. As another poem from the same group makes clear, 'what's required here is the death-defying number' ('was gewünscht wird, ist die Todesnummer'):[37] it is the prospect of a nose-dive that makes it possible to establish who is who – to risk a definition of the lyrical self, on paper and in words.

Like Heine in *Buch der Lieder* or in the ambiguity of 'Karl I' in the 'Tales' of *Romanzero*, Rühmkorf's fertile enthusiasm for parody and the principle of variation sets a measure for the condition of *contemporary* language by seeing the present and tradition in a prismatic relationship with each other. Like Heine, he too marks his modernity and ours in the space opened up between the canonical texts and contemporary memory. This, one might say, had been the argument of 'Jehuda ben Halevy' also, as it observes the shifts in aesthetic value accompanying the transmission of great poetry through history.

Such issues are addressed by the poems more or less explicitly. However, Rühmkorf's poetic method reveals another kind of affinity to Heine's work. His essays on the writing process 'Einfallskunde' ('Doctine of Notions'),[38] 'Über die Arbeit' ('On Work'),[39] as well as *Aus der Fassung* ('From the Drafts'/ 'Losing Control'), the massive textual complex from which 'Selbst III' emerged, all reveal his process of composition as accumulative:

As a matter of fact, poems are not – as Gottfried Benn could perhaps still think – 'made of words', but of ideas you get, as well as from fairly complicated word associations that are already live; and instead of dealing with inorganic ready-mades, I encounter nervous organisms.[40]

The constructive process passes into a stage when individual insights, phrases, fragments relate to each other in rhythmical, semantic, or ideological ways, until a third and final phase is reached in which the emerging poem attains to its own dialogical and dialectical coherence. Rühmkorf's very clear account of his own procedures in relation to the phrase, the 'notion' – 'luminous quanta' or 'lyrids', as he calls these elementary lyrical particles – is borne out by the pattern of his work. His use of rhymed stanzas with fairly strong end-stopping has the effect of emphasizing the moment of linguistic insight which then dazzles by its word-play and phrase-making.

Rühmkorf's poetological account of his own methods is remarkably close to the remarks of the old lizard in Heine's *Die Stadt Lucca*:

. . . as a result of my observations, experiments and anatomical comparisons, I can assure you: no human being thinks, it's just that every now and again something occurs to them through no fault of their own, and they call these notions thoughts, and the process of stringing them together is what they call thinking . . . (B 2, 480).

This attack on the standing of Hegel and Schelling as *thinkers* is, we now know, also an account of Heine's own working methods. As he said himself, 'People talk about inspiration, enthusiasm and the like – I work like a goldsmith making a chain, one little link after another, each through the other'.[41] Heine's own working habits involved the accumulation of 'a confusing and chaotic bundle of papers including the most heterogeneous sketches on all kinds of themes'.[42] Such a combinatory process draws together subtle detail in a calculated overall composition. It depends on the verbal units from which larger effects can be built up. And it is just such writing, composed of 'Einfälle' or notions, that Karl Kraus takes for his target in 'Heine and the consequences', when he suggests that a poem could be constructed by reading alternate lines from facing pages in *Buch der Lieder*. Such individual moments, however brilliant, can never be a substitute for the organic integrity of art, in Kraus's view, or for the personal depth which it uniquely reveals. It is Heine, we recall, who is supposedly guilty of introducing this method of montage borrowed from the stylistic habits of French, where 'everone enjoys the pleasures of the feuilleton. [French] is an idler in thought. The most level head is not safe from notions [ist nicht einfallsicher], if it has to do with her.'[43]

The linguistic turn of events that Kraus identifies can now be acknowledged as a significant feature of Heine's work. His notions/'Einfälle' become the stuff of his patchwork prose-style and of his lyrical confrontation with exhausted cliché and dead metaphor. Heine's 'Einfälle', Kraus's belief that German art needs to be safe from notions ('einfallsicher'), and Rühmkorf's doctrine of notions ('Einfallskunde') give a common name to the changing status of poetic language in modernity. Peter Rühmkorf's practice and critical engagement with the poetic tradition presents more than an authentic parallel to Heine's enterprise, for his work re-enacts the troubled relation to modernity which, as Kraus realized with so much alarm, Heine was among the first to articulate. And in that respect Heine's critical lyric and mastery of style have lost none of their edge or relevance in the continuing struggle for poetry's engagement with modern experience.

# Notes

INTRODUCTION

1 Jeffrey L. Sammons, *Heinrich Heine* (Sammlung Metzler 261) (Stuttgart: Metzler, 1991), pp. 166–9; see also his 'The Exhaustion of Current Heine Studies: Some Observations, Partly Speculative' in Mark H. Gelber (ed.), *The Jewish Reception of Heinrich Heine* (Tübingen: Niemeyer, 1992), pp. 5–19.

2 *'Ich bin ein Neger'. Diskussion mit Heiner Müller* (Darmstadt: Verlag der Georg Büchner Buchhandlung, 1986), p. 20.

3 Theodor W. Adorno, 'Die Wunde Heine' in *Noten zur Literatur* I, *Gesammelte Schriften*, ed. Rolf Tiedemann, 20 vols. (Frankfurt am Main: Suhrkamp, 1974), vol. XI, pp. 95–100; 'Heine the Wound' in *Notes to Literature*, trans. Shierry Weber Nicholsen, 2 vols. (New York: Columbia University Press, 1991), vol. I, pp. 80–5.

4 In *The Sociology of Georg Simmel*, trans., ed. and with an introduction by Kurt H. Wolff (New York: The Free Press, 1964), pp. 409–24; 'Die Großstädte und das Geistesleben', *Jahrbuch der Gehe-Stiftung Dresden* 9 (1903), pp. 185–206.

5 In this study I have used Klaus Briegleb's edition, *Heinrich Heine. Sämtliche Schriften*, 6 vols. in 7 (Munich: Hanser, 1968–76). Quotations from this text are indicated by the letter B, followed by volume number and page. Other editions are indicated as follows: DHA = *Heinrich Heine. Sämtliche Werke. Düsseldorfer Ausgabe*, ed. Manfred Windfuhr, 16 vols. (Hamburg: Hoffmann & Campe, 1973–97); HSA = *Heinrich Heine: Werke &c. Säkularausgabe*, ed. Nationale Forschungs- und Gedenkstätte der klassischen deutschen Literatur, Weimar, and the Centre national de la recherche scientifique, Paris, 27 vols. (Berlin: Akademie Verlag, 1970–). HSA is exclusively used for Heine's correspondence. Heine's conversation and the reports of his contemporaries are cited from Michael Werner (ed.), *Begegnungen mit Heine: Berichte der Zeitgenossen. In Fortführung von H. H. Houbens 'Gespräche mit Heine'*, 2 vols. (Hamburg: Hoffmann & Campe, 1973), cited as Werner/Houben, giving volume and page numbers.

6 *Critique of Cynical Reason*, trans. Michael Eldred, with a foreword by Andreas Huyssen (London: Verso, 1988). See section 5.

7 The phrase is Andreas Huyssen's in his introduction to the English translation of Sloterdijk's work.

8 I follow recent practice in translating *Denkschrift* (to echo its proximity to *Denkmal* – monument) as *Memorial.*

9 'O Schilda, mein Vaterland', B 4, 83–4 (repeatedly!).

10 Nietzsche's comments may be found in section 4 of the second essay in *Ecce Homo*, 'Why I Am So Clever', Friedrich Nietzsche, *Werke*, ed. Karl Schlechta, 3 vols. (Munich: Hanser, 1969), vol. III, pp. 1088–9. Thomas Mann, 'Notiz über Heine' (1908), in *Ludwig Börne und Heinrich Heine. Ein Deutsches Zerwürfnis*, ed. Hans Magnus Enzensberger (Nördlingen: Greno, 1986).

## I THE BIOGRAPHICAL IMPERATIVE: KARL KRAUS

1 See Helmut Arntzen, *Karl Kraus und die Presse* (Munich: Fink, 1975) *contra* Mechthild von Borries, *Ein Angriff auf Heinrich Heine* (Stuttgart: Kohlhammer, 1971).

2 See Sammons, *Heinrich Heine* (Sammlung Metzler 261), p. 154.

3 'Heine und die Folgen', 'Um Heine', 'Der Reim' ('Rhyme'), along with the other texts of Kraus's polemics are usefully collected in Dietmar Goltschnigg (ed.), *Die Fackel ins wunde Herz* (Vienna: Passagen, 2000). References here are to the standard edition: Karl Kraus, *Schriften*, ed. Christian Wagenknecht, 12 vols. (Frankfurt am Main: Suhrkamp, 1989). 'Heine und die Folgen' with its afterword and concluding words appears in vol. IV, *Untergang der Welt durch schwarze Magie* ('The End of the World through Black Magic', first collected in 1922), pp. 185–219.

4 See 'Vom Nutzen und Nachteil der Historie', in Nietzsche, *Werke*, vol. I, pp. 234–7.

5 Kraus, *Untergang der Welt*, p. 211.

6 'eine Sehnsucht, die sich irgendwo reimen muß', ibid., p. 185.

7 Jay F. Bodine, 'Heinrich Heine, Karl Kraus and "die Folgen". A Test Case of Literary Texts, Historical Reception and Receptive Aesthetics', *Colloquia Germanica*, 17 (1984), pp. 14–59.

8 Kraus, *Untergang der Welt*, p. 186.

9 Ibid., p. 187. Kraus's phrase is 'nicht einfallsicher': not inured to notions. Kraus, as we shall see, has an acute sense of aesthetic structure in connection with these 'notions'.

10 Ibid., p. 187.

11 'Der Autor der fremde Kostüme ausklopft, kommt dem stofflichen Interesse von der denkbar bequemsten Seite bei' (ibid., p. 187): 'stofflich' here seems to be a pun which anticipates the next stage of Kraus's analysis, for to beat, or perhaps more appropriately to 'shake down', foreign costumes, is to take a short cut to attractive topics for narrative – but it is also to reveal a merely superficial interest in the 'Stoff', the material in the sense of cloth! Wagenknecht's commentary in his Kraus anthology identifies the allusion to Kipling; see Karl Kraus, *Heine und die Folgen. Schriften zur Literatur*, ed. Christian Wagenknecht (Stuttgart: Reclam, 1986), p. 302.

12 Kraus, *Untergang der Welt*, p. 188.

13 Adolf Loos, 'Ornament und Verbrechen' in *Sämtliche Schriften*, ed. Franz Glück (Vienna and Munich: Herold Verlag, 1962), p. 284: translated in *Ornament and Crime, Selected Essays*, selected and with an introduction by Adolf Opel, trans. Michael Mitchell (Riverside, CA: Ariadne Press, 1998), p. 172 (modified).

14 See Alfred Pfabigan, *Karl Kraus und der Sozialismus* (Vienna: Europaverlag, 1976), p. 136, on the Wittgenstein house.

15 'die Hülle der schlechten Absicht gefällig zu machen', Kraus, *Untergang der Welt*, p. 189.

16 Karl Kraus, *Nachts* (Vienna and Leipzig: [Kurt Wolff] Verlag der Schriften von Karl Kraus, 1924), p. 67. The idea of an aesthetics of the phrase has been deployed by two unorthodox monographs on Kraus: Pfabigan's study, which cites the case of Bahr's beard (p. 137), and, following him, Manfred Schneider's psycho-biography *Die Angst und das Paradies des Nörglers* (Frankfurt am Main: Syndikat, 1977). Pfabigan illustrates Kraus's resistance to the 'phrase' in the context of Loos's idea of ornament, which Kraus understands, in human terms, as costume and fashion. Thus the popularity of the beard is attacked as no more than the self-stylization of those who like to think of themselves as artists.

17 Walter Benjamin, 'Karl Kraus' in *Selected Writings*, trans. Rodney Livingstone and others, ed. Michael W. Jennings, Howard Eiland, and Gary Smith, 3 vols. (Cambridge, MA and London: Belknap Press of Harvard University Press, 1999), vol. II: *1927–1934*, p. 435 (slightly modified); *Gesammelte Schriften*, ed. Rolf Tiedemann and Hermann Schweppenhäuser, 7 vols. (Frankfurt am Main: Suhrkamp, 1977), vol. II.1, pp. 336–7.

18 Kraus, *Untergang der Welt*, p. 190.

19 Pfabigan, *Karl Kraus und der Sozialismus*, p. 141, citing Jürgen Habermas, *Strukturwandel der Öffentlichkeit* (Neuwied: Luchterhand, 1971), p. 227.

20 See Wilhelm Gössmann, Hans P. Keller, Hedwig Walwei-Wiegelmann (eds.), *Geständnisse: Heine im Bewußtsein heutiger Autoren* (Düsseldorf: Droste, 1972), pp. 46–7.

21 Alf Jörgensen, *Karl Kraus. Der Heinefresser und die Ursachen* (Flensburg: Schütze und Schmidt, n.d. [?1912]), p. 13.

22 Pfabigan, *Karl Kraus und der Sozialismus*, p. 21; see also p. 17.

23 Hans Mayer, 'Karl Kraus und die Nachwelt', in *Ansichten. Zur Literatur der Zeit* (Reinbek bei Hamburg: Rowohlt, 1962), p. 74.

24 Kraus's term 'prompte[r] Bekleider' (*Untergang der Welt*, p. 197) suggests both the earlier metaphors of clothing and costume, as of a superficial effect, and of Heine fulfilling a role in the sense of 'ein Amt bekleiden' – to hold an (already existing) office.

25 Walter Benjamin, *The Origin of the German Tragic Drama*, trans. John Osborne (London: Verso, 1985), p. 162; *Ursprung des deutschen Trauerspiels, Gesammelte Schriften*, vol. I.1, p. 339. See Heinz Schlaffer, *Faust Zweiter Teil. Die Allegorie des 19. Jahrhunderts* (Stuttgart: Metzler, 1981).

26 Strikingly enough, Adorno, recalling a remark of Proust, will note the same sense of embarrassment himself vis-à-vis Kraus's own *Sittlichkeit und*

*Kriminalität.* See *Gesammelte Schriften*, vol. XI (*Noten zur Literatur* III), p. 383; *Notes to Literature*, vol. II, p. 53.

27 Kraus, *Untergang der Welt*, p. 200.

28 Ibid., p. 204.

29 This has been succinctly summarized, with reference to the role of Liliencron as a model in the argument, by Uta Schaub, in 'Liliencron und Heine im Urteil von Karl Kraus. Ein Beitrag zum Problem der literarischen Wertung', *HJb* 18 (1979), pp. 191–201

## 2 THE BIOGRAPHICAL IMPERATIVE: THEODOR ADORNO

1 Adorno, *Gesammelte Schriften*, vol. XI, pp. 95–100: p. 100; *Notes to Literature*, vol. I, p. 85.

2 See Derrida's remark: 'Comment dater ce qui ne se répète pas si la datation fait aussi appel à quelque forme de retour, si elle rappelle dans la lisibilité d'une répétition? Mais comment dater autre chose que cela même qui jamais ne se répète?' in *Schibboleth* (Paris: Editions du Seuil, 1986), p. 13.

3 See Gerhard Höhn, 'Adorno face à Heine ou le couteau dans la plaie', *Revue d'ésthetique*, n.s. 8 (1985), pp. 137–44. My account is greatly indebted to this paper.

4 Adorno, *Gesammelte Schriften*, vol. XI, p. 95; *Notes to Literature*, vol. I, p. 80.

5 Paul Peters suggests Adorno's complicity in this anti-Semitism, but presents little textual evidence of George's anti-Semitic position. See *Heinrich Heine 'Dichterjude'. Die Geschichte einer Schmähung* (Frankfurt am Main: A. Hain, 1990), pp. 160, 166–71.

6 Adorno, *Gesammelte Schriften*, vol. XI, p. 95; *Notes to Literature*, vol. I, p. 80.

7 Kraus, *Untergang der Welt*, p. 196.

8 Adorno, *Gesammelte Schriften*, vol. XI, p. 96; *Notes to Literature*, vol. I, p. 81.

9 Peters notes Kraus's self-distancing from the 'proletarian' Heine, *Heinrich Heine 'Dichterjude'*, p. 152. Heine's resistance to puritanical politicians is evident in his polemic against Börne: see chapter 5 below.

10 Adorno, *Gesammelte Schriften*, vol. XI, p. 97; *Notes to Literature*, vol. I, p. 82.

11 Adorno, *Gesammelte Schriften*, vol. XI, p. 96; *Notes to Literature* vol. I, p. 83 (translation modified).

12 Adorno, *Gesammelte Schriften*, vol. XI, pp. 96–7; *Notes to Literature* vol. I, p. 81.

13 Benjamin, *Gesammelte Schriften*, vol. II.1, pp. 336–7; 'Karl Kraus', p. 435.

14 See Erich Mayser, *H. Heines 'Buch der Lieder' im 19. Jahrhundert* (Stuttgart: Akademischer Verlag Heinz, 1978); Alberto Destro, 'Das *Buch der Lieder* und seine Leser' in Luciano Zagari and Paolo Chiarini (eds.), *Zu Heinrich Heine* (Stuttgart: Klett, 1981), pp. 59–73. For an overview, see Gerhard Höhn, *Heine Handbuch. Zeit – Person – Werk*, 2nd edition (Stuttgart: Metzler, 1997), pp. 76–79.

15 Adorno, *Gesammelte Schriften*, vol. XI, p. 97; *Notes to Literature*, vol. I, p. 82.

16 Adorno, *Gesammelte Schriften*, vol. XI, p. 96; *Notes to Literature*, vol. I, p. 81.

17 Adorno, *Gesammelte Schriften*, vol. XI, p. 97; *Notes to Literature*, vol. I, p. 82.
18 See Schaub, 'Liliencron und Heine', p. 197.
19 Adorno, *Gesammelte Schriften*, vol. XI, p. 97; *Notes to Literature*, vol. I, p. 82.
20 See Theodor W. Adorno, *Gesammelte Schriften*, vol. VII, pp. 38–9; *Aesthetic Theory*, translated by C. Lenhardt (London: Routledge and Kegan Paul, 1984), p. 31.
21 See Höhn, 'Adorno face à Heine', p. 141. Peters provides evidence of Benjamin's 'anti-Semitic' prejudice, *Heinrich Heine 'Dichterjude'*, pp. 164–6. For further discussion of Adorno's reading of Heine in relation to Benjamin's *Passagen-Werk*, see chapter 10 below.
22 Weber Nicholsen translates Adorno's phrase as 'words now defunct', 'In Memory of Eichendorff', *Notes to Literature*, vol. I, p. 73.
23 Adorno, *Gesammelte Schriften*, vol. XI, p. 98; *Notes to Literature*, vol. I p. 83.
24 Adorno, *Gesammelte Schriften*, vol. XI, p. 98; *Notes to Literature*, vol. I, p. 82.
25 Ritchie Robertson, *The 'Jewish Question' in German Literature* (Oxford: Oxford University Press, 1999), pp. 194, 259–62, and *passim*; on Adorno, p. 320.
26 Adorno, *Gesammelte Schriften*, vol. XI, p. 98; the book is the preferred reading in *Notes to Literature*, vol. I, p. 83.
27 Ibid.: 'Heines Mutter, die er liebte, war des Deutschen nicht ganz mächtig.'
28 See Franz Futterknecht, *Heinrich Heine. Ein Versuch* (Tübingen: Narr, 1985), and Peter Rühmkorf's 'Heinepreisrede', 'Suppentopf und Guillotine', in Rühmkorf, *Dreizehn deutsche Dichter* (Reinbek: Rowohlt, 1989), pp. 7–35.
29 Jeffrey L. Sammons, *Heinrich Heine. A Modern Biography* (Princeton: Princeton University Press, 1979), pp. 15–16.
30 See Klaus Briegleb, *Opfer Heine? Versuch über Schriftzüge der Revolution* (Frankfurt am Main: Suhrkamp, 1986), pp. 31–40; Sammons, *Heinrich Heine* (Sammlung Metzler 261), p. 49.
31 See Futterknecht, *Heinrich Heine* , pp. 105–6; 124ff.
32 Jeffrey L. Sammons in *Heinrich Heine: The Elusive Poet* (New Haven and London: Yale University Press, 1969) fiercely demonstrates the fabricated nature of Heine's account (pp. 256–7).
33 Adorno, *Gesammelte Schriften*, vol. XI, p. 98; *Notes to Literature*, vol. I, p. 83 (translation modified).
34 Johann Wolfgang von Goethe, *Werke* (Hamburger Ausgabe), ed. Erich Trunz, 14 vols. (Munich: C. H. Beck, 1994), vol. V, p. 166.
35 Adorno, *Gesammelte Schriften*, vol. XI, p. 100; *Notes to Literature*, vol. I, p. 85.
36 Adorno, *Gesammelte Schriften*, vol. XI, pp. 98–9; *Notes to Literature*, vol. I, p. 83.
37 See Robertson, *The 'Jewish Question' in German Literature*, pp. 314–20.
38 It seems to me that George F. Peters, in his useful survey *The Poet as Provocateur: Heinrich Heine and His Critics* (Rochester, NY, and Woodbridge: Camden House, 2000), mistakes Adorno's argument when he suggests that he 'effectively dismisses Heine's poetry in a neo-Marxist revitalization of the old argument that it is insincere' (p. 128).

### 3 THE BIOGRAPHICAL IMPERATIVE: HELMUT HEIẞENBÜTTEL–*PRO DOMO*

1 The Latin tag comes from an essay in an earlier collection of critical essays, Helmut Heißenbüttel, *Über Literatur* (Freiburg: Olten, 1966).
2 Helmut Heißenbüttel, *Zur Tradition der Moderne. Aufsätze und Anmerkungen* (Neuwied: Luchterhand, 1972), p. 59
3 Michael Perraudin, *Heinrich Heine: Poetry in Context. A Study of Buch der Lieder* (Oxford, New York, Munich: Berg, 1989), p. 48.
4 Helmut Heißenbüttel, *Von fliegenden Fröschen, libidinösen Epen, vater-ländischen Romanen, Sprechblasen und Ohrwürmern* (Stuttgart: Klett-Cotta, 1982).
5 Cited in ibid., pp. 20–1.
6 Heißenbüttel, *Zur Tradition der Moderne*, p. 64
7 I have gratefully used the translation by Hal Draper, *The Complete Poems of Heinrich Heine* (Cambridge, MA: Suhrkame / Insel, and Oxford: Oxford University Press, 1982), cited in the text as D, with page numbers.
8 Heißenbüttel, *Zur Tradition der Moderne*, p. 67.
9 There are other striking examples. See the discussion of 'Der Apollogott' or the subversions of balladesque narrative in 'Jehuda ben Halevy' below in chapter 10.
10 Heißenbüttel, *Von fliegenden Fröschen*, p. 185
11 Ibid., p. 79.
12 Ibid., p. 78.
13 The phrase 'ewiger Vorrat' used by Heißenbüttel, ibid., p. 80 and in *Zur Tradition der Moderne*, p. 69, is the translation of Palgrave's term 'treasury' adopted by Borchardt in the title of his own well-known anthology; see below, chapter 6: 'How to become a symbolist'.
14 Heißenbüttel, *Von fliegenden Fröschen*, p. 80.
15 Ibid., p. 82.
16 See Heine, *Memoiren*, B 6/1, 564–5.

### 4 FROM THE PRIVATE LIFE OF EVERYMAN: SELF-PRESENTATION AND AUTHENTICITY IN *BUCH DER LIEDER*

1 HSA XX, 91
2 See Hans Robert Jauß, *Literaturgeschichte als Provokation* (Frankfurt am Main: Suhrkamp, 1970): 'Das Ende der Kunstperiode – Aspekte der literarischen Revolution bei Heine, Hugo und Stendhal', pp. 107–43: pp. 107–9.
3 Norbert Altenhofer, 'Ästhetik des Arrangements. Zu Heines "Buch der Lieder"', in *Die verlorene Augensprache. Über Heinrich Heine*, ed. Volker Bohn (Frankfurt am Main: Insel, 1993), pp. 156–7.
4 See Werner/Houben, I, 192.
5 *Deutsche Vierteljahrsschrift* of 1838, quoted by Werner Kraft, *Heine der Dichter* (Munich: Text + Kritik, 1983), p. 15; the notion of the mosaic and of the

'montaged' personality seems to originate in Schiller's review of Bürger's poems, which he describes as 'more a conjunction of ideas, a compilation of characteristics, a kind of mosaic, than ideals' ('mehr einen Zusammenwurf von Bildern, eine Kompilation von Zügen, eine Art Mosaik als Ideale') (Johann Friedrich von Schiller, *Sämtliche Werke*, 3rd edition, ed. Gerhard Fricke and Herbert G. Göpfert in association with Herbert Stubenrauch, 5 vols. (Munich: Hanser, 1962), vol. V, p. 980). Before Schiller the idea appears in Winckelmann's *Gedanken über die Nachahmung der griechischen Werke*.

6 See Michael Perraudin, 'The "Doppelgänger" Poem and Its Antecedents: A Short Illustration of Heine's Creative Response to His Romantic Precursors', *Germanisch-Romanische Monatsschrift* 35 (1985), pp. 342–8.

7 This is S. S. Prawer's suggestion in *Heine: Das Buch der Lieder* (London: Edward Arnold, 1960), p. 37.

8 Perraudin, 'The "Doppelgänger" Poem', 347.

9 In the last of the 'Zeitgedichte' ('Poems for the Times') in the *Neue Gedichte*, 'Nachtgedanken' ('Night Thoughts'), this metaphor is explicit: 'Es kommt mein Weib, schön wie der Morgen' ('My wife comes in, fair as the morrow' (B 4, 433; D 408)). On allegorical possibilities see Stefan Bodo Würffel, *Der produktive Widerspruch* (Bern: Francke, 1986), p. 209.

10 Prawer, *Heine: Das Buch der Lieder*, pp. 12–13.

11 See DHA I/2, 1238.

12 Johann Wolfgang von Goethe, 'Gefunden', *Werke*, vol. I, p. 254.

13 Conversely, in a very concentrated discussion of this 'remarkable poem', Paul Peters identifies in the Sphinx Heine's experience of the 'ultimate shock of the female and the feminine': 'A Walk on the Wild Side', in Roger F. Cook (ed.), *A Companion to the Works of Heinrich Heine* (Rochester, NY, and Woodbridge: Camden House, 2002), pp. 55–103: pp. 68–9.

14 Frank Lentricchia, *Ariel and the Police* (Madison: University of Wisconsin Press, 1988), p. 3.

15 Heine describes his project in this way in his letter to Merckel, 16 November 1826 (HSA XX, 274–6: 276).

16 Adorno, *Gesammelte Schriften*, vol. XI, p. 370; *Notes to Literature*, vol. II, p. 43.

17 Kraus, *Untergang der Welt*, p. 194: 'Wohl aber überbietet ihn heute jeder Itzig Witzig in der Fertigkeit, ästhetisch auf Teetisch zu sagen und eine kandierte Gedankenhülse durch Reim und Rhythmus zum Knallbonbon zu machen.'

18 Kraus's criticism of Heine's commercial approach to language is anticipated by Ludwig Börne when he explains Heine's lack of personal convictions: 'Herr Heine is merely a phrase merchant who presents his offering to anyone and everyone, with businesslike neutrality. He is never concerned about the right, the justice of a cause; he only bothers about his word trade' (Ludwig Börne, *Sämtliche Schriften*, ed. Inge and Peter Rippmann, 5 vols. (Dreieich: Melzer, 1977), vol. II, p. 897.) See also Würffel, *Der produktive Widerspruch*, p. 262.

19 Grappin quotes a letter to Immermann of 14 January 1823 about his tea-time scourging in relation to this scenario. HSA XX, 65

20 Peters, 'A Walk on the Wild Side', p. 63.

21 See Grappin's commentary, DHA, I/2, 819.

22 Würffel identifies this early poem as a 'desperate search for new forms of expression': *Der produktive Widerspruch*, p. 83; see also p. 98.

23 Laura Hofrichter, *Heinrich Heine, Biographie seiner Dichtung*, (Göttingen: Vandenhoeck und Ruprecht, 1966), pp. 33–4

24 See B 1, 713, and in particular Briegleb's 'Vermerke zu Textähnlichkeiten in den zyklischen Zusammenhängen' (B 1, 676–7).

25 See note, B 1, 732.

26 Briegleb, *Opfer Heine?*, p 19. Briegleb's biographical prolegomena give an account of Heine's 'biblical mode of writing'. This method makes his textual apparatus dense with chain-references. See also Sammons's tart remarks on the procedure as adopted in the Hanser edition, in *A Modern Biography*, pp. 357–8.

27 Perraudin, *Poetry in Context*, p. 48.

28 Briegleb (B 1, 713) reminds us of the substance of the myth, quoting Herder's *Paramythien*, according to which Apollo grants the bird the song it never had and, in its death, immortality. He does not make explicit the other association that would link the star of love (Venus) to the dying swan as an animal sacred to Aphrodite, though he notes this meaning of the swan in his list of 'Bild-Chiffren', B 1, 670.

29 DHA I/2, 777.

30 Perraudin comments on the 'multiplication of the figure of the beloved' as also the 'cumulative effect of the *Buch der Lieder* poetry as a whole': '"Anfang und Ende meines lyrischen Jugendlebens": Two Key Poems of Heine's Early Years', *Seminar* 32/1 (1986), p. 52.

31 Benjamin, *Ursprung des deutschen Trauerspiels, Gesammelte Schriften*, I.1, p. 352; *Origin of the German Tragic Drama*, p. 176.

32 Martin Walser, 'Heines Tränen', in *Liebeserklärungen* (Frankfurt am Main: Suhrkamp, 1983), pp. 195–6.

33 See Grappin's commentary, DHA I/2, 845.

34 See B 1, 722.

35 Briegleb, *Opfer Heine?*, p. 235.

36 'Die Bindung des Textes an die Erlebnisstruktur eines (außerliterarischen) Subjekts wird ersetzt durch den (innerliterarischen) Bezug auf andere Texte, der in Heines lyrischen Zyklen meist die Form des selbstkritischen oder poetologischen Kommentars in Versen annimmt' (Altenhofer, 'Ästhetik des Arrangements', p. 157).

37 See William Empson, *Some Versions of Pastoral* (Harmondsworth: Penguin, 1974), especially chapter 7 on *Alice in Wonderland*.

38 Grappin's allusion to *Des Knaben Wunderhorn* does not seem to me to throw any better light on the text (see DHA I/2, 919).

39 B 1, 716, 728; DHA I/2, 38.

40 It is particularly important to recognize these systematic erasures of reference in the light of Briegleb's complex decipherment of *Heimkehr* XXXV as a polemic partially addressed to J. B. Rousseau which is given more 'plastic' anti-Catholic expression in XXXVII (B 1, 725, 728).

41 Sammons, *Heinrich Heine: The Elusive Poet*, p. 73.

42 Perraudin, *Poetry in Context*, pp. 37–71. See particularly pp. 51–60; 64–71.

43 Höhn calls them 'völliges Neuland', *Heine-Handbuch*, p. 75.

44 See most recently Bernd Kortländer, 'Die Erfindung des Meeres aus dem Geist der Poesie: Heines Natur', in Joseph A. Kruse, Ulrike Reuter, and Martin Hollender (eds.), '*Ich Narr des Glücks*'. *Heinrich Heine 1797–1856. Bilder einer Ausstellung* (Stuttgart, Weimar: Metzler, 1997), pp. 261–9.

45 See B 1, 847–48.

46 See Jürgen Brummack (ed.), *Heinrich Heine. Epoche – Werk – Wirkung*, (Munich: C. H. Beck, 1980), pp. 108–10.

47 Apparat zur *Romantischen Schule*, DHA 8/2, 1314.

48 See B 2, 462–70.

49 Voß's attack on Friedrich von Stolberg's conversion to Roman Catholicism appeared in 1819; Wolfgang Menzel's attack on Voß in 1825.

50 Friedrich's painting is in the Nationalgalerie, Berlin. See Kortländer, 'Die Erfindung des Meeres', p. 268; Michael Perraudin takes a less optimistic view of this 'empty and bereft silence'. See 'The Experiential World of Heine's *Buch der Lieder*', in Cook (ed.), *A Companion*, pp. 44–5

51 The phrase is Perraudin's. See his definitive account of 'Heine's Byronism' in *Poetry in Context*, pp. 81–118. On *Nordsee*, pp. 98–103.

52 Perraudin, *Poetry in Context*, pp. 100–1.

53 This poem is a probable origin, via Nerval's translations, of Norwegian allusions in Rimbaud's 'Ophélie', and even among the Parnassians. On that unusual route it will subsequently bring Heine's modern sensibility to Heym's 'Ophelia' too, and eventually to Brecht's 'Vom ertrunkenen Mädchen'.

54 *Der Mann ohne Eigenschaften* in Robert Musil, *Gesammelte Werke*, 9 vols. (Reinbek: Rowohlt, 1978), vol. III, p. 1014.

55 Christoph Martin Wieland: *Werke*, ed. Fritz Martini and Hans Werner Seiffert, 5 vols. (Munich: Hanser, 1964–8), vol. IV, p. 325.

56 See B 1, 751 on 'Frieden' , with further discussion of *Heimkehr* XXXV.

57 Rolf Lüdi, *Heinrich Heines Buch der Lieder: Poetische Strategien und deren Bedeutung* (Frankfurt am Main, Bern, etc.: Peter Lang, 1979), draws attention to the parallel between *Junge Leiden* and Goethe's title; see also Charles Andler, *La Poésie de Heine* (Lyon: Bibliothèque de la société des études germaniques) 1948, pp. 69–70; Erich Mayser, *H. Heines 'Buch der Lieder'*, pp. 33–5. Höhn cites both, *Heine Handbuch*, p. 66, and further draws attention to Heine's letter to Straube of early March 1821 (HSA XX, 39–41), and the remarks revealing a social interest in *Werther* in a review (B 1, 431). The allusion to the 'patriarchalische Idee' appears in Werther's letter of 12 May in Book I (Goethe, *Werke*, vol. VI, p. 10).

58 See Perraudin, *Poetry in Context*, p. 98.

5 IN THE DIPLOMATIC SENSE: READING *REISEBILDER*

1 The underlying historical reach of the *Nordsee* III is identified as Hegelian in Jost Hermand, *Der frühe Heine. Ein Kommentar zu den* 'Reisebildern' (Munich: Winkler, 1976), pp. 84–7.

2 Compare Perraudin on the relationship between the poet and the Great Men of History, *Poetry in Context*, p. 69.

3 See B 2, 341; Wolfgang Preisendendanz, 'Der Funktionsübergang von Dichtung und Publizistik' in *Heinrich Heine. Werkstrukturen und Epochenbezüge*, 2nd edition (Munich: Universitätstaschenbücher, 1983), p. 63: part III of this essay (pp. 39–78) deals in a groundbreaking way with Heine's methods in the *Reisebilder*; Brummack, *Heinrich Heine. Epoche – Werk – Wirkung*, p. 133.

4 See B 2, 150–3. Compare in *Die Leiden des jungen Werther* Werther's reading of 'Colma', Goethe, *Werke*, vol. VI, pp. 107–9; the well-known reference to Klopstock appears in Book I, on 16 June.

5 Ibid., vol. I, p. 50. Hermand identifies the 'shears of a remorseless Fate' near the start of the final section of *Harzreise* as a direct reference to Goethe's poem: *Der frühe Heine*, p. 70.

6 The earlier comparison appears in relation to Voß, B 3, 389. For a full discussion of Heine's visit to Weimar and its implications for the parodies in *Harzreise* and for his subsequent self-understanding, see Hermand, *Der frühe Heine*, pp. 60–8; Helmut Koopmann, 'Heine in Weimar. Zur Problematik seiner Beziehung zur Kunstperiode', *Zeitschrift für deutsche Philologie* 91 (1972), Sonderheft *Heine und seine Zeit*, pp. 46–66.

7 Translations from the *Reisebilder* are my own. An elegant translation of *Die Harzreise, Ideen. Das Buch Le Grand*, and *Die Stadt Lucca* appears in Heinrich Heine, *Selected Prose*, trans. and ed. with introduction and notes by Ritchie Robertson (Harmondsworth: Penguin, 1993).

8 Goethe, *Werke*, vol. I, pp. 44–5.

9 For a subtle discussion of Heine's recurrent deployment of the Aeschylean imagery of Prometheus Bound, see Hans Blumenberg, *Arbeit am Mythos*, 3rd edition (Frankfurt am Main: Suhrkamp, 1984), pp. 644–54.

10 This is less innocent than it seems: for the place of Russia in Heine's subsequent account of European emancipation, see *Die Reise von München nach Genua*, chapter XXX (B, 2, 380–1).

11 B 2, 753 on 147–8 provides evidence of the censor's attempts to make Heine's criticism less explicit.

12 Parallel uses of the idea of 'esoteric' meaning can be found in *Die Reise von München nach Genua* (B 2, 353) (the esoteric meaning of Rossini's comic operas); in *Die Romantische Schule* (B 3, 367, 369) (medieval poetry and architecture); *Shakespeares Mädchen und Frauen* (*Shakespeare's Women and Maidens* (B 4, 175)) explicitly invokes the idea of an esoteric reader able to identify the conflict of Jerusalem and Athens, spirit and flesh, in current affairs as well as cultural history.

13 The language of the eyes that takes on the force of gestural communication here returns in Heine's view of Rahel Levin-Varnhagen von Ense. See his letter

of condolence to Varnhagen on the death of his sister, of 5 February 1840 (B 4, 753) discussed below, pp. 164–5; and Altenhofer, 'Ästhetik des Arrangements' pp. 58–75.

14 See Günter Häntzschel's editorial comments at B 2, 689. The volume appeared in 1969.

15 In his conclusion ('Schlußwort') Heine compares his use of the *Briefe aus Berlin* to Cellini's use of tin to bulk out the bronze cast of Perseus. See B 2, 602.

16 Klaus Briegleb has discussed the significance of Heine's acquisition of Prussian nationality in *Opfer Heine?*, pp. 45–70.

17 See 'Heine – (k)ein Berliner' in Höhn, *Heine-Handbuch*, p. 174.

18 Madame de Staël, *De l'Allemagne*, ed. La Comtesse Jean de Pange, 5 vols. (Paris: Hachette, 1958–60), vol. I, pp. 235–6.

19 I owe this last point to Rowland Cotterill.

20 On the non-simultaneity of the simultaneous, see Ernst Bloch, *Erbschaft dieser Zeit*, Werkausgabe, vol. IV (Frankfurt am Main: Suhrkamp, 1985), pp. 104–26.

21 See Christian Liedke, *Heinrich Heine* (Reinbek bei Hamburg: Rowohlt, 1997), p. 53.

22 See 'Von Karlsbad nach Berlin', in Höhn, *Heine Handbuch*, pp. 173–4.

23 See also Klaus Pabel, *Heines 'Reisebilder'. Ästhetisches Bedürfnis und politisches Interesse am Ende der Kunstperiode* (Munich: Wilhelm Fink, 1977), pp. 53–4.

24 For an alternative view, see Albrecht Betz, *Ästhetik und Politik. Heinrich Heines Prosa* (Munich: Hanser, 1971), p. 108. According to Betz, Heine falls victim to a temptation to write 'a potpourri of facts and anecdotes, served up with plenty of gags and word-play'.

25 Ibid., p. 32. Pabel claims to identify resistance to the form of the commodity in the emerging aesthetic of *Ideas. The Book of Le Grand* (*Heines 'Reisebilder'*, pp. 160–74).

26 Bernd Witte, 'Düsseldorf – London – Paris. Heinrich Heines allegorische Lektüre der großen Stadt', in: Kruse (ed.), *Ich Narr des Glücks*, pp. 122–5.

27 S. S. Prawer, *Frankenstein's Island. England and the English in the Writing of Heinrich Heine* (Cambridge: Cambridge University Press 1986), p. 81.

28 Kraus, *Untergang der Welt*, p. 191.

29 Sammons, *Heinrich Heine. A Modern Biography*, p. 149.

30 Prawer, *Frankenstein's Island*, p. 61.


6 HOW TO BECOME A SYMBOLIST HEINE AND THE ANTHOLOGIES OF
STEFAN GEORGE AND RUDOLF BORCHARDT

1 Lentricchia: *Ariel and the Police*, p. 21

2 'Doch keineswegs darf man ihm, der als Gegensatz allein Jean Paul verträgt, einen anderen beireihen – am wenigsten, wie man leider noch immer tut, Schiller oder Heine: jener der feinste Schönheitslehrer, dieser der erste Tagesschreiber, beide aber in diesem Zwölfgestirn eher die kleinsten als die grössten' (Stefan George, Karl Wolfskehl, *Das Jahrhundert Goethes* (Düsseldorf and Munich: Georg Bondi, 1964 [1902, 1910]), n.p.).

3 See Michael Hamburger, *The Truth of Poetry* (London: Methuen, 1982), p. 70.
4 See Perraudin, *Poetry in Context*, pp. 90, 94.
5 René Wellek, 'What is Symbolism?', in *The Symbolist Movement in the Literature of European Languages*, ed. Anna Balakian (Budapest: Akadémiai Kiado, 1984), p. 27.
6 Cited by Haskell M. Block, 'Heine and the French Symbolists', in *Creative Encounter*, ed. Leland R. Phelps and A. Tilo Alt (Chapel Hill: University of North Carolina Press, 1978), pp. 25–39: see p. 28.
7 Cited by Wellek, 'What is Symbolism?', pp. 26, 27.
8 Hamburger, *The Truth of Poetry*, p. 70.
9 B 1, 309: line 967; see also the editor's remarks on the sonnet, 765–6.
10 Bernhard Böschenstein, 'Wirkungen des französischen Symbolismus auf die deutsche Dichtung', *Euphorion* 58 (1964), p. 376.
11 Friedrich Gundolf, *George* (Berlin: Georg Bondi, 1930), p. 10.
12 Ibid., pp. 11, 6.
13 Rudolf Borchardt, *Ewiger Vorrat deutscher Poesie* (Munich: Verlag der Bremer Presse, 1926), p. 456.
14 Ibid., p. 452.
15 Ibid., p. 457.
16 Ibid., p. 443.
17 Kraus, *Untergang der Welt*, p. 185
18 Borchardt, *Ewiger Vorrat*, p. 459.
19 Borchardt's intuition reflects the derivative element in Heine's work documented by Michael Perraudin.
20 Borchardt, *Ewiger Vorrat*, pp. 458–9.
21 See Jacques Grange, *Rudolf Borchardt 1877–1945*, 2 vols. (Bern, Frankfurt am Main, New York: Peter Lang, 1983), vol. II, p. 893.
22 Borchardt, *Ewiger Vorrat*, p. 459. My italics.
23 It seems fanciful to suggest that this is supposed to attest 'la continuité de la vie intellectuelle et spirituelle allemande'. See Grange, *Rudolf Borchardt*, p. 884; Borchardt, *Ewiger Vorrat*, p. 25.
24 For a discussion of Borchardt's treatment of this poem, see Würffel, *Der produktive Widerspruch*, pp. 56–63.
25 Adorno, 'George', *Gesammelte Schriften*, vol. XI, p. 525; *Notes to Literature*, vol. II, p. 180.
26 'Manchmal jedoch redet wirklich aus George, wie ein letztes Mal, und wie andere es nur vortäuschten, Sprache selber.' Adorno, 'George', *Gesammelte Schriften*, vol. XI, p. 529; *Notes to Literature*, vol. II, p. 185.

7 THE REAL HEINE: *ATTA TROLL* AND ALLEGORY

1 'Das Barocke, das Saloppe, das unverschämt Prosaische an diesen Versen ist eben das Poetische' (B 6/2, 677).
2 Würffel summarizes the central themes as love (St Simonianism), politics, and the question of artistic quality (*Der produktive Widerspruch*, p. 201).

3 See ibid., p. 211.

4 See Briegleb's commentary, B 4, 987–8.

5 See HSA XXII, 43; 49–50. The further consequence of Klaus Briegleb's account is to see the sequence of work after the Börne *Denkschrift*, through *Atta Troll* to *Lutetia* as a negotiation of political failures. Briegleb's argument is as dispersed as the clues he reckons to find in Heine's work. See B 4, 891–3, 984–9, and compare *Opfer Heine?*, pp. 344–5. His point seems to be that the accession of Friedrich Wilhelm IV of Prussia, combined with press hostility in France as a result of her diplomatic defeat in the Near East crisis, led to a dangerous alliance of Prussian restoration politics with bourgeois and liberal democratic 'nationalism'.

6 See Briegleb's account of the variants, B 4, 997; compare Paralipomena A9 and A2 in Winfried Woesler's edition of *Atta Troll* (Stuttgart: Reclam, 1977), pp. 106, 99.

7 Briegleb, B 4, 988, is inclined to see this remark as also designed to distract Laube from the more extreme 'communist' parts of the poem.

8 Similarly Heine's letter of 9 September 1840 (HSA XXI, 381) makes it quite clear that he recognizes his own responsibilities 'to act as a midwife' in the 'transitional crisis'.

9 See the classic account of Kurt Weinberg, *Henri Heine. Romantique défroqué. Héraut du symbolisme français* (New Haven and Paris: Yale, 1954).

10 This sense would echo Goethe's understanding of the Olympian gods: 'The god became a man in order to raise man to the status of god. One glimpsed the highest dignity and was inspired for the highest beauty' ('Der Gott war zum Menschen geworden, um den Menschen zum Gott zu erheben. Man erblickte die höchste Würde, und ward für die höchste Schönheit begeistert') (*Winckelmann*, in Goethe, *Werke*, vol. XII, p. 103).

11 D 420 (modified): 'in vaterländischen Dienst zu treten, etwa als Marketenderinnen der Freiheit oder als Wäscherinnen der christlich-germanischen Nationalität' (B 4, 494).

12 This is addressed in *Deutschland. Ein Wintermärchen*, V, lines 19–36.

13 Sammons, *The Elusive Poet*, p. 276.

14 Sammons, *Heinrich Heine* (Sammlung Metzler 261), p. 110.

15 This is the view of S. S. Prawer in *Heine. The Tragic Satirist. A Study of the Later Poetry* (Cambridge: Cambridge University Press, 1961), pp. 60–89.

16 Manfred Windfuhr, *Heinrich Heine. Revolution und Reflexion*, 2nd edition (Stuttgart: Metzler, 1976), p. 221. Walter Killy has taken a similar line in *Die Wunde Deutschland. Heinrich Heines Dichtung* (Frankfurt am Main: Insel, 1990), p. 216.

17 'Da sprechen die Leute von Eingebung, von Begeisterung und dergleichen, – ich arbeite wie der Goldschmied, wenn er eine Kette anfertigt, – ein Ringelchen nach dem anderen, – eines in das andere', Werner/Houben I, 232–3, cited by Erhardt Weidl, *Heinrich Heines Arbeitsweise. Kreativität der Veränderung* (Hamburg: Hoffmann und Campe: Heine-Studien, 1974), p. 41.

18 'Die kleinteiligen sprachlichen Versatzstücke werden probend in immer neuen Kombinationen montiert, variiert und dabei abgeschliffen' (ibid., p. 56).
19 HSA XX, 184, 267, 271, 227.
20 Weidl, *Arbeitsweise*, p. 74.
21 Compare Woesler's commentary, following Werner Vordtriede, in his edition: *Atta Troll. Ein Sommernachtstraum* (Stuttgart: Reclam, 1977), p. 144.
22 Friedrich Gottlieb Klopstock, *Ausgewählte Werke*, ed. Karl August Schleiden (Munich: Hanser, 1962), p. 90.
23 Woesler (ed.), *Atta Troll*, p. 143, on lines 41–8.
24 E. T. A. Hoffmann, *The Golden Pot and Other Tales*, trans. Ritchie Robertson (Oxford and New York: Oxford University Press, 1992) p. 5; *Der goldne Topf*, in *Fantasie- und Nachtstücke* (Düsseldorf and Zürich: Winkler, 1996), p. 183.
25 See B 4, 760. This note is also offered as a gloss on the *Atta Troll* passage, where it is called 'diese grundsätzliche Rede-Einstellung' (B 4, 1007).
26 See Woesler's commentary, *Atta Troll*, p. 53.
27 See my 'Goethe's "Euphrosyne" and the Theatres of *Faust* Part II', *PEGS* 59 (1988–9), pp. 59–78.
28 Jürgen Walter, 'Poesie und Zeitkritik' in Brummack (ed.), *Heinrich Heine. Epoche – Werk – Wirkung*, p. 227: 'Bild vom sittig-religiösen Bettlermantel'.
29 See Woesler (ed.), *Atta Troll*, Paralipomena B1; Briegleb's 'Streichungen' a, B 4, 989, includes an additional stanza.
30 B 3, 391: 'bemerkten lächelnd, daß . . . die Goetheschen Helden schwerlich als moralisch zu vertreten wären, daß aber diese Beförderung der Moral, die man von Goethe's Dichtungen verlange, keineswegs der Zweck der Kunst sei: denn in der Kunst gäbe es keine Zwecke, wie in dem Weltbau selbst.'
31 B 6/2, 706; cited with commentary in Höhn, *Heine-Handbuch*, p. 88.
32 The women on the balconies of Cauterets at the beginning of *Atta Troll* anticipate and unmask the aestheticism glimpsed by Würffel in 'Valkyren' from *Romanzero* (B 6/1, 20–1). See Würffel, *Der produktive Widerspruch*, p. 272.
33 Woesler (ed.), *Atta Troll*, p. 157 on lines 93–100.
34 'noch viele solche, nur noch "tendenzlosere" poetische Produktionen' (DHA 4, 396), cited by Höhn, *Heine-Handbuch*, p. 93.

8 VENTRILOQUISM IN *LUDWIG BÖRNE: EINE DENKSCHRIFT*

1 Gillian Rose, *The Broken Middle* (Oxford: Blackwell, 1992), p. 20: on Kierkegaard, pseudonymously *inter et inter*. My account of Heine's *Denkschrift* owes a great deal to the broad outline of Rose's argument, and all too little to her detailed expositions.
2 For a brief summary of the relationship, see Höhn, *Heine-Handbuch*, pp. 421–4.
3 Thomas Mann, 'Notiz über Heine' (1908), in *Ludwig Börne und Heinrich Heine. Ein deutsches Zerwürfnis*, p. 317. This anthology is cited hereafter in the text as *DZ* with page numbers.
4 Heinrich Heine, *Beiträge zur deutschen Ideologie*, ed. Hans Mayer (Frankfurt am Main: Ullstein, 1971).

5 Lothar Jordan, 'Heine und Enzensberger', *HJb* 32 (1993), pp. 127–43

6 Hans Magnus Enzensberger, *Mittelmaß und Wahn. Gesammelte Zerstreuungen* (Frankfurt am Main: Suhrkamp, 1988), p. 212.

7 *Merkur* 448 (June 1986), pp. 453–68; subsequently in Habermas, *Kleine politische Schriften*, 10 vols. (Frankfurt am Main: Suhrkamp, 1987), vol. VI: *Eine Art Schadensabwicklung.* 'Heinrich Heine and the Role of the Intellectual in Germany', in *The New Conservatism: Cultural Criticism and the Historians' Debate*, ed. and trans. Shierry Weber Nicholsen (Cambridge, MA: MIT Press, 1989), pp. 71–99.

8 Walser, *Liebeserklärungen*, pp. 197–207.

9 See B 4, 696–7.

10 Sammons, *A Modern Biography*, p. 238.

11 See Werner/Houben I, p. 417. Paolo Chiarini in 'Heine contra Börne ovvero Critica dell'impazienza rivolutionaria', *Studi germanici*, n.s., 10 (1972), pp. 355–92) recognizes the importance of style for Heine (p. 365) but nevertheless reads the strategy of the *Denkschrift* as a miscalculation (p. 369, n. 20). Most recently, see Zvi Tauber, 'Ästhetik und Politik: Der Streit zwischen Heine und Börne', in Frank Stern and Maria Gierlinger (eds.), *Ludwig Börne. Deutscher, Jude, Demokrat* (Berlin: Aufbau, 2003), pp. 203–21, who settles, as its central theme, for the 'absurd dilemma' of the conflict Heine perceives between justice and beauty, and projects into his relations with Börne.

12 See Heinrich Brockhaus's diary entry in November 1840 (*DZ* 290; Werner/Houben I, 457–8.)

13 Sammons notes in *A Modern Biography*, 'It demands a careful and attentive reading of a sort it has only seldom received' (p. 238). Sammons himself discusses the work in *The Elusive Poet*, pp. 248–73; Inge Rippmann, 'Heines Denkschrift über Börne: ein Doppelporträt', *Heine Jahrbuch* 12 (1973), pp. 41–70, concentrates on a substantial exposition of the notion of the Nazarene, while seeking to reconcile Heine and Börne through what they hold in common in the *Zeitgeist*. Rippmann has returned to the theme of exile in '"Sie saßen an den Wassern Babylons". Eine Annäherung an Heinrich Heines "Denkschrift über Ludwig Börne"', *Heine Jahrbuch* 34 (1995), pp. 25–47.

14 See Rose, *The Broken Middle*, p. 161 and the context of argument pp. 161–4.

15 The phrase is Briegleb's, 'überstürzte und sogleich formalisierte Volksbefreiung': see B 4, 803–4 on the first of the letters from Heligoland included in the *Memorial* (1 July 1830), B 4, 38.

16 This is the connection stressed by Tauber in relation to the French Preface to *Lutetia*. See 'Ästhetik und Politik', pp. 204, 219–20.

17 Michael Werner's 'Frères d'armes ou frères ennemis? Heine et Boerne à Paris', *Francia* 7 (1979), pp. 251–70) also stresses Heine's close relations with leading émigrés in Paris – Venedey, Garnier, Pistor. Briegleb discusses the linking of Heine's name with Börne in '"Ich trug an Bord meines Schiffes die Götter der Zukunft". Versuch über Heinrich Heines Abschied von Ludwig Börne in Frankfurt am 16. November 1827', in Stern and Gierlinger (eds.), *Ludwig Börne*, pp. 222–68. See pp. 227–33.

18 *DZ* 16; Börne, *Sämtliche Schriften*, V, 11.

19 Sammons recognizes different impulses but insists that they are in conflict as 'two different attitudes, one political and democratic, the other aesthetic and aristocratic' (*The Elusive Poet*, p. 250).

20 See Helmut Koopmann's commentary, DHA 11, 327.

21 Rose, *The Broken Middle*, p. 165. My use of the term 'authorship' is derived in particular from chapter 5, 'Love and the State'.

22 See Werner, 'Frères d'armes ou frères ennemis?', p. 254.

23 HSA XXI, 28, cited by Wolfgang Hädecke, *Heinrich Heine, eine Biographie* (Munich: Hanser, 1985), p. 283.

24 Börne, *Sämtliche Schriften*, vol. II, p. 898

25 Inge Rippmann points out that in *Shakespeares Mädchen und Frauen* Heine attacks the same combination of 'ascetic religious zeal and republican fanaticism' (B 4, 176) in English Puritanism. See Rippmann, 'Heines Denkschrift über Börne', p. 49.

26 See Hädecke, *Heinrich Heine*, p. 276; Sammons, *A Modern Biography*, p. 190.

27 The passage is so construed by Briegleb, B 4, 774n.

28 HSA XXIV, 105; cf. XXIVK, 90 *ad loc.*

29 See Campe's letters of 13 March 1832; 16 March, 25 June, 3 December 1833 (HSA XXIV, 114–18, 159, 178–83, 228–31); and Heine's letters to Campe of 16 January 1834; 20 December 1836 (HSA XXI, 74, 172–3) – 'When people named your most recent author to me, I covered my face' – though it is not certain that Campe was right in reading this as a reference to Börne; 23 January 1837 (HSA XXI, 174–5).

30 Sammons was one of the first to evaluate this aspect of the *Denkschrift*. For a summary see *A Modern Biography*, pp. 238–9.

31 My account of Rahel Levin's 'language' owes a great deal to Norbert Altenhofer's study in the posthumous collection named after it, *Die verlorene Augensprache*, pp. 58–75: particularly pp. 58–60. Altenhofer's essay concentrates on an exposition of *Ideen. Das Buch Le Grand*.

32 For a full discussion of the paradoxes of political stylistics in the early part of the nineteenth century see Briegleb on 'jenes . . . Lächeln', B 4, 765–6.

33 Letter to Fouqué of 26 July 1809, see Rahel Varnhagen, *Im Umgang mit ihren Freunden (Briefe 1793–1833)*, ed. Friedhelm Kemp (Munich: Kösel, 1967), pp. 295–7. Gillian Rose cites this extraordinary letter in *The Broken Middle*, p. 192.

34 See Briegleb, *Opfer Heine?*, pp. 157–78 on the 'Diskurs der Ausgrenzung'.

35 Rose, *The Broken Middle*, pp. 187–8.

36 '*Geheimnis, Verschweigen, Zensurrücksicht* und *Selbstzensur, Lächeln, Augensprache* usw.', B 4, 948; compare 753–4.

37 Compare Rose: 'Remaining within the agon of authorship they [Rahel Varnhagen, Rosa Luxemburg, Hannah Arendt] cultivate aporetic universalism, restless affirmation and undermining of political form and political action, which never loses sight of the continuing mutual corruption of the state and civil society . . .' (*The Broken Middle*, p. 155).

38 See Judith Purver, 'Revolution, Romanticism, Restoration' in *A History of Women's Writing*, ed. Jo Catling (Cambridge: Cambridge University Press, 2000), p. 82.

39 See Koopmann's comments, DHA 11, 622, on 121:1–2. Other references to Buffon, especially in *Communism, Philosophy and the Clerics* (*Lutetia*, Anhang II: 8 Juli 1843; B 5, 509), explicitly reject the direct bond between style and character in favour of imagery of disguise: 'sometimes the only thing hidden in the fox's clothing of Jesuitism is a limited little donkey' ['so steckt im Fuchspelz des Jesuitismus manchmal nur ein beschränktes Grauchen']! Heine is recycling a quip first used in his review of the concert season in 1841 (B 5, 360).

40 This is sufficient internal evidence to confirm Stefan Bodo Morawe's speculation in 'List und Gegenlist: Heine als politischer Schriftsteller', *Euphorion* 82 (1988), pp. 281–315; see in particular p. 294.

41 Börne, *Sämtliche Schriften*, vol. I, p. 597.

42 Ibid., p. 594.

43 See the materials gathered in the documentation of B 4, 651–739.

44 Sammons's account of the affair is illuminating, *A Modern Biography*, pp. 228–33; particularly pp. 232–3.

45 Briegleb (B 4, 769; and compare 816, 824) identifies the denunciation of the priests of Baal, who drank when the people thirsted, with two fragments from Börne.

46 Werner makes the point in 'Frères d'armes ou frères ennemis', p. 267: 'Heine projette une partie de son propre passé sur celui qu'il présente pourtant comme un antithèse vivante'. This was anticipated by Walter Hinderer, 'Nazarene oder Hellene. Die politisch-ästhetische Fehde zwischen Heine und Börne', *Monatshefte für den Deutschunterricht* 66 (1974), pp. 355–65: p. 362.

47 See Koopmann's commentary: DHA 11, 437, 656–8.

48 Sammons identifies the same strategy: 'Börne often seems to speak with Heine's voice' to produce a kind of discursive 'mutual interaction' (*The Elusive Poet*, p. 261), but understands the exchange of voices as evidence of the jealousy Heine supposedly felt for Börne's public position.

49 See DHA 11, 425.

50 B 2, 626–7 gives the source in the 'Nachlese' as one of the sketches for *Die Bäder von Lucca*; B 4, 778–81 presents the parallel passages in tabular form.

51 Sammons, *A Modern Biography*, p. 238.

52 B 4, 826 lists parallels to *Französiche Zustände*, B 3, 96. There was an earlier plan to quote Börne *contra* Raumer in 'Menzel der Franzosenfresser' (Menzel, devourer of Frenchmen): DHA 11, 500–5 and compare Paralipomena 395–6.

53 The Book 4 instance may be close to Heine's original memoirs: see B 4, 867 *ad* 118.

54 See Karl Marx, *On the Jewish Question*, in *Early Writings*, introduced by Lucio Coletti, trans. Rodney Livingstone and Gregory Benton (London and Baltimore: Penguin, 1975), pp. 236–7; 'Zur Judenfrage', in Karl Marx and Friedrich Engels: *Werke*, ed. Institut für Marxismus-Leninismus beim ZK der SED, 43 vols. (Berlin: Dietz-Verlag, 1956–74) vol. I, pp. 372–3.

55 See Dolf Sternberger, *Heinrich Heine und die Abschaffung der Sünde* (Frankfurt am Main: Suhrkamp, 1976), pp. 156–7.

56 See Rose, *The Broken Middle*, p. 186.

57 At B 4, 833–4, 'die "Propaganda"' is the name given by restoration ideology to a supposed liberal conspiracy; the Catholic origin of the word sustains the religious language Heine has deployed since the account of Nazarene mentality in Book 1. Heine had punned on the *montagnards* of the French Revolution as 'later sermonizers on the Mount' in *Englische Fragmente* (B 2, 598).

58 See DHA 11, 635; cf. 231–62; on secrecy B 4, 871 and 918–19 ('Zentralverweis').

9 SCHEHERAZADE'S SNAPSHOTS: *LUTETIA*

1 'einen großen Teil Neues habe ich bereits hingeschrieben, ich möchte fast sagen hinzugedichtet (was aber unter uns bleibt) . . .' (HSA XXIII, 220); 'Ich bin mir bewußt in meinem Buche "Lutetia", das fast aus lauter Tatsachen besteht, kein einziges Faktum ohne geprüfte Zeugnisse und Gewährschaft mitgeteilt zu haben' (HSA XXIII, 448).

2 See in particular the Hegelian reflections which open Article VI of *Französische Zustände* and the discussion of republicanism and modernism in Article IX (B 3, 165–7; 210–15). Cf. Rutger Booß, *Ansichten der Revolution. Paris-Berichte deutscher Schriftsteller nach der Juli-Revolution 1830* (Cologne: Pahl-Rugenstein, 1977).

3 Kraus, *Untergang der Welt*, p. 193.

4 Karl Marx, *Surveys from Exile*, edited and introduced by David Fernbach (London and Baltimore: Penguin, 1973), pp. 146–249; Marx and Engels, *Werke*, vol. VIII, pp. 115–208.

5 Such classical and imperial pretensions were still vivid in the last decade of the nineteenth century: Benjamin notes in the *Passagen-Werk* that Maxime du Camp's administrative history of Paris in the second half of the century takes its inspiration from comparison and competition with antiquity – the memory of the imperial past in Athens, Carthage, Alexandria or Rome (Benjamin, *Passagen-Werk*, *Gesammelte Schriften*, vol. V/1, pp. 143–4 [C4]). Benjamin's paragraph numbers readily identify quotations in the English translation: Walter Benjamin, *The Arcades Project*, trans. Howard Eiland and Kevin McLaughlin (Cambridge, MA and London: Belknap Press of Harvard University, 1999).

6 See Roger Magraw, *France 1815–1914. The Bourgeois Century* (London: Fontana, 1983), pp. 58–63.

7 Compare *Augsburger Allgemeine Zeitung* text at B 5, 1018, where the suggestion that Rothschild promotes only dead authors (who cost less to support) is more sharply made.

8 *Pace* Hansen's commentary in DHA 13/2, 1729, which identifies a renewal of the eighteenth-century formula 'je ne sais quoi'.

9 See Preisendanz, *Werkstrukturen*, p. 86; Briegleb, *Opfer Heine?*, pp. 18–20 and *passim*.

10 I translate Heine's German draft. The French version gives: 'Voilà pourquoi mes lettres contiennent beaucoup d'historiettes et d'arabesques, dont le sens symbolique n'est pas intelligible pour tout le monde, et qui ont pu paraître aux yeux du lecteur superficiel comme un ramassis de jaseries mesquines et de notices de gobe-mouche' (B 5, 222–3).

11 In 'Der politische Schriftsteller und die (Selbst-)Zensur', *Heine Jahrbach* 26 (1987), pp. 29–53, Michael Werner has suggested that the paintings of the 1843 Salon can be compared to metonymy.

12 Sammons, *A Modern Biography*, p. 330.

13 Briegleb borrows the term 'allégorie réelle', the subtitle of Courbet's painting 'L'Atelier du peintre', as a description of Heine's realism. See *Opfer Heine?*, pp. 131–45.

14 The image for a loss of support for the July Monarchy first appears, in connection with Louis-Philippe himself, in *Französische Zustände*, V (B 3, 156).

15 The metaphor of *falling* in relation to Guizot is a good deal more respectful here than in *Französische Zustände*, where the possibility of his fall is presented as the diarrhoea ('Durch*fall*') of the cholera epidemic.

16 This ironic use of the lost meaning of the hieroglyph in a society which actively reorganizes the semiotic for its own ends suggests that the hermeneutic crisis analysed by Norbert Altenhofer is not limited to personal identity. See 'Chiffre, Hieroglyphe, Palimpsest: Vorformen tiefenhermeneutischer und intertextueller Interpretationen im Werk Heines', in *Texthermeneutik. Aktualität, Geschichte, Kritik*, ed. Ulrich Nassen (Munich: UTB, 1979), p. 178.

17 See David H. Pinkney, *The French Revolution of 1830* (Princeton: Princeton University Press, 1972), pp. 168–72. Lucienne Netter in 'La Genèse des articles XL et XXV de "Lutetia" ou les anachronismes de Heine', *Etudes germaniques*, 29 (1974), pp. 83–8, identifies the source of Heine's citation in a review of Blanc's work published by the royalist *Gazette de France*. See DHA 13/2, 1287.

18 On Heine's relationship to Louis-Philippe in *Lutetia* see Sammons, *The Elusive Poet*, pp. 239–47.

19 See Briegleb's commentary, B 5, 484 and 1078.

20 DHA 14/1, 629; 14/2, 839.

21 See Altenhofer, 'Chiffre, Hieroglyphe', p. 150: 'Heine has had an astonishingly powerful, for the most part, it should be said, subcutaneous effect, which can be pursued all the way to theories of intertextuality influenced by Marx, Freud, and Nietzsche.' Sander L. Gilman's essay 'Freud Reads Heine Reads Freud', in Gelber (ed.), *Jewish Reception*, pp. 77–94, traces some of Heine's presence to Freud.

22 See Benjamin, *Gesammelte Schriften*, vol. V/1, p. 517: L2a, 4; and compare L5, 5: p. 522.

23 Gerhard Höhn makes the suggestion in *Heine-Handbuch*, p. 240.

24 P. N. Furbank's description of 'the form that reflection took' in Diderot's *Salons* as 'the abundant rush of ideas, the lateral swervings, the extempore

fantasies and glimpses of new laws, and the blithe turnings back upon himself in irony' could well apply to Heine. See P. N. Furbank, *Diderot. A Critical Biography*, (London: Secker and Warburg, 1992), p. 277.

25 Ibid., pp. 87, 132.

26 Cf. Briegleb, *Opfer Heine?*, p. 288.

27 DHA commentary (14/1, 365f. *ad* 20, 29–31) confuses the reference to St John 10, 16 ('and there shall be one fold and one shepherd') with the allusion to Revelation 12, 5: 'a male child who is to rule all the nations with a rod of iron'; cf. Revelation 2, 27 and Revelation 19, 15.

28 See DHA 13/1: 627, citing the *Memoirs of Lady Hester Stanhope* (London, 1846)!

29 See J. Derrida, 'Envois: May 1979', from *The Post Card: From Socrates to Freud*, in *A Derrida Reader. Between the Blinds*, ed. Peggy Kamuf (London: Harvester Wheatsheaf, 1991), p. 511:

> Knowing well how to play with the *poste restante*. Knowing how not to be there and how to be strong for not being there right away. Knowing how not to deliver on command, how to wait and make wait, for as long as what there is that is strongest in one demands – and to the point of dying without mastering anything of the final destination. The post is always *en reste*, and always *restante*. It awaits the addressee who might always, *by chance*, not arrive.

10 MATHILDE'S INTERRUPTION: ARCHETYPES OF MODERNITY IN
HEINE'S LATER POETRY

1 Adorno, *Gesammelte Schriften*, vol. XI, p. 97; *Notes to Literature*, vol. I, p. 82.

2 See Benjamin, *Gesammelte Schriften*, vol. V/1, p. 315: J8a,2; p. 377: J38a,5. See Gerhard R. Kaiser, 'Baudelaire *pro* Heine *contra* Janin', *Heine Jahrbuch* 22 (1983), pp. 134–78.

3 Theodor Adorno and Walter Benjamin, *Briefwechsel, 1928–1940*, ed. Henri Lonitz (Frankfurt am Main: Suhrkamp, 1994), pp. 145–6.

4 Compare Benjamin, *Gesammelte Schriften*, vol. V/1 p. 99: A7a, 1 and 2; Benjamin evidently knew the poem well enough to trace other references to shawls. The letter in which Adorno sent the quotation has not been preserved.

5 Adorno and Benjamin, *Briefwechsel*, p. 35.

6 I follow recent practice in using the common English spelling of Jehuda Halevi.

7 Benjamin, 'Paris, die Hauptstadt des XIX. Jahrhunderts', IV: 'Louis Philippe oder das Interieur', *Gesammelte Schriften*, vol. V/1, pp. 52–3; *The Arcades Project*, pp. 19–20.

8 See Hofrichter, *Heinrich Heine. Biographie seiner Dichtung*, p. 136; Ritchie Robertson, *Heine* (London: Weidenfeld and Nicholson (Peter Halban), 1988), p. 95; Wolfgang Preisendanz, *Werkstrukturen*, p. 115.

9 Roger F. Cook, *By the Rivers of Babylon: Heinrich Heine's Late Songs and Reflections* (Detroit: Wayne State University Press, 1998) gives an elaborate commentary on 'Jehuda ben Halevy', pp. 307–49. Cook interprets the poem as the assertion of Heine's belief in poetry as a critical and resistant force, after

his abandonment of Hegelian philosophy and in the course of his religious (re)turn. Cook ingeniously reads the poem with post-colonial theory and alongside Freud's *Moses and Monotheism*.

10 See above p. 130. (As Cook notes, p. 307, Heine also expressed great satisfaction with the poem, HSA XIII, 112.) Joachim Bark has noted other connections with the earlier comic epic in 'Die Muse als Krankenwärterin', his 'Nachwort' to Heinrich Heine, *Romanzero*, (Munich: Goldmann, 1988), pp. 260–1. I give a fuller account of structural and thematic parallels between the poems as well as in the similarity of their genesis in 'The State of the Art: Heine's *Atta Troll* and "Jehuda ben Halevy"', *Oxford German Studies* 33 (Special Number for T. J. Reed) (2004), pp. 177–94.

11 See Briegleb, *Opfer Heine?*, pp. 98–9, 255–6.

12 For a fuller, and different, account of the role of Minnesang as a false and abstract idealism in contrast to Halevi's preservation of a primitive Jewish ethical tradition, see Cook, *By the Rivers of Babylon*, pp. 325–7.

13 Wolfgang Preisendanz discusses memory and self-representation in the poem in 'Memoria als Dimension lyrischer Selbstrepäsentation in "Jehuda ben Halevy"', in *Memoria: Vergessen und Erinnern* (Poetik und Hermeneutik XV), ed. Anselm Haverkamp and Renate Lachmann (Munich: Fink, 1993), pp. 338–58

14 Karlheinz Fingerhut briefly draws attention to this pattern in 'Spanische Spiegel: Heinrich Heines Verwendung spanischer Geschichte und Literatur zur Selbstreflexion des Juden und des Dichters', *Heine Jahrbuch* 31 (1992), pp. 106–36; here p. 128: 'The treasures of the ancient and feudal worlds are thus transformed, just like poetry itself, into the commodities of the bourgeoisie'.

15 Bark (ed.), *Romanzero*, p. 412n., cites Jonas Fränkel's commentary from Walzel's edition: 'The historian's precipitate assurance that the unhappy suitor could not have travelled far provoked Heine to make him wander quite precisely to the remotest parts and richly to embroider his experiences.'

16 Cook gives a brilliant account of the failed assimilation of the schlemiel in German as a focus for Heine's resistance to dominant and oppressive *Leitkulturen* (mainstream cultures). See *By the Rivers of Babylon*, pp. 332–9.

17 Hans Kaufmann recognizes the problem without acknowledging its structural force in 'Heinrich Heine. Poesie, Vaterland und Menschheit', in *Heinrich Heine: Werke und Briefe*, ed. Hans Kaufmann, 10 vols. (Berlin and Weimar: Aufbau, 1980), vol. X, p. 143.

18 See Sammons, *A Modern Biography*, pp. 278–85.

19 See Sammons, *Heinrich Heine* (Sammlung Metzler 261), p. 126; Edda Ziegler, *Julius Campe – Der Verleger Heinrich Heines* (Hamburg: Hoffmann und Campe, 1976), pp. 202–3.

20 See Bark, 'Die Muse als Krankenwärterin', p. 237.

21 On this logic of proliferation, see Luciano Zagari '"Das ausgesprochene Wort ist ohne Scham". Der späte Heine und die Auflösung der dichterischen Sprache', in *Zu Heinrich Heine*, ed. Zagari and Paolo Chiarini (Stuttgart: Klett, 1981)

pp. 124–38; and Zagari's 'La "Pomare" di Heine e la crisi del linguaggio "lirico"' in *Studi germanici* 3 (1965), pp. 5–38: pp. 9–10.

22 These terms are derived from Adorno's later essay on tradition, 'Über Tradition'. See *Ohne Leitbild. Parva Aesthetica, Gesammelte Schriften*, vol. X/1, pp. 310–20.

23 See Benno von Wiese, 'Mythos und Historie in Heines später Lyrik' in *Internationaler Heine-Kongreß 1972*, ed. Manfred Windfuhr (Hamburg: Hofmann und Campe, 1973), pp. 121–46: p. 126.

24 Cook, *By the Rivers of Bablylon*, pp. 191–201, by identifying the opening of the poem as an inversion of the Lorelei scenario, stresses Heine's transition from the Romantic, and sees in the fate of the 'Apollogott' Heine's distance after 1848 from his earlier 'self-aggrandizing' (p. 15) Greek aspirations.

25 See Bark (ed.), *Romanzero*, p. 300n.

26 My discussion of 'Karl I' is indebted to Hans-Peter Bayerdörfer, '"Politische Ballade". Zu den "Historien" in Heines *Romanzero*', *Deutsche Vierteljahrsschrift* 46 (1972), pp. 435–68; in particular see pp. 440–68. For a more sceptical view see Alberto Destro's commentary, DHA 3/2, pp. 600–2.

27 Würffel identifies a similar temporal openness in Heine's poem 'Die Tendenz' (B 4, 422–3: 'For the cause', D 400). The poem acknowledges a claim of art to general truth, he suggests, in that 'on the one hand, as a "poem for the times" it takes up a direct relationship to the current problems of political poetry, and on the other, thanks to its interpretative openness can effortlessly outlast the time in which it was composed' (*Der produktive Widerspruch*, p. 203). Würffel also identifies a critical reworking of the ballad tradition in the 'Historien' of *Romanzero*; see pp. 268–70.

28 See W. Hinck, *Die deutsche Ballade von Bürger bis Brecht* (Göttingen: Vandenhoeck und Ruprecht, 1968), p. 57.

29 This is the case in a more extreme form in 'Das Sklavenschiff' from *Gedichte 1853 & 1854* (B 6/1, 194–9). For Benjamin the *prostitute* is the key figure of this process of commoditization; however, he also neglects the historical precedent of the slave trade. See also Walter Klaar's remarks on 'Das Sklavenschiff' at B 6/2, 71.

30 Charles Baudelaire, *The Flowers of Evil*, trans. by James McGowan (Oxford: Oxford University Press, 1993), p. 60.

31 'Pomare' moves Heine's sense of Parisian eroticism beyond the thrilling expectation Paul Peters identifies in the *Verschiedene* poem 'In der Frühe'. See 'A Walk on the Wild Side', pp. 79–82.

32 Briegleb identifies a sense of satirical resignation after 1848: 'satirisch-resignative Nachmärzgedichte'. See B 6/2, 57 on 'Im Oktober 1849'. Also: Dolf Oehler, *Ein Höllensturz der alten Welt*, Frankfurt am Main (Suhrkamp, 1988), pp. 239–53.

33 'Die Pforte *knarrt*, und niemand kommt herein': *Faust*, 11419.

34 Frauke Bartelt (DHA 3/2, 1503) identifies a sudden change of direction in 'Der Scheidende'; it is equally plausible to see the departure of the audience for domestic pleasures as the unheroic alternative to the dying poet's lot.

35 Bark (ed.), *Romanzero*, p. 388n., offers a paraphrase of the dull, thin sound of 'ein schollernd schnöder Klang' as 'ein [von stürzenden Steinen] dumpf rollender gemeiner Klang' (a dull rolling coarse sound, as of falling stones)..

36 Baudelaire, *Flowers of Evil*, pp. 144–5.

37 It is perhaps this residual pathos that leads Cook to limit this demise to an earlier *Romantic* Heine. See *By the Rivers of Babylon*, pp. 291–2.

38 For a full discussion, see ibid., pp. 21–6, 51–61, and *passim*.

39 Letter of 24 October 1851: 'In einem Buche, welches in diesem Augenblicke zu Hamburg von mir herausgegeben wird, habe ich ganz brühwarm benützen können, was Sie über Swedenborg sagten' (HSA XX–XXVIIR (Register, Nachträge), 337). The Fichtes' visit is described in Werner/Houben, vol. II, pp. 276–86, cited in DHA 3/2, 979, and – to different effect – in B 6/2, 63! Given Heine's orchestration of his letters for their respective recipients, it need come as no surprise that, in writing to Georg Weerth, Heine insists that he is dying as a *poet* who needs neither religion nor philosophy and eschews both ('der weder Religion noch Philosophie braucht und mit beiden nichts zu schaffen hat') (5 November 1851: HSA XXIII, 147).

40 See the 'Waterloo-Fragment', B 6/1, 505. Würffel underlines the concatenation of dates – the tension between July 1830, 1848, and Heine's 'Afterword' of 1851 – as an indication of Heine's simultaneous scepticism and optimism with regard to the revolutionary cause: *Der produktive Widerspruch*, pp. 253–4.

41 Würffel gives a concentrated account of the dialectic of the everyday and the transcendent in ibid., pp. 281–2.

42 Cook, *By the Rivers of Babylon*, pp. 349, 363.

43 For a helpful summary of Benjamin's understanding of 'Modernity and Tradition', see Peter Osborne, 'Small-scale Victories, Large-scale Defeats' in *Walter Benjamin's Philosophy*, ed. Andrew Benjamin and Peter Osborne (London: Routledge, 1994), pp. 81–5.

44 Michael Werner, in *Interpretationen. Gedichte von Heinrich Heine*, ed. Bernd Kortländer (Stuttgart: Reclam, 1995), p. 188.

45 See Peter Osborne, on *Passagen-Werk* N 11, 3, 'Small-scale Victories', p. 68.

## 11 THE TRIBE OF HARRY: HEINE AND CONTEMPORARY POETRY

1 Ben Jonson, *The Complete Poems*, ed. George Parfitt (Harmondsworth: Penguin, 1975), p. 191.

2 Kraus, *Untergang der Welt*, p. 193.

3 See Sammons, *Heinrich Heine* (Sammlung Metzler 261), p. 154.

4 Bertolt Brecht, *Werke* (Große kommentierte Berliner und Frankfurter Ausgabe), ed. Werner Hecht, Jan Knopf, Werner Mittenzwei, Klaus-Detlef Müller *et al.*, 30 vols. (Berlin and Frankfurt: Aufbau and Suhrkamp, 1988–2000), vol. XXVI, p. 416 (22 August 1940); *Journals*, trans. Hugh Rorrison, ed. John Willett (London: Methuen, 1993), p. 90.

5 Thomas Brasch, 'Heine' in *Hermannstraße 14*, 4. Jahrgang (1981), H.6, 19.

6 Georg Heym, 'Ophelia', *Dichtungen und Schriften*, ed. Karl Ludwig Schneider, 3 vols. (Munich and Hamburg: Heinrich Ellermann, 1960–64), vol. I, p. 160.

7 See John Felstiner, *Paul Celan. Poet, Survivor, Jew* (London and New Haven: Yale University Press, 1995), p. 36.

8 Ursula Krechel, *Nach Mainz!* (Munich: dtv, 1983), p. 29

9 Alfred Andersch, 'Hans Magnus Enzensberger, "Landesprache"' in *Über Hans Magnus Enzensberger*, ed. Joachim Schickel (Frankfurt am Main: Suhrkamp, 1970), pp. 68–7.

10 Wolf Biermann, *Verdrehte Welt – das seh' ich gern* (Munich: dtv, 1985), p. 109. Celan made the same pilgrimage with Nelly Sachs, see Felstiner, *Paul Celan*, p. 159.

11 Biermann, *Verdrehte Welt*, p. 108

12 Wolf Biermann, 'Brief an Robert Havemann' in *Nachlaß I* (Cologne: Kiepenheuer & Witsch, 1977), pp. 7–20: 'I couldn't understand the words, but you can judge the attitude from the tone of the music. Somehow the raucous, agitatory character of these songs confused me, made me feel envious and rejected . . . Envious because I thought "How lucky they are! They are singing in a key that is really mine too, but which I can't get into, the key of public political struggle, the rhythm of people on the street who are moved and move independently"' (p. 10).

13 Biermann, *Nachlaß I*, p. 471. See also 'Deutsches Misere (Das Bloch-Lied)', in Biermann, *Preußischer Ikarus* (Munich: dtv, 1981), pp. 201–8.

14 Uwe Timm's novel *Heißer Sommer* (Königstein: Autoren Edition, 1977), is an unlikely and extreme case of such a search for Italian solidarity after the collapse of the student movement.

15 Kruse, Reuter and Hollender (eds.), *"Ich Narr des Glücks"*, pp. 96–101.

16 Günter Kunert, *Fremd daheim* (Munich: Hanser, 1990), p. 75.

17 Peter Rühmkorf, *Wer Lyrik schreibt ist verrückt. Alle Gedichte 1953–75* (Reinbek bei Hamburg: Rowohlt, 1979), p. 133.

18 Ibid., p. 133.

19 Peter Rühmkorf, *TABU I. Tagebücher 1989–1991*, (Reinbek bei Hamburg: Rowohlt, 1995), p. 116. Rühmkorf's insight is confirmed by Würffel's account of the aporetic relation between the political and the private subject in Heine: see *Der produktive Widerspruch*, p. 209.

20 Rühmkorf, *TABU I*, p. 171.

21 Ibid., p. 174.

22 Rühmkorf, *Dreizehn deutsche Dichter*, pp. 7–34.

23 Peter Rühmkorf, *Mein Lesebuch* (Frankfurt am Main: Fischer, 1986), pp. 45–51.

24 See Rühmkorf, *TABU I*, pp. 20, 24–8.

25 Peter Rühmkorf, *Irdisches Vergnügen in g* (Reinbek bei Hamburg: Rowohlt, 1959), reprinted in *Gesammelte Gedichte*, subsequently *Wer Lyrik schreibt ist verrückt*, p. 44.

26 Peter Rühmkorf, *Die Jahre die Ihr kennt* (Reinbek bei Hamburg: Rowohlt, 1972), p. 7.

27 The German original is worth quoting:

> Man verstehe: Da wird mit Vorbedacht zween Herren gedient und mit gespaltener Zunge gesungen, da machen Strophen sich die Zwielichtigkeit zum Programm, und besondere seelische Ambivalenzen versuchen, sich in ästhetischen Mischeffekten, Reibetönen und Interferenzen darzutun.

This account, 'Paradoxe Existenz', appeared in *Mein Gedicht ist mein Messer. Lyriker zu ihren Gedichten*, ed. Hans Bender (Munich: List, 1961), pp. 149–55. An excerpt is reprinted in Peter Rühmkorf, *Selbstredend und selbstreimend*, ed. Peter Bekes (Stuttgart: Reclam, 1987), pp. 28–31. The 'Gedenklied' has also been admirably analysed by Rolf Schneider for Marcel Reich-Ranicki's *Frankfurter Anthologie*, vol. IV (Frankfurt am Main: Insel, 1979), pp. 213–16.

28 Peter Rühmkorf, *Über das Volksvermögen. Exkurse in den literarischen Untergrund* (Reinbek bei Hamburg: Rowohlt, 1967).

29 'Selbstporträt 1958', originally in *Irdisches Vergnügen in g*, reprinted in *Wer Lyrik schreibt ist verrückt*, p. 16; 'Selbstporträt' in Peter Rühmkorf, *Haltbar bis Ende 1999* (Reinbek bei Hamburg: Rowohlt, 1979), p. 9; 'Mit den Jahren . . . Selbst III/88' in Peter Rühmkorf, *Einmalig wie wir alle* (Reinbek bei Hamburg: Rowohlt, 1989), p. 129.

30 A footnote appended to the poem 'Hochseil' in the anthology *Komm raus!*, ed. Klaus Wagenbach (Berlin: Wagenbach, 1992), p. 73.

31 Rühmkorf, *Haltbar bis Ende 1999*, p. 3: 'Wenn ein Lyriker *ICH* sagt, kann schon einmal die Meinung aufkommen, der Herr Soundso spräche von sich. Die kunstvoll oder mühsam ins Gewand der Poesie gehüllte Erstepersoneinzahl bietet genügende und oft genug berechtigte Gründe zur Verkennung, handelt es sich hier doch um einen Wechselbalg von Persönlichkeit, halb der Natur entsprungen, halb ins Kostüm verwickelt, und wo man dem Schatten auf die Schleppe tritt, zuckt manchmal ein richtiger Mensch zusammen.'

32 See Leslie Meier poems such as 'Was seine Freunde sagen', 'Wir singen zum Eingang' and finally 'Waschzettel' (*Wer Lyrik schreibt ist verrückt*, pp. 19, 39, 106); Doletzki had been killed off in an imaginary car crash when Rühmkorf was still a multiple author for the journal *Zwischen den Kriegen* which he edited with Werner Riegel; see *Die Jahre, die Ihr kennt*, p. 44. Finally, and after some deliberation, Doletzki makes a return appearance in 'Mit den Jahren. Selbst III/88': see Rühmkorf, *Einmalig wie wir alle*, p. 136 and compare the earlier drafts of this extraordinary poem published as *Aus der Fassung, Selbst/III* (Zurich: Haffmanns, 1989).

33 Rühmkorf, *Wer Lyrik schreibt ist verrückt*, p. 34; (with Werner Riegel), *Heiße Lyrik* (Wiesbaden: Limes, 1956).

34 See Peter Rühmkorf, 'Fredmans Epistel Nr 27', *Frankfurter Allgemeine Zeitung*, 29 October 1997, p. 41.

35 Rühmkorf, *Wer Lyrik schreibt ist verrückt*, p. 133.

36 Rainer Maria Rilke, *Werke*, ed. Manfred Engel and Ulrich Fülleborn, 4 vols. (Frankfurt am Main: Insel, 1996), vol. II, p. 214. Translation by Naomi Segal

in Roger Paulin and Peter Hutchinson (eds.) *Rilke's Duino Elegies* (London: Duckworth, 1996), p. 211.

37 Rühmkorf, 'Zirkus', *Wer Lyrik schreibt ist verrückt*, p. 134.
38 Rühmkorf, *Haltbar bis Ende 1999*, pp. 91–121.
39 Peter Rühmkorf, *Akzente* 34 (1987), H.1, 22–38.
40 Rühmkorf, *Haltbar bis Ende 1999*, p. 108.
41 Werner/Houben I, 232.
42 See Weidl, *Arbeitsweise*, p. 70: 'ein verwirrend-chaotisches Zettelkonvolut mit den heterogensten Aufzeichnungen zu den verschiedensten Themen'.
43 Kraus, '*Untergang der Welt*, pp. 186–7.

# Bibliography

The following abbreviation are used for journals:
*DVjs Deutsche Vierteljahrsschrift*
*GRM Germanisch-Romanische Monatsschrift*
*HJb Heine Jahrbuch*
*MoH Monatshefte für den Deutschunterricht*
*ZfdP Zeitschrift für deutsche Philologie*

Adorno, Theodor W., *Ästhetische Theorie, Gesammelte Schriften*, ed. Rolf Tiedemann, 20 vols. Frankfurt am Main: Suhrkamp, 1974, vol. VII.
*Noten zur Literatur* I–III, *Gesammelte Schriften*, ed. Rolf Tiedemann, 20 vols. Frankfurt am Main: Suhrkamp, 1974, vol. XI.
*Aesthetic Theory*, trans. C. Lenhardt, London: Routledge and Kegan Paul, 1984.
*Notes to Literature*, trans. Shierry Weber Nicholsen, 2 vols. New York: Columbia University Press, 1991, 1992.
Adorno, Theodor W., and Benjamin, Walter, *Briefwechsel, 1928–1949*, ed. Henri Lonitz, Frankfurt am Main: Suhrkamp, 1994.
Altenhofer, Norbert, 'Chiffre, Hieroglyphe, Palimpsest. Vorformen tiefenhermeneutischer und intertextueller Interpretation im Werk Heines', in *Texthermeneutik. Aktualität, Geschichte, Kritik*, ed. Ulrich Nassen, Munich: UTB, 1979, pp. 149–93.
'Ästhetik des Arrangements. Zu Heines "Buch der Lieder"', in *Die verlorene Augensprache. Über Heinrich Heine*, ed. Volker Bohn, Frankfurt am Main: Insel, 1993.
Andersch, Alfred, 'Hans Magnus Enzensberger, "Landesprache"' in Schickel (ed.), *Über Hans Magnus Enzensberger*, pp. 68–9.
Andler, Charles, *La Poésie de Heine*, Lyon: Bibliothèque de la société des études germaniques, 1948.
Arntzen, Helmut, *Karl Kraus und die Presse*, Munich: Fink, 1975.
Balakian, Anna (ed.), *The Symbolist Movement in the Literature of European Languages*, Budapest: Akadémiai Kiado, 1984
Bark, Joachim, 'Heine im Vormärz: Radikalisierung oder Verweigerung', *Der Deutschunterricht* 31 (1979), pp. 47–60.
'"Versifizirtes Herzblut". Zur Entstehung und Gehalt von Heines *Romanzero*', *Wirkendes Wort* 36 (1986), pp. 86–103.

'Die Muse als Krankenwärterin', 'Nachwort' to Heinrich Heine, *Romanzero*, Munich: Goldmann, 1988.

Baudelaire, Charles, *The Flowers of Evil*, trans. James McGowan, Oxford: Oxford University Press, 1993.

Bayerdörfer, Hans-Peter, 'Fürstenpreis im Jahre 48. Heine und die Tradition der vaterländischen Panegyrik', *ZfdP* 91 (1972) Sonderheft *Heine und seine Zeit*, pp. 163–205.

'"Politische Ballade". Zu den "Historien" in Heines *Romanzero*', *DVjs* 46 (1972), pp. 435–68.

Bender, Hans (ed.), *Mein Gedicht ist mein Messer. Lyriker zu ihren Gedichten*, Munich: List, 1961.

Benjamin, Walter, *Gesammelte Schriften*, ed. Rolf Tiedemann and Hermann Schweppenhäuser, 7 vols., Frankfurt am Main: Suhrkamp, 1977.

*The Origin of the German Tragic Drama*, trans. John Osborne, London: Verso, 1985.

'Karl Kraus' in *Selected Writings*, vol. II: *1927–1934*, trans. Rodney Livingstone and others, ed. Michael W. Jennings, Howard Eiland, and Gary Smith, Cambridge MA and London: Belknap Press of Harvard University Press, 1999.

*The Arcades Project*, trans. Howard Eiland and Kevin McLaughlin, Cambridge, MA and London: Belknap Press of Harvard University, 1999.

Betz, Albrecht, *Ästhetik und Politik. Heinrich Heines Prosa*, Munich: Hanser, 1971.

'Marchandise et modernité. Notes sur Heine et Benjamin', in *Walter Benjamin et Paris*, ed. Heinz Wismann, Paris: Editions du Cerf, 1986, pp. 153–62.

Biermann, Wolf, *Nachlaß I*, Cologne: Kiepenheuer & Witsch, 1977.

*Preußischer Ikarus*, Munich: dtv, 1981.

*Verdrehte Welt – das seh' ich gern*, Munich: dtv, 1985.

Bloch, Ernst, *Erbschaft dieser Zeit* (Werkausgabe, vol. IV), Frankfurt am Main: Suhrkamp 1985.

Block, Haskell M., 'Heine and the French Symbolists', in *Creative Encounter*, ed. Leland R. Phelps and A. Tilo Alt, Chapel Hill: University of North Carolina Press, 1978, pp. 25–39.

Blumenberg, Hans, *Arbeit am Mythos*, third edition, Frankfurt am Main: Suhrkamp, 1984.

Bodine, Jay F., 'Heinrich Heine, Karl Kraus and "die Folgen". A Test Case of Literary Texts, Historical Reception and Receptive Aesthetics', *Colloquia Germanica* 17 (1984), pp. 14–59.

Booß, Rutger, *Ansichten der Revolution. Paris-Berichte deutscher Schriftsteller nach der Juli-Revolution 1830*, Cologne: Pahl-Rugenstein, 1977.

Borchardt, Rudolf, *Ewiger Vorrat deutscher Poesie*, Munich: Verlag der Bremer Presse, 1926.

Börne, Ludwig, *Sämtliche Schriften*, ed. Inge and Peter Rippmann, 5 vols., Dreieich: Melzer, 1977.

Borries, Mechthild von, *Ein Angriff auf Heinrich Heine*, Stuttgart: Kohlhammer, 1971.

Böschenstein, Bernhard, 'Wirkungen des französischen Symbolismus auf die deutsche Dichtung', *Euphorion* 58 (1964), pp. 375–95.

Brasch, Thomas, 'Heine' in *Hermannstraße 14*, 4 (1981), Heft 6, p. 19.

Brecht, Bertolt, *Werke*, ed. Werner Hecht, Jan Knopf, Werner Mittenzwei, Klaus-Detlef Müller *et al.*, 30 vols., Berlin and Frankfurt: Aufbau and Suhrkamp, 1988–2000.

*Journals*, trans. Hugh Rorrison, ed. John Willett, London: Methuen, 1993.

Briegleb, Klaus, 'Schriftstellernöte und literarische Produktivität. Zum Exempel Heinrich Heine', in *Neue Ansichten einer künftigen Germanistik*, ed. Jürgen Kolbe, Munich: Hanser, 1973, pp. 121–59.

*Opfer Heine? Versuche über Schriftzüge der Revolution*, Frankfurt am Main: Suhrkamp, 1986.

*An den Flüssen Babels*, Munich: Deutscher Taschenbuchverlag, 1997.

'"Ich trug an Bord meines Schiffes die Götter der Zukunft". Versuch über Heinrich Heines Abschied von Ludwig Börne in Frankfurt am 16. November 1827', in Frank Stern and Maria Gierlinger (eds.), *Ludwig Börne. Deutscher, Jude, Demokrat* (Berlin: Aufbau, 2003), pp. 222–68.

Brummack, Jürgen, 'Heines Entwicklung zum satirischen Dichter', *DVjs* 41 (1967), pp. 98–116.

(ed.), *Heinrich Heine. Epoche – Werk – Wirkung*, Munich: Beck, 1980.

Chiarini, Paolo, 'Heine contra Börne ovvero critica dell'impazienza rivoluzionaria', *Studi germanici*, n.s., 10 (1972), pp. 355–92.

Cook, Roger, *By the Rivers of Babylon: Heinrich Heine's Late Songs and Reflections*, Detroit: Wayne State University Press, 1998.

(ed.), *A Companion to the Works of Heinrich Heine*, Rochester, NY, and Woodbridge: Camden House, 2002.

Davies, Norman, *Europe. A History*, Oxford: Oxford University Press, 1996.

Derrida, Jacques, *Schibboleth*, Paris: Editions du Seuil, 1986.

'Envois: May 1979', from *The Post Card: From Socrates to Freud*, in *A Derrida Reader. Between the Blinds*, ed. Peggy Kamuf, London: Harvester Wheatsheaf, 1991, pp. 510–12.

Destro, Alberto, 'L'attesa contradetta. La svolta finale nelle liriche del *Buch der Lieder* di Heinrich Heine', *Studi tedeschi* 1 (1977), pp. 7–127.

'*Das Buch der Lieder* und seine Leser', in Zagari and Chiarini (eds.), *Zu Heinrich Heine*, pp. 59–73.

'Öffentlich und privat. Die Beurteilung des *Romanzero*', in Gössmann and Kruse (eds.), *Der späte Heine*, pp. 58–68.

Donnellan, Brendan, 'The Structure of *Atta Troll*', *HJb* 21 (1982), pp. 78–88.

Empson, William, *Some Versions of Pastoral*, Harmondsworth: Penguin, 1974.

Enzensberger, Hans Magnus (ed.), *Heinrich Heine und Ludwig Börne. Ein deutsches Zerwürfnis*, Nördlingen: Greno, 1986.

*Mittelmaß und Wahn. Gesammelte Zerstreuungen*, Frankfurt am Main: Suhrkamp, 1988.

Epping-Jäger, Cornelia, 'Mythos Paris? – Heinrich Heines daguerreotypische Schreibart', in Kruse, Witte, and Füllner (eds.), *Aufklärung und Skepsis*, pp. 408–21.

Espagne, Michel, '"Autor und Schrift paßten nicht mehr zusammen". Heines Selbstauslegung in den deutschen Manuskripten der *Geständnisse*', *HJb* 20 (1981), pp. 147–57.

   *Federstriche. Die Konstruktion des Pantheismus in Heines Arbeitshandschriften*, Hamburg: Hoffmann und Campe, 1991.

Fairley, Barker, *Heinrich Heine: An Interpretation*, Oxford: Clarendon Press, 1954.

Feise, Ernst, 'Form and Meaning of Heine's Essay *Die Nordsee*', in Feise (ed.), *Xenion. Themes, Forms, and Ideas in German Literature*, Baltimore: Johns Hopkins University Press, 1950, pp. 90–104.

Felstiner, John, *Paul Celan. Poet, Survivor, Jew*, London and New Haven: Yale University Press, 1995.

Fingerhut, Karlheinz, *Standortbestimmungen. Vier Untersuchungen zu Heinrich Heine*, Heidenheim: Heidenheimer Verlagsanstalt, 1971.

   'Spanische Spiegel. Heinrich Heines Verwendung spanischer Geschichte und Literatur zur Selbstreflexion des Juden und des Dichters', *HJb* 31 (1992), pp. 106–36.

Fuld, Werner, *Walter Benjamin. Zwischen den Stühlen. Eine Biographie*, Munich and Vienna: Hanser, 1979.

Furbank, P. N., *Diderot. A Critical Biography*, London: Secker and Warburg, 1992.

Futterknecht, Franz, *Heinrich Heine. Ein Versuch*, Tübingen: Narr, 1985.

Gelber, Mark H. (ed.), *The Jewish Reception of Heinrich Heine*, Tübingen: Niemeyer, 1992.

George, Stefan and Wolfskehl, Karl, *Das Jahrhundert Goethes*, Düsseldorf and Munich: Georg Bondi, 1964.

Gille, Klaus F., 'Heines *Atta Troll* – "Das letzte freie Waldlied der Romantik"?', *Neophilologus* 62 (1978), pp. 416–33.

Gilman, Sander L., *Inscribing the Other*, Lincoln and London: University of Nebraska Press, 1991.

   'Freud Reads Heine Reads Fraud', in *The Jewish Reception of Heinrich Heine*, ed. Gelber, pp. 77–94.

Goethe, Johann Wolfgang von, *Werke* (Hamburger Ausgabe), ed. Erich Trunz, 14 vols., Munich: Beck, 1994.

Goltschnigg, Dietmar (ed.), *Die Fackel ins wunde Herz*, Vienna: Passagen, 2000.

Gössmann, Wilhelm, Keller, Hans P., and Walwei-Wiegelmann, Hedwig (eds.), *Geständnisse: Heine im Bewußtsein heutiger Autoren*, Düsseldorf: Droste, 1972.

   and Kruse, Joseph A. (eds.), *Der späte Heine, 1948–1856. Literatur–Politik–Religion*, Hamburg: Hoffmann und Campe, 1982.

Grab, Walter, *Heinrich Heine als politischer Dichter*, Heidelberg: Quelle & Meyer, 1982.

Grange, Jacques, *Rudolf Borchardt 1877–1945*, 2 vols., Bern, Frankfurt am Main, New York: Peter Lang, 1983.

Grubačić, Slobodan, *Heines Erzählprosa. Versuch einer Analyse*, Stuttgart: Kohlhammer, 1975.

Gundolf, Friedrich, *George*, Berlin: Georg Bondi, 1930.

Guy, Irene, *Sexualität im Gedicht. Heinrich Heines Spätlyrik*, Bonn: Bouvier, 1984.

Habermas, Jürgen, *Strukturwandel der Öffentlichkeit*, Neuwied: Luchterhand, 1971.

'Heinrich Heine und die Rolle des Intellektuellen in Deutschland', *Merkur* 448 (June 1986), pp. 453–68.

*Kleine politische Schriften*, 10 vols. (Frankfurt am Main: Suhrkamp, 1987).

'Heinrich Heine and the Role of the Intellectual in Germany', in *The New Conservatism: Cultural Criticism and the Historians' Debate*, Cambridge, MA: MIT Press, 1989, pp. 71–99.

Hädecke, Wolfgang, *Heinrich Heine, eine Biographie*, Munich: Hanser, 1985.

Hamburger, Michael, *The Truth of Poetry*, London: Methuen, 1982.

Hansen, Volkmar, 'Der Wolf, der Kreide frißt. Lüge und Wahrheit in Heines politischer Publizistik der vierziger Jahre als Editionsproblem', *ZfdP* 101 (1982), pp. 64–79.

Heine, Heinrich, *Heinrich Heine. Sämtliche Schriften*, ed. Klaus Briegleb, 6 vols. in 7, Munich: Hanser, 1968–76.

*Heinrich Heine: Werke &c. Säkularausgabe*, ed. Nationale Forschungs- und Gedenkstätte der klassischen deutschen Literatur, Weimar, and the Centre national de la recherche scientifique, Paris, 27 vols., Berlin: Akademie Verlag, 1970–).

*Heinrich Heine. Sämtliche Werke. Düsseldorfer Ausgabe*, ed. Manfred Windfuhr, 16 vols., Hamburg: Hoffmann & Campe, 1973–97.

*The Complete Poems of Heinrich Heine*, trans. Hal Draper, Cambridge, MA: Suhrkamp/Insel, and Oxford: Oxford University Press, 1982.

*Selected Prose*, trans. and ed. with introduction and notes by Ritchie Robertson, Harmondsworth: Penguin, 1993.

Heißenbüttel, Helmut, *Über Literatur*, Freiburg: Olten, 1966.

*Zur Tradition der Moderne. Aufsätze und Anmerkungen*, Neuwied, Berlin: Luchterhand, 1972.

*Von fliegenden Fröschen, libidinösen Epen, vaterländischen Romanen, Sprechblasen und Ohrwürmern*, Stuttgart: Klett-Cotta, 1982.

Hermand, Jost, 'Napoleon im Biedermeier', in Hermand, *Von Mainz nach Weimar*, Stuttgart: Metzler, 1969, pp. 99–128.

*Streitobjekt Heine: Ein Forschungsbericht 1945–1975*, Frankfurt am Main: Athenäum, 1975.

*Der frühe Heine. Ein Kommentar zu den 'Reisebildern'*, Munich: Winkler, 1976.

'Erotik im Juste Milieu', in Kuttenkeuler (ed.), *Heinrich Heine: Artistik und Engagement*, pp. 86–104.

Heym, Georg, *Dichtungen und Schriften*, ed. Karl Ludwig Schneider, 3 vols., Munich and Hamburg: Heinrich Ellermann, 1960–4.

Hinck, Walter, *Die deutsche Ballade von Bürger bis Brecht*, Göttingen: Vandenhoeck und Ruprecht, 1968.

'Exil als Zuflucht der Resignation. Der Herrscher-Dichter-Konflikt in der Firdusi-Romanze und die Ästhetik des späten Heine', in Hinck, *Von Heine zu Brecht. Lyrik im Geschichtsprozeß*, Frankfurt am Main: Suhrkamp, 1978, pp. 37–59

*Die Wunde Deutschland. Heinrich Heines Dichtung*, Frankfurt am Main: Insel, 1990.

Hinderer, Walter, 'Nazarene oder Hellene. Die politisch–ästhetische Fehde zwischen Heine und Börne', *MoH* 66 (1974), pp. 355–65.

Hoffmann, E. T. A., *The Golden Pot and Other Tales*, trans. Ritchie Robertson, Oxford and New York: Oxford University Press, 1992.

*Fantasie– und Nachtstücke*, following the text of the first edition with corrections from the editions of Carl Georg Maassen and Georg Ellinger, Düsseldorf and Zurich: Winkler, 1996.

Hofrichter, Laura, *Heinrich Heine. Biographie seiner Dichtung*, Göttingen: Vandenhoeck und Ruprecht, 1966.

Hohendahl, Peter Uwe, 'Geschichte und Modernität. Heines Kritik an der Romantik', *Jahrbuch der deutschen Schillergesellschaft*, 17 (1973), pp. 318–61.

'Talent oder Charakter: die Börne-Heine-Fehde und ihre Nachgeschichte', *Modern Language Notes* 95 (1980), pp. 609–26.

Höhn, Gerhard, 'Adorno face à Heine ou le couteau dans la plaie', *Revue d'ésthetique*, n.s. 8 (1985), pp. 137–44.

'Heinrich Heine, intellectuel moderne', *Revue de métaphysique et de morale*, 2 (1989), pp. 151–64.

*Heinrich Heine: un intellectuel moderne*, Paris: Presses Universitaires de France, 1994.

*Heine-Handbuch. Zeit – Person – Werk*, 2nd edition, Stuttgart: Metzler, 1997.

(ed.), *Heinrich Heine. Ästhetisch-politische Profile*, Frankfurt am Main: Suhrkamp, 1991.

Holub, Robert, 'Heine's Sexual Assaults: Towards a Theory of Total Polemic', *MoH* 73 (1981), pp. 415–28.

Hosfeld, Rolf, *Die Welt als Füllhorn: Heine. Das neunzehnte Jahrhundert zwischen Romantik und Moderne*, Berlin: Oberbaum, 1984.

Jauß, Hans Robert, *Literaturgeschichte als Provokation*, Frankfurt am Main: Suhrkamp, 1970.

Jonson, Ben, *The Complete Poems*, ed. George Parfitt, Harmondsworth: Penguin, 1975.

Jordan, Lothar, 'Heine und Enzensberger', *HJb* 32 (1993), pp. 127–43.

Jörgensen, Alf, *Karl Kraus. Der Heinefresser und die Ursachen*, Flensburg: Schütze und Schmidt, n.d. [?1912].

Kaiser, Gerhard R., 'Baudelaire *pro* Heine *contra* Janin', *HJb* 22 (1983), pp. 134–78.

Kaufmann, Hans, 'Die Denkschrift *Ludwig Börne*', in *Internationaler Heine-Kongreß 1972*, ed. Manfred Windfuhr, Hamburg: Hoffmann und Campe, 1973, pp. 178–89.

'Heinrich Heine. Poesie, Vaterland und Menschheit', in *Heinrich Heine: Werke und Briefe*, ed. Hans Kaufmann, 10 vols., Berlin and Weimar: Aufbau, 1980, vol. X, pp. 5–166.

Klopstock, Friedrich Gottlieb, *Ausgewählte Werke*, ed. Karl August Schleiden, Munich: Hanser, 1962.

Kolk, Rainer, 'Über die Aufgabe des Geschichtsschreibers. Heines *Ludwig Börne. Eine Denkschrift* im Kontext', in Kruse, Witte, and Füllner (eds.), *Aufklärung und Skepsis*, pp. 86–101.

Koopmann, Helmut, 'Heine in Weimar. Zur Problematik seiner Beziehung zur Kunstperiode', *ZfdP* 91 (1972), Sonderheft *Heine und seine zeit*, pp. 46–66.

'Heines Romanzero', *ZfdP* 97 (1978), Sonderheft, pp. 51–70.

(ed.), *Heinrich Heine*, Darmstadt: Wissenschaftliche Buchgesellschaft, 1975.

Kortländer, Bernd, 'Der Sphinx im Märchenwald' in Kortländer (ed.), *Interpretationen. Gedichte von Heinrich Heine*, Stuttgart: Reclam, 1995, pp. 15–31.

'Die Erfindung des Meeres aus dem Geist der Poesie: Heines Natur', in Kruse, Reuter, and Hollender (eds.), *'Ich Narr des Glücks'*, pp. 261–9.

(ed.), *Interpretationen. Gedichte von Heinrich Heine*. Stuttgart: Reclam, 1995.

Kraft, Werner, *Heine der Dichter*, Munich: Text + Kritik, 1983.

Kraus, Karl, *Nachts*, Vienna and Leipzig: [Kurt Wolff], Verlag der Schriften von Karl Kraus 1924.

*Heine und die Folgen. Schriften zur Literatur*, ed. with commentary and afterword by Christian Wagenknecht, Stuttgart: Reclam, 1986.

*Schriften*, ed. Christian Wagenknecht, 12 vols., Frankfurt am Main: Suhrkamp, 1989.

Krechel, Ursula, *Nach Mainz!* Munich: dtv, 1983.

Kruse, Joseph A., 'Der große Judenschmerz. Zu einigen Parallelen wie Differenzen bei Börne und Heine' in *Ludwig Börne: 1786–1837*, ed. Alfred Estermann, Frankfurt am Main: Buchhändler-Vereinigung, 1986, pp. 189–97.

and Reuter, Ulrike, Hollender, Martin (eds.), *'Ich Narr des Glücks'. Heinrich Heine 1797–1856. Bilder einer Ausstellung*, Stuttgart, Weimar: Metzler, 1997.

and Witte, Bernd, Füllner, Karin (eds.), *Aufklärung und Skepsis. Internationaler Heine-Kongreß 1997 zum 200. Geburtstag*, Stuttgart: Metzler, 1999.

Kunert, Günter, *Fremd daheim*, Munich: Hanser, 1990.

Kuttenkeuler, Wolfgang (ed.), *Heinrich Heine: Artistik und Engagement*, Stuttgart: Metzler, 1977.

Lamping, Dieter, 'Das "sogenannt Persönliche" und die "geistigen Erscheinungen"', *ZfdP* 109 (1990), pp. 199–217.

Lefebvre, Jean-Pierre, 'Der RomanZero oder Götzens Enfant perdu', afterword to Heinrich Heine, *Romanzero, Gedichte 1853 und 1854*, ed. Bernd Kortländer, Stuttgart: Reclam, 1997, pp. 272–86.

Lentricchia, Frank, *Ariel and the Police*, Madison: University of Wisconsin Press, 1988.

Levin Varnhagen, Rahel, *Im Umgang mit ihren Freunden (Briefe 1793–1833)*, ed. Friedhelm Kemp, Munich: Kösel, 1967.

Liedke, Christian, *Heinrich Heine*, Reinbek bei Hamburg: Rowohlt, 1997.

Loos, Adolf, *Sämtliche Schriften*, ed. Franz Glück, Vienna and Munich: Herold Verlag, 1962.

*Ornament and Crime, Selected Essays*, selected and with an introduction by Adolf Opel, trans. Michael Mitchell, Riverside, CA: Ariadne Press, 1998.

Lüdi, Rolf, *Heinrich Heines Buch der Lieder: Poetische Strategien und deren Bedeutung*, Frankfurt am Main, Bern, etc.: Peter Lang, 1979.

Magraw, Roger, *France 1815–1914. The Bourgeois Century*, London: Fontana, 1983.

Marx, Karl, *On the Jewish Question*, in *Early Writings*, introduced by Lucio Coletti, trans. Rodney Livingstone and Gregor Benton, London and Baltimore: Penguin, 1975.

*Surveys from Exile*, ed. and introduced by David Fernbach, Harmondsworth and Baltimore: Penguin, 1973.

and Engels, Friedrich, *Werke*, ed. Institut für Marxismus-Leninismus beim ZK der SED, 43 vols., Berlin: Dietz-Verlag, 1956–74.

Mayer, Hans, 'Karl Kraus und die Nachwelt', in *Ansichten. Zur Literatur der Zeit*, Reinbek bei Hamburg: Rowohlt, 1962, pp. 71–84.

(ed.), *Heinrich Heine, Beiträge zur deutschen Ideologie*, Frankfurt am Main: Ullstein, 1971.

Mayser, Erich, *H. Heines 'Buch der Lieder' im 19. Jahrhundert*, Stuttgart: Akademischer Verlag Heinz, 1978.

Mende, Fritz, 'Heine, Guizot und der "geregelte Fortschritt"', *HJb* 29 (1990), pp. 54–75.

Morawe, Stefan Bodo, 'List und Gegenlist: Heine als politischer Schriftsteller', *Euphorion* 82 (1988), pp. 281–315.

Müller, Heiner, *'Ich bin ein Neger'. Diskussion mit Heiner Müller*, Darmstadt: Verlag der Georg Büchner Buchhandlung, 1986.

Musil, Robert, *Gesammelte Werke*, 9 vols., Reinbek: Rowohlt, 1978.

Netter, Lucienne, 'La Genèse des articles LX et XXV de "Lutezia" ou les anachronismes de Heine', *Etudes germaniques* 29 (1974), pp. 83–8.

*Heine et la peinture de la civilisation parisienne 1840–1848*, Frankfurt am Main: Peter Lang, 1980.

Nietzsche, Friedrich, *Werke*, ed. Karl Schlechta, 3 vols., Munich: Hanser, 1969.

Oehler, Dolf, *Pariser Bilder I 1830–1848. Antibourgeoise Ästhetik bei Baudelaire, Daumier und Heine, Frankfurt am Main*: Suhrkamp, 1979.

*Ein Höllensturz der alten Welt*, Frankfurt am Main: Suhrkamp, 1988.

Oellers, Norbert, 'Die zerstrittenen Dioskuren. Aspekte der Auseinandersetzung Heines mit Börne', *ZfdP* 91 (1972), Sonderheft *Heine und seine Zeit*, pp. 66–90.

Osborne, Peter, 'Small-scale Victories, Large-scale Defeats' in *Walter Benjamin's Philosophy*, ed. Andrew Benjamin and Peter Osborne, London: Routledge, 1994, pp. 59–109.

Pabel, Klaus, *Heines 'Reisebilder'. Ästhetisches Bedürfnis und politisches Interesse am Ende der Kunstperiode*, Munich: Wilhelm Fink, 1977.

Paulin, Roger and Hutchinson, Peter (eds.), *Rilke's Duino Elegies*, London: Duckworth, 1996.

Perraudin, Michael, 'The "Doppelgänger" Poem and Its Antecedents: A Short Illustration of Heine's Creative Response to His Romantic Precursors', *GRM* 35 (1985), pp. 342–8.

'"Anfang und Ende meines lyrischen Jugendlebens": Two Key Poems of Heine's Early Years', *Seminar* 32/1 (1986), p. 52.

*Heinrich Heine. Poetry in Context. A Study of Buch der Lieder*, Oxford, New York, Munich: Berg, 1989.

'The Experiential World of Heine's *Buch der Lieder*', in Roger F. Cook (ed.), *A Companion to the Works of Heinrich Heine*, Rochester, NY, and Woodbridge: Camden House, 2002.

Peters, George F., *The Poet as Provocateur. Heinrich Heine and His Critics*, Rochester, NY, and Woodbridge: Camden House, 2000.

Peters, Paul, *Heinrich Heine 'Dichterjude'. Die Geschichte einer Schmähung*, Frankfurt am Main: A. Hain, 1990.

'A Walk on the Wild Side', in Roger F. Cook (ed.), *A Companion to the Works of Heinrich Heine*, Rochester, NY, and Woodbridge: Camden House, 2002, pp. 55–103.

Pfabigan, Alfred, *Karl Kraus und der Sozialismus*, Vienna: Europaverlag, 1976.

Phelan, Anthony, 'The State of the Art: Heine's *Atta Troll* and "Jehuda ben Halevy"', *Oxford German Studies* 33 (2004) (Special Number for T. J. Reed), pp. 177–94.

Pinkney, David H. *The French Revolution of 1830*, Princeton: Princeton University Press, 1972.

Prawer, S. S., *Heine: Das Buch der Lieder*, London: Edward Arnold, 1960.

*Heine The Tragic Satirist. A Study of the Later Poetry 1827–1856*, Cambridge: Cambridge University Press, 1961.

*Heine's Jewish Comedy*, Oxford: Clarendon Press, 1983.

*Frankenstein's Island. England and the English in the Writings of Heinrich Heine*, Cambridge: Cambridge University Press, 1986.

Preisendanz, Wolfgang, 'Ironie bei Heine', in *Ironie und Dichtung. Sechs Essays*, ed. Albert Schaefer, Munich: Beck, 1970, pp. 85–112.

*Heinrich Heine. Werkstrukturen und Epochenbezüge*, 2nd edition, Munich: Universitätstaschenbücher, 1983.

'Memoria als Dimension lyrischer Selbstrepräsentation in Heines "Jehuda ben Halevy"', in *Memoria: Vergessen und Erinnern* (Poetik und Hermeneutik XV), ed. Anselm Haverkanp and Renate Lachmann, Munich: Fink, 1993, pp. 338–58.

Purver, Judith, 'Revolution, Romanticism, Restoration' in *A History of Women's Writing*, ed. Jo Catling, Cambridge: Cambridge University Press, 2000.

Reeves, Nigel, 'Heine and the Young Marx', *Oxford German Studies* 7 (1972/3), pp. 44–97.

*Heinrich Heine. Poetry and Politics*, Oxford: Oxford University Press, 1974.

'Atta Troll and his Executioners', *Euphorion* 73 (1979), pp. 388–409.

Reich-Ranicki, Marcel (ed.), *Frankfurter Anthologie*, vol. IV, Frankfurt am Main: Insel, 1979.

Rilke, Rainer Maria, *Werke*, ed. Manfred Engel and Ulrich Fülleborn, 4 vols., Frankfurt am Main: Insel, 1996.
Rippmann, Inge, 'Heines Denkschrift über Börne', *HJb* 12 (1973), pp. 41–70.
' "Sie saßen an den Wassern Babylons". Eine Annäherung an Heinrich Heines "Denkschrift über Ludwig Börne"', *HJb* 34 (1995), pp. 25–47.
Robertson, Ritchie, *Heine*, London: Weidenfeld and Nicolson (Peter Halban), 1988.
*The 'Jewish Question' in German Literature*, Oxford: Oxford University Press, 1999.
Rose, Gillian, *The Broken Middle*, Oxford: Blackwell, 1992.
Rose, William, *The Early Love Poetry of Heinrich Heine: An Enquiry into Poetic Inspiration*, Oxford: Clarendon Press, 1962.
Rühmkorf, Peter (with Werner Riegel), *Heiße Lyrik*, Wiesbaden: Limes, 1956.
'Paradoxe Existenz' in Hans Bender (ed.), *Mein Gedicht ist mein Messer*, pp. 149–55.
*Über das Volksvermögen. Exkurse in den literarischen Untergrund*, Reinbek bei Hamburg: Rowohlt, 1967.
*Die Jahre die Ihr kennt*, Reinbek bei Hamburg: Rowohlt, 1972.
*Haltbar bis Ende 1999*, Reinbek bei Hamburg: Rowohlt, 1979.
*Wer Lyrik schreibt ist verrückt. Alle Gedichte 1953–75*, Reinbek bei Hamburg: Rowohlt, 1979 (originally published 1976 as *Gesammelte Gedichte*).
*Mein Lesebuch*, Frankfurt am Main: Fischer, 1986.
*Selbstredend und selbstreimend*, ed. Peter Bekes, Stuttgart: Reclam, 1987.
'Über die Arbeit', *Akzente* 34 (1987), H.1, pp. 22–38.
*Aus der Fassung. Selbst/III*, Zurich: Haffmanns, 1989.
*Dreizehn deutsche Dichter*, Reinbek bei Hamburg: Rowohlt, 1989.
*Einmalig wie wir alle*, Reinbek bei Hamburg: Rowohlt, 1989.
*Komm raus!* ed. Klaus Wagenbach, Berlin: Wagenbach, 1992.
*TABU I. Tagebücher 1989–1991*, Reinbek bei Hamburg: Rowohlt, 1995.
'Fredmans Epistel Nr 27', *Frankfurter Allgemeine Zeitung*, 29 October 1997, p. 41.
Sammons, Jeffrey L., *Heinrich Heine: The Elusive Poet*, New Haven and London: Yale University Press, 1969.
*Heinrich Heine. A Modern Biography*, Princeton: Princeton University Press, 1979.
*Heinrich Heine* (Sammlung Metzler 261), Stuttgart: Metzler, 1991
'The Exhaustion of Current Heine Studies: Some Observations, Partly Speculative', in Gelber (ed.), *The Jewish Reception of Heinrich Heine*, pp. 5–19.
'Jewish Reception as the Last Phase of American Heine Reception' in Gelber (ed.), *The Jewish Reception of Heinrich Heine*, pp. 197–214.
Sauder, Gerhard, 'Blasphemisch-religiöse Körperwelt. Heinrich Heines "Hebräische Melodien"', in Kuttenkeuler (ed.), *Heinrich Heine: Artistik und Engagement*, pp. 118–43.
Schanze, Helmut, 'Noch einmal: Romantique défroqué. Zu Heines *Atta Troll*, dem letzten freien Waldlied der Romantik', *HJb* 9 (1970), pp. 87–98.

Schaub, Uta, 'Liliencron und Heine im Urteil von Karl Kraus. Ein Beitrag zum Problem der literarischen Wertung', *HJb* 18 (1979), pp. 191–201.

Schickel, Joachim (ed.), *Über Hans Magnus Enzensberger*, Frankfurt am Main: Suhrkamp, 1970.

Schiller, Johann Friedrich von, *Sämtliche Werke*, 3rd edition, ed. Gerhard Friche and Herbert G. Göpfert in association with Herbert Stubenrauch, 5 vols., Munich: Hanser, 1962.

Schlaffer, Heinz, *Faust Zweiter Teil. Die Allegorie des 19. Jahrhunderts*, Stuttgart: Metzler, 1981.

Schneider, Manfred, *Die Angst und das Paradies des Nörglers*, Frankfurt am Main: Syndikat, 1977.

*Die kranke schöne Seele der Revolution. Heine, Börne, das 'Junge Deutschland', Marx und Engels*, Frankfurt am Main: Syndikat, 1980.

Schneider, Rolf, 'Linke Narren aller Säkula' in Reich-Ranicki (ed.), *Frankfurter Anthologie*, vol. IV, pp. 213–16.

Schneider, Ronald, ' "Themis und Pan". Zu literarischer Struktur und politischem Gehalt der "Reisebilder" Heinrich Heines', *Annali*, Sezione germanica, 3 (1975), pp. 7–36.

Secci, Lia, 'Die Götter im Exil – Heine und der europäische Symbolismus', *HJb* 15 (1976), pp. 96–114.

Sengle, Friedrich, ' "Atta Troll". Heines schwierige Lage zwischen Revolution und Tradition', in Windfuhr (ed.), *Internationaler Heine-Kongreß 1972*, pp. 23–49.

Simmel, Georg, 'Die Großstädte und das Geistesleben', *Jahrbuch der Gehe-Stiftung Dresden* 9 (1903), pp. 185–206.

*The Sociology of Georg Simmel*, trans. and ed. Kurt H. Wolf, New York: The Free Press, 1964.

Sloterdijk, Peter, *Critique of Cynical Reason*, trans. Michael Eldred, London: Verso, 1988.

Staël, Madame de (Anne-Louise-Germaine). *De l'Allemagne*, ed. La Comtesse Jean de Parge, 5 vols., Paris: Hachette, 1958–60.

Sternberger, Dolf, *Heinrich Heine und die Abschaffung der Sünde*, 2nd edition, Frankfurt am Main: Suhrkamp, 1976.

Tauber, Zvi, 'Ästhetik und Politik: Der Streit zwischen Heine und Börne', in Frank Stern and Maria Gierlinger (eds.), *Ludwig Börne. Deutscher, Jude, Demokrat*, Berlin: Aufbau, 2003, pp. 203–21.

Teraoka, Takanori, 'Der Stildiskurs in Heines Denkschrift über Börne', *HJb* 27 (1988), pp. 66–85.

Timm, Uwe, *Heißer Sommer*, Königstein: Autoren Edition, 1977.

Veit, Philipp F., 'Heine's Imperfect Muses in *Atta Troll*', *Germanic Review* 39 (1964), pp. 262–80.

Walser, Martin, 'Heines Tränen', in *Liebeserklärungen*, Frankfurt am Main: Suhrkamp, 1983.

Weidl, Erhard, *Heinrich Heines Arbeitsweise*, Hamburg: Hoffmann und Campe, 1974.

Weinberg, Kurt, *Henri Heine. Romantique défroqué. Héraut du symbolisme français* (New Haven and Paris: Yale, 1954).

Wellek, René, 'What is Symbolism?', in *The Symbolist Movement in the Literature of European Languages*, ed. Ann Balakian, Budapest: Akadémiai Kiado, 1984, pp. 17–28.

Werner, Michael, 'Das "Augsburger Prokrustesbett". Heines Berichte aus Paris 1840–1847 ("Lutezia") und die Zensur', *Cahiers Heine* 1 (1975), pp. 42–65.

'Frères d'armes ou frères ennemis? Heine et Boerne à Paris', *Francia* 7 (1979), pp. 251–70.

'Der politische Schriftsteller und die (Selbst-)Zensur', *HJb* 26 (1987), pp. 29–53

'"Enfant perdu"' in Kortländer (ed.), *Interpretationen. Gedichte von Heinrich Heine*, pp. 181–94.

(ed.), *Begegnungen mit Heine: Berichte der Zeitgenossen. In Fartführung von H. H. Houbens 'Gespräche mit Heine'*, 2 vols., Hamburg: Hoffmann & Campe, 1973.

Wieland, Christoph Martin, *Werke*, ed. Fritz Martini and Hans Werner Seiffert, 5 vols., Munich: Hanser, 1964–8.

Wiese, Benno von, 'Mythos und Historie in Heines später Lyrik', in Windfuhr (ed.), *Internationaler Heine-Kongreß 1972*, pp. 121–46.

*Signaturen. Zu Heinrich Heine und seinem Werk*, Berlin: Erich Schmidt Verlag, 1976.

Windfuhr, Manfred, (ed.), *Internationaler Heine-Kongreß 1972*, Hamburg: Hoffmann und Campe, 1973.

*Heinrich Heine. Revolution und Reflexion*, 2nd edition, Stuttgart: Metzler, 1976.

*Rätsel Heine. Autorprofil – Werk – Wirkung*, Heidelberg: Universitätsverlag C. Winter, 1997.

Witte, Bernd, 'Düsseldorf – London – Paris. Heinrich Heines allegorische Lektüre der großen Stadt', in Kruse, Reuter, and Hollender (eds.), *'Ich Narr des Glücks'*, pp. 122–5.

Woesler, Winfried, 'Heines "köstliche" Trolliaden', *HJb* 15 (1976), pp. 52–66.

*Heines Tanzbär*, Hamburg: Hoffmann und Campe, 1978.

(ed.), Heinrich Heine, *Atta Troll. Ein Sommernachtstraum*, Stuttgart: Reclam, 1977.

Wolf, Ruth, 'Versuch über Heines "Jehuda ben Halevy"', *HJb* 18 (1979), pp. 84–98.

Würffel, Stefan Bodo, *Der produktive Widerspruch*, Bern: Francke, 1986.

Zagari, Luciano, 'La "Pomare" di Heine e la crisi del linguaggio "lirico"', *Studi germanici*, 3 (1965), pp. 5–38.

'"Das ausgesprochene Wort ist ohne Scham". Der späte Heine und die Auflösung der dichterischen Sprache', in Zagari and Chiarini (eds.), *Zu Heinrich Heine*, pp. 124–38.

and Chiarini, Paolo (eds.), *Zu Heinrich Heine*, Stuttgart: Klett, 1981.

Zantop, Susanne (ed.), *Paintings on the Move. Heinrich Heine and the Visual Arts*, Lincoln, Nebraska, and London: University of Nebraska Press, 1989.

Ziegler, Edda, *Julius Campe – der Verleger Heinrich Heines*, Hamburg: Hoffmann und Campe, 1976.

Zlotkowski, Edward A., *Heinrich Heines* [sic] *Reisebilder: The Tendency of the Text and the Identity of the Age*, Bonn: Bouvier, 1980.

# Index